Imagining the Public in Modern South Asia

In South Asia, as elsewhere, the category of 'the public' has come under increased scholarly and popular scrutiny in recent years. To better understand this current conjuncture, we need a fuller understanding of the specifically South Asian history of the term. To that end, this book surveys the modern Indian 'public' across multiple historical contexts and sites, with contributions from leading scholars of South Asia in anthropology, history, literary studies and religious studies. As a whole, this volume highlights the complex genealogies of the public in the Indian subcontinent during the colonial and postcolonial eras, showing in particular how British notions of 'the public' intersected with South Asian forms of publicity. Two principal methods or approaches—the genealogical and the typological—have characterized this scholarship. This book suggests, more in the mode of genealogy, that the category of the public has been closely linked to the sub-continental history of political liberalism. Also discussed is how the studies collected in this volume challenge some of liberalism's key presuppositions about the public and its relationship to law and religion.

This book was originally published as a special issue of *South Asia: Journal of South Asian Studies*.

Brannon D. Ingram is Assistant Professor of Religious Studies at Northwestern University, USA. He specializes in the study of Islam in modern South Asia and South Africa, focusing particularly on Sufism and traditionally educated Muslim scholars ('*Ulama*'). Ingram's publications can be found in journals such as *Modern Asian Studies* and *The Muslim World*.

J. Barton Scott is Assistant Professor of Religion and Historical Studies at the University of Toronto, Canada. His current research interests include print culture in colonial India, the legal regulation of media publics, and the reception of liberalism among colonial Hindu reformers. He is the author of *Spiritual Despots: Modern Hinduism and the Genealogies of Self-Rule* (University of Chicago Press, 2016).

SherAli K. Tareen is Assistant Professor of Religious Studies at Franklin and Marshall College, USA. He received his PhD in Religion/Islamic Studies at Duke University and his BA at Macalester College. His work centers on Muslim intellectual thought in modern South Asia with a focus on intra-Muslim debates and polemics on crucial questions of law, ethics, and theology. He is currently completing a book project entitled "Polemical Encounters: Competing Imaginaries of Tradition in Modern South Asian Islam" that explores polemics over the boundaries of heretical innovation (*bid'a*) among leading nineteenth century Indian Muslim scholars ('*Ulama*'). His articles have appeared in the *Journal of Law and Religion*, *Muslim World*, *Political Theology*, and *Islamic Studies*.

Imagining the Public in Modern South Asia

Edited by
Brannon D. Ingram, J. Barton Scott and
SherAli K. Tareen

LONDON AND NEW YORK

First published 2016
by Routledge
2 Park Square, Milton Park, Abingdon, Oxon, OX14 4RN, UK

and by Routledge
711 Third Avenue, New York, NY 10017, USA

Routledge is an imprint of the Taylor & Francis Group, an informa business

© 2016 South Asian Studies Association of Australia

All rights reserved. No part of this book may be reprinted or reproduced or utilised in any form or by any electronic, mechanical, or other means, now known or hereafter invented, including photocopying and recording, or in any information storage or retrieval system, without permission in writing from the publishers.

Trademark notice: Product or corporate names may be trademarks or registered trademarks, and are used only for identification and explanation without intent to infringe.

British Library Cataloguing in Publication Data
A catalogue record for this book is available from the British Library

ISBN 13: 978-1-138-64882-1

Typeset in Times
by RefineCatch Limited, Bungay, Suffolk

Publisher's Note
The publisher accepts responsibility for any inconsistencies that may have arisen during the conversion of this book from journal articles to book chapters, namely the possible inclusion of journal terminology.

Disclaimer
Every effort has been made to contact copyright holders for their permission to reprint material in this book. The publishers would be grateful to hear from any copyright holder who is not here acknowledged and will undertake to rectify any errors or omissions in future editions of this book.

Contents

Citation Information		vii
Notes on Contributors		ix
1.	What is a Public? Notes from South Asia *J. Barton Scott and Brannon D. Ingram*	1
2.	Rethinking the Public through the Lens of Sovereignty *David Gilmartin*	15
3.	How to Defame a God: Public Selfhood in the Maharaj Libel Case *J. Barton Scott*	31
4.	Crises of the Public in Muslim India: Critiquing 'Custom' at Aligarh and Deoband *Brannon D. Ingram*	47
5.	Contesting Friendship in Colonial Muslim India *SherAli K. Tareen*	63
6.	Booklets and *Sants*: Religious Publics and Literary History *Francesca Orsini*	79
7.	Ambedkar, Marx and the Buddhist Question *Ajay Skaria*	94
8.	Jurisprudence of Emergence: Neo-Liberalism and the Public as Market in India *Ritu Birla*	110
9.	A Different Kind of Flesh: Public Obscenity, Globalisation and the Mumbai Dance Bar Ban *William Mazzarella*	125
10.	Commissioning Representation: The Misra Report, Deliberation and the Government of the People in Modern India *Rupa Viswanath*	139
11.	Postscript: Exploring Aspects of 'the Public' from 1991 to 2014 *Sandria B. Freitag*	156
Index		169

Citation Information

The chapters in this book were originally published in *South Asia: Journal of South Asian Studies*, volume 38, issue 3 (September 2015). When citing this material, please use the original page numbering for each article, as follows:

Chapter 1
What is a Public? Notes from South Asia
J. Barton Scott and Brannon D. Ingram
South Asia: Journal of South Asian Studies, volume 38, issue 3 (September 2015)
pp. 357–370

Chapter 2
Rethinking the Public through the Lens of Sovereignty
David Gilmartin
South Asia: Journal of South Asian Studies, volume 38, issue 3 (September 2015)
pp. 371–386

Chapter 3
How to Defame a God: Public Selfhood in the Maharaj Libel Case
J. Barton Scott
South Asia: Journal of South Asian Studies, volume 38, issue 3 (September 2015)
pp. 387–402

Chapter 4
Crises of the Public in Muslim India: Critiquing 'Custom' at Aligarh and Deoband
Brannon D. Ingram
South Asia: Journal of South Asian Studies, volume 38, issue 3 (September 2015)
pp. 403–418

Chapter 5
Contesting Friendship in Colonial Muslim India
SherAli K. Tareen
South Asia: Journal of South Asian Studies, volume 38, issue 3 (September 2015)
pp. 419–434

CITATION INFORMATION

Chapter 6
Booklets and Sants: *Religious Publics and Literary History*
Francesca Orsini
South Asia: Journal of South Asian Studies, volume 38, issue 3 (September 2015) pp. 435–449

Chapter 7
Ambedkar, Marx and the Buddhist Question
Ajay Skaria
South Asia: Journal of South Asian Studies, volume 38, issue 3 (September 2015) pp. 450–465

Chapter 8
Jurisprudence of Emergence: Neo-Liberalism and the Public as Market in India
Ritu Birla
South Asia: Journal of South Asian Studies, volume 38, issue 3 (September 2015) pp. 466–480

Chapter 9
A Different Kind of Flesh: Public Obscenity, Globalisation and the Mumbai Dance Bar Ban
William Mazzarella
South Asia: Journal of South Asian Studies, volume 38, issue 3 (September 2015) pp. 481–494

Chapter 10
Commissioning Representation: The Misra Report, Deliberation and the Government of the People in Modern India
Rupa Viswanath
South Asia: Journal of South Asian Studies, volume 38, issue 3 (September 2015) pp. 495–511

Chapter 11
Postscript: Exploring Aspects of 'the Public' from 1991 to 2014
Sandria B. Freitag
South Asia: Journal of South Asian Studies, volume 38, issue 3 (September 2015) pp. 512–523

For any permission-related enquiries please visit:
http://www.tandfonline.com/page/help/permissions

Notes on Contributors

Ritu Birla is Associate Professor of History and the Richard Charles Lee Director of the Asian Institute, Munk School Global Affairs, University of Toronto, Canada. She has also served as Director of the Centre for South Asian Studies housed at this Institute. Her research has sought to build the global study of capitalism, its cultures, and forms of governing. Her first book, *Stages of Capital: Law, Culture, and Market Governance in Late Colonial India* (Duke University Press, 2009 and Orient Blackswan India, 2010), was winner of the 2010 Albion Book Prize. Her writing has addressed the gendered social and legal imaginaries of economic modernity; "embedded" value-systems in processes of economization and financialization; non-western engagements with political and economic liberalism; postcolonial intellectual history; and political, legal, and feminist theory.

Sandria B. Freitag is Teaching Associate Professor of History at North Carolina State University, Raleigh, USA. She teaches courses on Visual Culture and Interdisciplinary studies, and is editor of the book, *Culture and Power in Banaras: Community, Performance, and Environment, 1800–1980* (University of California Press, 1992) and more recently of *The Visual Turn in South Asian Studies* (Routledge, 2015).

David Gilmartin is Professor in History at North Carolina State University, Raleigh, USA. He specializes in the history of modern India and Pakistan. His most recent book is *Blood and Water: The Indus River Basin in Modern History* (University of California Press, 2015).

Brannon D. Ingram is Assistant Professor of Religious Studies at Northwestern University, USA. He specializes in the study of Islam in modern South Asia and South Africa, focusing particularly on Sufism and traditionally educated Muslim scholars ('*Ulama*'). His publications can be found in journals such as *Modern Asian Studies* and *The Muslim World*.

William Mazzarella is Professor of Anthropology at the University of Chicago, USA. He is the author of *Shoveling Smoke: Advertising and Globalization in Contemporary India* (Duke University Press, 2003), *Censorium: Cinema and the Open Edge of Mass Publicity* (Duke University Press, 2013) and, to be published in 2017, *The Mana of Mass Society*.

NOTES ON CONTRIBUTORS

Francesca Orsini is Professor of Hindi and South Asian Literature at the School of Oriental and African Studies, University of London, UK. Her research interests include modern and contemporary Hindi literature, book history, and the multilingual literary history of north India. Francesca is author of *The Hindi Public Sphere: Language and literature in the age of nationalism* (Oxford University Press, 2002) and *Print and Pleasure: Popular literature and entertaining fictions in colonial north India* (Permanent Black, 2009).

J. Barton Scott is Assistant Professor of Religion and Historical Studies at the University of Toronto, Canada. His current research interests include print culture in colonial India, the legal regulation of media publics, and the reception of liberalism among colonial Hindu reformers. He is the author of *Spiritual Despots: Modern Hinduism and the Genealogies of Self-Rule* (University of Chicago Press, 2016).

Ajay Skaria is Professor of South Asian History at the University of Minnesota, USA. His research has focused on such areas as postcolonial theory, intellectual history, adivasi history, Ghandi, and twentieth century Hinduism. He is the author of *Hybrid Histories: Forests, Frontiers and Wildness in Western India* (Oxford University Press, 1999) and *Unconditional Equality: Gandhi's Religion of Resistance* (University of Minnesota Press, 2016).

SherAli K. Tareen is Assistant Professor of Religious Studies at Franklin and Marshall College, USA. He received his PhD in Religion/Islamic Studies at Duke University and his BA at Macalester College. His work centers on Muslim intellectual thought in modern South Asia with a focus on intra-Muslim debates and polemics on crucial questions of law, ethics, and theology. He is currently completing a book project entitled "Polemical Encounters: Competing Imaginaries of Tradition in Modern South Asian Islam" that explores polemics over the boundaries of heretical innovation (*bid'a*) among leading nineteenth century Indian Muslim scholars (*'Ulama'*). His articles have appeared in the *Journal of Law and Religion*, *Muslim World*, *Political Theology*, and *Islamic Studies*.

Rupa Viswanath is Professor of Indian Religions at the Centre for Modern Indian Studies at the University of Göttingen. Her research interests include histories of unfreedom in South and Southeast Asia, comparative secularisms, theories of caste and race, and democratic theory in the global south. She is the author of *The Pariah Problem: Caste, Religion and the Social in Modern India* (Columbia University Press, 2014).

What is a Public? Notes from South Asia

J. BARTON SCOTT, *University of Toronto, Ontario, Canada*

BRANNON D. INGRAM, *Northwestern University, Evanston, Illinois, USA*

In South Asia, as elsewhere, the category of 'the public' has come under increased scholarly and popular scrutiny in recent years. To better understand this current conjuncture, we need a fuller understanding of the specifically South Asian history of the term. Toward this end, our discussion begins by considering more than two decades of scholarship that have worked to excavate this history. We propose that two principal methods or approaches—the genealogical and the typological—have characterised this scholarship. We then suggest, more in the mode of genealogy, that the category of the public has been closely linked to the subcontinental history of political liberalism. Finally, we discuss how the essays collected in this special issue challenge some of liberalism's key presuppositions about the public and its relationship to law and religion.

Reimagining the Public

That the past decade has seen a surge of scholarly interest in publics is hardly surprising: global culture in the early twenty-first century has complicated the distinction between public and private in seemingly unprecedented ways. In South Asia, as elsewhere, new technologies have opened up intimate life to public scrutiny, whether through state surveillance of 'terrorist' networks, the digital self-fashioning encouraged by websites like shaadi.com, or 'biometric' identity cards that mark the body itself as a form of public information. Gender politics, meanwhile, have determined who can move safely in public, as the 2012 rape and murder of a Delhi college student on a city bus so tragically demonstrated. Here, too, sudden inversions of public and private have been the order of the day, whether in the 2009 'pink *chaddi* campaign' (in which hundreds of women mailed underwear to a spokesman for the Sri Rama Sena to protest threats against couples caught 'being together in public' on Valentine's Day), or in the abrupt re-closeting of gays and lesbians after the Supreme Court upheld Section 377 of the Indian Penal Code in 2013. Finally, ongoing debate about the proper place of religion has occasioned still more contests over the limits of the public. On the one hand, the highly-publicised flesh of figures like Baba Ramdev and Anna Hazare was rendered a

---

The authors would like to thank the participants in the May 2014 workshop 'Imagining the Public in Colonial India', hosted by Northwestern University, Illinois, especially Laura Brueck, Daniel Elam, Sandria Freitag, Dilip Gaonkar, Rajeev Kinra and Rama Mantena. We refined the argument of this introduction in close conversation with Leo Coleman, who deserves particular thanks. Finally, we would like to thank SherAli Tareen for his help in conceiving and executing this special issue and Kama Maclean and Vivien Seyler for their help in producing it.

symbol for bringing corruption to light; on the other, the call to censor Wendy Doniger's *The Hindus* hailed a public defined by that which it would prefer to keep hidden.

In the twenty-first century, it seems, 'the public' is a site where matter is perpetually out of place. In such a context, public culture as a 'zone of debate' becomes fixated on policing the borders of the public, even as those borders remain in perpetual flux.[1] During the nineteenth century, as Partha Chatterjee has influentially argued, the 'inner' domain of religion, literature and domesticity incubated an anti-colonial politics that erupted into public view only later.[2] The abrupt inversions of publicity and privacy that mark our contemporary moment recall this longer history, even as they point towards an undetermined future.

To understand the current conjuncture, then, we need a fuller sense of the genealogy of 'the public' in South Asia. This collection of essays provides one set of possible starting points for such an inquiry. In doing so, it echoes and complements other recent work that asks how fundamental categories of modern thought ('culture', 'the social') have been adapted in the subcontinent.[3] As a whole, these essays suggest that South Asia is not just a special 'case' for the articulation of modern notions of the public; rather, we hope to show that by theorising the public from South Asia, we gain unique perspectives on how this central category of modern thought can be re-imagined today.

This collection revisits and expands the project begun by Sandria Freitag's influential 1991 special issue of the journal *South Asia* on 'Aspects of "the Public" in Colonial South Asia'.[4] Much, of course, has changed since 1991—not least, the 'liberalisation' of the Indian economy that began in July of that year. The major argument of the 1991 volume, however, remains as pertinent today as it was nearly 25 years ago. As Freitag insists, we should work to provincialise 'the public'—approaching it less as a normative model for modern society than as a culturally peculiar notion caught up with the particular history of the North Atlantic region (i.e. 'the West'). The chief task confronting the scholar, by this account, is one of translation. We should, in Freitag's words, try to identify the 'indigenous bases onto which western European notions of "the public" could have been grafted'.[5] In his contribution to the 1991 volume, Dipesh Chakrabarty provides an example that helpfully illustrates the analytic issues involved in such an effort. As he shows, it is possible to describe the streets of Banaras as a 'public' space. In doing so, however, one risks effacing the culturally-specific distinction between 'inside' and 'outside', between home and bazaar, and the world of meanings (about family, ritual cleanliness, auspiciousness, etc.) that this distinction implies. To sound this cautionary note is not to deny the potential analogy between the concepts of 'public' and 'outside'; it is simply to point out that, in drawing analogies, we need to remain aware of what gets lost in translation.[6]

---

[1] Arjun Appadurai and Carol Breckenridge, 'Why Public Culture?', in *Public Culture*, Vol. 1, no. 1 (1988), pp. 5–11.
[2] Partha Chatterjee, *The Nation and Its Fragments: Colonial and Postcolonial Histories* (Princeton, NJ: Princeton University Press, 1993), pp. 5–6.
[3] Andrew Sartori, *Bengal in Global Concept History: Culturalism in the Age of Capital* (Chicago, IL: University of Chicago Press, 2008); and Rochona Majumdar, 'A Conceptual History of the Social: Some Reflections from Colonial Bengal', in Michael Dodson and Brian Hatcher (eds), *Transcolonial Modernities in South Asia* (London: Routledge, 2012), pp. 165–88.
[4] *South Asia: Journal of South Asian Studies*, special issue on 'Aspects of "the Public" in Colonial South Asia', Vol. XIV, no. 1 (June 1991).
[5] Sandria B. Freitag, 'Introduction: "The Public" and its Meanings in Colonial South Asia', in *South Asia: Journal of South Asian Studies*, Vol. XIV, no. 1 (June 1991), p. 7.
[6] Dipesh Chakrabarty, 'Open Space/Public Place: Garbage, Modernity, and India', in *South Asia: Journal of South Asian Studies*, Vol. XIV, no. 1 (June 1991), pp. 15–31.

In revisiting the project laid out in the 1991 special issue, we also necessarily revise it, in part by resisting too strict a distinction between North Atlantic and South Asian materials. The British 'public' was never a totalising sociological reality; rather, it was an unstable assemblage of shifting ideas and institutions, defined as much by its internal contradictions as by its normative force. South Asian culture, for its part, was no less dynamic. Thus, in designating particular South Asian cultural forms as analogous to North Atlantic 'publics', we need to be careful not to reify either set of materials or to abstract them from their complex and contested histories. What is more, we need to consider how the Anglophone term 'public' has, since the nineteenth century, become an integral part of the South Asian scene. As the essays collected here demonstrate, 'the public' is seldom a neutral descriptor; rather, as a term with legal, political and cultural ramifications, it often shapes the objects that it describes.

Freitag's 'Aspects of the Public' highlighted 'two key areas' of inquiry: urban space and literary form. In complementary fashion, this set of essays highlights two key areas as well as two key problematics. While they call attention to the continued importance of print culture and religious polemics in defining 'the public', especially in the colonial period, they also suggest how the legal regulation of publics and the presence of religion in the 'secular' public sphere trouble the normative presumptions of classical liberalism (the body of thought with which the concept of 'the public sphere' is most closely associated). Where liberalism posits the public as independent from the state and defines religion as constitutively 'private', the essays collected here suggest a much more complex set of entanglements among these domains.

In this introductory discussion, we have three principal aims: first, we consider how scholars working in South Asian studies have approached the question, 'What is a public?'; second, we discuss the entanglement of 'the public' with the history of liberalism in the subcontinent; third and finally, we turn to our two major themes—law and religion—in order to challenge one of liberalism's dominant narratives about the public. According to one standard line of thought, the public is both constitutively separate from the state as well as linked to it; public debate places a check on the potential abuses of state power, even as the state legitimates its rule through its claim to represent the public's interests. The essays that follow from this introduction (arranged in roughly chronological order) complicate this picture by a variety of means, including by positioning the public as the object, rather than the agent of cultural regulation.

Locations of 'the Public': Genealogy or Typology?

Broadly speaking, we submit that there are two ways in which scholars have gone about studying South Asian publics: the typological method and the genealogical method. Both methods, perhaps inevitably, take North Atlantic notions of 'the public' as a primary point of reference, but their approach to these notions differs significantly. The typological approach looks for moments when South Asian ideas and practices seem similar to, or function like, North Atlantic ideas and practices of 'the public'. Broadly social scientific in spirit, it tries to apply 'the public' as a generalisable concept to South Asian materials. The genealogical approach, conversely, rejects the impulse to divorce the concept of 'the public' from its convoluted history. Instead, it works to further historicise the concept and practice of the North Atlantic 'public' by asking how this notion travelled to South Asia and how it was adapted from within particular institutions and power structures. These two approaches cannot, of course, be neatly separated. Nonetheless, they do remain distinct orientations within the study of South Asian publics.

To clarify the distinction between these two approaches, we turn to another English-language term that has gained considerable purchase in South Asia: 'religion'. As recent scholarship has emphasised, this distinctively modern concept constrains our analysis of South Asian culture, as by implying a clear distinction between the 'sacred' and the 'secular'. Consequently, scholars of early modern India have increasingly sought out alternate terms (e.g. 'ritual'), which allow them to sidestep 'religion' in approaching topics like sacred kingship.[7] For the colonial and post-colonial periods, however, the problem is more complicated: no longer a culturally foreign concept that we as scholars impose on South Asian materials, 'religion' becomes part of the conversation *in* South Asia, actively shaping modern cultural practice in significant ways. This was especially true for groups like the Arya Samaj, which deployed the English word strategically in their publications and adjusted their usage of the Hindi word *dharm* either to approximate it more closely or to avoid its semantic reach.[8]

Surely something similar is at play with the concept of 'the public'. Like 'religion', this term has come to shape South Asian cultural practice. On the one hand, its prominence in colonial and post-colonial legal codes has made the concept of 'the public' a tool for the juridical management of society. Thus, as William Mazzarella shows here, notions of 'public place' and 'public morality' determined the types of dance that were deemed legally permissible in Mumbai in the mid 2000s. In a slightly different vein, as Ritu Birla demonstrates in her contribution, the legal concept of 'public interest' was central to the emergence of neo-liberal administrative power in the 1990s. On the other hand, the concept of the public also shaped civil society institutions like the press. This was in part because newspapers rhetorically aligned themselves with the courtroom as a model for disinterested 'public' judgement on 'private' matters (see David Gilmartin and J. Barton Scott, this volume). But there were also lines of influence that did not run through the state or civil society. For example, nineteenth-century intellectuals like Sayyid Ahmad Khan consciously emulated the style of the same English newspapers (*Tatler*, *The Spectator*) that are now hailed as paradigmatic for the Enlightenment 'public sphere' *per se* (see Brannon Ingram, this volume).

Not surprisingly, colonial and post-colonial thinkers have struggled with how best to translate the concept of 'the public' into South Asian languages. Appearing at first in English (as in Ram Mohan Roy's 'Appeal to the Christian Public' of 1820), the word began to enter the various vernaculars by mid century. In the 1850s, journalist Karsandas Mulji tried to translate 'public spirit' into Gujarati (Scott, this volume). In the 1880s, journalist and novelist Abdul Halim Sharar began to speak of a nascent '*Islami pablik*' in Urdu.[9] Transliteration was easy enough, but how 'the public' was to be translated into South Asian languages remained something of a puzzle. Did it, as Mulji suggested, denote the 'outward' or 'apparent' (*jaher*) aspect of something? Or was it better, as Ashraf 'Ali Thanvi seemed to do in the 1910s, to align 'the public' with '*'awamm*'—a term that traditionally distinguished lay Muslims from the scholarly elite (*'ulama*) and connoted 'commonness', 'ordinariness' and 'generality' (Ingram, this volume)? As Francesca Orsini has argued elsewhere, Hindi-language writers

---

[7] For an example of this approach, see A. Azfar Moin, *The Millennial Sovereign: Sacred Kingship and Sainthood in Islam* (New York: Columbia University Press, 2012).

[8] For discussions of how the Arya Samaj managed the political semantics of religion in two different contexts, see C.S. Adcock, 'Sacred Cows and Secular History: Cow Protection Debates in Colonial North India', in *Comparative Studies in South Asia, Africa, and the Middle East*, Vol. 30, no. 2 (2010), pp. 297–311; and J. Barton Scott, 'Aryas Unbound: Print Hinduism and the Cultural Regulation of Religious Offense', in *Comparative Studies in South Asia, Africa, and the Middle East*, Vol. 35, no. 2 (2015), forthcoming.

[9] C. Ryan Perkins, 'From the *Mehfil* to the Printed Word: Public Debate and Discourse in Late Colonial India', in *The Indian Economic and Social History Review*, Vol. 50, no. 1 (2013), p. 52.

'struggling to find equivalents for this crucial word in the political vocabulary of modernity' ended up distinguishing between two distinct senses of the term: 'public' in the sense of pertaining to the government (*sarkari*), and in the sense of 'pertaining to the community' (*jati, janta, lok, sarvasadharan*) (cf. Orsini, this volume).[10]

Even in the North Atlantic world, the meaning of 'the public' was never fixed. The standard etymology of the word 'public' begins with the Latin *publicus* ('of or belonging to the people as a whole, common, universal').[11] This term entered Anglo-Norman in the thirteenth century and eventually accrued an array of meanings: 'open to general observation'; 'in print'; 'prominent, well-known'; 'official, professional'; 'carried out or made on behalf of the community by the government or State'; 'the body politic'; 'a writer's readership' or a 'performer's audience'. In Habermas' estimation, the modern sense of 'public' emerged in English only in the late seventeenth century, spreading to German and French in the eighteenth. During this period, 'public opinion' came to refer to 'the critical reflections of a public competent to form its own judgments'. It was thus defined against the less 'enlightened' beliefs of the unlettered masses.[12] In short, by the time the Anglophone 'public' came to India, the term was already a site where multiple meanings and histories intersected, without ever quite adding up into a single entity. Indeed, 'the public' is a term that is most often defined in terms of what it is not—a marker of conceptual instability if ever there was one.

This conceptual instability is all the more evident when we move from genealogy to typology—that is, from tracing how the North Atlantic 'public' travelled to South Asia to identifying concepts and practices that seem to qualify as 'publics' in a generalisable social scientific sense. Here too, translation is key. Thus, even while proposing *loka* ('the people' or 'the world') as an appropriate Sanskrit-Marathi rendering of 'public', Christian Novetzke notes the semantic distance between these two terms.[13] To help ease such problems, some scholars have suggested that 'publicity' may be more elastic than 'the public'. Farhat Hasan, for instance, draws on Mughal-era examples as diverse as Islamic sermons in Surat, the elaborate forms of intercommunication between a seventeenth-century Sufi master and his students in the Deccan, and the celebration of Holi in Ahmedabad to make a case for 'a vibrant space of publicity' in which 'normative claims could be raised, redeemed, or rejected' among non-elites in a way that made it a far cry from Habermas' 'liberal public sphere'.[14]

Indeed, we do not suggest that there is a moment when 'the public' triumphantly 'arrives' in South Asian contexts. Like modernity itself, its lineages are far too muddled to trace in such a fashion.[15] Recent scholarship has demonstrated the substantial continuity between pre-colonial and colonial 'publics'—or, more precisely, practices that can be described as constituting 'publics'. As C.A. Bayly and others have shown, indigenous forms of what can be

---

[10] Francesca Orsini, 'What Did They Mean by "Public"? Language, Literature, and the Politics of Nationalism', in *Economic & Political Weekly*, Vol. 34, no. 7 (1999), pp. 409–16.

[11] The term retains traces of what to modern readers might seem like a transgression of the boundary between public and private: *poplicus* became *publicus* in association with *pubes*, in the sense of 'adult men'. As Michael Warner puts it, 'public membership' becomes linked to 'pubic maturity' in a manner starkly at odds with contemporary English's demarcation of 'privates' and 'privy' as definitively non-public. See Michael Warner, *Publics and Counterpublics* (New York: Zone Books, 2002), p. 23.

[12] Jürgen Habermas, *The Structural Transformation of the Public Sphere: An Inquiry into a Category of Bourgeois Society* (Thomas Burger, trans.) (Cambridge, MA: MIT Press, 1989), pp. 26, 89–102.

[13] Christian Novetzke, *Religion and Public Memory: A Cultural History of Saint Namdev in India* (New York: Columbia University Press, 2008), pp. 13–5.

[14] Farhat Hasan, 'Forms of Civility and Publicness in Pre-British India', in Rajeev Bhargava and Helmut Reifeld (eds), *Civil Society, Public Sphere and Citizenship* (Delhi: Sage Publications, 2005), pp. 94–5.

[15] Dipesh Chakrabarty, 'The Muddle of Modernity', in *The American Historical Review*, Vol. 116, no. 3 (2011), pp. 663–75.

termed 'the public' not only predated the British, but were profoundly resilient in the face of colonialism. At least during the first half of the nineteenth century, the British 'informational order' did not so much displace these forms as augment them; the British state had to rely on pre-colonial modes of information gathering, just as colonial print culture built on existing economies of knowledge, ranging from astrology to medicine.[16] The rise of print culture in the nineteenth century likewise built on existing cultural practices. Vernacular newspapers in Persian and Urdu maintained striking continuities with Mughal-era *akhbarat*.[17] Just as importantly, print was shaped by the subcontinent's thriving cultures of orality.[18] The commitment of Allahabad's Belvedere Press to the publication of Awadhi *sant* poetry, for example, indicates how early modern oral devotionalism defined the printed canon of Hindi literature (Orsini, this volume).

Meanwhile, 'public' debate continued to proliferate in a variety of forms (e.g. *shatrarth*, *munazara*, *majalis*, *musha'ira*), even as (in Avril Powell's narrative) they moved from royal courts and the homes of the nobility to broader forums. In villages, festivals and town fairs, and in lithographed screeds and tracts, Muslims debated Hindus, Christians debated Muslims, Hindus debated Christians, and members of each debated each other, reifying religious boundaries both internal and external.[19] If by the end of the nineteenth century, the native informant, spy and news-runner had mostly been displaced by the postal system, telegraph and railway, the cultural worlds that they had established lived on, albeit in altered form. Like modernity itself—'a global and *conjunctural* phenomenon' in Sanjay Subrahmanyam's words, 'not a virus that spreads from one place to another'—the public assumed multiple forms in multiple contexts that resist neat teleologies.[20]

Any good typological account of South Asian publics, of course, needs to consider the extent to which they are 'split'—fractured along lines of language, caste, class, religion and gender.[21] In the colonial period, the 'middle class' constituted itself as such partly by establishing 'a public sphere, where alone its political opinion could form and represent itself'.[22] This vernacular public sphere, whether in Hindi or Telugu, was caught up with the question of language reform.[23] It was also caught up with questions of caste. This latter

---

[16] C.A. Bayly, *Empire and Information: Intelligence Gathering and Social Communication in India, 1780–1870* (Cambridge: Cambridge University Press, 1996).

[17] Margrit Pernau and Yunus Jaffery (eds), *Information and the Public Sphere: Persian Newsletters from Mughal Delhi* (Oxford: Oxford University Press, 2009), p. 2; and Gail Minault, 'From Akhbar to News: The Development of the Urdu Press in Early Nineteenth Century Delhi', in Kathryn Hansen and David Lelyveld (eds), *A Wilderness of Possibilities: Urdu Studies in Transnational Perspective* (Delhi: Oxford University Press, 2005), pp. 101–21.

[18] Anindita Ghosh, 'An Uncertain "Coming of the Book": Early Print Cultures in Colonial India', in *Book History*, Vol. 6 (2003), pp. 23–55. In North India, some Muslim scholars attempted to preserve accents of orality, central to classical Islamic education, well into the twentieth century. See Brannon D. Ingram, 'The Portable Madrasa: Print, Publics and the Authority of the Deobandi 'Ulama', in *Modern Asian Studies*, Vol. 48, no. 4 (2014), pp. 845–71.

[19] Kenneth W. Jones (ed.), *Religious Controversy in British India: Dialogues in South Asian Languages* (Albany: State University of New York Press, 1992); and Avril Powell, *Muslims and Missionaries in Pre-Mutiny India* (Richmond, Surrey: Curzon Press, 1993).

[20] Sanjay Subrahmanyam, 'Hearing Voices: Vignettes of Early Modernity in South Asia, 1400–1750', in *Daedalus*, Vol. 127, no. 3 (Summer 1998), pp. 99–100; emphasis in original.

[21] Arvind Rajagopal, *Politics after Television: Hindu Nationalism and the Reshaping of the Public in India* (Cambridge: Cambridge University Press, 2001).

[22] Vasudha Dalmia, *The Nationalization of Hindu Traditions: Bharatendu Harischandra and Nineteenth-Century Banaras* (Delhi: Oxford University Press, 1997), p. 31.

[23] Rama Sundari Mantena, 'Vernacular Publics and Political Modernity: Language and Progress in Colonial South India', in *Modern Asian Studies*, Vol. 47, no. 5 (2013), pp. 1678–705.

question has become increasingly prominent in recent years, as when a Dalit literary group symbolically burned a Premchand novel in 2004.[24] Here, we see the formation of a 'counterpublic' in Nancy Fraser's sense, in which a 'subordinated social group' establishes a 'parallel discursive arena' in order to 'circulate counterdiscourses' about a dominant social group.[25] To make sense of such fissures in the public, we can turn to Neeladri Bhattacharya, who presents modern Indian publics as caught between competing forces of 'homogenization and segmentation'.[26] Never unitary, 'the Indian public' is also more than the sum of its discrete parts.

If there is one lesson to be drawn from all this, it is that 'the public' is never simply an empirical object. It is always also a category of interpretation. 'The public', moreover, is not an external category that scholars impose on modern Indian materials. Rather, precisely as an English-language term, it is very much internal to the self-understanding of colonial and post-colonial South Asia. To use a slightly old-fashioned scholarly idiom, 'the public' has been an 'emic' rather than an 'etic' term in South Asia since at least the 1820s. As scholars, we are inheritors of this history and should situate our work accordingly—including by clearly differentiating among three distinct questions. First, what are the major forms of collectivity in modern South Asia? Second, to what extent is 'the public' an adequate model for conceptualising these forms? Third, what is the history of interpretation whereby these forms of collectivity have been directly or indirectly shaped by concepts of the public? Of course, if the concept of 'the public' has shaped collective life in modern South Asia, it has also, and just as surely, been re-shaped by its multiple South Asian interpreters. It is partly in order to recover this history of interpretation that we call attention to the specifically South Asian genealogy of the term—a genealogy inseparable from the history of liberal political thought in the subcontinent.

Liberalism and the Public Sphere

Jürgen Habermas' *The Structural Transformation of the Public Sphere* (1962) remains a touchstone for the study of publics. Its belated English translation in 1989 occasioned an interdisciplinary debate about the rise and fall of the public sphere that lasted well into the 1990s, providing the conceptual framework for, among other things, Freitag's 'Aspects of "the Public" in Colonial South Asia'.

For Habermas, the 'public sphere' (*Öffentlichkeit*) is a historically specific formation that emerged in the late seventeenth century and declined in the late nineteenth with the rise of mass culture and modern bureaucracy. His book's ostensible aim was one of immanent critique: by analysing how the internal contradictions of the Enlightenment public sphere ultimately caused that sphere's dissolution, Habermas hoped to recuperate for contemporary political thought the utopian kernel at the heart of the Enlightenment. Throughout his later career, Habermas has remained among the most articulate champions of political liberalism, even while modifying some of his earlier claims (including, for example, his claims about religion).[27]

---

[24] Laura R. Brueck, *Writing Resistance: The Rhetorical Imagination of Hindi Dalit Literature* (New York: Columbia University Press, 2014), p. 4.
[25] Nancy Fraser, 'Rethinking the Public Sphere: A Contribution to the Critique of Actually Existing Democracy', in Craig Calhoun (ed.), *Habermas and the Public Sphere* (Cambridge, MA: MIT Press, 1993), pp. 109–42.
[26] Neeladri Bhattacharya, 'Notes Towards a Conception of the Colonial Public', in Rajeev Bhargava and Helmut Reifeld (eds), *Civil Society, Public Sphere and Citizenship* (Delhi: Sage Publications, 2005), p. 142.
[27] Craig Calhoun, Eduardo Mendieta and Jonathan VanAntwerpen (eds), *Habermas and Religion* (Cambridge: Polity Press, 2013).

There are many criticisms of Habermas' work. Some scholars question the historical accuracy of his narrative.[28] Others insist that his fundamental categories should be re-thought, as through feminist or queer theory.[29] In keeping with both types of critique, we would point to a particularly striking omission from Habermas' account (and one of obvious importance for the essays collected here): empire. As two generations of scholars have argued, to study Britain and France in isolation from their overseas colonies is to provide a history of modernity that is both historically dubious and analytically impoverished. To understand modernity, we need to understand how the cross-currents of empire shaped colony and metropole alike.[30] Political liberalism, after all, has been a global affair since at least the eighteenth century.[31] So, presumably, has the concept of the 'public sphere'. Indeed, there are good reasons to think that interaction began even earlier than this. For example, John Roe's reports on the interreligious civility of the Mughal court may have informed seventeenth-century English debates about religious 'toleration'. If this is the case, Akbar's late-sixteenth-century parliaments of religion would not just have mirrored liberalism, they would have directly influenced it.[32] Regardless, it seems clear that by the late eighteenth century, imperial scandals like the Warren Hastings trial were formative for the self-conception of a British public increasingly defined by its moral relationship to the colonies.[33]

Liberalism, as is now well known, was one of the principle idioms of empire. The colonies provided a laboratory for the experimental social reforms proposed by Utilitarians and others, especially in the early nineteenth century. Liberalism also, in its expansively universalist spirit, proved a principal means of denying cultural difference so as to enable British cultural hegemony. It is not that liberalism and empire always paired together. On the contrary, as Karuna Mantena argues, the imperial state largely abandoned liberal justifications for British rule in India after 1857, preferring instead to emphasise culture as an 'alibi' of empire. What is more, as Andrew Sartori reminds us, tensions internal to liberalism have allowed it to emerge as a key means of critiquing imperial capital, as by insisting on the integrity of small landholders' property rights. Liberalism is not reducible to the state-backed *laissez-faire* policies of either the nineteenth or the twenty-first centuries.[34]

It is not our intention to intervene directly in these debates. We simply want to point out that the idea of 'the public' was central to colonial liberalism (and remains so to post-colonial neo-liberalism, as Birla shows in her essay here). Indeed, the ideal of 'government by discussion'—to invoke Walter Bagehot's 1872 definition of parliamentary democracy—lived

---

[28] Craig Calhoun (ed.), *Habermas and the Public Sphere* (Cambridge, MA: MIT Press, 1992); and Harold Mah, 'Phantasies of the Public Sphere: Rethinking the Habermas of Historians', in *The Journal of Modern History*, Vol. 72, no. 1 (2000), pp. 153–82.

[29] Michael Warner's *Publics and Counterpublics* is exemplary in this regard.

[30] Peter van der Veer, *Imperial Encounters: Religion and Modernity in India and Britain* (Princeton, NJ: Princeton University Press, 2001).

[31] C.A. Bayly, *Recovering Liberties: Indian Thought in the Age of Liberalism and Empire* (Cambridge: Cambridge University Press, 2011).

[32] Rajeev Kinra, 'Handling Diversity with Absolute Civility: The Global Historical Legacy of Mughal *Sulh-i Kull*', in *The Medieval History Journal*, Vol. 16, no. 2 (2013), pp. 251–95; and Amartya Sen, *The Argumentative Indian* (London: Penguin, 2005).

[33] Nicholas Dirks, *The Scandal of Empire* (Cambridge, MA: Harvard University Press, 2006).

[34] Eric Stokes, *The English Utilitarians and India* (Oxford: Clarendon Press, 1959); Thomas R. Metcalf, *Ideologies of the Raj* (Cambridge: Cambridge University Press, 1994); Uday Singh Mehta, *Liberalism and Empire: A Study in Nineteenth-Century British Liberal Thought* (Chicago, IL/London: University of Chicago Press, 1999); Karuna Mantena, *Alibis of Empire: Henry Maine and the Ends of Liberal Imperialism* (Princeton, NJ: Princeton University Press, 2010); and Andrew Sartori, *Liberalism in Empire: An Alternative History* (Berkeley: University of California Press, 2014).

on in colonial public culture even after the imperial state, by Mantena's account, abandoned liberalism as a justification for empire. To approach liberalism via 'the public' is thus to highlight the extent to which the history of liberalism in India exceeds the history of the state: precisely because the colonial state asked that Indian elites internalise liberalism's political lexicon, this lexicon dispersed beyond the state's immediate purview, even as it continued to orient itself toward the state. 'Much of local politics', as Douglas Haynes observes, 'involved conflicting attempts by elites to construe the meaning of the concept *public* among themselves and in negotiation with the Anglo-Indian rulers'. This was true, moreover, both in English and in the vernacular languages. To understand the 'development of democratic cultural forms in India', then, we need to unpack what 'local figures meant when they used terms such as *public opinion, the public good*, and *the nation*'.[35]

One clue is to be found in a speech, 'On the Means of Ascertaining Public Opinion in India', that Sir Bartle Frere delivered in 1871 to Dadabhai Naoroji's East India Association. Frere opens with a question that he notes is 'almost always asked in a tone which rather implies an inevitable negative answer': 'Is there such a thing as public opinion in India?' He then proceeds to distinguish between 'public opinion' and 'published opinion', defining the former as 'any opinion which is not personal nor peculiar, and which is shared and more or less expressed by large bodies of men'. The only difference between English and Indian public opinion, he argues, is that the latter is 'less articulate'; its many voiceless subalterns have yet to be trained to speak in a way that would help the colonial state avoid another Mutiny. The 'Press', which 'represents the opinions of a mere fraction of the masses of India', does not resolve this problem to Frere's satisfaction. Instead, he proposes a layered system of councils (village, district, provincial), each of which would be tasked with 'representing' the opinions of its constituents to its superior body.[36] Here, we see how the concept of 'public opinion' shapes state practice. Frere invokes it to argue for a system of representative government that recalls the parliamentary ideal of open critical discussion, even while working to ensure that discussion reinforces the authority of the state, both symbolically (these councils position the state, not the press, as the guardian of public opinion) and practically (by augmenting the state's access to information that will safeguard its power). If Frere's remarks invoke the symbolic authority of 'government by discussion' while sidelining its substance, they perhaps anticipate the function of the 'commission as form' in the post-colonial period (see Rupa Viswanath, this volume).

The strong 'associational culture' that arose in colonial India thus often echoed the liberal rhetoric of the British state. The proliferating voluntary societies of the late nineteenth century were institutionally similar to the system that Frere proposed, structured as they were into regional branches organised by the liberal logic of 'representation'.[37] Some of these organisations claimed not only to represent 'public opinion', but also (as one such society in Lucknow would have it) the 'public good' (*rifah-i 'am*).[38] Quintessentially liberal, these societies emphasised debate, deliberation and the civic agency of the self-determining individual.

---

[35] Douglas Haynes, *Rhetoric and Ritual in Colonial India: The Shaping of a Public Culture in Surat City, 1852–1928* (Berkeley, CA: University of California Press, 1991), p. x; emphasis in original.

[36] Sir Bartle Frere, 'On the Means of Ascertaining Public Opinion in India', in *Journal of the East India Association*, Vol. 5, no. 4 (1871), pp. 102–4, 109–15.

[37] For further discussion of these themes, see Scott, 'Aryas Unbound'.

[38] Ulrike Stark, 'Associational Culture and Civic Engagement in Colonial Lucknow: The Jalsah-e Tahzib', in *The Indian Economic and Social History Review*, Vol. 48, no. 1 (2011), pp. 1–33.

Despite its universal aspirations, however, the public comprised of these voluntary societies was a bourgeois phenomenon defined through its contrast with the 'public arenas' of the streets.[39] It was also prototypically male, more often taking women as the object of reform than as speaking subjects in their own right.[40] Starting in the late nineteenth century, the question of how best to conjoin these various publics came to preoccupy nationalist thinkers like B.G. Tilak, whose promotion of the Ganesh festival is emblematic in this regard.[41] By the early decades of the twentieth century, movies and other mass media had begun to displace publics formed around print and civic associations. Increasingly, the 'crowd' was becoming the face of the public, in India as elsewhere.[42]

The resulting crisis in liberal notions of the public prompted a flowering of public sphere theory in the 1920s. While Walter Lippmann dismissed the deliberative public as a 'phantom' and Carl Schmitt claimed that 'modern mass democracy has made argumentative public discussion an empty formality', John Dewey sprang to the defence of publics as fundamental to democracy.[43] It would be extremely interesting to read India back into this scene. How, one might ask, did these debates inform the work of Dewey's former student, B.R. Ambedkar? Ambedkar once told his friends that if 'Dewey died, I could reproduce every lecture verbatim'.[44] Should we hear echoes of Dewey, then, in Ambedkar's later claim that caste 'has killed public spirit...[and] made public opinion impossible'?[45] As Ajay Skaria suggests in his contribution to this volume, Ambedkar's conversion to Buddhism can be read as an effort to create a 'civil religion' in the tradition of Dewey, 'concretising the abstractness of the rights of man' in a way that calls attention to the place of the Dalit as a 'minor' figure. How else might nationalist leaders have re-thought 1920s liberalism in relation both to the particular conditions of modern India and its commonalities with the wider world?

The essays collected here do not share a single perspective on any of these questions. Taken as a whole, however, they indicate the prominence of two themes in current thinking about publics: law and religion. Both themes suggest inadequacies in the liberal notion of the public sphere. Where liberalism posits a public entirely independent of the state, these essays indicate the extent to which the public is defined and regulated through juridical institutions. Where liberalism stipulates that religion remain a private affair, these essays demonstrate the vibrancy of public religion.

---

[39] Sandria B. Freitag, *Collective Action and Community: Public Arenas and the Emergence of Communalism in North India* (Berkeley, CA: University of California Press, 1989); and Sumanta Banerjee, *The Parlour and the Streets: Elite and Popular Culture in Nineteenth Century Calcutta* (Calcutta: Seagull Books, 1989).

[40] Charu Gupta, *Sexuality, Obscenity, Community: Women, Muslims, and the Hindu Public in Colonial India* (New Delhi: Permanent Black, 2001); and Faisal Devji, 'Gender and the Politics of Space: The Movement for Women's Reform in Muslim India, 1857–1900', in *South Asia: Journal of South Asian Studies*, Vol. XIV, no. 1 (1991), pp. 141–53.

[41] Raminder Kaur, *Performative Politics and the Cultures of Hinduism: Public Uses of Religion in Western India* (Delhi: Permanent Black, 2003).

[42] William Mazzarella, *Censorium: Cinema and the Open Edge of Mass Publicity* (Durham, NC: Duke University Press, 2013).

[43] Walter Lippmann, *The Phantom Public* (New York: Harcourt, Brace, and Co., 1925); John Dewey, *The Public and Its Problems* (Athens: Ohio University Press, [1927] 1954); and Carl Schmitt (Ellen Kennedy, trans.), *The Crisis of Parliamentary Democracy* (Cambridge, MA: MIT Press, [1923] 1985), p. 6.

[44] Arun P. Mukherjee, 'B.R. Ambedkar, John Dewey, and the Meaning of Democracy', in *New Literary History*, Vol. 40, no. 2 (Spring 2009), p. 347.

[45] B.R. Ambedkar (Valerian Rodrigues, ed.), *The Essential Writings of B.R. Ambedkar* (New Delhi: Oxford University Press, 2004), p. 275.

Constituting the Public: Entanglements of Law and Religion

Since the colonial period, the Indian public has typically been imagined as a 'deficient entity, to be contained, improved, or transcended, rather than one to be meaningfully engaged by the state'.[46] It was thus consistently the object of what William Mazzarella and Raminder Kaur term 'cultural regulation'.[47] Indian publics were seldom thought to be 'public' enough. They had to be educated, reformed and reworked before they could aspire to the name. From this vantage point, far from self-constituting, the public emerges here as something that comes into being when regulated from without.

Instead of taking this apparent deficiency as an idiosyncrasy of colonialism, it perhaps makes more sense to see it as telling us something important about publics more generally: they are constituted by overlapping networks of state and civil regulation. Take, for example, the set of civil laws governing the market economy. As Ritu Birla has argued, 'market governance' promoted a 'concept of the public' that functioned 'as a shorthand for the supra-local terrain of market exchange'. This terrain, comprised of economic actors disembedded from traditional communities, did not emerge spontaneously; rather, it was produced partly through the force of the law itself.[48] Where Birla's earlier work analyses the legal constitution of the market-as-public in late colonial India, her article here tracks how a series of court decisions in the 1990s redefined 'public interest' in a manner closely aligned with the emergent administrative style of neo-liberal governmentality. By attending to the legal regulation of the market, Birla challenges the presumed distinction between the state and the economy, demonstrating not only the historical contingency of the 'public' and the 'private', but also the extent to which both domains are tools of juridical administration. Here, 'the public' appears simultaneously as the object of the state's 'benevolent authority' and the 'instrument' of the juridico-economic order.

Much the same can be said for religious publics. In order to grant freedom to religion, the secular state must first determine what precisely counts as 'religion', thus adjudicating whether a given text or practice qualifies for state protection. Ironically, then, religion can only be free from state interference once it has received the state's imprimatur.[49] One way to see how this dynamic played out in British India is to examine how colonial actors finessed their political rhetoric to take advantage of the Raj's principle of 'non-interference'. As C.S. Adcock has shown, Arya Samajis were especially adept at devising a 'political semantics' that manipulated the Anglophone distinction between 'religion' and 'politics' to their advantage.[50]

Even the institution of the secret ballot, as David Gilmartin suggests, demonstrates how the rational–critical public emerges in tandem with the state.[51] As a theatrical space, the voting booth helps stage a drama in which the sovereign individual exercises her critical judgement free (at least apparently) from the external constraints of state and society. Far from preceding

---

[46] Arvind Rajagopal, 'Introduction', in Arvind Rajagopal (ed.), *The Indian Public Sphere: Readings in Media History* (New Delhi: Oxford University Press, 2009), p. 8.

[47] William Mazzarella and Raminder Kaur, 'Between Sedition and Seduction', in William Mazzarella and Raminder Kaur (eds), *Censorship in South Asia: Cultural Regulation from Sedition to Seduction* (Bloomington, IN: Indiana University Press, 2009), pp. 1–28.

[48] Ritu Birla, *Stages of Capital: Law, Culture and Market Governance in Late Colonial India* (Durham, NC: Duke University Press, 2009), pp. 4–5.

[49] Winnifred Fallers Sullivan, *The Impossibility of Religious Freedom* (Princeton, NJ: Princeton University Press, 2007); and Winnifred Fallers Sullivan and Robert Yelle (eds), *After Secular Law* (Stanford, CA: Stanford University Press, 2011).

[50] C.S. Adcock, *The Limits of Tolerance* (New York: Oxford University Press, 2013).

[51] David Gilmartin, 'Towards a Global History of Voting: Sovereignty, the Diffusion of Ideas, and the Enchanted Individual', in *Religions*, Vol. 3, no. 2 (2012), pp. 407–23.

the state, however, this atomised (or, in Elaine Hadley's terms, 'abstract') individual is in fact the product of an elaborate set of institutional procedures devised and guaranteed by the state.[52] The self-abstracted voter, we might say, lives a 'double life'. As Karl Marx argues in 'On the Jewish Question', the modern person 'lives in the *political community*, where he regards himself as a *communal being*, and in *civil society*, where he is active as a *private individual*'. He is split down the middle, both *bourgeois* (a private economic actor) and *citoyen* (an abstract public being).[53] For Marx, the attendant self-alienation renders politics fundamentally akin to religion: both entail 'man's' living simultaneously in heaven (i.e. through the medium of God or state) and on earth. The contradiction between these two terms (*bourgeois* and *citoyen*) underpins Habermas' account of the rise and fall of the Western European public sphere.[54] And, as Skaria suggests here, by reading 'On the Jewish Question' alongside Ambedkar's writings on Buddhism, it also sheds light on the place of 'the public' in modern India.

Gilmartin gives us a strong argument as to why this should be the case in his article here. Notions of 'the public' and 'the people' exist simultaneously in heaven and on earth. They conjure visions of a grandly unified entity that is the transcendent ground of state legitimation; at the same time, they also denote an empirical object that is defined by its heterogeneity, its ability to encompass multiple distinct voices vying for political precedence. As Gilmartin explains, the modern public, precisely in its 'double life', inherits and reshapes the more venerable problem of the 'king's two bodies': mediaeval and early modern political theology 'hinged on a distinction between *legitimation*, that is, a claim to authority transcending the everyday, and *governance*, the mundane process of actually managing and bringing order to society'. In slightly different terms, one might describe this as the distinction between the king's transcendent 'glory' and his immanent managerial power.[55] With the transition to modern democratic politics, this distinction was not eliminated; rather, a new set of abstract entities ('reason', 'the people') came to occupy the position of the king's spiritual body, granting the state its legitimacy by seeming to stand outside of and prior to the domain of governance.[56] Gilmartin's great intervention here is to suggest that, if we want to transpose this narrative to India, we need to push Ernst Kantorowicz's Christian kings onto transnational terrain (which, historically speaking, was surely their natural habitat). Drawing on recent work by Azfar Moin and Mithi Mukherjee, Gilmartin poses a series of highly suggestive questions. How, for example, might the ritual vocabulary of Mughal–Safavid sovereignty that lingered on into the nineteenth century have overlapped with the ritual vocabulary of the British Raj? Did ritual enactments of 'the people' vary between regions, inflected by culturally variable understandings of the sacred sovereign? Finally, how did the Raj's own internal distinction between 'imperial' and 'colonial' power inflect the political constitution of 'the people' in South Asia?

---

[52] Elaine Hadley, *Living Liberalism: Practical Citizenship in Mid-Victorian Britain* (Chicago, IL: University of Chicago Press, 2010), pp. 175–228.

[53] Karl Marx, 'On the Jewish Question', in Rodney Livingstone and Gregor Benton (trans.), *Early Writings* (London/New York: Penguin, 1974), p. 220; emphasis in original.

[54] See, for instance, Habermas, *The Structural Transformation of the Public Sphere*, pp. 116–26.

[55] See Giorgio Agamben, *The Kingdom and the Glory: For a Theological Genealogy of Economy and Government* (Stanford, CA: Stanford University Press, 2011).

[56] Of course, as several scholars have argued, 'the people' is only performatively constituted as such via documents like the US Declaration of Independence, which are often explicitly linked to the state. See, for example, Jason Frank, *Constituent Moments: Enacting the People in Postrevolutionary America* (Durham, NC: Duke University Press, 2010).

One point of entry into these questions is the debates around the caliphate and Islamic law that preoccupied Muslim reformers and others during the 1910s and 1920s. As SherAli Tareen suggests here, Abul Kalam Azad sought to anchor Indian Muslim identity in the symbol of the sovereign caliph, whereas Ahmad Raza Khan sought to relocate the basis of community to the 'practice of everyday life', thus opening the everyday to new forms of moral regulation. Similarly, we see in Ingram's article how nineteenth-century Islamic legal critiques of 'custom' conceived of certain everyday life habits as constituting a 'counter-normativity' that 'impinged on the normativity of the Qur'an and Sunna' by forming its 'own faux Shari'a', a *nomos* or law to rival that of official tradition. How to read this intensified regulation of daily life remains something of an open question. But one could suggest that it was precisely the shift to using the 'masses' (*'awamm*) as a symbol of political legitimacy that made these masses' mundane behaviour into a public or political problem.

A different point of entry is suggested by the legal regulation of 'the public' in the post-colonial period. Here too we see the conceptual gap between 'the public' as a general or transcendent entity and as an empirical object. As Mazzarella suggests in his discussion of the 2005 Mumbai dance bar ban, the legal statutes that define obscenity as causing 'annoyance' to the public entail a key ambiguity. Which 'public' are we talking about? The group of people who happen to be in attendance at an allegedly obscene performance? Or some representative sampling of 'the people' as a whole? A different version of this problem is to be found in the 2007 Misra Commission, as discussed by Viswanath. Here, we see how the state uses commissions to represent 'the public' in both its bodies. The commission 'represents representation'—that is, it does the 'performative work of representing the people *as a whole* and of suturing antagonistic divisions'.[57] But it also documents the empirical variation of the people by demanding the production of social scientific knowledge about oppressed groups. Here, a 'representational logic' familiar from the scholarship on colonial ethnology continues to operate in a 'formal democracy'. The commission blurs the line between these two types of public, converting social scientific fact into a symbol of state legitimacy. It is empirical variation and not transcendent unity that provides the symbolic ground of state power, precisely through its veneer of completeness.

In yet a different vein, we might ask how Ambedkar's effort, according to Skaria, to formulate Buddhism as a religion after secularism intervened in the Schmittian problematic of political theology. If part of the problem with the secular 'public' as the basis of legitimation for the modern state is the way in which it lays claim to an impossible position of generality or universality that effaces the minority, then Ambedkar's response is to 'search for another universalism' based on a principle of 'unruly spectrality'. He uses religion, Skaria argues, to recuperate a notion of the politically 'minor', of 'participation without a part, without sovereignty'.

Finally, we should ask how the print public fashioned itself, on the model of the court, as an institution wherein 'the people' can engage in the quintessentially sovereign act of imaginatively 'standing apart from the state and providing commentary' on the political and social world (Gilmartin, this volume). Insofar as it models itself on courts, 'the public' cannot be said to exist prior to the state. Rather, it emerges in tandem with the state, as an institution of modern governance. The affinity between court and press was on vivid display during the 1862 Maharaj Libel Case, during which judges and reformers aligned against what they perceived as a shared enemy: traditional religion. As Scott shows here, the affinity between press and court structured the rhetoric of 'exposure' that dominated the affair. One should be

---

[57] The language here is taken from the version of this essay presented on 18 May 2014 as part of the Northwestern University workshop, 'Imagining the Public in Colonial India'.

careful, however, to clarify that reformers like Karsandas Mulji were not characteristic of the print public as a whole. Many purveyors of print media explicitly aligned themselves with the sort of religious tradition that Mulji had maligned. Indeed, as Francesca Orsini shows here, 'old texts' were at least as important as new ones in defining the contours of the colonial public sphere. Whatever theoretical account we might want to give of the 'sovereign public' thus needs to consider how bhakti lives on into the modern period as a key means of thinking the relationship between self and society.

To bring the 1991 and 2015 special issues together is to showcase the diversity of possible approaches to the study of South Asian 'publics'. It is also to suggest promising areas for future research. As Freitag notes in her 'Postscript', even while bringing needed attention to topics like law and religion, the present collection places relatively less emphasis on the popular and performative aspects of public culture in South Asia. This is a significant omission, given the continued vibrancy of the 'visual turn' in South Asian studies, as well as the importance of visual culture to the history of legal concepts like 'public good' and 'public obscenity'. Both here and in her other recent work, Freitag reviews a number of ways in which visual sources can broaden and enrich the study of publics, as of South Asian history more generally.[58] It is a fitting way to conclude the current collection—gesturing toward the necessary incompletion and open-endedness of any inquiry into how the category of 'the public' functions in modern culture.

What is a public? This is a question that has to remain unanswered. Our aim here has simply been to outline a range of approaches to it in order to open a 'zone of debate'. We hope, in somewhat circular fashion, that this question can convene its own public, however fleeting or provisional, so that, as scholars, we might better appreciate the range of voices both within and beyond South Asia that have joined together to fashion this central term of modern thought.

---

[58] See especially the essays in Sandria B. Freitag (ed.), 'The Visual Turn in South Asian Studies', special issue of *South Asia: Journal of South Asian Studies*, Vol. XXXVII, no. 3 (Sept. 2014).

Rethinking the Public through the Lens of Sovereignty

DAVID GILMARTIN, *North Carolina State University, Raleigh, USA*

The interrelationships of the various, seemingly contradictory, uses of the public as a concept are best understood by relating the concept to sovereignty. The concept of the public thus gained particular structural meaning in colonial India through the state's efforts to legitimise its authority as the embodiment of a discourse of reason in the nineteenth century, with the courts serving as a critical model for the public. With the emergence of the concept of the sovereignty of the people in the twentieth century, the nature of the public was significantly transformed, and gained increasing significance as an arena for the open performance of the autonomous self.

The term 'public' has many different contemporary usages, in modern South Asia as elsewhere. On one level, the term relates to a particular form of state action (as in the phrases 'public works' or 'public policy') indexed to a particular claim to modern state legitimacy. On another level, it relates to a particular form of community standing *apart* from the state (as in 'public opinion', or 'the public'), and constituted by self-directed individuals; indeed, it can even refer to the distinctive individual orientations and sensibilities associated with participation in such a community (as in 'public-spirited'). On a third—and more structural—level, it can refer also to a particular *arena* (or space) of debate and action that stands conceptually *between* the state and society, a *space* (both physical and metaphorical) characterised by its *openness*, as in the phrases 'public sphere', 'public spaces', or simply, 'in public'. Here it is a 'zone' of interaction,[1] within which the power of the state can be held up to scrutiny (or legitimised) in intersection with a community of autonomous persons.

The argument here is that the relationship of these interconnected meanings can best be understood by invoking another critical concept—sovereignty—and the ways that sovereign authority operates in the mundane political world. This provides a critical framework for understanding how 'public', as a concept, operates simultaneously—and in critically interlinked ways—*both* as a descriptive term *and* as a normative term, defining both structures of open debate and norms for holding power to account. But in doing so, it also embodies a conundrum, rooted in the public's simultaneous significance as an arena of open contestation and as a concept framing the projection of a unified societal voice. If there has been a new direction in studies of the public over the last twenty years, it has been in efforts to come to terms with this contradiction. This was perhaps most clearly opened up by the arguments of

---

In addition to the comments of the other conference participants, I would like to acknowledge in particular the suggestions of Sandria Freitag, Pamela Price, Brent Sirota, and two anonymous *South Asia* readers in revising this article.

[1] This was the term used by Arjun Appadurai and Carol Breckenridge in their framing of 'public culture'. See Arjun Appadurai and Carol A. Breckenridge, 'Why Public Culture?', in *Public Culture Bulletin*, Vol. 1, no. 1 (Fall 1988), p. 6

Harold Mah, who noted the deep contradictions in a space of debate defined, in its fundamental nature, by struggles for access and precedence, which nevertheless seemed to transform, by an almost miraculous alchemy, these conflicting voices into a unity ('the public')—and one critical to state legitimation.[2]

Habermas, Sovereignty, and the Public Sphere

There is no better place to begin a discussion of this than with the classic narrative of the emergence of the modern 'public sphere' in western Europe provided by Jurgen Habermas, but to re-inflect this story (and to shape its distinctive departures when applied to colonial India), by linking it directly to the history of sovereignty—for it is in linking the public to notions of sovereignty that we can best explore the roots of this conundrum. Habermas's narrative is a relatively simple and compelling one: the development of European commerce and the emergence of a growing culture of print (and literacy), gave rise in the eighteenth century to a sphere of reasoned discussion existing apart from the authority of the state, conducted both in the press and in other 'open' venues such as coffee houses or associations. Critical to the model was that this was a sphere of independent men, fortified by their control of a 'private', domestic sphere. Rooted in the history of expanding commerce, the 'public sphere' was also, in Habermas's account, a quintessentially bourgeois phenomenon. Yet, critically, this sphere was also in principle an open one, defined *not* (in imagining) by social or political or class status (however critical these were to its *actual* historical moorings), but by the independent discourse of reason itself. And as such, it constituted a framework/structure for bringing independent reason to bear as a form of surveillance over the power of the state.[3]

Habermas himself recognised that the concept of the 'public sphere', though cast in his account as an emergent historical product, could in many ways be better understood as a 'normative concept' than as a strictly descriptive one.[4] But the significance of the 'public sphere' as, in effect, a normative, ideological assertion about legitimate power, can be better highlighted if we move outside Habermas's own frame to ground his account in the longer history of sovereignty, which is best understood in a broader, worldwide perspective. The key to sovereignty as a global concept, was that it was a form of legitimation rooted in the appeal to sources of power, divine and cosmic, located *outside* the contexts of immediate politics and everyday social life. It hinged on a distinction between *legitimation*, that is a claim to authority transcending the everyday, and *governance*, the mundane process of actually managing and bringing order to society. The key to Habermas's 'public sphere' in this context was his delineation of a structural frame in which reason itself could be projected as a touchstone for sovereign authority, as it too transcended everyday politics/social relations in a manner parallel to the operation of these divine and cosmic powers. Central to its relation to sovereignty was thus the fact that it stood structurally outside—and from that position operated upon—the realm of politics and worldly power.

If we re-inflect his argument, the concept of the 'public sphere' can thus be read in Habermas's formulation as, at root, a marker of a critical shift in substantive understandings of

---

[2] Harold Mah, 'Phantasies of the Public Sphere: Rethinking the Habermas of Historians', in *Journal of Modern History*, Vol. 72, no. 1 (March 2000), pp. 154–8. Mah in fact is critical of the primacy given in most analyses to the interpretation of 'the public' as a space.

[3] Jurgen Habermas, *The Structural Transformation of the Public Sphere: An Inquiry into a Category of Bourgeois Society* (trans. Thomas Burger) (Cambridge, MA: MIT Press, 1989).

[4] Jurgen Habermas, 'Popular Sovereignty as Procedure', in James Bohman and William Relg (eds), *Deliberative Democracy: Essays on Reason and Politics* (Cambridge, MA: MIT Press, 1997) p. 57.

sovereignty operating in the early modern period. Such older forms of sovereignty were multiple and are best projected onto a canvas far broader than Habermas's largely Eurocentric focus. If the role of 'divine right' in legitimising sovereignty in Europe was a subject of broad debate in European political theorising during the seventeenth and eighteenth centuries, the linking of sovereignty to multiple cosmic and divine formulations was also widespread in the Islamic world, as Azfar Moin has delineated. Most importantly, such ideas on sovereignty were in considerable Eurasian interaction—and in considerable flux; as Moin's work illustrates.[5] But whatever its multiple forms, sovereign authority was imagined in most contexts as an expression of the underlying conundrum of state power—a conundrum rooted in the need for sovereigns to be effective agents of order (and governance) in the mundane political world (and thus to be effectively engaged with all the community's conflicts and divisions), and yet at the same time to imaginatively transcend all society's conflicts and divisions, standing apart from them and embodying the community (and the polity) *as a unity*. This was the case whether theories of sovereignty were derived from connections to divine forces or from an imagined social contract. Whether reflected in the 'conundrum of the king's authority' (as the defining feature of pre-Islamic sovereignty in India as described by J.C. Heesterman), or in the imagining of the 'king's two bodies' in mediaeval Europe (as described by Ernst Kantorowicz), sovereignty entailed the *simultaneous* (and contradictory) projection of deep political engagement (and force) on the one hand, and apolitical detachment (even renunciation of the social world) on the other.[6]

Critically, the emerging framing of the 'public sphere' in the eighteenth century did not point in this context to the 'public' itself as a new *source* of sovereignty, but rather to the 'public sphere' as the imagined discursive zone of debate dramatising sovereignty's emerging forms—and its ongoing conundrums. Discursive reason, in its basic objectifying Cartesian dynamics, itself provided an increasingly important touchstone for legitimate sovereign authority. 'Reason' here hardly excluded 'irrational' elements—and was often mobilised for polemical purposes—but it defined a *discursive realm of evaluative argument* standing between (and—critically—apart from) state *and* society, a 'zone' from which an emerging 'public' could interrogate both. But the imagining of such a 'public sphere'—apart from both state and social power—remained bound in sovereignty's conundrums for such a zone of discursive reason could never, in its own structures (including law and rationalising bureaucracy), fully escape the pressures of politics and worldly influence. It thus embodied 'the conundrum of the king's authority' in new form, defining *both* a 'space' of worldly conflict and debate and—at the very same time—an image of unity implicit in the idea of a 'public' voice. This tension in fact shaped the moral and aesthetic dynamics of Habermas's account—an account driven by an image of the politics of discursive reason emerging in the eighteenth century as a lodestar of human progress, and yet one perpetually open to 'corruption' (or debasement) by the politicised and market-inflected flows of discourse as it encountered the real, changing social and political world during the course of the nineteenth and twentieth centuries, a reflection of sovereignty's underlying conundrum—a point to which we will return.

---

[5] Azfar Moin, *The Millennial Sovereign: Sacred Kingship and Sainthood in Islam (1400–1700)* (New York: Columbia University Press, 2012).
[6] For a further elaboration of this, see David Gilmartin, 'Towards a Global History of Voting: Sovereignty, the Diffusion of Ideas, and the Enchanted Individual', in *Religions*, Vol. 3, no. 2 (2012), pp. 407–23. The references are to J.C. Heesterman, *The Inner Conflict of Tradition: Essays in Indian Ritual, Kingship, and Society* (Chicago: University of Chicago Press, 1985); and Ernst H. Kantorowicz, *The King's Two Bodies: A Study in Mediaeval Political Theology* (Princeton: Princeton University Press, 1997).

I. Sovereignty, Society and the State: The Public as Discourse

If our reinflected account from Habermas provides an important theoretical backdrop for thinking about the 'public', it points also to the importance of addressing in India the specific character of colonial sovereignty. For our purposes, a rough outline of the central features of sovereignty in British India can be drawn from Mithi Mukherjee's recent account. As Mukherjee sees it, arguments on sovereignty in early British India (particularly those mobilised by Burke in Warren Hastings' impeachment trial), crystalised a structure of sovereign thinking based on the juxtaposition of two interconnected—yet in critical ways contradictory—components of sovereign order. These were, in Mukherjee's terminology, the 'imperial' and the 'colonial'. 'Imperial sovereignty', as she put it, was cast precisely in the language of detachment from the pragmatics of territorial administration and grounded in appeals to 'natural law' (a cosmic vision linked to science, morality and reason). 'Colonial sovereignty', on the other hand, was cast in terms of 'state necessity', or, to put it another way, in terms of the politics of everyday order.[7] As a basically Hobbesian vision, colonial sovereignty enmeshed the state in the structures of power it encountered on the ground in India. Yet, at the very same time, imperial sovereignty gained meaning as it positioned the British state as a force apart from such particularities, an agency of idealised reason and progress whose claims to authority (like those deriving from divine and cosmic forces) stood outside the everyday worlds of power in the society it ruled. These two elements, the 'imperial' and the 'colonial', were *both* critical to the state's authority and legitimacy, but their juxtaposition points toward the same inner conundrum of sovereignty we have just discussed.

Most intriguing in Mukherjee's argument is her attempt to develop a structural understanding of how, in such a context, sovereignty operated—and it is here that she sees the operationalisation of this conflicted vision of sovereignty as most clearly embodied in the model of the colonial law court. It is this model, she argues, that significantly shaped Burke's original framing of 'imperial' sovereignty, as sovereign authority most powerfully inhered in the figure of the judge, adjudicating power and social relations but himself standing conceptually apart from the 'colonial' realm of administration and force. By the late nineteenth century this model had powerfully shaped an idea she calls 'justice as equity', a fundamental framework for the projection of sovereign authority in which 'justice' was linked preeminently to *impartiality* and *detachment* (rather than to substantive, *social* ideas), a projection perhaps most clearly articulated in Queen Victoria's 1858 proclamation signalling the end of Company rule and justifying Crown rule—for all its founding violence during the suppression of the 1857 revolt—preeminently in these terms.

Subsequently, 'colonial' and 'imperial' rule in fact intersected in various ways. The most noteworthy administrative manifestation of this intersection lay in the attempted British objectification of indigenous cultural categories, a central strategy through which the British sought to assimilate a fragmented social order to their rule through detached, 'objective' reason.[8] But, as Mukherjee argues, the most powerful model for the projection of sovereign authority lay in the law court, whose structure shaped deeply indigenous thinking on legitimate rule—and thus influenced significantly the form of early Indian National Congress challenges to British rule.[9] This is not to say that most in the Congress actually believed that

---

[7] Mithi Mukherjee, *India in the Shadow of Empire: A Legal and Political History, 1774–1950* (Delhi: Oxford University Press, 2010), pp. 42–4, 58–9.

[8] Bernard S. Cohn, 'The Census, Social Structure and Objectification in South Asia', in *An Anthropologist among the Historians and Other Essays* (New York: Oxford University Press, 1987), pp. 224–54.

[9] Mukherjee, *India in the Shadow of Empire*, pp. 72–150.

'justice as equity' was, *in practice*, what the British legal regime actually delivered—far from it. Nor were legal issues the only focus for early Congress discourse. But a view of 'justice' as hinging fundamentally on *detachment* from partiality or particularity came to define a powerful sensibility, a sensibility given meaning precisely by the principles of sovereignty asserted by the British themselves, which allowed key Indian elites to position themselves as standing apart from the pressures of social divisions and hierarchical power (in which they were otherwise deeply enmeshed) and to participate, however partially, in a discourse of disinterested oversight of the operation of the state—and of society—in the name of a discourse of reason. In a society in which the bourgeois transformations emphasised by Habermas remained limited, it was the imagined intersection of law and sovereignty, in other words, that most powerfully structured an emerging vision of an Indian 'public' located between the 'state' and 'society', and offering an ongoing critique of both.

Courts and Law as Central to the Emerging Public in India

To point to this structure is not to deny the importance of new networks of print linking India, Britain, and many other parts of the world in shaping these processes, as C.A. Bayly has made clear.[10] Nor is it to deny the importance of existing, indigenous traditions of detached, literate oversight of authority, linked in particular to networks of high-caste (particularly Brahman) elites, whose self-definition suggested the powerful exclusions shaping such newly-emerging 'public' visions as well.[11] But it was the structuring of law (and the courts) that proved most critical as to the public sphere's emerging nineteenth-century form. As litigation brought the inner workings of social life (and social power) into open court, publicity also brought the public audience for court cases (as they were covered in the press, commented upon in pamphlets, and evaluated in innumerable venues of gossip and discussion) into the subjective, structural position of judges. It was the publicising of court cases (which were in their very structure *open*) that perhaps more than anything else provided the model for the sensibilities defining an emergent 'public' whose principles mirrored the sovereign claims of the state.

We can illustrate the impact of models of law on emerging conceptions of the 'public'—and suggest the significant anomalies the concept embodied—in multiple ways. These include three key areas: (a) the distinctive way that the 'public' took on meaning in India in juxtaposition with an emerging 'private', domestic realm that arose out of the 'fragmentation' of the older visions of sacred kingship associated with 'little kings'; (b) the distinctive ways that 'religion' itself was reconfigured as a category as religious authority came to be subject to colonial litigation; and (c) the distinctive ways that conceptions of sovereignty in 'public arenas' (arenas of open religious performance, as Sandria Freitag has delineated them) were re-shaped by being made subject to colonial legal and administrative adjudication. In all these areas, the role of the law and the courts shaped emerging visions of the 'public' in its distinctly Indian manifestations.

---

[10] See C.A. Bayly, *Empire and Information: Intelligence Gathering and Social Communication in India, 1780–1870* (Cambridge: Cambridge University Press, 1996), pp. 180–224, for a discussion of an emerging 'Anglo-Indian public sphere'.

[11] For earlier Brahman networks, see the important work of Rosalind O'Hanlon, 'Contested Conjunctures: Brahman Communities and "Early Modernity" in India', in *American Historical Review*, Vol. 118, no. 3 (June 2013), pp. 765–87.

Court Cases, the 'Private' Realm, and the Reconstruction of Sovereignty

Inheritance cases in prominent landed families and lineages were particularly ubiquitous in late nineteenth-century India. But their importance lay not just in shaping the history of landholding in India, but in shaping the distinction between the 'public' and the 'private' that was to become central to the new sovereign order. Such cases provide, in fact, a critical window on how new, law-framed formulations of colonial sovereignty depended on new distinctions between private and public even as older visions of sovereignty were called into question by the very exercise of law-based proceduralism.

The dynamics of this have been illustrated perhaps most clearly in the work of Pamela Price on inheritance-based litigation in prominent South Indian landed families. As Price argues, inheritance cases in such families were never *just* about property (though property was at their heart) but were also about the nature of authority in landed domains. 'The rhetoric of litigation, simultaneously universalizing and individualizing', Price argues, had critical implications for the images of sovereignty that had historically defined authority in these estates, for it redefined the relationship between divine and human realms, undercutting the imagining of a world in which kingship was shared within nesting domains. In the process of being subjected to the courts' procedural authority, 'monarchical cosmologies' were, she writes, called into question, and their taken-for-granted power challenged. A critical by-product of exposure to the sovereign structure of detached court-based 'justice' was, in other words, to significantly 'fragment', as Price puts it, existing understandings of sovereign authority linked to older cosmologies.[12]

Equally critically, such cases also demonstrated how the 'public' authority of the state (as reflected in the courts) was also linked to a parallel, discursive 'public' ream, standing apart from the state and providing commentary on its actions (and on the 'private' social realms it opened to 'public' inspection). As Price suggests, the impact of high-profile inheritance cases in prominent families lay in the fact that the inner details of internal family politics were, through court procedures, *exposed* to public view. 'Litigation at district level took political competition beyond the realm of the estate or *samastanam* (kingdom)'. When taken to Madras on appeal, such cases became the subject of increasing 'newspaper reportage', in the process shaping the 'values and categories' defining 'the discourses of the public sphere in the Presidency capital'.[13] One effect of such cases was thus to transform the internal politics of landed families, now subjected to 'public' surveillance, from contests over the symbols of sovereignty linked to divine cosmologies, to simply 'private' disputes within what was increasingly viewed as a *social class* of landed families comprising the 'native aristocracy'. The irony, of course, was that the constitution of the 'private' sphere that defined these 'families' was itself constituted by the existence of a detached 'public' that could now imagine itself standing outside the social to evaluate this realm according to rational criteria, paralleling the *proceduralism* of the courts themselves. Such cases thus helped to instantiate new visions of imperial sovereignty linked to detached, reasoned surveillance over what was increasingly seen as a distinct 'social' realm. This was in fact part of a process by which 'society' was delineated as a distinctive realm, existing apart from the state, even as the 'public' occupied a conceptual space in between.

Critical here were thus the larger structural parallels between court-based authority (as central to the constitution of colonial sovereignty), and the emerging structure of a nineteenth-century 'public'. Property cases helped to shape the idea of the 'private' (or the domestic) as

---

[12] Pamela G. Price, *Kingship and Political Practice in Colonial India* (Cambridge: Cambridge University Press, 1996), p. 75.
[13] *Ibid.*, pp. 41–2.

the realm of the *social* par excellence (and one in which women were particularly important, as Price's case studies make clear), with the 'public' linked to a vision of sovereignty standing apart from this world and rooted in the autonomous realm of discourse (associated particularly with men).[14] But also critical was that such processes were not simply a product of action from above—by a 'modernising' and 'secularising' colonial state—but were equally a product of actions by the litigants *themselves*, whose appeals to the courts in local struggles for property and status facilitated the gradual devitalisation (or at least reformulation) of older sovereign cosmologies as British visions of 'justice as equity' (which had, of course, their own indigenous analogues) penetrated into 'public' consciousness.[15] The structure of the 'public' thus emerged as a reflection not only of the structure of colonial sovereignty itself, but also as a product of the actions of Indians themselves who, through their own social conflicts, gave this structure increasing ideological meaning.

Court Cases and the Reconstruction of Religion

This is not to say, as Price's account also makes clear, that such developments were without ambiguities, for the images of monarchical authority embodied in religious ritual continued to carry powerful popular meanings in South Indian society, whatever their relationship to an emerging 'public'. But such processes can be seen even more clearly in the direct intersection of courts and 'public' discourse regarding religious leadership and, indeed, with respect to changing meanings of 'religion' itself. The operation of court cases dealing with religious property and inheritance contests were in many ways similar to those involving the 'property rights' of 'little kings'. Control over property was critical to a variety of religious institutions in India, influencing struggles for authority in Hindu *maths* as much as Sufi shrines. Court cases thus opened the inner workings of these institutions to 'public' discussion and commentary just as they did in other landed property disputes. Indeed, the very structure of these cases—and the publicity attending them—underscored the juxtaposition of the 'social' (and the 'private') against the 'public', thus shaping, in some cases, the very meanings attached to legitimate 'religious' leadership. Cases of litigation involving religious leaders were in fact often linked to the concomitant delineation of 'corrupt' forms of religion, forms that were now associated with—and often perceived as being determined by—the 'social' (or by 'custom'), as juxtaposed with the detached (and 'uncorrupted') sensibilities of a reasoned, 'public' approach to religion.[16]

Once again, the effect of publicised court proceedings was thus, in effect, to re-orient the relationship between divine and human realms, and to open older forms of 'religious' leadership to the discipline of new public definitions of 'religion' associated with the detached judgment and discursive reason that defined the new locus for sovereign colonial authority. And in the context of many cases, this 'public' surveillance over the social worlds of religious practice was now broadened by reference to the larger rationalising trends in the ongoing academic study of religions, marked by detachment and objectivity, that shaped metropolitan scholarship in this era—and which influenced court judgments as well. As Tomoko Masuzawa

---

[14] For a probing analysis of the complex dynamics of the law's role in this process, see Rachel Sturman, *The Government of Social Life in Colonial India: Liberalism, Religious Law, and Women's Rights* (Cambridge: Cambridge University Press, 2012).

[15] This is an argument made in somewhat different form by Lauren Benton, *Law and Colonial Cultures: Legal Regimes in World History, 1400–1900* (Cambridge: Cambridge University Press, 2002).

[16] See J. Barton Scott, *Spiritual Despots: Modern Hinduism, Priestcraft, and the Genealogies of Self-Rule* (Chicago: University of Chicago Press, forthcoming).

has argued, the intellectual analysis of 'religion' in the late nineteenth century was associated with the widespread projection of rationalising, 'world-wide' categories for making sense of the messy worlds of local religious practice.[17] The projection of external, Cartesian templates for making comparative sense of religion, drawn from the realm of discursive reason, significantly influenced the courts, a process suggesting, in fact, the broader intellectual significance of scientific and academic social scientific discourse in shaping the redefinitions of sovereignty marking this period more generally. A prime example of this came with the famous Aga Khan case of 1866, whose result was largely to remove the Aga Khan's leadership from its particular 'social' context—a context defined by the cosmological intersection of divine and human domains in the social world—and to ground it instead in the detached, rationalised frame of 'public', discursive reason, shaped by the court's judgment that the practice of the Khojas had to be evaluated in terms of their place within a rationalised structure of world 'religions', as a 'sect' of Muslim Ismailis.[18]

It was not, of course, exclusively property disputes that led to such cases, as Bart Scott's work on the Maharaj Libel case illustrates.[19] Criminal cases revealing the 'private' lives of religious leaders, such as the Tarakeswar murder case of 1873, had similar effects.[20] But by directing a spotlight on the social embeddedness of religious leaders, property cases played perhaps the most pervasive and critical role in highlighting the contrast between a detached 'public' vision of religious leadership and the potential 'corruption' entailed in the absorption of religion into the 'social' world of power and property—not least because, as in the case of 'little kings', it was the actions of religious leaders themselves (and their relatives) in filing property cases that opened their authority to 'public' scrutiny. Property was thus the most important concept driving religion into the courts, and in the process transforming its meanings. Associated with these transformations was the emergence of a new 'public' religious sensibility (one might even say a 'secular' religious sensibility, in the sense of one conceptually separated from the immediacy of everyday social entanglements[21]), that was aligned with a new set of sovereign ideals—and that defined a new vision of 'public' religion linked to these ideals.

Public Arenas, the Law, and the Oversight of Religion

But the ambiguities in the 'public's' relationship to new forms of sovereignty can perhaps be seen most clearly of all if we turn to the operation of the open arenas of action associated with the ritual calendars of Hinduism and Islam that Sandria Freitag has labelled 'public arenas'. As Freitag argues, there were critical parallels between Habermas's vision of an open realm of 'public' discourse for the reasoned, moral critique of the state (and thus the exercise of moral surveillance over it) and the structuring of public observances evoking templates of 'good rule' embodied in the open performance of powerful moral (even, 'civilisational') stories such as those of the Ramayana or the martyrdom of Husain at Karbala. Like Habermas's public, these stories contained within them templates of justice that stood apart from—and thus

---

[17] Tomoko Masuzawa, *The Invention of World Religions, or, How European Universalism was Preserved in the Language of Pluralism* (Chicago: University of Chicago Press, 2005).

[18] Teena Purohit, *The Aga Khan Case: Religion and Identity in Colonial India* (Cambridge, MA: Harvard University Press, 2012).

[19] See Bart Scott's article in this issue.

[20] Tanika Sarkar, 'Talking about Scandals: Religion, Law and Love in Late Nineteenth Century Bengal', in *Studies in History*, Vol. 13, no. 1 (1997), pp. 63–95.

[21] For the elaboration of such a view of the 'secular', see Humeira Iqtidar, *Secularizing Islamists: Jamaat-e-Islami and Jamaat-ud-Dawa in Urban Pakistan* (Chicago: University of Chicago Press, 2011).

offered an external frame for the evaluation of—everyday politics and rule.[22] The 'public' nature of these performances was in fact further enhanced by their extensive links in the late nineteenth and early twentieth centuries to the emerging, discursive realms of social and political commentary *in print*, for which they provided a reservoir of images that were powerfully evoked in both literary and visual allusion. The theatricality of these 'public arena' realms in fact played a critical role in shaping significantly the sensibilities of the new 'public sphere' of print, within which the inter-generic connections between print and public performance were extensive.[23] One critical reason to pay attention to such 'public arena' performances in this sphere was thus, as Freitag has strongly emphasised, that their roles suggested a genealogy for the 'public' in India that was hardly a product *wholly* of the Eurocentric transformations underscored by Habermas, or of the structure of colonial rule.

Yet, at the same time, the development of such public arenas in eighteenth- and nineteenth-century India suggests the centrality of shifting conceptions of sovereignty to the meanings such public arenas carried. The degree to which the historical development of these public arena performances was itself a product of shifting visions of sovereignty as the Mughal Empire gave way to the regional eighteenth-century successor states who sponsored the expansion of such performances, remains a subject that needs considerably more exploration. But critical also is the question as to how the meanings of such public arena performances (and thus of the 'public' itself) were inflected as they were encompassed within the structuring of British 'imperial' visions of rule and within an ideal of sovereignty linked to the 'rule of law'. On one level, structures of British dispute settlement played a vital role in encompassing such performances too—and access to 'public' spaces more generally—within a broader, detached vision of sovereign *impartiality*, a framework of legitimate rule standing apart from the distinctive *substantive* content of the very templates of 'good rule' that such public arena performances embodied. And once again, local leaders were themselves often responsible for facilitating the penetration of such a vision of detached sovereign authority into elite consciousness, for it was they who often took the initiative in appealing to the courts—and to British administrators—to adjudicate public arena disputes (about procession routes, access to particular public spaces, etc.). For their part, British administrators (and courts) generally looked to the precedence of 'custom' in making their decisions in these disputes, thus making clear their own linking of the *substance* of these performances not to images of cosmic order or to sovereignty, but to the *social* world of religious difference and *particularity*. This underscored their own sovereign grounding in a detached, *procedural* realm that transcended the substantive particularism of which the common appeal to 'custom' in British colonial law was a powerful marker.

And yet, the relationship of these sites to the development of the 'public' in colonial India was one of considerable ambiguity, for even as these public arena performances were, in a sense, encapsulated within the larger structures of colonial sovereignty—and the 'rule of law'—they operated in ways that could never be fully encompassed by such a structure. Perhaps most important was their grounding in structures of cyclical time that brought cosmic powers to earth within structures of imagining that could not be fully contained by colonial

---

[22] Sandria B. Freitag, *Collective Action and Community: Public Arenas and the Emergence of Communalism in North India* (Berkeley: University of California Press, 1989).

[23] As Freitag puts it, 'the connections [of live performances] to two-dimensional visual media are fascinating and astonishingly obvious'. Sandria B. Freitag, 'Visions of the Nation: Theorizing the Nexus between Creation, Consumption and Participation in the Public Sphere', in Rachel Dwyer and Christopher Pinney (eds), *Pleasure and the Nation: The History, Politics and Consumption of Public Culture in India* (Delhi: Oxford University Press, 2001), p. 46.

adjudication. As Freitag argues, public arena activities in open spaces accessed an overarching vision of sovereign community—standing apart from the divisions of the everyday socio-political world—through the imagined movement from social structure to *communitas* (in the language of Victor Turner), that is, from mundane to sacred time, and then back again. Their operation was thus predicated on visions of sovereign authority, situated apart from the social, that yet lived in popular consciousness as participants returned to their everyday social and political worlds.[24]

The operation of such 'public arenas' thus raises questions relating to a problem long debated with respect to theories of the public, that is, whether we can imagine a world in which multiple 'publics' (in the *plural*) emerged, in this case rooted in their relationship to different touchstones of sovereignty. The existence of multiple 'publics' (or 'counterpublics') within Habermas's framework was a question raised long ago by critics of Habermas's emphasis on the bourgeois public sphere as an imagined unity. Noting the deeply exclusionary nature of this public sphere in reality, these critics tracked the supposedly plural character of 'publics' in Europe and elsewhere as they emerged among subaltern groups in response to these exclusions.[25] Such exclusionary influences have shaped writing on the public in India too, where the sensibilities associated with detached, evaluative reason were ones with powerful exclusionary biases, linked to gender, class, caste and other deep-seated social distinctions—including religion—whose operation spawned sometimes fragmented spaces of public discussion.

Yet, as other critics have noted, an emphasis on multiple 'publics', as distinctive spaces of assertion and debate, can easily deflect attention from the transformative power of the emergent concept of the 'public' as a unifying process and ideal.[26] In the case of 'public arenas', the question was thus something quite different. Here the issue related not just to the boundaries and exclusions in *spaces* of debate, but to whether and how 'publics' linked to religious templates of cosmic power and 'good rule' retained their own universalising sovereign pretensions even in the face of the new detached, encapsulating sovereign visions associated with British rule. The operation of 'public arenas' seemingly pointed to colonial sovereign structures that sought to encapsulate not just individuals but entire 'religious communities' with their own universalising visions, thus defining a world of differentiated 'publics' operating with incommensurable frameworks of sovereign value—a structure perhaps pointing toward an emerging world of Indian 'communalisms'.

And yet, even in these circumstances, the 'public sphere' also provided a site where Indian actors renegotiated these older, cosmic framings of sovereign authority in interaction with the sensibilities of detached, objective reason that defined the new claims to sovereignty modelled by science and the 'rule of law'. For some leaders of the Arya Samaj concerned with cow protection, for example, the 'public sphere' was *both* an arena for reasoned discussions of the universal moral orientations derived from a particular (Hindu) 'scripture' *and* a frame for broader discussions about the reform of society and the state transcending religious particularity.[27] In a similar vein, champions of Urdu language could sometimes see their mission as a universalising one, linking to a cosmopolitan and secular vision, even as they

---

[24] Freitag, *Collective Action and Community*, pp. 85–97.
[25] Nancy Fraser, 'Rethinking the Public Sphere: A Contribution to the Critique of Actually Existing Democracy', in Craig Calhoun (ed.), *Habermas and the Public Sphere* (Cambridge, MA: MIT Press, 1992), pp. 109–42.
[26] Mah, 'Phantasies of the Public Sphere', pp. 156–68.
[27] C.S. Adcock, 'Sacred Cows and Secular History: Cow Protection Debates in Colonial North India', in *Comparative Studies of South Asia, Africa and the Middle East*, Vol. 30, no. 2 (2010), pp. 297–311.

grounded this in a commitment to the particularity of Urdu's distinct cultural history as a language.[28] In this, they echoed emerging languages of nationalism, which cast the particularity of the nation as itself a manifestation of the universalism of human difference.[29] None of this eliminated the ongoing tension between the particularising power of objectifying imperial sovereignty and the ongoing, universalising meanings still attached to older, cosmic religious visions. But such new approaches suggested the critical transformations in the 'public' that new visions of sovereignty entailed.

II. Sovereignty and the 'People': The Public as Performance

To understand the twentieth-century relationship of sovereignty to the 'public', however, we must introduce another critical concept into the story, the idea of the 'sovereignty of the people'. In some ways, the sovereignty of the 'people', and the sovereignty of discursive reason and the law had long been intellectually linked. But to appeal to the people's sovereignty, as increasingly embodied in the twentieth-century spread of mass elections, was to appeal not to reasoned *discourse* itself as the locus of sovereignty, but to the embedding of sovereignty in physical bodies, whose sovereign authority was linked to a newly-emerging concept of the individual person, viewed as the bearer of an almost mystical *autonomy*. This is in no way to suggest that appeals to the discourse of reason disappeared—for such appeals remained central throughout the twentieth century to the state's projection of its 'public' authority. But an image of what I have elsewhere called the 'enchanted individual', an individual defined by an ineffable essence transcending his or her social existence, gained increasing significance.[30] And along with this came important shifts in the meaning and operation of the concept of the 'public', not as a *source* of sovereignty but as a stage for the *performance* of a *non-discursive* human essence, the kernel of autonomy and freedom, that defined the self-controlled and desiring individual as the theoretical bedrock of the 'people's sovereignty'.[31]

The Enchanted Individual and Public Performance

There were, of course, older traditions of performance that had marked the public realm, as we have already seen. But the key to performances linked to the invocation of the people's sovereignty was that these were essentially performances of the self, public projections of the imagined, enchanted individual who was the key to a new vision of order (one might even say, cosmic order). As these performances of the self played out in the public sphere in India in the twentieth century, they took (at least) two distinctive forms linked to different (though hardly fixed) concepts of the person, each defined—in different ways—by the autonomy and freedom that allowed the individual to be imagined as an enchanted entity transcending the world of social and power relations—and indeed, the world of discourse itself. The first concept was one of enchanted self-mastery, whose performance projected the self-controlled person as a

---

[28] Kavita Datla, *The Language of Secular Islam: Urdu Nationalism and Colonial India* (Honolulu: University of Hawaii Press, 2013).

[29] Charles Taylor, 'The Politics of Recognition', in Amy Gutman (ed.), *Multiculturalism: Examining the Politics of Recognition* (Princeton: Princeton University Press, 1994), pp. 25–73.

[30] See Gilmartin, 'Towards a Global History of Voting', pp. 411–14, for a discussion of the introduction of the secret ballot in these terms.

[31] The argument here is an elaboration, but with analytical attention to the sovereignty concept, of the one made in David Gilmartin, 'Democracy, Nationalism and the Public: A Speculation on Colonial Muslim Politics', in *South Asia: Journal of South Asian Studies*, Vol. XIV, no. 1 (June 1991), pp. 123–40.

universalising microcosm for political order, and thus the key to sovereign authority. This was a vision dramatised most spectacularly in the years following 1919–20 by the public performances of Mahatma Gandhi. The second was a vision of autonomous personhood linked to the transformative power of individual desire, whose public enactment, whether through market-based consumption or the open performance of devotional commitment, projected once again an enchanted core of sovereign personhood in public that was imagined to operate as an existential human essence existing apart from the social. Both of these visions had roots going back much earlier than 1920, *both* in India *and* in nineteenth-century European thinking. But they nevertheless took on new vitality in the twentieth century with the gradual emergence of the idea of the sovereign 'people' as a touchstone for legitimate rule on a worldwide scale.

The Self as Microcosm Defined by Autonomous Self-Mastery

As Mithi Mukherjee has argued, Gandhi's politics were built on a distinctive idea of human freedom as renunciation, which represented, she argues, a distinctively Indian approach to liberty that was in sharp contrast to dominant 'western' ideas of liberty based on 'individual rights, private property, representative Government, national identity, and the nation-state'.[32] But an emphasis on the 'non-Western' roots of Gandhi's thinking should not divert us from the ways that Gandhi's ideas were also deeply linked to international ideas on popular sovereignty (both 'Western' and 'non-Western', terms it is best to leave behind here) as a form of legitimate authority linked to an image of autonomous personhood, standing apart (in essence) from the socio-political world. This is what gave Gandhi's emphasis on renunciation-in-the-world its powerful political significance in twentieth-century India. Gandhi's model of the *satyagrahi* was based on persons whose moral essence was detached from the social influences of the world even as their actions engaged with and provided a *model for* sovereignty's operation in that world as an ideal. Gandhi's idea of *swaraj*, or self-rule, drew, in other words, on the image of an autonomous, sovereign self, with *satya* (truth) at its enchanted core—and this provided the underpinnings for the larger concept of the sovereignty of the 'people' in India, defined by an essence that stood apart from the conflicts of everyday politics and interest—in which the worldly self was at the same time engaged.

The 'public sphere' thus took on new meanings as a stage for the projection of this vision of sovereignty, which Gandhi's Non-Cooperation movements themselves soon occupied. The realm of print no doubt remained a vital site for the discursive critique of both state and society in these movements (as the voluminous writings of Gandhi and other Congress leaders show), but there was an important shift in emphasis: the 'public' character of these movements lay less in their appeal to discursive reason than in their performative character, with India itself—its open spaces, its pilgrimages, its clothed bodies, its criss-crossing railways—as the public stage on which *satyagraha* played out. Nothing illustrated this more clearly than the relationship of these movements to the 'rule of law', the touchstone of colonial sovereignty in the past. Gandhi by no means rejected the concept of the rule of law. But he was scathing in his denunciations of what the structure of 'justice' had come to mean under the British. Far from 'justice as equity', British courts, he declared, had brought slavery to India.[33] But Gandhi's *satyagraha* was based on a different definition of law: for the

---

[32] Mithi Mukherjee, 'Transcending Identity: Gandhi, Nonviolence, and the Pursuit of a "Different" Freedom in Modern India', in *American Historical Review*, Vol. 115, no. 2 (April 2010), pp. 453–73.
[33] M.K. Gandhi, *Hind Swaraj and Other Writings* (Antony Parel, ed.) (Cambridge: Cambridge University Press, 1997), p. 58.

satyagrahi, the commitment to rules (procedures) was rooted in the construction of the self, in the self-denial and self-discipline that was the essence of *swaraj*.

Gandhi made this clear in his famous distinction between 'mobocracy' and 'democracy', the latter defined by what Gandhi called 'people's law' (the law, though Gandhi did not put it exactly this way, that lay at the heart of the people's claim to sovereignty). This was law that was not an emanation of the procedural rationalism of a detached, equitable state—or of reason as an autonomous discourse. It was rather an internalised property of the self, of 'the people's ability to control themselves', as Gandhi put it.[34] It too thus emanated from a place outside the social, but it was to be made 'public' (however much it was also rationally explained) primarily through performance rather than through discourse. In describing the proper mode of action for Lahoris protesting in 1921 the infamous John Lawrence statue on the Mall in Lahore, for example, whose inscription asked them to choose whether they would 'have the pen or the sword', Gandhi seemingly rejected both, seeing the people's mystical sovereign unity (their action 'as one man', as he put it, the individual the microcosm of the whole) lying in the *performance* of an internal self-discipline that transcended both force *and* reasoned discourse. They 'must not *argue*', he said, 'but merely court arrest'. Removal of the statue must be the ultimate result, but the immediate aim was that 'men and women offer themselves as a sacrifice'.[35] Here the 'public' became almost (but not quite, given the highly politicised context) a *ritual* platform precisely for the performance of sacrifice not only for India's freedom, but also to the ultimate principle of sovereignty, a 'people' constituted by the primacy of the enchanted, self-mastering self.

New visions of the 'people' as sovereign thus shaped newly emerging framings of the public realm as a stage for the performance of popular sovereignty based on principles that the colonial state could hardly *openly* repudiate in the international climate of the years after World War I. The British state had, indeed, gestured toward this definition of sovereignty with the introduction of important provincial elections in 1920 (however limited the franchise). But once again, it was a stage whose performances were directed *both* toward calling the state to account according to these new sovereign principles *and* toward educating a people whose worldly social selves represented an ever-present threat to the enchanted, extra-social moral essence that defined the people's own sovereign claims, a threat captured strikingly by Gandhi's derogatory use of the term 'mobocracy'. The term, in fact, points also to the continuities in Gandhi's thinking with nineteenth-century liberalism. The 'people' were, for Gandhi, in a process of *becoming*, always challenged by the lower social instincts that needed discipline and education. The public—as an idea and as an arena—thus lay in its links to a vision of sovereignty that allowed for detachment from (and thus a position for critique of) state and society alike.

The Self as Defined by Autonomous Desire

But the vision of the autonomous sovereign individual also took another powerful form in this era, and one in sharp tension to the one projected by Gandhi, a vision of sovereign autonomy linked less to self-control than to public devotionalism: to the making of an autonomous core

---

[34] M.K. Gandhi, 'Democracy "versus" Mobocracy', *Young India* (8 Sept. 1920), in *The Collected Works of Mahatma Gandhi* (ebook), Vol. 21, 1 July–21 Nov. 1920 (New Delhi: Publications Division Government of India, 1999), pp. 245–49 [http://www.gandhiserve.org/cwmg/VOL021.PDF, accessed 16 Dec. 2014].

[35] M.K. Gandhi, 'The Pen or the Sword', *Young India* (17 Nov. 1921), in *The Collected Works of Mahatma Gandhi* (ebook), Vol. 25, 27 Oct.1921–22 Jan. 1922 (New Delhi: Publications Division Government of India, 1999), pp. 113–15 [http://www.gandhiserve.org/cwmg/VOL025.PDF, accessed 16 Dec. 2014]. Emphasis added.

of individual desire public. Again, this was a form of action with deep historical roots, as the histories of both Sufism and bhakti suggest. But what was critical in this era was its new linking to the *performance* of popular sovereignty on a public stage.

A critical element in this new vision of the public was provided by middle-class consumerism. No one has captured this more clearly than Markus Daechsel in his study of the Urdu middle-class milieu. As Daechsel argues, the years after World War I witnessed a new form of political action he calls the 'politics of self-expression'. This drew strength from consumer-related self-fashioning, a politics that 'denied the social and political nature of humanity', as he puts it, and saw the 'self-expression' of 'inner essences', or identities, as the central purpose of political action.[36] In this sense, he describes a politics driven by the same sovereign, autonomous, enchanted self—a vision of the self transcending the social—that shaped the ideas of Gandhi. But far more than in the case of Gandhi, this was a politics built, as Daechsel sees it, on the outright *rejection* of discursive reason, a politics with important family ties to European fascism in the interwar years.

Daechsel's account in fact self-consciously echoes the earlier commentaries of the Frankfurt School (and Habermas) on the role of mass consumption in producing a 'degeneration' of the reasoned public sphere in an era of mass consumption. With a vision of political action defined increasingly *not* by the negotiation of complex social relations, but by the performance of a 'unitary and inner (individual) essence', the idea of a communicative 'public sphere', as Daechsel sees it, effectively 'ceased to function' (at least when it came to forms of political 'self-expression').[37] This was reflected in many of the characteristic political movements of this era, such as that of Allama Mashriqi and the Khaksars (with its emphasis on militarised organisation and loyalty to a leader), or the devotional movements attached to symbols like the Shahidganj mosque, or, indeed, the Pakistan Movement itself, driven less by reasoned discourse than by the cosmic power of *desire and longing* to transcend (and in the process re-make) the world.

Yet of course the appeal to a discourse of sovereign reason hardly disappeared in this era. Daechsel's work is important rather in underscoring the depth of the tension between a 'public' realm defined by discursive reason and one defined by the open *performance* of inner identity, a development Daechsel sees, following Baudrillard, as a product of the expanding world of individual consumption. Yet it is important to see these developments also as linked to the tensions inherent in the sovereignty of the 'people' itself, as it gained traction in India in this era. It was not merely rising middle-class consumption (which, in any case, still remained relatively limited), but a post-World War I crisis in the foundations of sovereignty on a world-wide scale, shaping both empire and democracy, that was critical. Even as the sovereignty of the 'people' was given increasingly normative value in international circles after World War I (a deeply irrational war now projected, after the fact, to have been fought to make the world 'safe for democracy'), the fundamental tension in visions of sovereignty linked to the discourse of reason (and order) on the one hand, and to the cosmic importance of individual autonomy on the other, 'performed' in popular movements, were played out on the public stage.

But in India such tensions also took on distinctive form, reflecting the old structure of colonial sovereignty. Even in invoking an individualising universalism, performances of the self frequently invoked also the cosmic languages (and symbols) of older religious traditions, which had retained their sovereign vitality during the colonial era. To exemplify the tensions

---

[36] Markus Daechsel, *The Politics of Self-Expression: The Urdu Middle-Class Milieu in Mid-Twentieth Century India and Pakistan* (New York: Routledge, 2006), p. 1.
[37] *Ibid*. pp. 8-9.

this entailed, we can perhaps find no more appropriate thinker than Muhammad Iqbal. Few intellectuals in India captured so clearly the vision of the enchanted, sovereign individual as Iqbal. Deeply influenced by those European thinkers such as Nietzsche and Bergson, who had grappled with the meaning of a sovereign self (and an individual consciousness) imagined—somehow—to exist outside the normal worlds of objectified social reality, Iqbal captured this conception in his own notion of *khudi*.[38] For Iqbal, as Iqbal Sevea puts it, 'individual personality was the central fact of the universe',[39] and his 'reconstruction' of Islam was fundamentally cast with a cosmic vision of this individual personhood at its core.[40]

And yet, Iqbal's place as a 'public' figure in India was ambiguous and contradictory. On one level, his intellectual claims were universalising, and his vision of the sovereign power of human desire was powerfully cast in this frame, as reflected in one of his most famous *shers*:

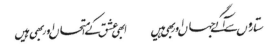

Beyond the stars, there are still more worlds
For now, there are still more tests of love.

This was an evocation of individual desire as a cosmic force permeating the universe, transcending all particularities and played out in 'tests of love'—one whose scope extended well beyond India's Muslims.[41] Indeed, Iqbal developed a liberating vision of Islam itself powerfully cast within this universalising frame. And yet, it was a vision that remained also deeply embedded in the particular language and history of Islam. Despite Iqbal's undoubted universalism, his ideas were thus publicly mobilised after his death in 1938 (and, indeed, before) in the name of a distinctly particularised Muslim vision of community, notably as he became an icon for the Pakistan Movement. In few cases was the tension between universalising and particularising ideas so marked as in the works of Iqbal as they entered into the public realm.

Such contradictions were a product of the distinctive nature and structure of the public realm itself—and the concept of the 'public'—as it had developed in India. As Iqbal's important career suggests, this ambiguity between the particular and the universal was built into the very conception of the 'public' in India, precisely because it was a space defined in relationship to universalising principles of sovereignty, imagined by the state as transcending the social realm, with all its particularities, even as those principles continued to be debated within the framing of *particular* languages of cosmic authority and symbolism linked to

---

[38] For a discussion of Nietzsche's influence, see Iqbal Singh Sevea, *The Political Philosophy of Muhammad Iqbal: Islam and Nationalism in Late Colonial India* (Cambridge: Cambridge University Press, 2012), esp. pp. 111-12. For Bergson's influence, see Naveeda Khan, *Muslim Becoming: Aspiration and Skepticism in Pakistan* (Durham, NC: Duke University Press, 2012), pp. 70–7.

[39] Sevea, *The Political Philosophy of Muhammad Iqbal*, p. 111.

[40] Allama Muhammad Iqbal, *The Reconstruction of Religious Thought in Islam* (Lahore: Sh. Muhammad Ashraf, [1930], 1971).

[41] This *sher*, which was used by the Muslim League in its appeals for Pakistan during the 1946 Punjab elections, is from a poem in *Bal-i Jabril* (*Gabriel's Wing*), 1935. See Mustansir Mir, *Tulip in the Desert: A Selection of the Poetry of Muhammad Iqbal* (Lahore: Iqbal Academy, 1990), pp. 113–14. It continues: '…You are an Eagle, flight is your vocation: You have other skies stretching out before you. Do not let mere day and night ensnare you.…'

distinctive socially-grounded visions of religious community in India.[42] For scholars, the relationship between these particularised communities and notions of the 'public' as a universal touchstone for sovereign legitimacy remains a central question to be grappled with as studies of the public in colonial and post-colonial India move forward.

Conclusion

To be meaningful the concept of the public must thus be recognised not simply as a descriptive term, nor even a normative one, but as embodying a conundrum linked to the fundamental nature of sovereignty itself. Whether viewed as a space for the projection of ideas of state legitimacy, an individual orientation, or an open 'zone' of interaction, the paradoxical tension of the public—as an arena for open debate and displays of difference *and* for the production of an image of imagined community unity—is central to its modern meanings. In this sense, the concept has captured in modern form the deep historical—and ultimately unresolvable—tensions between the particular and the universal, between difference and commonality that have defined the nature of sovereignty. But to say this is hardly to imply that visions of the public have been static. In the nineteenth century they reflected sovereignty's colonial constructions, in which the model of a structure of reason, law and procedure detached from the substance of social relations—and from the everyday violence of the state itself—was central. In the twentieth century to such visions were added a vision of sovereignty linked to the 'people' and to constructions of individual autonomy and self-control/self-rule. Such visions, in all their contradictions, remain central to the structuring of Indian democracy today.

---

[42] These contradictions in the application of Iqbal's ideas to society were thus summed up in the 1940s in W.C. Smith's acute analysis of Iqbal as *both* a 'progressive' figure (projecting the individual as a solvent on existing social hierarchies) and as a 'reactionary' figure (with no appreciation of the social forces actually shaping the 'conflict of personality with personality'). See Wilfred Cantwell Smith, *Modern Islam in India: A Social Analysis* (Lahore: Sh. Muhammad Ashraf, [1946], 1963), pp. 116–35, 155–66.

How to Defame a God: Public Selfhood in the Maharaj Libel Case

J. BARTON SCOTT, *University of Toronto, Ontario, Canada*

This article argues that competing ideas about the nature of public selfhood structured the Maharaj Libel Case, as well as colonial publics more broadly. Jadunathji Maharaj had, in effect, lost his libel suit even before it went to court. For libel law, the essence of the human person is a private self that owns various forms of property, including the public persona known as 'reputation'. For the Hindu Pushtimarg, meanwhile, the Maharaj was considered an incarnation of Krishna; his religious or public self preceded and was the ontological ground for his merely personal being. To compare these two conceptualisations of the self is to see how selfhood became an important site for the articulation of the public in colonial India.

Hailed as 'the greatest trial of modern times since the trial of Warren Hastings', the Maharaj Libel Case of 1862 remains an emblematic event in the history of modern Hinduism.[1] The basic facts of the case are simple enough. The defendant was reform-minded journalist Karsandas Mulji, whose 1860 newspaper article, 'The Primitive Religion of the Hindus and the Present Heterodox Opinions', questioned the legitimacy of the Pushtimarg or Vallabhacharya *sampradaya*, a Hindu sect prevalent among Bombay's Gujaratis. The plaintiff was Jadunathji Brizratanji, the eponymous Maharaj (the religious title given to leaders of the sect), whom the article accused of having 'defiled' his female devotees.[2] To clear his good name, the Maharaj took the unprecedented step of filing a libel suit in the Bombay Supreme Court. As is often the case with libel hearings, the court's attention quickly turned away from the defendant and toward the plaintiff: to determine whether Mulji's defamatory publication qualified as libel (the written form of the tort of defamation), the two judges had to assess the truth of its claims. Experts like missionary scholar John Wilson contrasted Pushtimargi teachings with those of more 'orthodox' Hindu texts. Much more damningly, several witnesses vividly described Jadunathji's erotic escapades. The Maharaj's fate was sealed when two different doctors testified to having treated him for syphilis by prescribing the external application of mercurial 'blackwash'. Based largely on the strength of this medical

---

Research for this article was made possible by grants from Montana State University and the American Institute for Indian Studies. For feedback on earlier versions of the essay, I would like to thank the participants in the 2014 Northwestern University workshop on 'Imagining the Public in Colonial India' and the 2014 National Humanities Center SIAS Summer Institute on 'Cultural Encounters'. I would also like to thank the two peer reviewers for *South Asia*, as well as Mitch Numark, Dan Sheffield, Amrita Shodhan, Usha Thakkar, and especially Mitra Sharafi.

[1] B.N. Motiwala, *Karsondas Mulji: A Biographical Study* (Bombay: Karsondas Mulji Centenary Celebration Committee, 1935), p. 33.

[2] *Report of the Maharaj Libel Case and of the Bhattia Conspiracy Case, Connected With It* (Bombay: Bombay Gazette Press, 1862), p. 3; henceforth referred to as *MLC*.

evidence, both judges acquitted Mulji of the charge of libel, although on slightly different grounds. They agreed that the defamatory article was 'justified', and thus not libellous, in that its allegations were true; they disagreed as to whether its publication to a broad reading audience was appropriate.

For most of a century, the trial was typically understood as 'an eloquent sermon on religion and pseudo-religion', in which the reformist Mulji liberated his caste fellows from oppressive priestly rule.[3] A more recent scholarship has shown that this is, at best, a partial story: 'liberation' from priestly rule facilitated the emergence of new forms of social control, ranging from the codification of an Orientalist-juridical Hinduism that could meet the bureaucratising demands of the colonial state, to the regulation of female domesticity by bourgeois Hindu men.[4] One of just a handful of events in the history of modern Hinduism that has begun to accrue a relatively thick interpretive tradition in which different layers of cultural criticism (reformist–liberal, feminist, post-colonial) overlap and intersect, the Maharaj Libel Case helps us to see not only how several generations of scholars have construed the problematic of 'Hindu modernity', but also how the colonial archive can continue to structure contemporary theoretical debates—including, as I will suggest, debates about the genealogy of 'the public' in South Asia.

The Maharaj Libel Case is typically seen as a classic drama of colonial misrecognition, and with good reason: representatives of the Pushtimarg could not speak in court without their words taking on unanticipated shape, changing meanings as they changed context. This article confirms and elaborates on this narrative by arguing that British libel law and Pushtimargi devotionalism implied distinct and mutually-incompatible models of human personhood that were in substantial tension during the trial. At the same time, however, I also ask whether cultural encounters like this one created the conditions of possibility for the emergence of novel social forms that cut across the familiar divide between coloniser and colonised. Here, I suggest that the colonial print public and Pushtimargi theology relied on remarkably parallel epistemologies of exposure that could, perhaps, have been productively combined. This did not happen. But, as I explore in greater depth elsewhere, by positioning the self as a key site for the articulation of the colonial public, the Maharaj Libel Case did anticipate what would later become a major idiom of colonial politics: the early-twentieth-century 'ethical turn' perhaps most famously associated with M.K. Gandhi's writings on 'self-rule'.[5] In their Gujarati-language writings of the late 1850s and early 1860s, Mulji and the Maharaj had both

---

[3] *Maharaj Libel Case: Including Bhattia Conspiracy Case* (Bombay: D. Lukhmidass, 1911), p. i; see also Charles Heimsath, *Indian Nationalism and Hindu Social Reform* (Princeton, NJ: Princeton University Press, 1964), pp. 103–5; and Makrand Mehta, 'Maharaj Libel Case: A Study in Social Change in Western India in the Nineteenth-Century', in *Indo-Asian Culture*, Vol. 19, no. 4 (1970), pp. 26–39. For a reconsideration of this narrative, see J. Barton Scott, 'Luther in the Tropics: Karsandas Mulji and the Colonial "Reformation" of Hinduism', in *Journal of the American Academy of Religion*, Vol. 83, no. 1 (2015), pp. 181–209.

[4] David L. Haberman, 'On Trial: The Love of the Sixteen Thousand Gopees', in *History of Religions*, Vol. 33, no. 1 (1993), pp. 44–70; Jürgen Lütt, 'From Krishnalila to Ramarajya: A Court Case and Its Consequences for the Reformulation of Hinduism', in Vasudha Dalmia and Heinrich von Stietencron (eds), *Representing Hinduism: The Construction of Religious Traditions and National Identity* (New Delhi: Sage Publications, 1995), pp. 142–53; Amrita Shodhan, 'Women in the Maharaja Libel Case: A Re-Examination', in *Indian Journal of Gender Studies*, Vol. 4, no. 2 (1997), pp. 123–39 and Usha Thakkar, 'Puppets on the Periphery: Women and Social Reform in 19th Century Gujarati Society', in *Economic & Political Weekly*, Vol. 32, nos. 1–2 (Jan. 1997), pp. 46–58.

[5] Shruti Kapila, 'Self, Spencer, and *Swaraj*: Nationalist Thought and Critiques of Liberalism, 1890–1920', in *Modern Intellectual History*, Vol. 4, no. 1 (2007), pp. 109–27.

positioned the self as the primary object of religious reform and did so in a way that drew on Hindu, Protestant and liberal techniques of self-formation.[6] Here, in complementary fashion, I hope to show that religious reformers were not alone in problematising the self at this time; major public institutions were doing much the same. Indeed, it was only by reshaping selfhood that the colonial 'public' could emerge as such.

A Public Spirit

In his much-quoted closing opinion, Puisne Judge Joseph Arnould pronounced that Mulji had only been doing his 'duty' when he exposed the Maharaj's misdeeds: 'A public journalist is a public teacher: the true function of the press, that by virtue of which it has rightly grown to be one of the great powers of the modern world—is the function of teaching, elevating and enlightening those who fall within the range of its influence'.[7] Arnould's remarks might seem common-sensical. Implicitly defining the public as consisting of 'those who fall within the range' of newspapers, Arnould renders the phrase 'public journalist' all but redundant: print and the public are constitutively interlinked. Here, contrary to standard accounts of the liberal public sphere as independent of the state, we can see how the British state worked to define and regulate the Indian public through institutions like the courts.

Arnould's claim about print is, of course, culturally and historically specific, caught up with the extension of the eighteenth century's republic of letters from Britain to its overseas colonies, including India.[8] To provincialise it, we need only follow it in its travels. Like other terms in the cultural lexicon of modern English (e.g. *religion*), *public* cannot be translated into South Asian languages without significant remainder.

Apparently aware of this fact, some colonial writers simply transliterated the word (as *pablik*) into languages like Hindi.[9] Others sought vernacular equivalents to it. Karsandas Mulji, our defendant, is a case in point. In an 1858 essay, he chided Bombay for its 'Want of Public Spirit and Independence'.[10] This is a title with an implicit double meaning. Not only, according to Mulji, do some of Bombay's most prominent citizens lack the courage to stand up for their views on controversial topics like widow remarriage, but Gujarati even lacks words for what Mulji positions as distinctively British 'virtues' (*gun*). In translating *public* into Gujarati, however, Mulji cannot quite close this gap: to translate is to proliferate shades of meaning.

Mulji is hardly the only person to have identified 'public spirit' as central to the political life of modern Britain; Jürgen Habermas does much the same.[11] But in trying to translate 'the public', Mulji disarticulates two distinct senses of the word that the English liberal tradition

---

[6] J. Barton Scott, *Spiritual Despots: Modern Hinduism and the Genealogies of Self-Rule* (Chicago, IL: University of Chicago Press, forthcoming).

[7] *MLC*, p. 205.

[8] For an analysis of one corner of this colonial world, see Michael Warner, *The Letters of the Republic: Publication and the Public Sphere in Eighteenth Century America* (Cambridge, MA: Harvard University Press, 1992). Anglo-Indian newspapers situated themselves within the larger world of Enlightenment letters by a number of means, including literary quotation. The *Poona Observer*'s motto, for instance, quotes Daniel Defoe's claim that the 'impartial writer' dedicated to 'truth' should 'expect martyrdom on both sides': *Poona Observer* (15 Feb. 1862), p. 79.

[9] See, for example, Shriman Munshi Dayaram Sahib, *Maharsi Dayanandcaritamrt* (Meerut: Swami Press, 1904), pp. i–ii; and Lala Lajpat Ray (Gopaldas Devgun Sharma, trans.), *Maharsi Svami Dayanand Sarasvati aur Unka Kam* (New Delhi: Sarvadeshak Arya Pratinidhi Sabha, [1898] 1967), p. 275.

[10] Karsandas Mulji, *Nibandhmala* (Mumbai: Union Press, 1870), pp. 95–8.

[11] Jürgen Habermas (Thomas Burger, trans.), *The Structural Transformation of the Public Sphere* (Cambridge, MA: MIT Press, 1989), pp. 93–5.

had only provisionally reconciled. According to the *Oxford English Dictionary*, the word *public* can be used to describe that which is 'open to observation' and 'carried out without concealment', as well as anything 'of or relating to the people as a whole'. Mulji's Gujarati '*jaher himat*' ('public spirit') has a much greater affinity for the first of these meanings. Derived from the Arabic verb *to appear*, the Urdu adjective *zahir* denotes the outward, exterior, apparent, open or overt.[12] While in contemporary Gujarati, it can indicate that which belongs to all people (the *sarvajanak*), as in the phrases for 'public transit' (*jaher vahan*) and 'public service' (*jaher seva*), etymologically, its more fundamental sense is as the opposite of 'secret' (*gupt*, which is in turn not entirely equivalent to the Urdu *batin*).[13] That *jaher* cannot quite encompass both senses of the English *public* is suggested by Mulji's translation of Judge Arnould's closing speech: 'A public writer (*jaher lakhnar*) is counted as the people's public teacher (*lokono jaher shikshak*)'.[14] In English, a 'public teacher' can, however tautologically, address 'the public' (i.e. a set of persons defined by having been so addressed). In 1860s Gujarati, it would seem, *jaher* could not designate audience in quite this way; to be fully public, in the doubled sense of that term, an 'open writer' must be tied to 'the people' (*lok*) explicitly.

The public here is that which sutures 'the people' to an attitude of openness, or which brings the people into being in relation to such an attitude. It is, in short, not just a social formation, it is also a formation of the subject. Publics imply an orientation of the self—whether a way of being *in public* that lays the self open to the scrutiny of unknown others, or a writing of the self into the outward surface of a text. To analyse the history of colonial publics, then, we also need to pursue the history of colonial subjectivity.

In what follows, I pursue two different inquiries related to this broader set of concerns. On the one hand, I distinguish between the two distinct models of human personhood implied by British libel law and Pushtimargi devotionalism; on the other, I suggest that both these cultural formations used parallel tropes of exposure, such that each can be understood as hailing a subject constituted by a desire for hidden or veiled knowledge. While my characterisation of both libel law and Pushtimargi devotion is necessarily schematic, I try to present the cultures that collided in this 1862 courtroom not as reified or timeless entities, but as the mobile products of ongoing histories; where I schematise, I do so in the hope that the use of heuristic ideal types can illuminate cultural phenomena, the complexity of which inevitably exceeds them.

Making the Bombay Public

The history of Bombay is inseparable from the economic expansion of the British Empire across South Asia and the Indian Ocean world. It is also inseparable from the history of religion—of the Hindus, Muslims, Jews, Jains, Christians and Parsis who criss-crossed India, Africa, and East and Southeast Asia to make their city one of the nineteenth century's most cosmopolitan. With modern technologies like the steamship and the printing press enabling a

---

[12] John T. Platts, *A Dictionary of Urdu, Classical Hindi, and English* (Oxford: Oxford University Press, 1974), p. 755.
[13] *Sarth Gujarati Jodanikosh* (Ahmedabad: Gujarat Vidyapith, 2006), p. 348. The standard antonym in Urdu would, of course, be *batin*.
[14] Karsandas Mulji (trans.), *Maharaj Laibal Kes, Tatha Eni Sathe Sambandh Sakhnar Bhatia Kanspiresi Kesno Riport* (Mumbai: Daftar Ashakara Chapakana, 1862), p. 176.

lush proliferation of devotional practices, religion became an especially productive cultural field during this period, whether politicised in a Ganesh festival or aestheticised on a cinema screen.[15]

Bombay changed profoundly during the nineteenth century, and perhaps never more rapidly than in the 1860s. This was the time of the cotton bubble, the transition to Crown rule and the formation of proto-nationalist groups like Dadabhai Naoroji's East India Association. Within twenty years, industrial cotton mills and neo-Gothic buildings constructed largely on infill would decisively transform the urban landscape. Other forces, meanwhile, were remaking the city's social terrain. Bombay had long been comprised of distinct communities demarcated by caste, language and religion. Parsis, Bohras, Bhattias and other groups intermixed in street and market, but the centre of civic life arguably lay elsewhere—in the *panchayats*, *mahajans*, and other bodies that governed these 'encapsulated' communities.[16] Indeed, the word 'community' has been said to obscure the way in which these groups functioned as self-governing political spaces; it is probably better, as Amrita Shodhan suggests, to term them 'caste polities'.[17]

Sometime after the 1850s, Bombay's centre of civic gravity shifted away from these polities and toward an emergent public sphere closely associated with the colonial milieu. There were several reasons for this shift, ranging from the relatively abstract pressure of the market (which, as a cultural form, required the reconstitution of communally-embedded subjects as autonomous individuals within an undifferentiated public) to more concrete changes in urban institutions.[18] Bombay's 'merchant princes', or *shetias*, had been collaborating across community lines for decades; after the 1850s, however, their 'concerted action' against the British (to use Naoroji's phrase) amplified the significance of this collaboration. Just as important was the rising tide of 'Young Bombay', the English-educated 'intelligentsia' that advocated for social reform in newly-founded newspapers, libraries and debating societies.[19] Together, these constellated institutions, which existed outside of and in tension with caste polities, comprised the colonial public.

The Maharaj Libel Case demonstrates in miniature how this transition occurred. Bania and Bhattia *mahajans* and the Pushtimargi Maharajas had traditionally worked together to resolve conflicts and enforce caste norms. As these traditional alliances began to erode, caste members increasingly turned to the colonial courts to adjudicate conflicts. In doing so, however, they undermined the caste polity's ability to self-govern. Colonial courts, after all, tended to interpret the community's efforts at self-governance as criminal interference with the law (this was especially clear in the Bhattia Conspiracy Case that preceded the Maharaj Libel trial proper). Eventually, as Shodhan argues, the shift in civic gravity prompted a transformation in how caste was understood. What had been 'recognized as a political space of debate, dispute, and hierarchy' was now seen primarily as an 'attachment' of an 'individual' subject defined by his or her place within a socially-undifferentiated public sphere. Henceforth, caste would

---

[15] Gyan Prakash, *Mumbai Fables* (Princeton, NJ: Princeton University Press, 2011); Nile Green, *Bombay Islam* (Cambridge: Cambridge University Press, 2011); Teena Purohit, *The Agha Khan Case: Religion and Identity in Colonial India* (Cambridge, MA: Harvard University Press, 2012); and Raminder Kaur, *Performative Politics and the Cultures of Hinduism* (Delhi: Permanent Black, 2003).

[16] J.C. Masselos, *Towards Nationalism: Group Affiliations and the Politics of Public Associations in Nineteenth-Century Western India* (Bombay: Popular Prakashan, 1974).

[17] Amrita Shodhan *A Question of Community: Religious Groups and Colonial Law* (Calcutta: Samya, 2001).

[18] Ritu Birla, *Stages of Capital: Law, Culture, and Market Governance in Late Colonial India* (Durham, NC: Duke University Press, 2009).

[19] Masselos, *Towards Nationalism*; and Christine Dobbin, *Urban Leadership in Western India: Politics and Communities in Bombay City, 1840–1885* (London: Oxford University Press, 1972).

function chiefly as a sociological descriptor or 'anachronistic identity' borne by subjects whose political being derived from elsewhere.[20]

The press played an important role in this process. Several kinds of publicity overlapped during the Maharaj Libel affair. Some were spectacular, like the quasi-theatrical spaces of the courtroom and police office, which at one point was so packed with 'vast masses of human beings' that it seemed like the floor might collapse.[21] Others were more intimate, like rumour and gossip. Still others were allegedly supernatural, as when a Poona medium claimed to have received the judges' final opinions days before they were read out in court.[22] But as a mass-mediated scandal, the Maharaj Libel affair was most quintessentially associated with print—especially Bombay's major English-language dailies, *The Times of India* and the *Bombay Gazette*, and the Gujarati-language *Rast Goftar and Satya Prakash*.

As Chief Justice Matthew Sausse observed, if Karsandas Mulji had sincerely wanted to reform his caste, he would have addressed his complaints only to its members. By broadcasting his critique to a wider reading public, Sausse argued, Mulji had renounced his claim to the sort of 'justifying occasion' that would absolve him of the charge of libel. The 'mode of publication', said Sausse, 'quite exceeded the bounds suited to the occasion'.[23] Mulji may well have agreed with this assessment. By at least one account, he had intended only to introduce reforms from 'within' his caste group, but, ultimately, 'found to his dismay that he had wrecked more than he had constructed'.[24] It is possible that he failed to realise that his message could not be readily separated from its medium: to critique caste customs from the pages of a newspaper was to alter the city's social terrain. It was, in the standard metaphor of the period, to open or 'expose' the caste polity to the prying eyes of the reading public.[25]

This rhetoric of 'exposure' had ample precedent. Consider Bombay Supreme Court Justice Erskine Perry's comment of the early 1850s:

> [I]n courts of justice the veil which shrouds the privacy of Oriental life is necessarily drawn aside, the strong ties which at other times bind together caste and family in pursuit of a common object are loosened under the pressure of stronger individual interests…[such that] the motives, reasonings, and actions of the native population of India are displayed in broad light.[26]

In annexing 'Oriental life' to the imperial information order, in other words, the act of unveiling also alters the subjectivities of those whom it opens to public scrutiny. The bonds of caste and tradition dissolve to reveal self-interested, atomised individuals. Like other such 'subtraction stories', this tale naturalises the liberal individual by implying that individuality was there all along, underlying the constraints of tradition. It thus draws attention away from the modern social imaginary that forms this individual—an imaginary that consists, among other things, of the very notion of a public sphere defined by an epistemology of exposure.[27]

---

[20] Shodhan, *A Question of Community*, pp. 118–9, 125.
[21] *Bombay Gazette* (24 Sept. 1861), p. 914; and *Bombay Gazette* (25 Oct. 1861), p. 1023.
[22] *Bombay Gazette* (12 May 1862), pp. 449–50.
[23] *MLC*, p. 199.
[24] N.A. Thoothi, *The Vaishnavas of Gujarat* (London: Longman, 1935), p. 97.
[25] *MLC*, p. 205.
[26] Erskine Perry, *Cases Illustrative of Oriental Life and the Application of English Law to India, Decided in H.M. Supreme Court at Bombay* (London: S. Sweet, 1853), p. iv.
[27] Charles Taylor, *A Secular Age* (Cambridge, MA: Harvard University Press, 2007); and Warner, *The Letters of the Republic*, p. 82. I analyse the epistemology of exposure in greater depth in my 'Miracle Publics: Theosophy, Christianity, and the Coulomb Affair', in *History of Religions*, Vol. 49, no. 2 (2009), pp. 172–96.

Press coverage of the Maharaj Libel Case relied heavily on such rhetoric. *The Times of India* was perhaps most expansive:

> Through a long night of superstition and darkness, vile creatures like this Maharaj have been able to make their dens of vice and debauchery seem to their spell-bound followers to be the holy temples of God. But as soon as the morning light comes, the place is found in full corruption and uncleanness; magical spells lose all effect; and all men of a better sort rise disgusted, and at any cost break loose from such a haunt.[28]

The press, we are to surmise, is a force for disenchantment, freeing humanity from magicians whose spells cannot withstand the light of truth. The *Bombay Gazette* likewise condemned the Maharajas' 'hidden works of darkness' and the 'disgusting and abominable things' that they did 'in secret'.[29] So did the reformist *Rast Goftar and Satya Prakash* (amalgamated from the longstanding Parsi newspaper and Mulji's Hindu reform paper). After the trial concluded, it revelled in its titular metaphor, noting that 'in the end, the truth will out. In the end, there is the light of truth'.[30] Or, as it observed some weeks later, 'Like the light of the sun, the light of the Maharaj's immorality has reached from one end of the earth to the other'.[31]

During the affair, these public exposures returned insistently to a single object: the body of the Maharaj. For both judges, the case hinged on the 'material fact' of Jadunathji's alleged case of the 'French pox'. Sausse concluded that the two doctors (one of whom was leading Bombay citizen Bhau Daji) were telling the truth. Not only had they rigorously kept themselves to giving medical evidence, but their testimony had been corroborated by Lakhmidas Khimji, 'one of the leading men in the sect of Vallabhacharyas in Bombay'. Weighing the conflicting evidence, Sausse ruled against the Maharaj. Reasoning that he must have allowed 'personal interests' to overcome his 'respect for truth', Sausse dismissed his entire testimony as compromised.[32] Arnould followed the senior judge's lead. Thus did the truth of the trial come to rest on a question of sexuality: Jadunathji's body divulged secrets that, once fixed by official forms of knowledge, determined how the public would understand Pushtimargi religion.

Indeed, the precise nature of the Maharaj's flesh was arguably the question at the centre of the trial. Was this man a god? A few years earlier, the *Rast Goftar* (translating the *Bombay Guardian*) had observed that if 'these divine avatar men enter a court of justice to give their testimony they will become unholy and their high status will be much lessened'.[33] Not surprisingly, then, Jadunathji's presence in court during the Maharaj Libel Case caused something of a sensation. When he entered the courtroom, heads craned, people stood, and a general whisper of 'he is coming' pulsed through the crowd.[34] After his arrival, his physical being remained at issue. While in the witness box, Jadunathji fretted that someone might brush up against him from behind. Thomas Anstey, the pleader for the defence, replied harshly: 'Why should you not be touched?.... You are not a God. As for me I won't touch you with a pair of tongs'.[35]

---

[28] *The Times of India* (2 May 1862), quoted in Karsandas Mulji, *History of the Sect of Maharajas, or Vallabhacharyas in Western India* (London: Trübner & Co., 1865), p. 134.
[29] *Bombay Gazette* (23 April 1862), p. 382.
[30] *Rast Goftar and Satya Prakash* (27 April 1862), p. 199.
[31] *Rast Goftar and Satya Prakash* (18 May 1862), p. 237.
[32] MLC, p. 203.
[33] *Rast Goftar* (11 Sept. 1859), p. 453.
[34] MLC, p. 166.
[35] Ibid., p. 173.

By at least one measure, the *Rast Goftar*'s prediction that the Maharaj's status would be diminished was necessarily fulfilled. Legally, this was not a case of blasphemy or offence against religion, it was a case of alleged libel. Jadunathji had sued to protect his 'private property of character'.[36] In so doing, he presented himself to the court as an ordinary individual and not a divine incarnation of Krishna. His flesh was thus legally transformed: no longer sacred, it was now a form of private property safeguarded by the British state and regulated through state-sanctioned truth procedures like those of scientific medicine.

Genealogies of Libel Law

One of several overlapping categories that modern states have used to regulate the public, libel also implies a historically and culturally specific vision of what it is to be a self. Libel law hinges on the notion of 'reputation'. This is a notion that, as legal theorist Robert Post explains, establishes 'an image of how people are tied together, or should be tied together, in a social setting', as well as 'an implicit theory of the relationship between the private and public aspects of the self'.[37] Two distinct and mutually-contradictory concepts of reputation, as explained by Post, are pertinent here: *property* and *honour*. As property, reputation is understood as a form of intangible wealth with implicit monetary value. In the words of one Anglo-Indian legal manual, '[a] man's reputation is his property and, if possible, more valuable than other property. No mere poetic fancy suggested the truth that a good name is rather to be chosen than great riches'.[38] Reputation can be cashed in either in everyday financial transactions (a good reputation translates into creditworthiness) or, in exceptional circumstances, through the award of pecuniary damages by a court. It is also the product of labour: an honest merchant or a skilled carpenter builds his reputation through hard work and, if he loses it, he can in theory build it again. Not so reputation-as-honour. Once lost, it cannot be remade. Whereas the property concept prevails in market-based industrial societies, the honour concept characterises 'deference societies' like that of early modern England. In such societies, a person does not produce his own honour; he claims honour based upon the status with which his social role is invested, thus blurring the distinction between private and public selfhood. The preservation of honour, relatedly, is essential to the maintenance of society as a whole and not just the individuals who comprise it.[39]

The tension between Post's two concepts can be seen concretely in the history of English defamation law (i.e. the law of libel, or written defamation, and slander, its oral counterpart). Although key aspects of English libel law have been said to date to the ancient Mediterranean world, and even to the dawn of writing itself, its most important principles are of more recent derivation. In particular, the early nineteenth century seems to have seen a decided shift away from an honour-based concept of reputation to a property-based concept. Here, I will sketch this shift in what is probably too stark a manner. In actuality, early modern legal forms persisted into the nineteenth century, interlayering with newer forms in complex ways.

Slander against the 'leading men' of England had been considered a crime since the thirteenth century and was a means of protecting a social order based on 'personal bonds of

---

[36] *Ibid.*, p. 198.
[37] Robert C. Post, 'The Social Foundations of Defamation Law: Reputation and the Constitution', in *California Law Review*, Vol. 74, no. 3 (May 1986), pp. 691–742.
[38] Ratanlal Ranchhoddas and Dhirajlal Keshavlal Thakore, *The English and Indian Law of Torts* (Bombay: Bombay Law Reporter Private Ltd, [1897] 1965), pp. 159, 164–5.
[39] Post, 'The Social Foundations of Defamation Law', pp. 700–2.

honour and loyalty'.[40] By the eighteenth century, this offence was termed 'seditious libel'. Notably, it refused truth as a defence: a true statement against a highborn man could be even more damaging to the social order than a false one.[41] It was not until the early nineteenth century that libel law, instead of restricting publication to protect the powerful, was reconceived as a means of protecting private persons. As late as 1818, Francis Holt's *Law of Libel* included only a single chapter on libel against private persons, devoting space instead to libel against the 'King's Government' (which warrants two chapters), the 'Two Houses of Parliament', the 'Courts of Justice', the 'Law of Nations', 'Morality and the Law of Nature', and the 'Christian Religion' (the line separating libel and blasphemy, or 'libel against religion', remained thin).[42] The flurry of treatises on libel that appeared in the 1810s seems to indicate that the concept was changing and in need of recodification at this time, however. As an 1815 review of four such books (including Holt's) quipped: 'The law of libel! There's no such thing. After an attentive perusal of all four of the above treatises, we are still constrained to say that the *law of libel* is rather a circumlocution-saving phrase than a description of an entity'.[43] The reviewer's specific complaint is that the treatises all based their conception of libel on the preservation of public peace, rather than on the standard of truth (i.e. the honour-concept, which preserves the social order at all costs, rather than the property-concept, which strives to correctly calibrate earned and actual reputation).

Libel law was the topic of lively, if sporadic, debate in parliament from the 1810s through the 1840s, culminating in the enactment of the Libel Act of 1843. Reformers were puzzled by what had come to seem like inconsistencies in defamation law. They were especially keen to align criminal defamation law with the body of civil law that had grown up alongside it to regulate the primarily oral defamation of merchants. For civil defamation suits, truth was an 'absolute justification', as the law could offer no recompense to a person who claimed a reputation he did not deserve.[44] Reformers wanted to eliminate the distinction between libel and slander (itself only codified in 1812); to introduce the standard of truth into criminal libel; and to temper the absoluteness of truth as justification in civil suits by penalising 'malicious' publications not in the public interest. In various iterations, these reforms were included in bills proposed between 1816 and 1843, when they were enacted into law—although in a much-reduced form that, as historian Paul Mitchell suggests, was a mere 'shadow' of the reforms proposed. As Mitchell goes on to argue, a fully reformed libel law would become a reality only in colonial contexts, as in New South Wales in 1847, where new laws could take hold more readily than they could in London.[45]

Traces of this history can be seen in the 1860 Indian Penal Code, Chapter 21 of which defines defamation as consisting 'in the injury offered to reputation, not in any breach of the peace or other consequence that may result from it'. Its 'essence' is the emotional 'pain' it produces.[46] This relatively narrow definition advances the property-concept over the honour-

---

[40] Norman L. Rosenberg, *Protecting the Best Men: An Interpretive History of the Law of Libel* (Chapel Hill: University of North Carolina Press, 1986), p. 4.
[41] Post, 'The Social Foundations of Defamation Law', p. 705.
[42] *Ibid.*, p. 702; and Francis Ludlow Holt, *The Law of Libel* (New York: Stephen Gould, [London, 1812] 1818).
[43] *A Review of the Late Publication on Libel of Messrs. George, Holt, Starkie, & Jones, by a Barrister of the Inner Temple* (London: Reed and Hunter, 1815), pp. 7–8.
[44] Rosenberg, *Protecting the Best Men*, pp. 5–6; and Peter Frederick Carter-Ruck, *Libel and Slander* (Hamden, CT: Archon Books, 1973), pp. 37–48.
[45] Paul Mitchell, 'The Foundations of Australian Defamation Law', in *Sydney Law Review*, Vol. 28, no. 3 (2006), pp. 477–504.
[46] W. Morgan and A.J. MacPherson, *The Indian Penal Code (Act XLV of 1860), with Notes* (Calcutta: G.C. Hay & Co., 1861), pp. 439–40.

concept, while also excluding previously common ideas like that of 'libel against religion'. Other reformist proposals are also in evidence: the Code erases the distinction between libel and slander; allows for justification in cases where defamatory claims are both true and their publication in the public good; and offers protection to those expressing 'any opinion whatever' about 'a public servant in the discharge of his public functions' (thus starkly inverting the older concept of 'seditious libel').[47]

As a civil suit, the Maharaj Libel Case was tried under common law and not the newly-enacted Indian Penal Code. Even so, the Code was part of the broader cultural field that shaped the trial. So were the many guides to the tort of defamation that had been published in the preceding decades, such as George Cooke's *Treatise on the Law of Defamation* (1844) and C.G. Addison's *Wrongs and their Remedies* (1860).[48] A full history of libel law in colonial India has, to the best of my knowledge, yet to be written. But given the range of cases during the 1860s alone that were tried or publicised under this rubric, including the Lucknow Libel Case (1860), the Nil Darpan Case (1861) and the Parsi Priest Defamation Case (1870), as well as the appearance of legal guides such as Jehangeer Merwanjee's Gujarati manual, *Libel and Slander*, apparently published on the heels of the Maharaj affair, it would seem that in India, as in Britain, 'libel' remained a relatively mobile concept, the boundaries of which were still in the process of being defined.[49]

For our purposes, we might describe libel as information out of place: it puts into print what should not be there. Libel law, then, tries to make information stay put, ordering it so as to safeguard privacy. But because libel necessarily links the private self to the law and, with it, the public domain, it ensures that the private can never be entirely excluded from public discourse. Rather, the private self is always at risk of being dragged into public to prove itself before the 'tribunal' of juridical and popular opinion.[50] If sexuality is one paradigmatic site whereby the potential for the private to become scandalously public becomes actualised, religion is another. To see how, we return to the Maharaj Libel Case—rejoining the trial *in medias res*.

Unbecoming Krishna

'By God, I mean Krishna', Jumnadas Sevaklal answered tersely, his pinched reply indicating irritation with Thomas Anstey's interrogation of his beliefs. The packed audience looked on as Sevaklal was threatened with a fine of Rs100 for evading cross-examination. Under pressure, he had little choice but to elaborate on his previous claim: 'In my opinion, the Maharaj is a representative of Krishna'. Anstey, not content to let the matter rest there, pushed further:

---

[47] The section of Macaulay's draft penal code of 1837 that handled sedition was omitted from the 1860 Indian Penal Code, allegedly 'by some unaccountable mistake'. This omission was corrected in 1870 with the addition of s. 124-A: see Walter Donagh, *The History and Law of Sedition and Cognate Offences* (Calcutta: Thacker, Spink, & Co., 1911), p. 1; and W.R. Hamilton, *The Indian Penal Code with Commentary* (Calcutta: Thacker, Spink, and Co., 1895), pp. 132–42. For speculation as to the reasons for the omission of the sedition statute, see Aravind Ganachari, *Nationalism and Social Reform in Colonial Situation* (Delhi: Kalpaz Publications, 2005), pp. 54–7. For a further discussion of the history of British colonial libel law, see Mitra Sharafi, *Law and Identity in Colonial South Asia* (Cambridge: Cambridge University Press, 2014), pp. 276–85.

[48] *MLC*, pp. 76, 60.

[49] *Action for Libel* (Lucknow: Newul Kishore Press, 1860); *Parsee Priest Defamation Case* (Bombay: Dorabjee Eduljee Tata, 1870); *The History of the Nil Darpan* (Calcutta: n.p., 1861); and Geoffrey Oddie, *Missionaries, Rebellion, and Proto-Nationalism: James Long of Bengal, 1814–87* (New York: Routledge, [1999] 2013). Merwanjee's *Libel and Slander* is mentioned in the *Bombay Gazette* (1 May 1862), p. 412.

[50] *MLC*, pp. 205, 209.

Mr. Anstey:	Do some Banias believe the Maharaj to be a God?
Witness:	We consider him to be our gooroo.
Sir M. Sausse:	Tell witness if he does not answer the question, he will be sent to jail.
Witness:	What is the precise question? (Interpreter explains.) Some consider the Maharaj a god in the shape of gooroo.
Mr. Anstey:	Is Gooroo a God?
Witness:	Gooroo is gooroo.
Sir M. Sausse:	Tell him if he does not answer the question, most indubitably he will go to jail.
Sir Joseph Arnould:	Tell him he is asked what others believe, not as to his own belief.
Witness:	I don't know if others believe him as God; I consider him simply a gooroo.[51]

Here, the semiotics of devotion strain under the weight of the colonial legal apparatus. Legal institutions were far from neutral or empty sets in which public dramas could unfold. The court was a technology of subjectivation or, rather, a set of such technologies—here, the witness stand functions as a sort of confessional booth, which imposes certain unstated rules on the person within it.

To find voice at court, bhakti (roughly, devotional Hinduism) had to translate itself into the language of propositional belief, reducing the rich relational network of lived religion into dry theological statements like 'Guru is God'. The juridical subject of belief necessarily precedes the proposition that he assents to; otherwise, he would not have the legal standing to grant his assent. Where the Pushtimarg had prized the ideal of 'self-surrender' (*atmanivedan*), the British court reduces religion to a set of beliefs that a sovereign subject can 'have', thus replacing a faith that unravels the self in the face of the other with a faith that presumes that integrity of the believing subject.

We might say that during the Maharaj Libel Case, the faith binding guru and devotee was rhetorically severed. Half of the relational bond was delivered to the devotees as 'belief'. The other half was given to the guru as his 'reputation'. What had served as a mode of relationship with a potential to erode the boundaries of the self is, in both cases, rendered a form of property that reinforces the sense of discrete personhood. By abstracting the complex web of an individual's social and professional relationships into a discrete object, reputation reifies a community's fluid perceptions as a form of property. In a sense, it inverts the process whereby a subject is hailed by her social order and offered a fixed position within it: one 'has' a reputation, rather than being had by it. In this context, Jumnadas Sevaklal's plaintive refrain ('Gooroo is gooroo') acquires an almost deictic force, pointing toward Jadunathji in his social immediacy as though to underscore the bond between teacher and disciple.

The property concept of reputation was not, of course, alien to India. A version of it had long been central to Gujarati merchant society, where 'the maintenance and improvement of reputation' (*abru*) was a matter with serious financial consequences.[52] But it was not a merchant's reputation that was on trial during the Maharaj Libel Case. Instead, the court found itself faced with the question of whether a 'spiritual' man like the Maharaj could be defamed in his capacity as a 'private' citizen. Is a priest legally equivalent to members of other, secular

---

[51] *Ibid.*, pp. 134–6.
[52] Douglas Haynes, *Rhetoric and Ritual in Colonial India: The Shaping of a Public Culture in Surat City, 1852–1928* (Berkeley: University of California Press, 1991), pp. 38, 56–8.

professions such as a 'tradesman'?[53] Did the Maharaj even qualify as a 'priest'? What, after all, is the nature of 'spiritual' personhood?

The trial opened with an argument about whether libel law could be applied in this case. Thomas Anstey, the pleader for the defence, pointed out that, in Britain, a defamed 'ecclesiastic' would file suit in the 'Courts Christian' and not the 'Court of Common Law'. In Bombay Presidency, which had no such courts, there was consequently 'no law of defamation of a spiritual man'.[54] Lyttelton Bayley, arguing for the prosecution, responded that 'this was a libel against the plaintiff not in his spiritual capacity, but in his private character'.[55] Chief Justice Sausse concurred: it 'was a libel against the plaintiff in his individual capacity, segregated from his character of priest'.[56] While the arguments made by both attorneys shifted somewhat during the trial (Bayley later claimed that the plaintiff had been libelled 'in his double capacity as man and as Maharaj'),[57] this basic logic held. There were two persons in court, analytically 'segregated' from one another: the 'spiritual' Maharaj and the 'private' Jadunath.

The court conceded that Mulji was well within his rights to disparage the first of these persons. Religion, all parties seemed to agree, must remain open to criticism. If calling a religious sect heretical was deemed illegal, argued Anstey, then every Protestant and Catholic journal in England and every philosopher from John Locke forward should be prosecuted, and 'the whole body of missionaries from the East to the West, who preach against the immorality of heathenism...would be brought up for libel every day!'[58] Judge Arnould added the biblical prophets and church fathers to this list of potential libellers.[59] In an earlier era of British law, 'libel against religion' was harshly censured. As one early-nineteenth-century writer reflected (in discussing a famous early modern case that centred on the claim that 'Christ is a whoremaster, and religion is a cheat'), 'libels against religion...may with equal propriety be said to be libels against the public at large'.[60] They dissolve the moral foundation of society and so endanger the peace to a unique degree.

The cast of characters assembled in the Bombay Supreme Court thought differently. For them, the 'public at large' cohered around a principle other than religion. As has often been observed, the government of British India was generally more secular than its metropolitan counterpart. The law of libel suggests one way in which this was the case. In place of a blasphemy statute (i.e. 'libel against religion'), the Indian Penal Code (Section 298) criminalises publications that wound 'the religious feelings of any person'. Here, protection of religion as a collective cultural form that founds and maintains 'the public at large' is replaced by the protection of the individual 'person', whom the statute presents as preceding her religion. Community, of course, was never far behind. But the wording of the statute does indicate an important shift in how religion was understood under secular law. Criticism of religion *per se* was now protected, in that it was deemed unthreatening to social order; criticism of the beliefs and feelings of private persons was carefully managed, implying that the social order was now anchored in the sanctity of the liberal individual.[61]

---

[53] *MLC*, p. 75.
[54] *Ibid.*, pp. 8–9.
[55] *Ibid.*, p. 16.
[56] *Ibid.*, p. 19.
[57] *Ibid.*, p. 167.
[58] *Ibid.*, pp. 19, 154–6.
[59] *Ibid.*, p. 428.
[60] *A Review of the Late Publication on Libel*, p. 27.
[61] For further consideration of s. 298 and 295-A, see J. Barton Scott, 'Aryas Unbound: Print Hinduism and the Cultural Regulation of Religious Offence', in *Comparative Studies of South Asia, Africa, and the Middle East*, Vol. 35, no. 2 (2015), forthcoming.

Bayley's response to Anstey's defence of the right to criticise religion is revealing in this regard. If the 'doctrine' implied by denying the Maharaj the right to sue for libel was allowed, he argued, then 'no Brahmin in the land would be safe; he could be slandered and libelled with impunity, and redress denied him because he happened to be a spiritual person'.[62] Here, 'Brahmin' is effectively redefined as an office distinct from the person who 'happens' to holds it. The check placed upon the criticism of religion derives from the legal distinction between a Brahman's 'public' capacity as priest and his 'private' character as an ordinary person: the priest can be criticised with impunity, the private person cannot. This distinction, of course, ignores how the ritual economy of caste Hinduism writes status into the flesh. If a Brahman has a private self that is analytically distinct from and more fundamental to him than his spiritual personhood, then we are dealing with something other than the traditional world of caste. 'Spiritual personhood' precedes the self, it does not follow from it.

Something similar holds for the Pushtimargi Maharajas, who were traditionally held to be incarnations of Krishna. A god cannot be libelled (at least in the modern sense of the term) because a god has no private self. To defame a god is to defame all that he represents (e.g. 'the public at large'), but not him personally. By turning 'spiritual personhood' into a mere office, the property-concept of libel prompted an important shift in the legal regulation of religion in that the sanctity of the individual came to replace the sanctity of religion *per se* as the primary object of legal protection. As long as no 'person' was offended or libelled, one could criticise religion at will.

Manifestly Divine

The Pushtimarg, or 'Way of Grace', had originated with Shri Vallabhacharya (1479–1530), one of the most important early modern exemplars of bhakti. Born to Telugu Brahmans, he travelled widely throughout the subcontinent, singing the praises of Krishna and initiating disciples into his *sampradaya*. In his substantial corpus of written works in Sanskrit and Braj Bhasha, he developed the philosophical system of Shuddhadvaita (pure non-dualism), which modified the earlier monism of Shankaracharya by eliminating the notion of *maya*. Additionally, Vallabhacharya married and had two sons, Gopinath (1512–42) and Vitthalnath (1515–85), a fact of decisive importance for his *sampradaya*, which does not prize celibacy as do many other Hindu lineages. When Vallabha died, his spiritual authority passed to these two heirs. Vitthalnath assumed greater authority and *his* seven sons (Vallabha's grandsons) established the 'Seven Houses' that remain the sect's major structuring institution. Control of the houses is inherited via primogeniture, although all of Vallabha's descendants through the male line are typically termed 'Maharajas'. From the sixteenth to the eighteenth centuries, these religious leaders pursued the patronage of commercial and political elites in Rajasthan, Gujarat and elsewhere in northern and western India, growing wealthy in the process.[63]

Pushtimargis consider both Vallabha and his son, Vitthalnath, to have been incarnations of Krishna. Their immediate followers, meanwhile, are considered incarnations of the *gopis* (the

---

[62] *MLC*, p. 16.
[63] Thoothi, *The Vaishnavas of Gujarat*, pp. 92–8; Richard Barz, *The Bhakti Sect of Vallabhacarya* (Faridabad: Thomson Press, 1976); and Shandip Saha, 'Creating a Community of Grace: A History of the Pushti Marga in Northern and Western India, 1479–1905', unpublished PhD thesis, University of Ottawa, 2004, pp. 107–27. A series of recent legal disputes in Rajasthan over whether Pushtimargi temples are 'public' or 'private' (*nij*) entities would provide an interesting topic for further research: see Peter Bennett, *The Path of Grace: Social Organization and Temple Worship in a Vaishnava Sect* (Delhi: Hindustan Publishing Corporation, 1993), pp. 83, 172–5.

cow-herding girls who were Krishna's consorts). When these first two generations of Pushtimargi devotees died, they resumed their divine play in heaven.[64] What happened next is controversial. As Jadunathji Brizratanji insisted during the Maharaj Libel Case, 'Vallabhacharya and his son Gosaijee (Vitthalnath) are regarded as incarnations of God but not so the sons of Gosaijee'.[65] Given the quantity of contradictory testimony, however, it seems likely that Jadunathji was misrepresenting popular belief in his community; many Banias and Bhattias in the 1850s and 1860s do seem to have considered these later Maharajas to be divine. Gopalldas Mahadevdass, the head of the Bania *mahajan*, probably summarised the situation fairly accurately when he explained to the court that '[s]ome people do say that they are gods, while some deny that they are'.[66]

The simple equation 'Guru *is* God', however, is too reductive a summary of what is going on here. The Maharaj was not divine in and of himself; he was divine insofar as he represented Krishna. To develop a more nuanced picture of the Pushtimarg's semiotics of devotion, we can turn to the religious practices described during the trial. By Mahadevdass' account, the Maharajas worship the 'idols', while ordinary men and women worship the Maharajas:

> They prostrate themselves at the Maharaj's feet. By worshipping the Maharaj, I understand applying to him scent and stuff, and offering him fruits and flowers, in the same way as the idols are worshipped. When we fall down before the Maharaj, he blesses us. One mode of worshipping the idol is by swinging it, and our women worship the Maharaj by swinging him.[67]

Additionally, devotees eat the 'remnants' of the Maharaj's food and *paan* and also drink 'the water rinsed and wrung' from his dhoti (termed *charanamrit*, or 'nectar of the feet'). Other witnesses gave similar testimony.

The question remains as to how one should read such practices. Was the Maharaj an index, an icon, or a symbol of the divine? One view would opt for the index: as an incarnation, the Maharaj has a direct physical relationship to Krishna. This indexical logic, moreover, permeates many of the religious practices discussed during the Maharaj Libel scandal, as Christopher Pinney has suggested: one eats the dust from the guru's feet because that dust is a physical trace of him; ingestion of it incorporates the guru into the self.[68] Here, the guru is semiotically porous, bleeding out into his followers via the same kind of indexical connection that links him to Krishna.

Another view would align the guru with the icon (i.e. the image that provides a likeness of Krishna). As the *Rast Goftar and Satya Prakash* explained: 'The Maharajas serve the image (*murti*), and devotees cannot serve the image, and so instead (*tene badale*) they serve the Maharaj' by rocking him in a swing or offering him flowers and fruit just as he does to the *murti*.[69] The use of the word *murti* here is tendentious. Within the Pushtimarg, as Richard Barz explains, the divine image is never referred to as a *murti* (representation), but rather as a *svarup* (the 'entity itself, not a likeness').[70] Devotional images are the self-manifestations of Krishna; like avatars, they participate indexically in the divine. Thus, while it might seem that

---

[64] Barz, *The Bhakti Sect of Vallabhacarya*, pp. 21, 38.
[65] *MLC*, p. 170.
[66] *Ibid.*, p. 62.
[67] *Ibid.*, p. 63.
[68] Christopher Pinney, *The Coming of Photography in India* (London: British Library, 2008), pp. 114–7.
[69] *Rast Goftar and Satya Prakash* (23 Feb. 1862), p. 91.
[70] Barz, *The Bhakti Sect of Vallabhacarya*, p. 9

there is an arbitrary exchange (*badal*) or substitution between two independent entities, in the mode of the symbol, what we actually see here are two entities that index a common referent; *murti* and *avatar* are two types of spark issuing from a single fire.

There are good metaphysical reasons for this. The phenomenal world, according to Vallabhacharya, comes to exist when Brahman (or the Ultimate) 'conceals part of himself'. This is the process that Vallabha calls *tirobhava* ('concealment, act of hiding, becoming invisible'; 'capability of not becoming an object of experience'). Brahman consists of three parts: being, consciousness and bliss (*sat*, *cit* and *ananda*). In the physical world, only being is in its 'manifest' or 'apparent' (*avirbhuta*) condition; in the soul (*jiva*), both being and consciousness are manifest. The problem of *samsara*, then, is a problem of wrong understanding: the soul understands that it exists, but not that it is part of Brahman-Krishna. Once it attains this understanding, it achieves bliss (or, rather, its innate bliss becomes manifest).[71] Shuddhadvaitic metaphysics, it would seem, precludes a strict ontological distinction between sign and referent: insofar as all beings participate in Brahman-Krishna, all beings bear an indexical relationship to one another. As a 1910 primer on Pushtimargi principles succinctly puts it, 'Nothing is distinct from the Ultimate Being (*parabrahm*)'.[72]

To say that the Maharaj is God, then, is simply to state the obvious: all entities are God, whether they realise it or not.[73] Such subtleties were, of course, lost on the Bombay Supreme Court. Even so, by reading the Pushtimarg to highlight the doctrine of 'concealment' (*tirobhava*), we discover a surprising resonance between its theology and colonial law: both were preoccupied with what we might, by creatively stretching our translations, term publicity. If the public (*jaher*) is that which is 'outward' or 'apparent', then the public is very much analogous to the 'manifest' (*avirbhuta*) aspects of the Pushtimargi divine. Both, in fact, take the 'secret' (*gupt*) as their primary antonym.[74] If the Maharaj is a manifestation of Krishna, a making visible of the divine in the world, then he is, by definition, always already *jaher*.

I do not, of course, mean to suggest that Advaitic metaphysics and the colonial public's epistemology of exposure are somehow the same. They are not. But by aligning them in this way, we can begin to develop an alternative narrative that presents religion as plying something other than (in the words of the *Bombay Gazette* and *The Times of India*) 'darkness'. Like colonial print culture, the Pushtimarg organises a particular distribution of the visible that likewise implies particular notions about the nature of human personhood. As Sandria Freitag has counselled, in constructing a genealogy of the public in colonial South Asia, we need to look for the 'indigenous bases onto which western European notions of "the public" could have been grafted'.[75] Pushtimargi metaphysics appears as one such base, especially when juxtaposed with Karsandas Mulji's translation of *public* as *jaher*.

---

[71] *Ibid.*, pp. 63–71; and Mrudula Marfatia, *The Philosophy of Vallabhacharya* (Delhi: Munshiram Manoharlal, 1967), pp. 48–54.

[72] Patvari Ranchoddas Vandravandas, *Pushtimargiya Siddhant Athava Shuddhadvaitna Multattva, Vol. 1* (Ahmedabad: Gujarat Printing Press, 1910), p. 101.

[73] Bennett, *The Path of Grace*, pp. 39–40, 59–60.

[74] Vandravandas' *Pushtimargiya Siddhant* seems to use *gupt* and *tirobhav* more or less interchangeably. *Avirbhav*, meanwhile, becomes *prakat* when shifted from technical to more ordinary Gujarati. It is possible that the author thought the Arabic root *jaher* too 'Islamic' to be used in a Hindu devotional context.

[75] Sandria Freitag, 'Introduction': "The Public" and its Meanings in Colonial South Asia', in 'Aspects of the Public in Colonial South Asia', *South Asia: Journal of South Asian Studies*, special issue, Vol. 14, no. 1 (June 1991), p. 7.

Conclusion

After the trial, Jadunathji Brizratanji and several other Maharajas quickly left Bombay, lest they be indicted for perjury.[76] Mulji, meanwhile, was feted for several months by his fellow reformists.[77] Eventually, however, he too moved on to new challenges—most notably, a voyage to England that furthered antagonised caste authorities. Some commentators predicted that the libel case would extinguish belief in the Maharaj, but its actual outcomes proved considerably more ambivalent. One newspaper noted that the scandal had 'only increased the ardour' of the Pushtimargis' devotion.[78] Years later, another critic complained that the 'incomprehensible psychological phenomenon' of 'Maharajism' had persisted unscathed.[79] In reality, this was not entirely true. The trial, as Jürgen Lütt has argued, presaged a widespread retreat from the erotics of Krishna devotion that became more pronounced by the early twentieth century.[80] The Pushtimarg seems to have participated in this general trend—at least in its self-presentation to the Gujarati print public. For instance, as its title suggests, the book, *Pushtimargi Principles, or the Original Form of Pure Non-Dualism* (1910), emphasises Vallabhacharya's monistic philosophy over the affective practices of Krishna worship. Strenuously denying the by-then common claim that *pushti* means 'to eat, to drink, and to become contented', its author set out to prove by copious textual example that Pushtimargi teachings are fully concordant with those of the *Vedas*, the *Gita* and other canonical scriptures.[81] One can see here how the trial shaped and constrained the Pushtimarg for years to come.

One might ask whether this story could have ended differently. For example, what would have happened if Mulji had reframed the Anglophone rhetoric of public 'exposure' in terms of the Pushtimargi notion of divine 'manifestation'? Could he, by more carefully managing not only his medium, but also the cultural idioms that accompanied it, have articulated a more effective critique of the Maharajas? Perhaps.

Regardless, it might seem safest to accept a piece of old advice that was revived during the trial: 'Better have no opinion of God at all than an injurious one'.[82] Upon closer inspection, however, one finds that this early modern maxim is not so easily transposed to the nineteenth century. Journalists in Victorian India frequently quoted English Enlightenment classics, but, in doing so, they tended to neglect how the world had changed since the days of Francis Bacon. This was certainly the case with respect to the state's management of religion. In 1862, it seems, 'injurious' opinions about God were, in themselves, legally permissible; injury to the reputation or feelings of the individual person, on the other hand, was the object of careful regulation.

---

[76] *Bombay Gazette* (3 May 1862), p. 420.
[77] *Bombay Gazette* (16 July1862), p. 672.
[78] *Poona Observer* (11 Mar. 1862), supplement, pp. 1–2.
[79] Behramji M. Malabari, *Gujarat and the Gujaratis* (Delhi: Mittal Publications, [1889] 1983), pp. 226–7.
[80] Lütt, 'From Krishnalila to Ramarajya', pp. 142–53.
[81] Vandravandas, *Pushtimargiya Siddhant*, pp. vi–vii, 2–5.
[82] Francis Bacon, as quoted in the *Bombay Gazette* (4 Dec. 1861), p. 1158.

Crises of the Public in Muslim India: Critiquing 'Custom' at Aligarh and Deoband

BRANNON D. INGRAM, *Northwestern University, Evanston, USA*

*This article argues that Sayyid Ahmad Khan (1817–98) and Ashraf 'Ali Thanvi (1863–1943) were, respectively, exemplars of what I will call the liberal critique of custom on the one hand, and the Islamic legal critique of custom on the other. I argue that a range of overlapping semantic fields in their Urdu works—'custom' (*rasm*), 'reform' (*islah*), 'decline' (*zawal, tanazzul*) and 'nation' or 'moral community' (*qawm*), among others—opens up new lines of inquiry in comparing Aligarh and Deoband, typically treated as incommensurable in their views, as institutions and movements. I suggest, additionally, that 'the public' (*'amm*) was a shared frame through which they envisioned implementing their respective projects. At the imagined centre of these publics, they located a new sort of Muslim: literate, self-regulating, self-fashioning, guided by rationality (*'aql*) and free, above all, of the moral and social entanglements of 'custom'.*

Introduction

In the aftermath of the revolt of 1857, the trope of 'decline'—whether political, intellectual, educational, aesthetic or religious—pervaded much of Indian Muslim thought. From Hali to Iqbal, narratives of decline became ubiquitous in Indian Muslim poetry, historiography and literature. The trope of the 'backward' Muslim began to proliferate in debates on Indian Islamic education, while Urdu language poetry became both the medium through which 'decline' was debated and, for some, evidence of the decline itself.[1] Within the framework of these narratives, the notion that such decline was due to Indian Muslims becoming mired in 'customs'—ranging from the baroque array of practices that coalesced around major life events like birth and marriage to the myriad forms of reverence towards Sufi saints at their shrines—became especially widespread.

This article explores how the two respective icons of the Aligarh and Deoband movements—Sayyid Ahmad Khan (1817–98), founder of the Muhammadan Anglo-Oriental College at Aligarh (now Aligarh Muslim University), and Ashraf 'Ali Thanvi (1863–1943), the preeminent Deobandi scholar of the colonial era—theorised 'custom', its effect on human rationality and agency, and its socio-legal status. It also shows how they saw the public, paradoxically, as both the space in which customs naturally proliferate *and* the venue through

---

I benefitted from comments on an initial draft of this paper at the conference 'Imagining the Public in Colonial India: Print, Polemics and the People' at Northwestern University, Evanston, Illinois, in May 2014. I also received valuable feedback presenting part of this article at the American Historical Association's annual conference in January 2015. I would especially like to thank Muzaffar Alam for his comments at the AHA.

[1] Sanjay Seth, *Subject Lessons: The Western Education of Colonial India* (Durham, NC/London: Duke University Press, 2007), pp. 109–28; and Iqbal Singh Sevea, *The Political Philosophy of Muhammad Iqbal* (Cambridge: Cambridge University Press, 2012), p. 74.

which they could be reformed. What makes this comparison compelling is the fact that scholarship often presents Aligarh and Deoband as two movements—the one 'modernist', the other 'traditionalist'—in 'diametrical opposition'.[2] Surely, in nearly every respect, they were. But the modernist–traditionalist dichotomy obscures the extent to which both movements were animated by similar vocabularies of reform.

The argument of this article runs as follows: Sayyid Ahmad Khan and Ashraf 'Ali Thanvi were exemplars of what I will call the liberal critique of custom on the one hand, and the Islamic legal critique of custom on the other. I argue that a range of overlapping semantic fields in their Urdu language works—not just 'custom' (*rasm*),[3] but also 'reform' (*islah*), 'decline' (*zawal, tanazzul*) and 'nation' or 'moral community' (*qawm*)—opens up new lines of inquiry in comparing Aligarh and Deoband as institutions and movements. I suggest, additionally, that 'the public' (*'amm*) was a shared frame through which they envisioned implementing their respective projects. At the imagined centre of these publics, they located a new sort of Muslim: literate, self-regulating, self-fashioning, guided by rationality (*'aql*) and, above all, free of the moral and social entanglements of 'custom'.

I will pose a set of interrelated questions here. What kind of idealised member of a Muslim public do these thinkers interpellate, whether embodying Sayyid Ahmad's 'civilised' rationalism or Thanvi's sober-minded piety? What does it mean to say that they addressed these publics as implicitly 'Muslim' first and foremost—that is, not 'Punjabi' or 'Deccani', not *ashraf* or *ajlaf*, but simply 'Muslim'—even as both appealed implicitly to nascent middle-class sensibilities, and explicitly to North Indian readers of Urdu? Who is the individual Muslim at the centre of this public? What notions of freedom, agency, moral autonomy and self-regulation were bound up in him or her?[4] For my purposes here, I see 'the public' as a space conjured by and through discourses and defined by modes of relationality. It was, therefore, not exclusively or even primarily a physical space—though it certainly could be, and often was—but was first and foremost a discursive one configured through the circulation of texts.[5]

Comparing Aligarh and Deoband

It is worth highlighting a certain irony in comparing Sayyid Ahmad and Thanvi in this vein. The Aligarh and Deoband movements have long been regarded as the archetypal intellectual rivals of nineteenth-century Indian Islam, the one representing 'modernist' and the other

---

[2] Margrit Pernau, *Ashraf into Middle Classes: Muslims in Nineteenth Century Delhi* (New Delhi: Oxford University Press, 2013), p. 274.

[3] The word most often used to signify 'custom' is *rasm* (pl. *rusum*), meaning 'to mark, trace or delineate', connoting established usage or law. But both Sayyid Ahmad and Thanvi also occasionally use *'adat*, from the Arabic root 'to return to', suggesting habit or convention; *rivaya*, derived from the Persian root 'to go', suggesting something that is current, tolerated or widely accepted; and *rivaj*, from the Arabic 'to be current' or 'in demand'. When they distinguish between these terms individually, I note it below.

[4] I say 'him or her' with the full understanding that the texts I explore here were overwhelmingly directed towards male readers. When directing their texts to female readers, reformist works were explicit in doing so (most famously, Thanvi's *Bihishti Zewar*). For an overview of such works, see Gail Minault, *Secluded Scholars: Women's Education and Muslim Social Reform in Colonial India* (New Delhi: Oxford University Press, 1998). I do not want to suggest, then, that I am taking these publics to be 'genderless' by any stretch, but gender will not be one of the major analytical frames of this article.

[5] Michael Warner, *Publics and Counterpublics* (New York: Zone Books, 2002).

'traditionalist' approaches to education, Islamic sciences, law and theology.[6] Whereas the latter emphasised 'traditional' Islamic education in North India (in brief, Qur'an, Hadith, Ash'ari-Maturidi theology and Hanafi law), even if in the context of an institutional setting modelled in part after British education,[7] the former supplemented religious sciences with 'English' education, and in his own writings, Sayyid Ahmad advanced self-consciously 'modern' (*jadid*) ideas that were roundly criticised by the Deobandi and other traditionally educated Islamic scholars (*'ulama*).

The rivalry was the occasion for mutual criticism. Sayyid Ahmad believed that Dar al-'Ulum Deoband woefully underserved the Muslims of India by offering only Islamic subjects.[8] Likewise, Deoband co-founder Muhammad Qasim Nanautvi (d. 1880) believed that Sayyid Ahmad's theological innovations were extremely dangerous, notably composing his *Tasfiyat al-Aqa'id* (*The Purification of Beliefs*) as a systematic critique of Sayyid Ahmad's approach to religious authority, scripture and tradition.[9] Indeed, Sayyid Ahmad's attempts to justify his theology to Nanautvi appear to have been in vain.[10] Thanvi, too, was clear about his approach to Aligarh and Sayyid Ahmad Khan. He blamed him for opening up a space for apostasy to flourish and even blamed his allegedly 'naturalist' (*nechari*)[11] theology for the rise of the despised Ahmadiyya sect. 'Because of Sayyid Ahmad Khan, much deviation has spread', stated Thanvi. '*Nechari* is the…root of which apostasy is one of the branches. The Qadian sect', as the Ahmadis were derisively termed, 'is the first prey of *nechari*'.[12]

But we must not let this obscure the common vocabularies of reform that animated both movements, or even the comparable social contexts in which they emerged.[13] Like the first generation of Deobandis, Sayyid Ahmad's early thought was galvanised by the reformist legacy of Sayyid Ahmad Barelvi (d. 1831) and Muhammad Isma'il (d. 1831).[14] The fact that Sayyid Ahmad had an early encounter, in 1853, with the spiritual mentor to the first two generations of Deobandis, Hajji Imdadullah al-Makki, who requested that Sayyid Ahmad

---

[6] Sayyid Ahmad was, for instance, the exemplary modernist in Fazlur Rahman's understanding of Islamic modernism. See Fazlur Rahman, *Islam and Modernity* (Chicago, IL: University of Chicago, 1982), p. 51; and Fazlur Rahman, 'The Impact of Modernity on Islam', in *Islamic Studies*, Vol. 5, no. 2 (1966), p. 116. The point is reiterated by Faisal Devji in 'Apologetic Modernity', in *Modern Intellectual History*, Vol. 4, no. 1 (2007), p. 66. On Deoband's 'tradition'-oriented reform, see Barbara Metcalf, *Islamic Revival in British India: Deoband, 1860–1900* (Princeton, NJ: Princeton University Press, 1982). By 'tradition' here, broadly, I mean to connote Deoband's emphasis on what early Deobandis termed the 'transmitted' (*manqulat*) bodies of knowledge (e.g. Qur'an, Hadith, *fiqh*) as opposed to the 'rational' (*ma'qulat*) bodies of knowledge (e.g. *falsafa*, logic).
[7] Metcalf, *Islamic Revival in British India*, p. 93.
[8] Sayyid Ahmad Khan, 'Madrasa Deoband ki Salana Report par Tabsirah', in Muhammad Isma'il Panipati (ed.), *Maqalat-i Sar Sayyid, Vol. 7* (Lahore: Majlis Taraqqi-yi Adab, 1962), pp. 278–88. This article first appeared in Sayyid Ahmad's journal, *Tahzib al-Akhlaq* (hereafter *TA*), on 27 July 1873.
[9] Muhammad Qasim Nanautvi, *Tasfiyat al-'Aqa'id* (Delhi: Matba'-i Mujtabai, 1934).
[10] See, for example, his letter of 1867 to Nanautvi reprinted in Mohammad Abdul Mannan (trans.), *Selected Letters of Sir Syed Ahmad* (Aligarh: Sir Syed Academy, 2007), pp. 116–20.
[11] *Nechari* is the pejorative term used most famously by Jamal al-Din al-Afghani to denote Sayyid Ahmad's alleged materialist philosophy. See Nikki Keddie (trans.), *An Islamic Response to Imperialism: Political Writings of Sayyid Jamal al-Din al-Afghani* (Berkeley, CA: University of California Press, 1983). The term is, in turn, adopted by Thanvi and other Deobandi scholars in their critiques of the Aligarh movement.
[12] Ashraf 'Ali Thanvi, *Al-Ifadat al-yawmiyya min al-ifadat al-qawmiyya, Vol. 6* (Multan: Idara-yi Ta'lifat-i Ashrafiyya, 2003), pp. 330–1.
[13] Muhammad Ikram, in particular, believes the opposition towards Sayyid Ahmad Khan from the *'ulama* has been overstated. See S.M. Ikram, *Mauj-i Kausar* (Lahore: Idara-yi Saqafat-i Islamiyya, 1990), pp. 90–1.
[14] His early treatise, *Rah-i sunnat aur rad-i bid'at* (*The Path of the Sunna and Refutation of Innovation*), was modelled after Muhammad Isma'il's *Idah al-Haq al-Sarih fi ahkam al-mayyit wa-l darih* (*Elucidation of the Clear Truth Concerning Rules about the Dead and Tombs*). See Christian Troll, *Sayyid Ahmad Khan: A Reinterpretation of Muslim Theology* (New Delhi: Vikas Publishing House, 1978), p. 40.

translate al-Ghazali's *Kimiya-i Sa'adat* into Urdu, is also telling.[15] These events date from the early period of his life, when he admitted that a certain 'Wahhabi' desire for purifying the faith captured his imagination.[16] But while he himself dismissed this as a youthful flirtation of sorts, a purist impulse to glean the 'fundamental' elements of Islamic belief and practice remained with him throughout his career. And upon Nanautvi's death, Sayyid Ahmad declared that Nanautvi 'worked for the welfare of the Muslim community' and regarded Dar al-'Ulum Deoband as 'a living monument of his services', adding 'it is incumbent on all to see that this *madrasah* continues and flourishes'.[17]

'Custom' in Late Colonial India: Three Overlapping Frames

Before proceeding to our comparison, let me place Sayyid Ahmad's and Thanvi's interventions into social and historical context with a brief overview of three intersecting frameworks for understanding 'custom' in late colonial India.[18]

The first is the Islamic legal critiques of 'custom' that animate early nineteenth-century treatises such as those of Muhammad Isma'il (d. 1831) and Khurram 'Ali (d. 1855), and whose critiques were revived in Deobandi, Ahl-i Hadis and other circles after 1857. These critiques saw custom as the preeminent space where the masses ascribed quasi-divine qualities to entities other than God (*shirk*) and performed certain acts with such regularity that they impinged on the normativity of the Qur'an and Sunna.[19] This counter-normativity insinuates itself into the masses' thinking: they feel obligated to uphold the custom and, worse, disparage those who do not.[20] For Muhammad Isma'il, the space of 'custom' is also one defined by the influence on Indian Islam of 'Hindu' practices, a notion that heavily impacted upon later debates on custom among the *'ulama*. Articulating fundamental elements of what Ashraf 'Ali Thanvi would shape into a nuanced Sunna-based critique of custom, Muhammad Isma'il lamented how 'in the present age, people have chosen myriad paths. Some follow the customs (*rasmen*) of their ancestors, while some follow the ways of pious men (*buzurg*). Some offer the self-proclaimed sayings of the scholars (*'ulama*) as their proof, while some pry into religious matters under the pretext of using their rationality (*'aql*)'. But the best path, he continued, was 'to take the Qur'an and Sunna as the standard' by which to assess 'the customs of society'.[21]

The second, which had a more abiding impact on Aligarh, located local customs within broader discourses of 'civilisations', in large part the outcome of North Indian Muslim intellectuals' engagements with Orientalist critiques of Islam and India. In the second half of the nineteenth century, translations of works such as Gustave Le Bon's *La civilisation des Arabes* (which entered Urdu as *Tamaddun-i 'Arab* in 1896) amplified a nascent discourse of civilisational 'decline' and 'progress' in Urdu.[22] Meanwhile, texts like Sayyid Ahmad

---

[15] Sayyid Ahmad Khan, 'Tarjuma Kimiya-i Sa'adat', in Muhammad Isma'il Panipati (ed.), *Maqalat-i Sar Sayyid, Vol. 5* (Lahore: Majlis Taraqqi-yi Adab, 1962), p. 430.
[16] Troll, *Sayyid Ahmad Khan*, p. 41.
[17] Ziya ul-Hasan Faruqi, *The Deoband School and the Demand for Pakistan* (New York: Asia Publishing House, 1963), pp. 42–3, n. 2.
[18] This is not meant to be at all exhaustive, but only to frame subsequent analysis for the purposes of this article. A more detailed foray would also include, for example, Hindu reformist critiques of 'custom'.
[19] Khurram 'Ali, *Nasihat al-Muslimin* (Lucknow: Dar al-Isha'at Islamiyya, 1964), pp. 35–9.
[20] Muhammad Isma'il, *Taqwiyat al-Iman ma' Tazkir al-Ikhwan* (Deoband: Dar al-Kitab Deoband, 1997), pp. 248–9.
[21] *Ibid.*, pp. 13–4.
[22] Gustave Le Bon (Sayyid 'Ali Bilgrami, trans.), *Tamaddun-i 'Arab* (Sargodha: Zafar Traders, 1975).

Dihlavi's *Rusum-i Dihli* (*Customs of Delhi*, 1905) catalogued the intricate customs that were thought to dominate certain aspects of Muslim life, an encyclopaedic impulse that was partly critical, partly nostalgic, and focused on 'Hindu' influence in Muslim cultural life.[23] This encyclopaedic mode reached its zenith in Abdul Halim Sharar's *Hindustan Men Mashriqi Tamaddun ki Akhiri Namuna, ya'ni Guzashta Lakhna'u* (*The Last Example of Eastern Civilization in India, or Lucknow of the Past*, 1913–20), which linked the decline of Muslim political power with the decline of 'culture' (*tahzib*) and reflected a range of new vocabularies among Urdu-speaking intellectuals—e.g. *akhlaq* (morals), *rusum* (customs), *rivaj* (practices), *riwayat* (traditions)—that came to be understood as various parts of a unifying whole, namely *tahzib* (culture) and *tamaddun* (civilisation).[24] Sayyid Ahmad Khan, particularly, emerged from and contributed to these discourses.

If the first would most directly frame the Islamic legal critique and the second, the liberal critique, the third formed a sort of semantic background for both: British ethnographic, administrative and legal observations of Indian customs. The British had long been interested in collecting data on Muslim customs. Early nineteenth-century studies—most notably Ja'far Sharif's *Islam in India, or the Qanun-i Islam: The Customs of the Musalmans of India* (1832), Meer Hassan Ali's *Observations on the Mussulmauns of India* (1832) and Garcin de Tassy's *Mémoires sur les particularités de la religion musulmane dans l'Inde* (1831)—were widely read and published in multiple editions. By the 1870s and 1880s, an armchair interest in custom was channelled into the apparatus of rule, in which British officials and ethnographers sought to map out local 'customs' directly, which they would then redact in the vein of British 'customary law'. Thus, the Punjab Laws Act of 1872, establishing 'customary law' as the basis for adjudicating disputes, expressed Lord Dalhousie's earlier vision of upholding 'Native Institutions and practices as far as they are consistent with the distribution of justice'.[25] Such an initiative was partially a reaction to earlier Orientalists' attempts to reconstruct 'Gentoo' and 'Muhammadan' law through texts, as opposed to practices, and to earlier liberal projects of inculcating 'Englishness' among the British Empire's subjects.[26] In this manner, the *Code of Gentoo Laws* of 1776 ultimately gave way to texts like Tupper's *Punjab Customary Law* of 1881. It was also, of course, an extension, in theory if not always in practice, of the post-1857 policy of 'non-interference' in native 'religious' affairs. Yet, as Nicholas Dirks has made clear, even as they believed mapping out customary practice could obviate another 'Mutiny', many remained suspect of the power of custom in the everyday lives of Indians, believing them to deprive individuals of agency and make them vulnerable to the caprices of 'public opinion' and mob rule—sentiments echoed by Sayyid Ahmad and Thanvi.[27]

---

[23] Sayyid Ahmad Dihlavi, *Rusum-i Dihli* (Rampur: Kitab Kar Publications, 1965), p. 38; and Gail Minault, *Secluded Scholars*, pp. 98–100.

[24] C.M. Naim, 'Interrogating "The East", "Culture", and "Loss" in Abdul Halim Sharar's *Guzashta Lakhna'u*', in Alka Patel and Karen Leonard (eds.), *Indo-Muslim Cultures in Transition* (Leiden/Boston, MA: Brill, 2012), pp. 196–9. By the 1920s, the discourse on civilisations had widened to encompass broader notions of 'Eastern civilisation' (*mashriqi tamaddun*), especially in Urdu works devoted to Japan as a model for becoming 'modern' without becoming 'Western'. See Nile Green, 'Anti-Colonial Japanophilia and the Constraints of an Islamic Japanology: Information and Affect in the Indian Encounter with Japan', in *South Asian History and Culture*, Vol. 4, no. 3 (2013), pp. 291–313.

[25] David Gilmartin, *Empire and Islam: Punjab and the Making of Pakistan* (Berkeley, CA: University of California Press, 1988), p. 14.

[26] Neeladri Bhattacharya, 'Remaking Custom: The Discourse and Practice of Colonial Codification', in R. Champakalakshmi and S. Gopal (eds), *Tradition, Dissent and Ideology: Essays in Honour of Romila Thapar* (Delhi: Oxford University Press, 1996), pp. 20–51.

[27] Nicholas Dirks, *Castes of Mind: Colonialism and the Making of Modern India* (Princeton, NJ: Princeton University Press, 2001), pp. 149–72.

The Liberal Critique of Custom: Rationality, Civility and the Power of Print

After Sayyid Ahmad Khan's sojourn in England in 1869–70, he returned to India where he set out to establish a 'reformist (*islahi*) journal in Urdu' that would facilitate 'the reform (*islah*) and progress (*taraqqi*)' of Indian Muslims along the lines of 'the refinement and civility (*tahzib o tamaddun*) of Europe'. First appearing on 24 December 1870, his long-running journal, *Tahzib al-Akhlaq* (*The Refinement of Morals*), was the outcome of this vision.[28] Consisting of short, morally-edifying essays written mostly (though not exclusively) by Sayyid Ahmad, the journal was modelled after the early eighteenth-century English periodicals, *The Spectator* and *Tatler*.[29]

Like other North Indian intellectuals of his era, Sayyid Ahmad Khan spoke of an Indian Muslim public culture in need of reform and imagined how the growing availability of cheap lithographed texts could be mobilised towards this end. He aimed to popularise a clear, unadorned Urdu that would be accessible to all.[30] According to Sayyid Ahmad's biographer, Hali, it was the same desire for simplicity and accessibility for the masses that drove Sayyid Ahmad's passion for 'public speaking', a phrase he transliterated into Urdu.[31] We can probably best understand Sayyid Ahmad's view of the 'newspaper'—*parcha*, the term he used to refer to *Tahzib al-Akhlaq*—as an extension of this desire for simplicity and accessibility; for Sayyid Ahmad, the newspaper was a liberatory mechanism by which one acquired the trappings of civilised society and which advanced 'national progress' (*qawmi taraqqi*).[32]

But who were the specific publics to whom Sayyid Ahmad directed his reformist project? Sayyid Ahmad believed—rightly, it turns out, according to Hali—that the impact of *Tahzib al-Akhlaq* would be most palpable among the emerging middle-class Muslims of the *qasbahs*, and specifically those who were neither among the *'ulama* nor among the nobility. For, he says, the *'ulama* were threatened by the journal's challenge to their authority, and the nobility was inured to its reformist message because of its decadence.[33] '*Tahzib al-Akhlaq* made its greatest impact on the Muslims of the middle class (*mutawasit daraja*)', explains Hali, who were 'neither completely illiterate nor highly intellectual and whose standard of living was neither very low nor very high. It made very little impression on the people of Delhi and Lucknow and the surrounding areas where the last few vestiges of the former glory of the Muslims still survived'.[34] Aligarh, like Deoband, was the product of intellectual and social

---

[28] It temporarily ceased publication in 1876; after a hiatus of three years, it resumed in 1879, coming out regularly until 1881. Sayyid Ahmad Khan, *Maqalat-i Sar Sayyid, ya'ni un 'ilmi, adabi, mu'ashiri, tamadduni, ta'miri aur islahi mazamin ka majmu'a-yi intikhab* (Khurja: Muhammad 'Abdullah Khan Khveshgi, 1962), pp. 13–4.

[29] See, for instance, his discussion of both periodicals in Sayyid Ahmad Khan, 'Maqasid-i Tahzib al-Akhlaq', in Muhammad Isma'il Panipati (ed.), *Maqalat-i Sar Sayyid, Vol. 10* (Lahore: Majlis Taraqqi-yi Adab, 1962), pp. 39–51 (*TA*, 11 Mar. 1872). *Tatler* was, of course, one of the 'moral weeklies' that Habermas took as perhaps the archetypal example of print in the English public sphere. Jürgen Habermas (Thomas Burger, trans.), *The Structural Transformation of the Public Sphere* (Cambridge, MA: MIT Press, 1991), pp. 42–3. *The Spectator*, moreover, is the journal that Michael Warner highlights in his argument on the reflexivity of publics. See Warner, *Publics and Counterpublics*, esp. pp. 99–108.

[30] David Lelyveld, *Aligarh's First Generation: Muslim Solidarity in British India* (Princeton, NJ: Princeton University Press, 1978), pp. 206–7.

[31] David Lelyveld, 'Sir Sayyid's Public Sphere: Urdu Print and Oratory in Nineteenth Century India', in Agnieszka Kuczkiewicz-Fras (ed.), *Islamicate Traditions in South Asia: Themes from Culture and History* (New Delhi: Manohar, 2013), pp. 153–7.

[32] Sayyid Ahmad Khan, 'Maqasid-i Tahzib al-Akhlaq', p. 39.

[33] According to Lelyveld, the most vociferous attacks on the journal came not from *'ulama* or nobles, but from two prominent Muslims who, like Sayyid Ahmad Khan, were sympathetic to the British, Sayyid Imdad Ali and Ali Bakhsh Khan: Lelyveld, *Aligarh's First Generation*, pp. 131–2.

[34] Khvajah Altaf Husain Hali, *Hayat-i Javid* (Lahore: 'Ishrat Publishing House, 1965), p. 166.

networks that bound the *qasbahs* of North India together in the latter half of the nineteenth century as 'nodal points traversing the worlds of the local, the larger Indian, and the global Islamic'.[35]

If Sayyid Ahmad saw a middle-class, Urdu-literate member of the North Indian *qasbah* as the public to which he directed his journal, he also situated him accordingly at the centre of a nexus of readers who were, in his view, free of both religious affect and pride in their lineage or social standing. These Muslims would be the vanguard of a new form of public debate, tempered and constrained. It would help move India's Muslims beyond the older forms of religious disputation (*munazara*), too fraught with 'religious zeal' (*josh mazhabi*),[36] towards print-mediated rational inquiry. 'When you are in an assembly (*majlis*) where there are people of various opinions', Sayyid Ahmad advised his readers, 'avoid altercation, dispute and disputation as much as possible'.[37]

In this idealised public, the task of curtailing the emotions depended, in turn, on Muslims forsaking their obsession with 'station and rank' (*halat aur rutba*).[38] Sayyid Ahmad was one among North Indian Muslim intellectuals who came to re-conceive nobility, according to Gail Minault, as a set of virtues rather than a birthright. *Sharif* (nobility), in the sense of birthright, 'gave way to "noble" in the sense of good character: honourable, upright, cultured, and respectable…pious without being wasteful, educated without being pedantic, and restrained in his expression of emotion'.[39] To submit one's own opinions to rational interrogation, one had to do so without respect to one's own 'wealth, position, power or knowledge' in a vein comparable to the classic Habermasian position. 'The very idea of the public', in these terms, 'was based on the notion of a general interest sufficiently basic that discourse about it need not be distorted by particular interests'.[40] Sayyid Ahmad sought to speak to his readers as individuals, not just '*in* the public' but '*as* the public'.[41]

One can witness in *Tahzib al-Akhlaq*, moreover, how mass affect had begun to shape public sentiment. At the same time that Sayyid Ahmad saw a public of readers as a salutary force, that very public was now prone to a new phenomenon: public opinion. He deplored mindless submission to 'mass opinion' (*jumhur ki ra'e*) and, indeed, critiqued those governed by custom for liking only 'what the public likes' (*jo 'amm pasand*) and conforming their 'taste and fundamental disposition' with custom itself.[42] Championing 'freedom of opinion' (*azadi*

---

[35] M. Raisur Rahman, 'Beyond Centre–Periphery: Qasbahs and Muslim Life in South Asia', in *South Asian History and Culture*, Vol. 5, no. 2 (2014), p. 164; see also Faisal Devji, 'Gender and the Politics of Space', in *South Asia: Journal of South Asian Studies*, Vol. XIV, no. 1 (1991), p. 149. Looking beyond the classic examples of Deoband and Aligarh, Justin Jones sees the late nineteenth-century *qasbah* as a centre of public debate in which the *munazara* acted as a means of vaunting the prestige of the *qasbah* and local *ashraf* nobility. See Justin Jones, 'The Local Experiences of Reformist Islam in a "Muslim" Town in India: The Case of Amroha', in *Modern Asian Studies*, Vol. 43, no. 4 (2009), pp. 871–908.
[36] Sayyid Ahmad Khan, 'Azadi Ra'e', in Muhammad Isma'il Panipati (ed.), *Maqalat-i Sar Sayyid, Vol. 5* (Lahore: Majlis Taraqqi-yi Adab, 1962), p. 214 (*TA*, 11 Feb. 1871).
[37] Sayyid Ahmad Khan, 'Bahs o takrar', *Maqalat-i Sar Sayyid, ya'ni un 'ilmi, adabi, mu'ashiri, tamadduni, ta'miri aur islahi mazamin ka majmu'a-yi intikhab* (Khurja: Muhammad 'Abdullah Khan Khveshgi, 1962), p. 192.
[38] Sayyid Ahmad Khan, 'Rasm o Rivaj ki Pabandi ke Nuqsanat', in Muhammad Isma'il Panipati (ed.), *Maqalat-i Sar Sayyid, Vol. 5* (Lahore: Majlis Taraqqi-yi Adab, 1962), p. 23 (*TA*, 23 Jan. 1871).
[39] Minault, *Secluded Scholars*, pp. 4–5.
[40] Craig Calhoun, 'Introduction: Habermas and the Public Sphere', in Craig Calhoun (ed.), *Habermas and the Public Sphere* (Cambridge, MA: MIT Press, 1992), p. 9. This version of Habermas' thought has long since been complicated by Habermas himself. See, among other examples, Habermas' reply in Craig Calhoun, Eduardo Mendieta and Jonathan VanAntwerpen (eds), *Habermas and Religion* (Cambridge: Polity Press, 2013).
[41] Harold Mah, 'Phantasies of the Public Sphere: Rethinking the Habermas of Historians', in *The Journal of Modern History*, Vol. 72, no. 1 (2000), pp. 167, 169.
[42] Sayyid Ahmad Khan, 'Rasm o Rivaj ki Pabandi ke Nuqsanat', p. 24.

ra'e) as 'an absolute right' of every human being, Sayyid Ahmad saw that very freedom as a bulwark against the corrosive power of public opinion; like social status and wealth, 'numbers of people' are no reliable criterion for truth. Only the 'power of sound reasoning' (*quwwat-i istidlal*) provides this criterion. The veracity of a claim depends not on the authority of the one making it, but on the claim itself.[43]

It is, finally, 'customs and habits' that most hinder the free circulation of rational thought in public. Sayyid Ahmad's critique of customs appears from the very first issue of *Tahzib al-Akhlaq*—in his essay 'Customs and Habits' ('Rusum o 'Adat')—and is a theme to which he returned repeatedly in subsequent issues. He distinguished between three words that are commonly glossed as 'custom': *rasm*, *rivaj* and *'adat*. A *rasm* is an action that people believe is passed down from their 'ancestors', the origins of which are now obscure. A *rivaj*, by contrast, is an action that people do out of habit or because it is fashionable, but lacks the temporal dimension of a *rasm*.[44] When a *rivaj* persists over a certain period of time, it becomes inscribed into the social polity in such a way that it acquires a certain historicity and takes on the semblance of an unstated 'law', thereby becoming a *rasm*. An *'adat*, finally, is ingrained in human nature itself, a tendency towards certain qualities, whether good or bad, that humans share by virtue of being human. Thus, he illustrates, the *rasm* of giving alms arises from the *'adat* of generosity.[45]

He advances three arguments about custom that are germane to the discussion here. First, not all customs are necessarily harmful; it is the resistance to questioning *all* customs, regardless of merit, that Sayyid Ahmad finds stifling. What worries him is that the masses and elites alike accept a *rasm* so unthinkingly as to be its 'slaves': 'The slave of God sometimes has the anxiety of disobedience, but the slaves of *rasm o rivaj* have no such anxiety'. Custom casts its allure over all, 'the learned and the unlearned, the ignorant and the wise'.[46] The reason is that custom's power derives from the power of narratives: they are thought to have existed since time immemorial. But that ahistoricity is an insidious fiction; our ancestors interrogated their *own* ancestors' customs, he says, and amended them accordingly. It is then the very *illusion* of timelessness that gives the *rasm* its power. 'And when our own ancestors reformed their ancestors' customs', he asks, 'then why can we not reform ours?'[47]

Second, if custom's pull exerts itself on the minds of individual Muslims, it casts its spell all the more over the collectivity—the *qawm* or nation. The *qawm*, according to Sayyid Ahmad, does not denote a political entity, let alone a geographic one. Rather, *qawm* is an imagined collectivity that sublimates internal divisions among Muslims, such as class and rank, as we saw above.[48] He assimilates the *qawm* into a narrative of civilisational progress that depends on a sort of communal introspection. 'We should not simply take the customs of our nation or country on faith to be good', he writes. 'Rather, we should test them with utmost freedom (*azadi*)'.[49] Civilised nations have undertaken a critical interrogation of their own

---

[43] Sayyid Ahmad Khan, 'Azadi Ra'e', p. 213.

[44] Sayyid Ahmad Khan, 'Rasm o Rivaj', *Maqalat-i Sar Sayyid, ya'ni un 'ilmi, adabi, mu'ashiri, tamadduni, ta'miri aur islahi mazamin ka majmu'a-yi intikhab* (Khurja: Muhammad 'Abdullah Khan Khveshgi, 1962), p. 93.

[45] *Ibid.*, pp. 93–4.

[46] *Ibid.*, p. 95.

[47] *Ibid.*, p. 104.

[48] Faisal Devji has suggested that Sayyid Ahmad's articulation of the *qawm* as classless is inseparable from a *sharif*-dominated political imaginary that projected its own perspectives as universal. Faisal Devji. 'The Idea of a Muslim Community: British India, 1857–1906', in Marcel Maussen, Veit Bader and Annelies Moors (eds), *Colonial and Postcolonial Governance of Islam* (Amsterdam: Amsterdam University Press, 2011), pp. 111–32.

[49] Sayyid Ahmad Khan, 'Rusum o 'Adat', in Muhammad Isma'il Panipati (ed.), *Maqalat-i Sar Sayyid, Vol. 5* (Lahore: Majlis Taraqqi-yi Adab, 1962), p. 13 (*TA*, 25 Dec. 1870).

customs and traditions, dispensing with those that encourage 'barbarity' (*wahshana*) and impede 'civility' (*shahyastagi*).[50] 'Civility', moreover, is a universal human (*insani*) value for Sayyid Ahmad; it is not limited to Muslims. God has endowed each individual with an 'intrinsic goodness' (*dili neki*) that, once the constraining power of custom has been removed, will lead to human flourishing.[51] 'Being bound to custom is everywhere a hindrance and obstacle to human progress (*insan ki taraqqi*)' and the 'basis for human decline (*insan ki tanazzul*)'.[52] For Sayyid Ahmad, India's Muslims 'have already reached the furthest limit in the era of decline, disgrace, and baseness' because they have lost the capacity to critically evaluate their own customs.[53]

Third, customs proliferate through 'imitation'—whether between individuals in public or between entire 'nations'. Indian Muslims have especially succumbed to its effects:

> It is often the case that a nation unintentionally adopts the customs of other nations because of mixing and interaction, without examining whether they are good or bad. This is especially the case of the Muslims of India. They have unthinkingly adopted thousands of customs from other nations in all matters of life as well as in some religious matters, or invented new customs that resemble other nations' customs. But if we want to elevate our own ways of life and civilisation (*tamaddun*) to the highest level of refinement (*tahzib*), so that those nations that are more refined than ours may not look upon us with scorn, we must critically examine all our customs and habits (*rusum o 'adat*), cast off those that are bad, and reform (*islah*) those that are worthy of reform.[54]

Unlike the subject bound by custom, the liberal subject is self-governing and self-regulating, one for whom 'helping one's self' (*apni madad ap*) is a paramount virtue[55] and who is not bound by 'imitation of others' (*dusron ki taqlid*) or 'thoughtless' (*be soche*) observance of customs. But breaking the spell of custom requires that individuals 'practise' (*mashq*) their faculties of moral discrimination.[56]

The notion of an ideal public being comprised of self-regulating, critical individuals is, of course, one that had become normative in the intellectual history of Europe by this time. Sayyid Ahmad was an enthusiastic reader of John Stuart Mill, founding a Scientific Society in Ghazipur that translated the works of Mill into Urdu.[57] He drew on Mill's belief that '[t]he

---

[50] Sayyid Ahmad Khan, 'Tariqa-yi Zindagi', in Muhammad Isma'il Panipati (ed.), *Maqalat-i Sar Sayyid, Vol. 5* (Lahore: Majlis Taraqqi-yi Adab, 1962), p. 35 (*TA*, 1 Sept. 1871): on his theory of civilisation generally, and its indebtedness to nineteenth-century liberal texts like J.S. Mill's *On Liberty*, see Avril Powell, *Scottish Orientalists and India: The Muir Brothers, Religion, Education and Empire* (Woodbridge: Boydell Press, 2010), pp. 206–11.
[51] Sayyid Ahmad Khan, 'Rusum o 'Adat', p. 14.
[52] Sayyid Ahmad Khan, 'Rasm o Rivaj ki Pabandi ke Nuqsanat', p. 25.
[53] *Ibid.*, p. 26.
[54] Sayyid Ahmad Khan, 'Rusum o 'Adat', pp. 16–7.
[55] Sayyid Ahmad Khan, 'Apni Madad Ap', in Muhammad Isma'il Panipati (ed.), *Maqalat-i Sar Sayyid, Vol. 5* (Lahore: Majlis Taraqqi-yi Adab, 1962), pp. 71–81 (*TA*, Sept. 1875).
[56] Sayyid Ahmad Khan, 'Rasm o Rivaj ki Pabandi ke Nuqsanat', pp. 20–1. On Sayyid Ahmad Khan's theory of progress on the level of states and civilisations, see also Hafeez Malik, 'Sir Sayyid Ahmad Khan's Doctrines of Muslim Nationalism and National Progress', in *Modern Asian Studies*, Vol. 2, no. 3 (1968), pp. 221–44, esp. pp. 234–44.
[57] J.M.S. Baljon, *The Reforms and Religious Ideas of Sir Sayyid Ahmad Khan* (Lahore: Sh. Muhammad Ashraf, 1964), p. 56, n. 1; and Shan Muhammad (ed.), *The Aligarh Movement: Basic Documents, 1864–1898, Vol. 1* (Meerut: Meenakshi Prakashan, 1978), p. 16.

human faculties of perception, judgment, discriminative feeling, mental activity, and even moral preference, are exercised only in making a choice. He who does anything because it is the custom, makes no choice'.[58] Similarly, Sayyid Ahmad argues, 'we should not think that those who prefer certain customs do so out of their own desire.... Rather, the truth is that they only prefer what is dictated by custom itself'.[59] He seems, in fact, to have adapted the language of Mill's *On Liberty* (1859) in his essay 'Azadi Ra'e' ('Freedom of Opinion'). Mill wrote:

> An enemy of free discussion may be supposed to say that there is no necessity for mankind in general to know and understand all that can be said against or for their opinions by philosophers and theologians. That it is not needful for common men to be able to expose all the misstatements or fallacies of an ingenious opponent. That it is enough if there is always somebody capable of answering them, so that nothing likely to mislead uninstructed persons remains unrefuted. That simple minds, having been taught the obvious grounds of the truths inculcated on them, may trust to authority for the rest, and being aware that they have neither the knowledge nor talent to resolve every difficulty which can be raised, may repose in the assurance that all those which have been raised have been or can be answered, by those who are specially trained to the task.[60]

In arguing against what he sees as the pernicious effect of 'imitation' (*taqlid*) on the minds of Muslims, Sayyid Ahmad writes, in a statement that directly paraphrases Mill:

> Opposition to a diversity of opinion has spread greatly among the Muslims, in connection to which a powerful but sly claim is made, namely: that it is neither necessary nor possible for all people to know what the great doctors (*hakim*), mystics (*ahl-i ma'rifat*), and men of religious knowledge (*'ulum-i din*) know and understand, nor that it is possible for a common man (*'amm admi*) to comprehend and refute all the errors of a clever and wise opponent, but that it is sufficient for him to grasp that there will always be someone else to provide answers to religious issues by means of which no opponent's idea will remain unrefuted. Thus for simple-minded people this alone is sufficient: that they should be taught the fundamentals and rely on others for the rest, and when they understand they do not have sufficient knowledge to solve all the difficulties which may be raised, they can be content in knowing that whatever difficulties or objections may arise, all the answers have already been provided or will be provided by great scholars.[61]

The Islamic Legal Critique of Custom: Normativity, Rationality and the Public 'Signs' of Islam

Sayyid Ahmad Khan's liberal critique of custom revolved around emancipating individual subjects from the narratives that enchant them and training them to evaluate customs critically. Ashraf 'Ali Thanvi, too, was critical of ancestral authority, blindly-held assumptions

---

[58] John Stuart Mill, *On Liberty* (London: John W. Parker and Son, 2nd. ed. 1859), p. 105.
[59] Sayyid Ahmad Khan, 'Rasm o Rivaj ki Pabandi ke Nuqsanat', p. 23.
[60] Mill, *On Liberty*, pp. 68–9.
[61] Sayyid Ahmad Khan, 'Azadi Ra'e', pp. 227–8. Powell notes a different passage from this essay that paraphrases Mill. Powell, *Scottish Orientalists and India*, p. 218, n. 51.

and traditions that pose as timeless 'law' when they are in fact contingent. But Thanvi's critique of custom revolves around it mimicking the normativity of the Sunna and the role of the *'ulama* in disabusing the masses of false beliefs.

Most of Thanvi's texts consulted here date from the turn of the century—such as *Islah al-Khayal* from 1901 and *Bihishti Zewar* from 1905—with the exception of his oral discourses (*malfuzat*) collected in 1932.[62] This first decade, what Francis Robinson called the 'high point of Muslim separatism', was of course a markedly different cultural environment than that of the 1870s, when Sayyid Ahmad composed the essays discussed above.[63] There is, of course, no space here to survey these seismic shifts in any depth. Briefly, a number of cultural, political and demographic changes are essential for understanding Thanvi's own context. The Survey of India (1878) and Census of India (1881), as numerous scholars have shown, inscribed new identities from above.[64] New religious sectarianisms, meanwhile, were in the process of being mobilised. The Arya Samaj, founded in 1875, did not yet exist when the first issues of *Tahzib al-Akhlaq* were published, whereas the Arya-supported Cow Protection Movement of 1893 and the ensuing sectarian riots transpired within increasingly contested public spaces.[65] New forms of political mobilisation, most crucially the founding of the All India Muslim League in 1906—based in part on Sayyid Ahmad's own evolving views of a separate Muslim '*qawm*'—grew out of a sense that the Indian National Congress could not adequately represent Muslim 'interests' in a new political landscape. And Deoband itself, still in its infancy in the 1870s, was by 1900 a major intellectual and political force among India's Muslims. All of these shifts would have made Sayyid Ahmad's liberal project less tenable to many, not least of whom was Thanvi himself.

This is, of course, not to say that if Thanvi had been writing in the 1870s, he would have been more accommodating of Sayyid Ahmad's liberalism. However, despite the striking contrast in historical contexts, Thanvi begins from similar premises in his critique of custom. Like Sayyid Ahmad, he understood, first of all, the power of print and its emergent publics. But to compare Sayyid Ahmad and Thanvi through the lens of 'the public' is also necessarily to evoke the problematic of translation, most evident in taking Thanvi's *'amm* as 'public' and *'awamm* as 'the public'. The meaning of *'amm* (and its obverse, *khass*, variously connoting 'elite' and 'private') has shifted depending on historical, social and legal contexts. We see it in the Mughal-era designations of the *divan-i 'amm* and *divan-i khass*, 'public' and 'private' audience halls, with the implication that the 'private' space of the latter conferred political capital on those who could access it.[66] For Thanvi, *'awamm* denotes 'the masses', and specifically those who are not among the scholarly elite. The 'elite' (*khawass*), in Thanvi's own work, almost always denotes the *'ulama*. It is precisely for this reason that those whom his written work purports to initiate into this rarefied scholarly discourse become part of a sort of quasi-public of 'middling' scholars—not quite the scholarly 'elite', but not entirely

---

[62] Other texts by Thanvi (e.g. *Islah al-Rusum* and *Aghlat al-'Awamm*, consulted here) do not provide original publication dates.
[63] Francis Robinson, *Separatism among Indian Muslims: The Politics of the United Provinces' Muslims, 1860–1923* (Cambridge: Cambridge University Press, 1974), pp. 133–74.
[64] Most famously shown by Bernard Cohn, 'The Census, Social Structure and Objectification in South Asia', in *An Anthropologist among Historians and Other Essays* (Delhi: Oxford University Press, 1987), pp. 224–54.
[65] Sandria B. Freitag, 'Contesting in Public: Colonial Legacies and Contemporary Communalism', in David E. Ludden (ed.), *Contesting the Nation: Religion, Community and the Politics of Democracy in India* (Philadelphia, PA: University of Pennsylvania Press, 1996), pp. 211–34.
[66] Margrit Pernau, 'From a "Private" Public to a "Public" Private Sphere: Old Delhi and the North Indian Muslims in Comparative Perspective', in Gurpreet Mahajan (ed.), *The Public and the Private: Issues of Democratic Citizenship* (New Delhi: Sage Publications, 2003), pp. 105–6.

'common' either. It is worth noting that Thanvi and Sayyid Ahmad's biographer, Hali, both use the same Urdu word, *mutawasit* (middling, midway, intermediate), to describe their respective audiences.[67] This is not to suggest that Thanvi's 'middling scholar' (*mutawasit 'alim*) and Sayyid Ahmad's 'middle class' (*mutawasit daraja*) readers necessarily overlapped, but the shared rhetoric of appealing to the sensibilities of new readers—neither elite nor common, neither rich nor poor—is suggestive.

At the nexus of Thanvi's public was a self-regulating, self-fashioning individual—or, more precisely, *partially* self-regulating, for the role of the *'ulama* in facilitating moral regulation and self-fashioning is indispensable. For Thanvi, the idealised member of his moral public is one armed with the religious knowledge necessary to distinguish between what is prophetic norm (*sunna*) and what is heretical innovation (*bid'a*), and the pious sensibilities to bring every sphere of life into accord with a normative ethical model. We can get a glimpse of Thanvi's popular readership with short texts like *Aghlat al-'Awamm* (*Errors of the Public*), a pamphlet in which Thanvi serially and systematically catalogued common errors of belief. It evinces, above all, the extent to which he sees the public as a space in which error naturally proliferates. 'Today', he states, 'the elements of religious knowledge are easily attained via printed religious books that are cheaply and widely available and translated into Urdu, and via *'ulama* who preach about the necessities of religion'. However, 'despite this there are also many among the masses, even some of the elite among the masses, for whom errors in religious knowledge, having no basis in the Shari'a, have become rampant'.[68]

Thanvi shared Sayyid Ahmad's suspicion of public opinion. But he was, by comparison, deeply ambivalent about print and its ramifications, seeing it as a vehicle for reform, but one that gave lay readers a dangerous sense of interpretive independence.[69] If Sayyid Ahmad saw the civilising potential in the newspaper, Thanvi was highly sceptical towards the newspaper as a 'worldly' instrument that trafficked in gossip and hearsay. 'Nowadays there is great clamour in the newspapers', he said. 'They are the root cause of corruption (*fasad*) in this country. Spreading unsubstantiated "stories" is what they do best'.[70] He saw religious tracts as, ideally, conferring just enough religious knowledge to allow readers to bring their belief and practice into accord with the Sunna. They were not equipped to debate publically any religious questions (*masa'il*), a provision that applied, above all, to the political questions of the day, for politics too was subsumed under the normative regulations of the Shari'a. He maligned the mass political movements of the first two decades of the twentieth century, for they were based on notions of 'majority opinion' (*kasrat-i ra'e*), which, in Thanvi's view, were abominable.[71]

His ambivalence about print is, then, the context for understanding the power of custom. Customs dull the very moral sensibilities that religious texts are meant to promote. Thanvi began his short work, *Islah al-Rusum* (*Reformation of Customs*), with the admonition that 'in this age, most Muslims see that we are so thoroughly bound to invented customs (*rusum ikhtira'iyya*) that, although carrying out necessary and compulsory religious duties has not been lost, customs have been given no less an equal status'.[72] Customs mimic the normativity of prescribed religious practices, whereas the Shari'a forbids 'restricting, stipulating, specifying,

---

[67] Ashraf 'Ali Thanvi, *Bihishti Zewar: Mudallal o Mukammal Bihishti Zewar ma' Bihishti Gauhar, Vol. I* (Karachi: Altaf and Sons, 2001), p. 4. For Hali, see footnote 34, above.

[68] Ashraf 'Ali Thanvi, *Aghlat al-'Awamm* (Deoband: Maktabah Nizamiyya, 1962), p. 3.

[69] Brannon D. Ingram, 'The Portable Madrasa: Print, Publics and the Authority of the Deobandi 'Ulama', in *Modern Asian Studies*, Vol. 48, no. 4 (2014), pp. 845–71.

[70] Thanvi, *Al-Ifadat al-yawmiyya, Vol. 2*, pp. 28–9.

[71] Ashraf 'Ali Thanvi, *Ashraf al-Jawab* (Deoband: Maktaba Thanvi, 1990), pp. 298–9.

[72] Ashraf 'Ali Thanvi, *Islah al-Rusum* (Delhi: Dini Book Depot, 1963), p. 9.

or making mandatory' any particular belief or action to the extent that it simulates or mimics the normativity of the law.[73] That is, to perform any action with the same degree, consistency or intentionality that one is expected to grant Sunna acts is prohibited.[74] Custom arrogates to itself its own *nomos*; it forms its own faux Shari'a, what Thanvi derisively calls a 'self-devised' (*man gharat*) Shari'a, a veritable contradiction in terms.[75]

In *Bihishti Zewar* (*Heavenly Ornaments*), Thanvi offers a typology of 'customs' in three categories: first, those the public knows to be a sin (*gunah*), but does anyway (e.g. dancing at weddings, fireworks); second, those that they believe to be permissible (*ja'iz*), when, in fact, they are not (e.g. the micro-customs that have formed around the circumcision rite); and third, those that have clustered around normative Islamic ritual practices (e.g. burial of the dead). What all customs have in common is their propensity to dull the senses of 'otherwise intelligent and rational' Muslims:

> From the moment one comes into this world until the last breath, most if not all customs are of the sort that have spread like a tempest among otherwise intelligent (*samajh-dar*) and rational (*'aql-mand*) people…. The only explanation for this is that these customs have become such common practice among the people that they have cast a veil upon their rationality (*'aql*).[76]

Thanvi is, ultimately, less trusting than Sayyid Ahmad of rationality or *'aql* to guide moral sensibilities. Rationality can be harnessed to sharpen faculties of moral discrimination, but it has its limits; his legal hermeneutics begins in the space where rationality ends, and the *'ulama* are those who claim—a claim not uncontested—to adjudicate that space.

As we have seen, for Sayyid Ahmad, customs insinuate themselves partly through the uncritical imitation of other 'nations' (*aqwam*). But Thanvi's foray into this discourse was far more pointed, oriented around the perils of 'imitation' for both the individual and on the societal level, in which Islamic law framed what constituted imitation and what did not. When Sayyid Ahmad derided 'imitation', the word he used was most often *taqlid*—commonly understood as the principle by which a Muslim jurist (*faqih*) defers to prior precedent within his specific school of law, as opposed to deriving law directly from the sources of law, the Qur'an and Sunna—but Sayyid Ahmad uses it in a more general sense. Ironically, this is one form of so-called 'imitation' that, for Thanvi, is the *sine qua non* of Islamic legal reasoning.[77] Thanvi's 'imitation' (*tashabbuh*), by contrast, transpired against a new public conscientiousness about the 'signs' (*shi'ar*) or 'marks' (*'alamat*) of Islam. For Thanvi, maintaining public distinction (whether in matters of clothing, eating habits, or buying and selling goods) was crucially bound up with Indian Islamic identity in an era of perceived threats to it. It was an effort, perhaps, to resist the 'fuzziness' of mass identity through a regime of regulating the visual, behavioural and performative dimensions of Islam in the context of a public life that he saw as increasingly dominated by Hindu signs and symbols.[78]

---

[73] *Ibid.*, p. 131.
[74] Ashraf 'Ali Thanvi, *Masa'il-i Tasawwuf Ahadis ki Roshni Men* (Deoband: Ittihad Book Depot Deoband, 2006), p. 180.
[75] Barbara Daly Metcalf, 'Islam and Custom in Nineteenth Century India: The Reformist Standard of Maulana Thanawi's *Bihishti Zewar*', in *Contributions to Asian Studies*, Vol. 17 (1982), p. 69.
[76] Thanvi, *Bihishti Zewar, Vol. 6*, p. 6.
[77] Thanvi, *Al-Ifadat al-yawmiyya, Vol. 1*, pp. 120–7.
[78] See especially Muhammad Qasim Zaman, *Ashraf Ali Thanawi: Islam in Modern South Asia* (Oxford: Oneworld, 2008), pp. 39–44. On 'fuzzy' and 'enumerated' identities, see Sudipta Kaviraj, *The Imaginary Institution of India: Politics and Ideas* (New York: Columbia University Press, 2010), pp. 13–4.

He was, for instance, troubled by certain *'ulama* attempting to placate Hindus by declaring the slaughter of cows to be forbidden (*haram*). These *'ulama*, in his view, found it 'permissible to abandon the outward marks of Islam (*shi'ar-i Islam*) for the sake of peace'.[79] It was all the more troublesome when they did so with reference to normative Islamic sources; Thanvi is particularly incensed by a certain *'alim* who cited Qur'an 6:108—'Do not insult those that they invoke other than Allah'—in forbidding cow sacrifice.

Sayyid Ahmad was deeply critical of prohibitions on 'imitating the unbelievers' (*tashabbuh bi-l kuffar*), even going so far as to question the authenticity of the Hadith—narrated from Abu Da'wud, 'Whoever imitates (*tashabbaha*) a nation (*qawm*) belongs to it'—on which the concept is based.[80] He noted, among other things, that the Prophet Muhammad wore robes associated with both Syrian Christians and Jews.[81] Thanvi did not accept Sayyid Ahmad's argument: 'Distinguishing the nation', he wrote, 'the maintenance of difference in our clothing, our manners, our way of speaking, and our behaviour' is mandated by the Shari'a. And yet, 'certain things are a sin even if they are not the characteristics of other nations', he argued. Thus, 'shaving the beard, wearing pants above the knees, and wearing shorts are all forbidden' to Muslims in any context. But, crucially, other features are prohibited, not for Muslims generally, but because they muddle specific public identities; some articles of clothing, for example, are sufficiently generic as not to be associated with a specific 'nation', but as soon as they do, 'it will become forbidden to adopt them, just as in our country wearing coat and pants, wearing *gurgabi*, tying a *dhoti* [around one's waist], and women wearing the *lahanga* are all things which are purely the characteristics of other nations (*aqwam*)'.[82]

He elaborates this idea in a *fatwa* dated 12 January 1917. For Muslims to wear English dress in England was perfectly acceptable, as indeed he conceded that some did, but wearing such clothing in India was forbidden, precisely because it compromised public distinctions between Muslims and others.[83] The point is that appearances matter. Thanvi explained the legal status of appearances with the following analogy: suppose a man fills an empty liquor bottle with water and drinks it in public. He is not consuming liquor, to be sure; nonetheless 'he is a criminal and, from the perspective of the Shari'a, a sinner, because he appears (*tashabbuh*) to be among the consumers of liquor'.[84]

Thanvi's response to a letter that he received from someone who advanced views remarkably akin to Sayyid Ahmad's spells out this idea in even starker detail. In this letter, the author believes civilisational 'progress' (*taraqqi*) is within reach of India's Muslims if they can only critically assess their own customs and adopt those of other nations. After the early period of Islam, 'other nations progressed', while Islam stagnated and, indeed, the Ottoman sultans retained power only by modelling their rule on Europe's example, unlike the Indian Muslims who atrophied from within.[85] The author of the letter then provides an example of

---

[79] Thanvi, *Al-Ifadat al-yawmiyya, Vol. 1*, pp. 35–6.

[80] Qari Muhammad Tayyib, *Islami Tahzib o Tamaddun* (Lahore: Idara-yi Islamiyya, 1980), pp. 228–32; see also Muhammad Khalid Masud, 'Cosmopolitanism and Authenticity: The Doctrine of *Tashabbuh Bi'l-Kuffar* (*Imitating the Infidel*) in Modern South Asian Fatwas', in Derryl N. Maclean and Sikeena Karmali Ahmed (eds), *Cosmpolitanisms in Muslim Contests: Perspectives from the Past* (Edinburgh: Edinburgh University Press, 2012), pp. 156–75.

[81] Tayyib, *Islami Tahzib o Tamaddun*, pp. 236–43.

[82] Ashraf 'Ali Thanvi, *Hayat al-Muslimin* (Karachi: Idara al-Ma'arif, 2005), pp. 186–7.

[83] Ashraf 'Ali Thanvi, *Imdad al-Fatawa, Vol. 4* (Karachi: Maktaba Dar al-'Ulum Karachi, 2007), p. 268.

[84] Ashraf 'Ali Thanvi, *Anfas-i 'Isa: Az Ifadat-i Hakim al-Ummat Hazrat Mawlana Shah Ashraf 'Ali Sahib Thanvi* (Deoband: Idara Ta'lifat-i Awliya, 1971), p. 359.

[85] Ashraf 'Ali Thanvi, *Islah al-Khayal* (Lahore: Kutub Khana-yi Jamila, 1965), p. 9.

this sort of atrophy: 'Islamic' clothing failed to adapt to 'the necessities of the time'. Therefore, Western clothing should now be not only permissible, but recommended for Muslims, drawing on the utilitarian calculus that new technologies of travel dictate new forms of dress. 'Every day I travel on horseback for four hours and by bicycle for three', he says, making Islamic clothing 'unpractical'.[86] This is, in other words, precisely what Sayyid Ahmad would have regarded as a 'dispensable' custom.

Thanvi replies that the author's argument is tantamount to claiming the Shari'a must change to adapt to a new law of 'nations'—that 'with a change in the times comes a change in the legal commands (*ahkam*)'. The author has confused the 'aims' (*maqasid*) of the Shari'a with the 'means' of attaining those aims. The means can change, but the aims cannot. Thus, Thanvi offers the example of the Haj: it is an 'aim' (*maqsad*) of the Shari'a that a Muslim must go on the Haj, but the means of doing so can change (for example, he says, one can now travel by train and steamship). While the means can change, fulfilling the Haj is a requirement that is timeless and universal, not subject to the whims of history. The prohibition on 'imitating the unbelievers' (*tashabbuh bi-l kufaar*) is like the Haj in this respect: it is an 'aim', grounded in the Qur'an and Sunna. Thus, bringing the argument full circle, Thanvi rejects the author's utilitarian argument for wearing 'coat and pants'.[87]

There is no space here to comment on the complex argumentation at work here—assimilating the prohibition on 'imitation of the unbelievers' to the aims of the Shari'a—and there are certainly pre-modern examples of Muslims' anxieties about maintaining public distinction from religious 'others'. Regardless, surely these anxieties were heightened, for Thanvi, by the lack of a Muslim polity to enforce these norms and the intermingling of vastly different communities enabled by colonial modernity, in addition to the new reifications of identity that this very modernity began to inscribe upon those communities themselves.

Conclusion

'With the colonial state providing no symbolic definition of Muslim community in India', David Gilmartin suggests, 'the assertion of "community" solidarity required that the individual Muslim himself bring his (or her) inner life and sense of identity under self-conscious personal and rational control'.[88] Sayyid Ahmad Khan, Ashraf 'Ali Thanvi, and the movements they both represented and in no small way defined, were preoccupied with a certain ambivalence: should the task of reform (*islah*) focus on the individual or the polity? To what extent could an imagined community of readers form a nexus for linking the two in time and space? Both envisioned the Muslim at the centre of that nexus as one with a critical disposition, educated and endowed with a discrete sense of 'self', empowered both to identify and resist 'custom' as a rival form of authority in private lives and public space. But whereas Thanvi's critique of authority—whether the authority of ancestral tradition, Sufi saints or popular belief—was partly a means of reconstituting *'ulama* authority at the same time, Sayyid Ahmad's 'apologetic modernity', to borrow Devji's phrase, subsumed the *'ulama*, too, within the purview of its critique, and posited a pure 'Islam' in their stead, one that 'transcended the remit of specific authorities like those of clerics, mystics and kings, but could

---

[86] *Ibid.*, p. 18.
[87] *Ibid.*, pp. 41–2.
[88] David Gilmartin, 'Democracy, Nationalism, and the Public: A Speculation on Colonial Muslim Politics', in *South Asia: Journal of South Asian Studies*, Vol. XIV, no. 1 (1991), pp. 128–9.

also become its own authority as an independent historical actor designating a new kind of moral community'.[89]

Let me conclude with an open-ended query of sorts. This article has aimed to gauge how two thinkers, both of whom were invested in reforming Muslim publics, drew on common vocabularies to chart markedly different routes to reform. It has stressed a certain commensurability of terms within a reformist lexicon and suggested ways in which 'two traditions', in this case Deoband and Aligarh, might 'come to recognise certain possibilities of fundamental agreement and reconstitute themselves as a single, more complex debate'.[90] Approaching both Deoband and Aligarh through the lens of a shared 'tradition' might complicate both the former's claim to be a seamless link with the past and the latter's to be radically new;[91] instead, it repositions both as two 'sides', perhaps, in an argument whose interlocutors deployed the full semantic range of key concepts—most notably *islah*—towards specific ends. And if the respective theologies of Deoband and Aligarh are, in the end, incompatible, it may be the case that the colonial public was a venue through which they attempted to translate those theologies into projects of mass reform and through which they, perhaps inadvertently, became unwitting interlocutors in a dialogue about the past, present and future of Islam.

---

[89] Devji, 'Apologetic Modernity', p. 64.
[90] Alasdair Macintyre, *Whose Justice? Which Rationality?* (Notre Dame, IN: University of Notre Dame Press, 1988), p. 12.
[91] These are, of course, ideal-typical self-understandings of the Deoband and Aligarh movements, probably best represented, on the one hand, by texts like Qari Muhammad Tayyib's *Maslak-i 'Ulama-yi Deoband* (Lahore: Aziz Publications, 1975) and, on the other hand, by Sayyid Ahmad Khan's essay, 'Mazhabi Khayal zamana-yi qadim aur zamana-yi jadid ka', in *Maqalat-i Sar Sayyid, Vol. 3* (Lahore: Majlis Taraqqi-yi Adab, 1961), pp. 23–7.

Contesting Friendship in Colonial Muslim India

SHERALI K. TAREEN, *Franklin & Marshall College, Lancaster, Philadelphia, USA*

This essay examines competing understandings of ideal publics in modern South Asian Islam by analysing a polemical debate among Muslim scholars about the boundaries of friendship between Muslims and non-Muslims. The specific context of this polemic was the pan-Islamic Khilafat movement and concomitant debates on the limits of friendship between Muslims, the British and Hindus. Through a close reading of this polemic, I show ways in which Muslim normative sources are mobilised and interpreted for radically contrasting ideological and political projects. The specific focus of this essay is on intra-Muslim contestations surrounding the category of muwalat *(friendship or clientage), and it shows the opposing ways in which this category was approached by Indian Muslim scholars as either friendship between different religious communities or in terms of a citizen's relationship to a modern state. These varied understandings of* muwalat, *I argue, corresponded to diverging imaginaries of a moral public. This essay particularly focuses on the thoughts of the towering Indian Muslim scholars, Ahmad Raza Khan (d. 1921) and Abul Kalam Azad (d. 1958).*

Introduction

On 26 October 1920, Maulvi Hakim 'Ali, a teacher at Islamiyya College in Lahore in British India, wrote a letter to the towering late-nineteenth and early-twentieth-century Indian Muslim thinker, Ahmad Raza Khan (d. 1921). Khan was terminally ill when he received this letter; he died only a year later in 1921. In his letter, Maulvi Hakim 'Ali sought Khan's guidance on a conundrum that had taken the Islamiyya College campus by storm. A few days earlier, Abul Kalam Azad (d. 1958), another prominent Indian Muslim scholar and political leader, had issued a juridical opinion that prohibited all Muslim schools and colleges in India from accepting any form of financial aid or support from the British colonial government. Moreover, he had declared that students at religious schools and colleges must annul their enrolments if their institutions did not decline all forms of financial support from the British, thus creating a good deal of confusion in colleges across the country, including at the Islamiyya College.[1]

Azad's exhortation was animated by the anti-colonial Non-Cooperation movement led by Gandhi and the Indian National Congress. The leaders of this movement called on all Indians,

---

I would like to thank all participants at the Imagining the Public workshop at Northwestern University in 2014 for their valuable feedback, and especially Barton Scott for his additional editorial help. Many thanks also for their comments and suggestions to Anna Bigelow, Bruce Lawrence, Ebrahim Moosa, Vincent Cornell, Tehseen Thaver, the anonymous reviewers, and to the audiences at the 2013 Annual South Asia Conference, the American Academy of Religion meeting, and at the 2014 Modern South Asia workshop at Yale, where different versions of this essay were presented.

[1] Ahmad Raza Khan, *Al-Mahajja al-Mu'tamana fi Ayah Mumtahana*, in Ahmad Raza Khan, *Fatawa Rizviyya*, Vol. 14 (Lahore: Raza Foundation, 1998), p. 417.

including Indian Muslims, to abandon any relationship of friendship, co-operation and service with the British. Azad was also a major protagonist of the Khilafat movement that was in full swing at this moment.[2] The Khilafat movement combined the anti-colonial fervour of the Non-Cooperation movement with the political mission of protecting the Ottoman caliphate from what its leaders saw as the colonising designs and aggression of the British in the Arab Middle East following World War I.

Azad and his compatriots' call for abandoning relations with the British catalysed a heated debate among Indian Muslims over the normative limits of friendship between Muslims and non-Muslims, a debate that often took the form of outright polemic. At the heart of this polemic were certain pressing questions for Muslim scholars. For instance, what were the limits of friendship for a colonised Muslim community that found itself in a moment of political crisis? Which unbelievers were worthy of friendship and which ones were not? In the context of colonial India, was there a distinction to be made between the British and the Hindus in terms of their normative allowance for friendship? And, perhaps most crucially, how was Indian Muslim identity to be imagined, performed and protected in the colonial public sphere?

This essay describes the opposing views of two major scholars who were at the centre of this polemic, Abul Kalam Azad and Ahmad Raza Khan, with the purpose of exploring the question of how competing imaginaries of friendship between Muslims and non-Muslims translated into competing understandings of a moral public in modern South Asian Islam. Approaching the public as a site of moral contestation, this essay shows how divergent readings of a discursive tradition generate varied imaginaries of a normative religious self and, by extension, of normative religious publics. To anticipate, Abul Kalam Azad argued that Indian Muslims must abandon all relations with the British and ally themselves squarely with Hindus and specifically with Gandhi, a gesture that was consistent with the larger anti-colonial project of the Non-Cooperation movement, of which he was a major protagonist. Ahmad Raza Khan, on the other hand, chastised Azad and the other leaders of the Khilafat and Non-Cooperation movements for what he saw as their undue doctrinal promiscuity in encouraging Hindu–Muslim intimacy and bringing destruction upon themselves by taking on a powerful imperial force.

Through a close reading of their arguments, I will show that underlying the disagreement between Azad and Khan were two divergent understandings of the idea of friendship or *muwalat* in Muslim thought. While Azad understood this category primarily in terms of citizenship as a form of alliance or clientage with the state, the focus of Khan's thought was on the civil dimension of friendship, as exhibited in how a community performed its religion in the public sphere in relation to its competing 'others'. These competing imaginaries of friendship, in turn, translated into opposing understandings of a moral public and that of a normative Indian Muslim identity in colonial modernity.

Pivotal to Azad's and Khan's polemical encounter was the question of how one should understand two specific verses in the Qur'an, verses 8 and 9 of chapter 60 (Surah Mumtahana), the relevant parts of which read as follows: 'God does not forbid you from showing kindness to those unbelievers who do not fight you on account of your faith and neither drive you forth from your homes…. God only forbids you to turn in friendship towards those [unbelievers] who do fight against you because of your faith and drive you forth

---

[2] Gail Minault, *The Khilafat Movement: Religious Symbolism and Political Mobilization in India* (New York: Columbia University Press, 1982); and Naeem Qureshi, *Pan-Islam in British Indian Politics: A Study of the Khilafat Movement* (Leiden: Brill, 1999).

from your homes or aid others in driving you forth'.[3] This chapter was revealed circa 629 CE, when the early Muslim community had developed into a formidable political entity under the leadership of Prophet Muhammad in the city of Medina. The title of chapter 60, 'The Woman Examined', refers to the steady migration of women from Mecca to Medina who had the intention of joining the fold of Islam. The faith of such women, God stipulated in this chapter, can only be examined and tested by God and not by any other entity; their declaration of having embraced Islam sufficed as evidence of the sincerity of their faith. It is from this moment in the Qur'an that we get the principle that the proclamation of embracing Islam serves as sufficient evidence for the validity of a Muslim's faith, as God is the sole arbiter on that question.

In addition to the issue of faith, a central theme of this chapter is the demarcation of the boundaries of Muslim identity in relation to non-Muslims. Verses 8 and 9 of Surah Mumtahana seem to authorise some degree of normative allowance and flexibility for engaging non-Muslims in friendship. However, as we will soon see, the question of who specifically falls under the purview of the category, *those who do not fight you on account of your faith*, has been a subject of intense contestation. In the remainder of this essay, I will try to navigate and bring into view how Abul Kalam Azad and Ahmad Raza Khan mobilised the Qur'an and the Muslim canonical tradition in radically contrasting ways as they disputed the normative boundaries of friendship in Islam. Let me begin by examining the thoughts of Abul Kalam Azad on the interaction of Muslim religious identity and secular citizenship in British India.

Negotiating Religious Identity and Secular Citizenship

Abul Kalam Azad was a journalist and scholar whose erudition and literary abilities were legendary. Having received a traditional Muslim education from his father, Azad later became increasingly critical of the Indian Muslim scholarly elite's inability to confront the political and moral challenges of modernity. For this reason, he, in turn, was viewed with some contempt by traditionalist Muslim scholars. Azad is perhaps best known for his widely-read commentary on the Qur'an entitled *Tarjuman al-Qur'an* (*The Qur'an's Translator*).[4] More relevant here is a less well-known work entitled *Jazirat al-'Arab* (*The Arabian Peninsula*), which strives to establish the necessity of the caliphate according to the Shari'a. Azad wrote this book in 1920, a moment when the Ottoman caliphate had considerably weakened politically, and six years after Britain and the allied forces had declared war against the Ottomans in World War I. As part of his larger project to establish the caliphate as a non-negotiable doctrinal imperative, Azad also offered Indian Muslims specific guidelines on how they must imagine the limits of their identity in relation to non-Muslims, especially in connection with the Khilafat movement.

The Khilafat movement was initiated in 1919 by a group of Muslim political leaders and intellectuals, several of whom were educated at Western institutions of learning. The specific objective of this movement was to pressure the British government to preserve the geographic boundaries and the spiritual/political authority of the Ottoman caliphate. The Khilafat movement was at once pan-Islamic and nationalist in orientation. On the one hand, at the centre of its platform was the pan-Islamic ideal of restoring the eroding symbolic capital and political power of the institution of the caliphate, an institution that the leaders of the Khilafat

---

[3] Q 60: 8–9, Muhammad Asad (trans.), *The Message of the Qur'an* (Bitton, UK: Book Foundation, 2003).
[4] Ian Douglas, *Abul Kalam Azad: An Intellectual and Religious Biography* (Oxford: Oxford University Press, 1975).

movement associated with the Ottoman state. Understood as God's and the Prophet's deputy on earth, the caliph has represented a figure pregnant with moral and symbolic significance throughout Muslim history. The scriptural basis of the institution of the caliphate comes from the well-known Qur'anic verse that states: 'Oh you who believe! Obey Allah, and Obey the Messenger and those charged with authority among you'.[5] The Prophet also is said to have foretold the onset of a caliphal era after his departure from the world.

Just as important as the textual foundations of the caliphate was its emotive status as the earthly representative of God. As the temporal mirror of divine sovereignty, the figure of the caliph was not only invested with immense political authority, but also suffused with extraordinary charisma. Thus, the appropriation of this symbol was an attractive mechanism for Islamicate dynasties and imperial kingships to authorise their sovereign authority, a mechanism that was often employed by multiple rulers simultaneously across Islamdom.[6] Therefore, in its vigorous defence of the Ottoman caliphate, the Khilafat movement drew on a symbol of political mobilisation with universal and transnational appeal. However, not all Muslims, in India or elsewhere, regarded the Ottoman state as a legitimate caliphate. Indeed, the mantle of caliph was avidly contested, with competing claimants to the caliphate such as the sharif of Mecca, Husayn bin 'Ali (d. 1931). But, despite its contested status, the caliphate was a particularly poignant symbol for Indian Muslim elites, whose sovereignty and social standing had been badly fractured by their brutal defeat by the British in the mutiny of 1857. However, as Gail Minault has best argued, the pan-Islamic dimension of the Khilafat movement was intimately connected with the decisively nationalist project of forging political unity and cohesion among Indian Muslims within the subcontinent. As she puts it:

> The Khilafat movement was primarily a campaign to unite the Indian Muslim community by means of religious and cultural symbols meaningful to all strata of society.... In the reasoning of the Khilafat leaders: Muslims in India, if united, could offset their minority status by their ability to bargain from a position of strength, whether with the British or with the Hindus in the Indian National Congress.[7]

Moreover, by positioning themselves as the custodians and defenders of the foremost symbol of Muslim political unity, the caliphate, the movement's leaders sought to legitimate their status as the most authoritative representatives of Indian Muslims. Gandhi and the Indian National Congress, in turn, found these Muslim leaders useful allies in their own anti-colonial project. Therefore, the alliance between the Khilafat and the Non-Cooperation movements brought together varied yet overlapping aspirations, glued together by a shared politics of anti-colonial nationalism.

In *The Arabian Peninsula*, Abul Kalam Azad sought to fashion a political theology that would authorise the ideological project of the Khilafat movement. His central argument was that the institution of the caliphate, currently represented by the Ottomans, constituted a foundational tenet of Islam. Moreover, he argued, since the caliph was the deputy of God and the Prophet, whoever abetted the caliph's enemy was like God's and the Prophet's enemy. Thus, any Muslim who did not submit to the sovereignty of the Ottoman caliph was outside the fold of Islam.

---

[5] Q 4: 59, 'Abdullah Yusuf 'Ali (trans.), *The Qur'an: Translation* (Washington, DC: Islamic Center of Washington, DC, 2001).
[6] Aziz Al-Azmeh, *Muslim Kingship: Power and the Sacred in Muslim, Christian, and Pagan Polities* (London/New York: I.B. Tauris, 1997), pp. 81–181.
[7] Minault, *Khilafat Movement*, p. 2.

Azad explained the caliphate's centrality to Islam with an evocative agricultural analogy. The institution of the caliphate, he argued, is the root of Shari'a, while obligatory practices like praying and fasting are its branches. The normative foundations of the religion depended on the existence of the caliphate. Therefore, while not praying or fasting constituted a sin, not aiding a Muslim caliph, especially during a time of war, made one a non-Muslim. As Azad emphatically put it, 'protecting the caliphate is more important than a thousand prayers or a thousand days of fasting. Why? Because disobedience towards the caliph is such a grave sin that a person who disobeyed the caliph, no matter how much he prayed or fasted, his prayers and fasts will not help his salvational prospects'.[8]

Azad's argument here was not without precedent. As Patricia Crone and Martin Hinds have argued, in the medieval era, the religious character of the Muslim community intimately depended on the existence of the caliph.[9] Notice the remarkable correspondence between Azad's views and the following declaration of a tenth-century Abbasid poet: 'He who does not hold fast to God's trustee will not benefit from the five prayers'.[10] The eleventh-century polymath, Abu Hamid al-Ghazali (d. 1111), too, had argued 'that if the caliphate was deemed to have come to an end, all religious institutions would be in a state of suspension and all acts performed under Islamic law deprived of their validity'.[11] Over time, however, and especially after the Mongol destruction of the Abbasid caliphate in 1258, Muslim jurists seem to have preferred the more centrist position that while departing from the caliphate was not inherently permissible, it was allowed under attenuating or dire circumstances.[12] Aside from the juridical dimensions of this issue, most central to Azad's project was the emotional and religious symbolism of the caliphate as the temporal representative of divine and prophetic authority.

Having established the caliphate as a doctrinal and political imperative, Azad proposed that defending the caliph when his sovereignty was challenged was obligatory for all Muslims. More specifically, he argued that when a non-Muslim force attacked, intended to attack, or injured the independence and sovereignty of a Muslim polity, it was incumbent on all Muslims to help their Muslim brothers. This was especially true in a situation where the aggressor was more powerful and the Muslim citizens or government that was attacked did not possess the capacity to fight back.[13] Similarly, Azad argued, it was incumbent on all Muslims to protect the Arabian Peninsula (hence, the title of his book) from all forms of non-Muslim aggression. In Azad's view, because the British had openly declared war against the Ottoman caliphate, it was an individual obligation (*fard al-ayn*) on all Indian Muslims to engage in jihad against the British. Interestingly, Azad emphasised the importance of Indian Muslims to participation in this endeavour by claiming that, in comparison to other Muslims, Indian Muslims were in a much better position politically and economically to do so.

But how were Indian Muslims supposed to negotiate their responsibilities as citizens of a colonial state with their religious obligation to wage war against that very state? Put more simply, how were Indian Muslims supposed to interact with the British state as part of their everyday lives? Azad's answers to these questions, to which I now turn, illustrate how he understood the intersection of religious identity, secularism and modern citizenship.

---

[8] Abul Kalam Azad, *Jazirat al-'Arab: Mas'ala-i Khilafat* (Delhi: Hali Publishing House, 1961), p. 231.
[9] Patricia Crone and Martin Hinds, *God's Caliph: Religious Authority in the First Centuries of Islam* (Cambridge/New York: Cambridge University Press, 1986), pp. 24–97.
[10] *Ibid.*, p. 34
[11] *Ibid.*
[12] Mona Hassan, 'Modern Interpretations and Misinterpretations of a Medieval Scholar: Apprehending the Political Thought of Ibn Taymiyya', in Yousef Rapoport and Shahab Ahmed (eds), *Ibn Taymiyya and His Times* (Karachi/New York: Oxford University Press, 2010).
[13] Azad, *Jazirat al-'Arab*, p. 218.

Good Non-Muslim, Bad Non-Muslim

According to Azad, in the political conditions that existed in 1920, it was no longer possible for Indian Muslims to remain loyal citizens of the British Empire while also fulfilling their religious obligations in the public sphere. Since the British had adopted a policy of active aggression against the Ottomans, Indian Muslims were obligated to abandon virtually any relationship with them. A key term that Azad mobilised in this context was what he called *tark-i muwalat*, meaning abandoning any relationship of friendship, love, intimacy or co-operation. The category of *muwalat* was critical to the larger debate over the boundaries of friendship between Muslims and non-Muslims. Derived from the Arabic roots *wa-la-ya*, *muwalat* refers to friendship and intimacy in an individual and civil sense, as well as indicating alliance or clientage in a more political sense. The terms for a 'friend of God' (*wali*), or a Muslim mystic, and 'sainthood' (*walaya*) also derive from the same roots.[14] For Azad, the civil and political meanings of the term were intertwined: the severing of political clientage mandated the abandonment of all public relations of service and co-operation towards the state.

Azad argued for abandoning friendship and intimacy by drawing on verses 8 and 9 in chapter 60 (Surah Mumtahana) of the Qur'an. In his view, these two verses provided clear guidance on the boundaries of friendship in Islam. As can be seen in these verses, Azad explained, the Qur'an divides non-Muslims into two distinct categories: 1) those non-Muslims who did not fight against Muslims, were not aggressively hostile towards them, and who did not harbour any designs to colonise them; and 2) those non-Muslims who displayed all of these antagonistic qualities.[15] Muslims must treat the first category with every kind of friendship, love, kindness and hospitality. In the context of colonial India, Azad specified, this category included Hindus, who had never attacked Muslim countries, fought them in religion, or been the cause of the expulsion of Muslims from their lands.[16] In stark contrast, the British, with their designs to colonise Arabia and destroy the Ottoman caliphate, exemplified non-Muslims of the second variety: those who fought Muslims in religion and expelled them from their homes.

Therefore, Azad extrapolated, Indian Muslims were forbidden to show any form of love, friendship or co-operation towards the British. He did not clarify whether by the British, he meant only those attached to the colonial state, or also ordinary British citizens. However, he left no shade of ambiguity in his declaration that Muslims who did engage the British in a relationship of friendship would themselves be counted as among the enemies and, hence, as enemies of God and the Shari'a. Azad summed up with the proclamation that 'in conditions of war between Muslims and non-Muslims, Muslims cannot abandon their brothers and become friends with their enemies'.[17]

In this situation, Azad argued, Indian Muslims had only two mutually exclusive options: loyalty to the British state or loyalty to their religion. In other words, it had become impossible for Indian Muslims to remain loyal citizens of British India without compromising their religious duties and obligations.

---

[14] Vincent Cornell, *Realm of the Saint: Power and Authority in Moroccan Sufism* (Austin: University of Texas Press, 1998).
[15] Azad, *Jazirat al-'Arab*, p. 232.
[16] *Ibid.*, p. 282.
[17] *Ibid.*, p. 233.

The Promise and Responsibility of Secularism

Azad further argued that by adopting a policy of aggression against the Ottoman caliphate, the colonial state had compromised its own promise of secularism and freedom of religion for all communities in India. By intervening in a matter of religious importance for Indian Muslims, the British had contravened the secular principle of the separation of religion and politics. Ostensibly, all religious communities in India, including Muslims, were granted complete freedom to fulfil their religious duties and obligations in the public sphere. That is why, he explained, Muslims in India 'had established mosques, the sound of the call to prayer could be heard throughout the country five times a day, and no ruler stopped them from saying their prayers'.[18] However, while granting Muslims the freedom to perform everyday religious practices, the British had assaulted the most foundational doctrinal tenet and institutional structure in Islam: the caliphate. As Azad dramatically put it: 'The British continue their assault on the Muslim caliphate, their naval ships march in the waters with the intention of destroying the caliphate to pieces, and their military continues to occupy Iraq. And despite all this they expect pitiful Muslims of India to remain loyal to them!'[19] While Indian Muslims were free to carry out minor religious observances, they could not invoke the right to religious freedom when it came to the most essential of their religious tenets. In effect, the British had forced Indian Muslims into an irresolvable conundrum whereby their religious obligations directly clashed with their obligations as citizens of the colonial state. As Azad poignantly summed up: 'in order to demonstrate their loyalty to the state, the British want [Indian] Muslims to commit treason against Islam'.[20]

The British, Azad warned, had to decide between two options. Either they should uphold the secular promise of separating religion from politics and not intervene in the religious lives of Indian Muslims, or they should openly announce that they had no regard for the religious obligations and injunctions of Muslims and stop pretending to be the slogan-bearers for secular ideals. He described the second option in vivid terms: 'They (the British government) should declare that all they care about is more land, more power, more oil from Mosul, and the end of the Muslim caliphate. Then it will be easy for the Muslims also to choose between their religion and their citizenship under the British government'.[21] What must be observed here is not only the content of Azad's arguments, but also the way he *framed* his arguments. More specifically, notice his valorisation of secularism as a normative ideal. For Azad, British aggression towards the Ottoman caliphate was most repugnant *because* of the way in which it undermined the secular ideals of religious freedom and the separation of religion and state. Leaving aside Azad's somewhat elementary conceptualisation of the secular, what I want to emphasise is how the normative desire for the secular was central to the organising logic of his argument. As Azad launched a scathing critique of the colonial state and of its policies and attitudes towards native religious communities, the grammar of that critique was indebted to the political and conceptual terrain of secular colonial modernity.

Azad's political and hermeneutical programme did not go unchallenged. Indeed, his call for Indian Muslims to boycott the British and to ally with the Hindus and Gandhi precipitated a massive backlash from a number of Indian *ulama*. But, perhaps, none was as scathing and comprehensive in his rebuke of Azad and his compatriots in the Khilafat and Non-Cooperation movements as the prolific North Indian Muslim scholar, Ahmad Raza Khan. A Hanafi jurist and Qadiri Sufi, Khan is among the most illustrious personalities in the

---

[18] *Ibid.*, p. 229.
[19] *Ibid.*
[20] *Ibid.*
[21] *Ibid.*, p. 239.

intellectual history of modern South Asian Islam. He is said to have composed over a thousand works on various subjects including law, theology, Hadith, philosophy and the Qur'an. Most of his writings are today preserved in a 32-volume collection of juridical opinions (*fatawa*) titled *Fatawa Rizviyya*. Khan was also the founder of what is known as the Barelvi school of thought in South Asia named after the North Indian town of Bareilly where he was from.[22]

Khan refuted Azad's views on the boundaries of friendship in an exegetical work entitled *The Convincing Proof on the Mumtahana Verse* (*al-Mahajja al-Mu'tamana fi Ayah Mumtahana*) (1920). It is said that Khan was on his deathbed when he wrote this book; he died less than a year after its publication. Khan wrote this text in response to a question by a teacher at Islamiyya College Lahore—Maulvi Hakim 'Ali, with whom we began this article. Hakim 'Ali had inquired about the normative status of Azad's *fatwa* forbidding Muslim schools and colleges in India from accepting British financial aid. In his response, while authorising the acceptance of such financial support from the colonial government, Khan launched a devastating attack against the religious and political project of Azad and other Muslim leaders of the Khilafat and Non-Cooperation movements. In contrast to Azad, whose book was largely focused on the Qur'an and Hadith, Khan mobilised a panoply of traditional normative sources, including the Qur'an, Hadith, Qur'an commentaries, and Hanafi and even non-Hanafi legal texts.[23] I next describe the central features of Khan's exegetical programme as a way of presenting a competing narrative of the boundaries of Islam and friendship in colonial modernity.

Friendship and Its Perils

Before seeking to undo Azad's hermeneutical arguments, Khan tried to dismantle Azad's credibility as a legitimate spokesperson for the Indian Muslim community. According to Khan, the ostensibly anti-colonial agenda of Muslim scholars attached to the Khilafat and Non-Cooperation movements was not only hermeneutically invalid, it was also outright hypocritical. In the guise of opposing the British, he argued, these scholars were merely interested in advancing their own political aspirations. Their opposition to the British was superficial; culturally, they were the slogan-bearers of a modernist world-view that was infested with Western values and normative ideals. To truly protect Islam in India from the threat of colonialism, mere financial non-cooperation with the British was not enough: 'If the objective is to abandon imitation of the British, then financial non-cooperation will not suffice. The West should also be abandoned in fashion, culture, atheism (*dahriyyat*) and naturalism (*nechari*)'.[24]

While pretending to act as the caretakers of Indian Muslims, Khan claimed, Azad and scholars of his ilk had always looked with disdain at traditional norms, institutions, and custodians of Muslim education in the country. Now, during a moment when it was politically convenient for them, these same scholars had donned the moralising garb of Islam's defenders against colonial power. As he fumed, 'Are these not the same people who, when you would

---

[22] Usha Sanyal, *Ahmad Riza Khan Barelwi: In the Path of the Prophet* (Oxford: Oneworld, 2005).
[23] Ahmad Raza Khan, *Al-Mahajja al-Mu'tamana fi Ayah Mumtahana*, p. 428.
[24] *Ibid.*, p. 431. '*Nechari*' is a clear reference to Sayyid Ahmad Khan, who was among Azad's major intellectual influences.

ask them why do you not educate your sons in the Qur'an, they would reply in condescension, "Why would we do that? Do we want our children to be eating chickpeas on the third day of someone's death (*siwam*)?'".[25] In Khan's view, the so-called defenders of Islam and tradition in the Khilafat and Non-Cooperation movements were themselves products of 'modern Western' education and values. Their rejection of financial aid from the British was only a ruse that masked their deep-seated cultural and moral intimacy with the normative horizons and desires of Western modernity. Having punctured the religious authority and credibility of his rivals, Khan then turned to the task of undoing their interpretive programme.

Hermeneutically, Khan drew a distinction between friendship/intimacy (*muwalat*) and mere pragmatic relations (*mujarrad-i mu'amalat*). The acceptance of financial aid from the British for religious schools fell squarely into the second category. Moreover, this kind of pragmatic relationship with non-Muslims was completely permissible so long as it did not promote any sort of unbelief or bring any harm to Islam and the Shari'a.

Tampering with the Shari'a

Khan's central charge against Azad and his compatriots was that they altered the logic of the Shari'a by obligating friendship with Hindus and forbidding mere pragmatic relations with the British. In effect, they had committed the minor sin of forbidding something permissible (pragmatic relations with British) and the major sin of obligating something forbidden (friendship with Hindus). What angered Khan the most, however, was the inclusion of Hindus in the category of *those who do not fight you in religion* (*lam yuqatilukum fi din*) by Gandhi's Muslim allies such as Azad. Khan emphatically declared that Hindus were without doubt active aggressors against Islam (*muharib bil fi'l*) who could not be excluded from the category of *those who do not fight you in religion* according to verse 8 of Surah Mumtahana.[26]

In assembling his argument, Khan mobilised two varieties of evidence: historical and practical. Historically, Khan sought to show that the Hindus of India did not match the characteristics of possible members of the category, *those who do not fight you in religion*. Citing the noted Companion of the Prophet and early Qur'an scholar, 'Abdullah bin 'Abbas (d. 687), Khan argued that there were three possible groups of people who could have been referred to in the statement 'those unbelievers who do not fight you on account of your faith and neither drive you forth from your homes':[27] 1) those Muslims who had not yet left Mecca and migrated to Medina; 2) members of the Banu Khuza'a tribe in Mecca with whom Muhammad had entered into a treaty; and 3) the women and children among the unbelievers who did not possess the capacity to fight. Hindus, Khan stated, did not correspond to any of these groups.

Practically, Khan reasoned, Hindus cannot be categorised among unbelievers who do not fight Muslims in religious war because they had indeed fought Muslims on numerous occasions, often in gruesomely violent ways. He reminded his readers that it was the same Hindus with whom Azad had called for friendship who had massacred and incinerated innocent Muslims over the issue of the sacrifice of cows. For anyone who was unpersuaded by

---

[25] *Ibid*. *Siwam* refers to the ritual of distributing food to the community, especially the destitute, on the third day after a person's death. A ritual that dominates Muslim India, its purpose is to transmit the spiritual rewards and blessings received from the charitable act of distributing food to the soul of the deceased. Before the food is consumed, usually, graduates and students of Muslim seminaries say some prayers over the food to sanctify it, hence Khan's reference here.

[26] *Ibid*., p. 436.

[27] Q 60: 8–9, Muhammad Asad (trans.), *The Message of the Qur'an*.

the brutality of Hindus towards Muslims, he proposed an experiment: 'Go to any city, district, or village and try sacrificing a cow; see then if these very dear brothers, elders, and leaders of yours do not become ready to break your bones into pieces'.[28] Khan addressed the Muslim leaders of the Khilafat movement with a set of comments that deserve to be quoted at some length because they capture the intensity of his protest in particularly vivid ways:

> O you leaders who sit on fancy stages and pretend to be Muslims and sympathisers of Islam. If you have any ounce of shame left, then go drown in the Ganges. Are not these Hindu polytheists whom you call your brothers, your confidantes, your well-wishers, is it not these same people who have time and again assaulted Islam, the Qur'an, and our Mosques. And today it is for these same people that you sell yourselves and celebrate your slavery to them.[29]

Khan climaxed his disgust for Azad and the leaders of the Khilafat movement with a lament that is untranslatable. He gasped: 'Uff Uff Uff, Tuff Tuff Tuff'.[30]

It is true that the Muslim leaders of the Khilafat and Non-Cooperation movements had acknowledged episodes of Hindu violence against Muslims, but they had been quick to assert that such episodes were individual, scattered and sporadic. Therefore, so their argument went, the Hindu community as a whole did come under the category of *those who do not fight you in religion*. Khan counter-argued that, for a community to be categorised as 'active aggressors' (*muharib bil fi'l*) against Islam, it was not necessary for every member of that community to physically fight or take up arms against Muslims. Were that the case, he reasoned, it was also unjustified for Azad to call for a boycott against the British; after all, not every British citizen had physically fought against Muslims. Similarly, Khan continued, during the time of the Prophet, not every unbeliever took to the battlefield or fought individually against the Muslim community.[31]

According to Khan, the category of active aggressor against Islam was applicable to any unbeliever who showed aggression towards Muslims through physical force, feeling or speech. Under this expansive definition, the Hindu 'polytheists' of India were clearly active aggressors against Islam. Even when they did not fight Muslims explicitly, their hearts were suffused with animosity towards them. 'Which Hindu's heart does not burn when it comes to the issue of the sacrifice of cows?' he asked.[32]

Duplicitous Stratagems

In Khan's view, the rhetoric of non-cooperation was a ruse devised by Gandhi and the Hindu nationalist leadership to decimate Muslims socially, financially and, indeed, physically: Gandhi had incited Muslim leaders to wage jihad against the British so that the Muslim community would be crushed in an uneven battle. When that plan failed, he tried to convince Muslims to emigrate from India so that their houses and property could be auctioned off to Hindus for paltry sums or simply be occupied. And when that also failed, he tried to rope Muslims into the Non-Cooperation movement. Seemingly a movement for political freedom, in fact, its underlying purpose was that Muslims would abandon their jobs, government posts

---

[28] Ahmad Raza Khan, *Al-Mahajja al-Mu'tamana fi Ayah Mumtahana*, p. 454.
[29] *Ibid.*, p. 452.
[30] *Ibid.*
[31] *Ibid.*, p. 453.
[32] *Ibid.*

and membership in council committees so that Hindus could usurp important positions of wealth, power and prestige. Ultimately, these measures were meant to rob Muslims of all positions of socio-economic and political strength and, as a result, to ensure the complete domination of Hindus in all domains of life.[33] Showcasing a mindset according to which Muslim decline necessarily meant and was inversely proportional to Hindu progress, Khan wrote: 'When Hindus usurp all Muslim jobs and property, the only work left for Muslims to do would be to work as baggage porters (*kulli* or *coolie*) at train stations'.[34]

According to Khan, the leaders of the Khilafat movement, either knowingly or unknowingly, had fallen right into Gandhi's trap; they advocated positions that were at once logically untenable, self-destructive and impossible. For instance, the idea of waging jihad against the British was only inviting catastrophe. But without waging war, how should Indian Muslims deal with a non-Muslim colonising force such as the British? In answering this question, Khan advocated the curious position that while engaging the British, Muslims should simply adopt an attitude of superficial or masked friendship (*muwalat-i suwariyya*), to be distinguished from substantive friendship based on affection and intimacy (*muwalat-i haqiqiyya*). This way, they would both safeguard the normative boundaries of friendship in Islam while also protecting their lives, property and interests.[35]

But, Khan insisted, to mount war against a towering imperial force, as Azad and his colleagues suggested, was not only logically dumbfounding, but also contravened the Islamic legal doctrine that states 'do not throw yourselves in the path of destruction (*la alqu anfusakum ila al-tahlaka*)'. Suppose a few hundred Muslims did indeed leave their jobs, abandon their landholdings and shut down their businesses. What harm would that do to the might of the British or what benefit would it bring to the already dwindling Ottoman state? All that Muslims would achieve would be to harm themselves by weakening their status and position.[36] And it was wishful thinking, Khan warned, that the Hindus would follow suit; they were sure to leave Muslims in the lurch while reaping the benefits of their departure.[37]

According to Khan, the Khilafat and Non-Cooperation movements were not only ill-conceived, but their leaders were insincere and dishonest. If the leaders of the Khilafat movement were truly serious about abandoning all relations with the British, they would also have abandoned the use of British technologies such as the postal system, the telegraph and the railways.[38] All that such selective anti-imperialism could achieve would be the wasting of large sums of money and resources for a lost political cause, and an assault on the livelihood of Muslim farmers, agriculturalists and labourers in the guise of non-cooperation, Khan grimly concluded.

Imperial Hermeneutics

Among the most fascinating aspects of Khan's hermeneutics was that he took for granted the imperial logic and context of medieval and early modern Islamic law, even at a moment when Muslims, in India or elsewhere, were no longer possessors of empire, but were, rather, colonised subjects. However, the current political reality seems to have escaped Khan's religious imaginary because he cited and invoked mediaeval and early modern Muslim legal

---

[33] *Ibid.*, p. 536.
[34] *Ibid.*, p. 537.
[35] *Ibid.*, p. 446.
[36] *Ibid.*, p. 532.
[37] *Ibid.*
[38] *Ibid.*, p. 535.

scholars whose understanding of the normative boundaries of friendship and relations between Muslims and non-Muslims were surely informed by the context of empire. This problem of conceptual translation is most visible in his discussion of the only kinds of relationships that Muslims could cultivate with Hindus.

More specifically, Khan addressed the question of when it was permissible for Muslims to seek the help or assistance of non-Muslims who were not among the People of the Book (Jews and Christians). According to him, there were three scenarios of relationships that might exist between the givers and receivers of assistance: imploration (*iltija*); reliance (*i'timad*); and domination (*istikhdam*).[39] Muslims, Khan argued, could only receive the help of Hindus in the case of domination, which he described as a situation in which 'an unbeliever is completely under the control of Muslim rule and has no power to oppose Islam and Muslims in any way'.[40] In this situation, when non-Muslim helpers are entirely subservient to Muslims, assistance can only elevate and exalt Islam, such as through the assistance of a Muslim army during war. In this situation, even if the non-Muslim harbours hatred towards Muslims, he will not be able to express that hate because of his absolute subservience to and extreme fear of Muslims. Khan likened such a subservient subject to a dog:

> ... the help of only those non-Muslims is permitted who are like domesticated dogs for Muslims. This situation would be analogous to a hunter seeking the help of a dog for hunting. A hunter would only use a dog that has been completely domesticated and has no interest except to help the hunter however he wished. Similarly, only those non-Muslims can be sought for help who are like hunting dogs, with no agency or interest of their own, and who are used as mere instruments by Muslims.[41]

The mediaeval and early modern Muslim legal texts that Khan cited to make his case clearly presumed the context of Muslim imperial rule. For instance, notice the reason presented as to why Muslims must not depend on the help of unbelievers (unless it was absolutely necessary) by the Syrian Hanafi jurist Ibn 'Abidin (d. 1836) in his famous commentary, 'Radd al-Muhtar', on the Hanafi legal text, 'Durr ul-Mukhtar', by al-Haskafi. Ibn 'Abidin argued that such dependence was prohibited because one could never erase the suspicion that unbelievers will commit treason (against the state) (*la yu'min ghadrahu*).[42] Similarly, Ibn 'Abidin recounted that when the second caliph in Sunni Islam, 'Umar Ibn al-Khattab, learnt that his associate Abu Musa Ash'ari had appointed an unbeliever as an official scribe, he 'repudiated this appointment with an arresting set of comments: "[I]t is not appropriate for us to take unbelievers as confidantes when God has declared them untrustworthy; we cannot elevate them when God has accorded them a lowly status, and we cannot exalt them when God has mandated them to pay [us] the poll tax (*jizya*) as a marker of their subservience"'.[43]

In both these examples, the assumption of Muslim imperial sovereignty is crucial to how the difference between Muslims and non-Muslims is understood. But in his mobilisation of these pre-modern sources of authority, Khan did not account for the political shift from a Muslim to a non-Muslim empire. For him, the canonical tradition was immune to the

---

[39] *Ibid.*, p. 509.
[40] *Ibid.*
[41] *Ibid.*, p. 510.
[42] Cited in *ibid.*, p. 514.
[43] Cited in *ibid.*

mutability of historical conditions. The task of hermeneutics was not creative translation, but, rather, the faithful recreation and re-enactment of the past in the present.

Preserving a Moral Public

Finally, Khan argued that even if one hypothetically assumed that no Hindu in India harboured any aggression towards Islam, Azad's efforts to cultivate a relationship of intimate friendship between Hindus and Muslims still contravened the Shari'a. This was so because although verse 8 of Surah Mumtahana permitted Muslims to show basic kindness to non-combative non-Muslims, it did not sanction a relationship of unrestrained intimacy.

However, in their zeal to please Gandhi, Azad and his compatriots had blatantly transgressed the limits of friendship sanctioned in Surah Mumtahana, Khan asserted.[44] They had done so by fostering a public sphere in which Muslim symbols and markers of distinction (*shi'ar-i Islam*) had all but been erased as Hindus were granted unbridled friendship, intimacy and privilege. Khan was particularly incensed by an episode in which the Muslim leaders of the Khilafat movement had invited Gandhi to a mosque on a Friday to address the gathered congregants. For him, this moment epitomised the complete disregard of these leaders for Muslim norms and traditions. By according Gandhi an elevated position of privilege in a Muslim mosque during Friday prayers, they had proven beyond doubt that they regarded him as their ultimate religious guide and leader (imam). Khan labelled Gandhi with the derogatory Qur'anic term *taghut*, or 'evil idol', declaring that Azad and his cohort of Muslim scholars had taken the '*taghut*' of the Hindus as their imam.[45] If left unchecked, Khan warned, the day was not far off when the leaders of the Khilafat movement would make Indian Muslims worship Gandhi as part of their religious lives. Soon, he predicted, the canonical supplication in the five daily prayers, '[Oh God] grant us the straight path (*ihdina al-sirat al-mustaqim*)', would be replaced with the statement, 'Grant us Gandhi's path (*ihdina al-sirat al-Gandhi*)'.[46]

The hyperbole of this suggestion aside, at the heart of Khan's protest was a very palpable anxiety over what he saw as a looming threat to the distinguishing signs and symbols of Islam in the public sphere. A key term that Khan repeatedly mobilised in his text was the 'symbols of Islam' ('*shi'ar-i Islam*'). In Khan's social imaginary, a moral economy in which the boundaries of religious identity were not carefully regulated was sure to extinguish the characteristic markers and symbols of that religion. Notice the combination of alarm and anxiety in the way Khan described the threat posed to Indian Muslim identity by a libertine attitude towards the boundaries of friendship with Hindus:

> This verse (verse 8 of Surah Mumtahana) only permits showing basic kindness to non-Muslims. It does not say make them your intimate friends, shower them with praise, make their *taghut* (Gandhi) your Imam, invite them to your mosques to give sermons on Fridays, say prayers for the salvation of their deceased, perform funeral prayers for them, shut down the market on the day of their death, not eat cow's meat for their happiness, ridicule those who do, treat cow's meat as if it were pork, and take the Qur'an and the Ramayana side by side to their temples.[47]

---

[44] *Ibid.*, p. 473.
[45] *Ibid.*
[46] *Ibid.*, p. 518.
[47] *Ibid.*

As this comment makes clear, what was at stake for Khan in his tussle with Azad was the imperative of protecting the normative purity of Islam from what he saw as the threat of internal and external 'others'. Most importantly, his position on the boundaries of friendship in the Qur'an was inextricably tied to the way he imagined a moral public and the public performance of Islam as a lived tradition. Another way of putting this is that, for Khan, of paramount if not exclusive importance about the category of *muwalat* was its civil dimension of friendship and intimacy with other religious communities.

Conclusion

There is a subtle, but important difference in the conceptual space occupied by the category of *muwalat* in Azad's and Khan's projects. For Azad, the political meaning of *muwalat*, of alliance or clientage, was of crucial significance, as reflected in his call for Muslims to dissociate themselves from the British state. In contrast, for Khan, the desire to patrol the rhythms and patterns of everyday communal and public life was of central importance.[48]

One may put this differently by arguing that at the heart of Azad's and Khan's disagreement were varied and at times opposing imaginaries of a moral 'Indian Muslim public'. In Khan's social imaginary, most crucial to the curation of a moral public was the practice of everyday life. Central to his discourse was the anxiety to guard the normative purity of public markers of distinction that, in his view, symbolised Muslim identity, and that he found urgently threatened by corruption and extinction. One may surmise that with the loss of Muslim political sovereignty in 1857, the focus of attention for religious reformers such as Ahmad Raza Khan shifted to quotidian practices and the everyday performance of religion in the public sphere. The practice of everyday life was increasingly seen as the linchpin and locus of religious authenticity. For Khan, preserving a distinct religious identity as manifested in the public choreography of religious practices trumped the importance of restoring political institutions such as the caliphate.[49]

On the other hand, Abul Kalam Azad's conception of the public brought together the local and the transnational. In his view, the integrity of Indian Muslim identity hinged on preserving what he saw as the foremost symbol of the universal Muslim community, the caliphate. It was not the purity of religious practices, but the symbolic capital of Muslim political unity that he found most critical for the sustenance of a moral public. The normative legitimacy of even obligatory practices like praying and fasting depended on securing the sovereignty of the caliph. In other words, political sovereignty, or more specifically caliphal sovereignty, represented a precondition for even the possibility of publically performing one's religion. In turn, the way Azad mobilised the idea of *muwalat* or friendship with reference to Indian Muslims was also informed by the political objective of restoring the sovereignty of the universal Muslim public. The local and the universal were mutually entangled. In short, both Azad's and Khan's understandings of friendship and its limits were inextricably tied to how they imagined the idea and boundaries of the public they sought to address, persuade and galvanise.

Let me end by highlighting two broader conceptual arguments I wish to make through this essay. First, I would like to argue that the polemic between Azad and Khan described in this essay cannot be canonised into such binaries as traditional/modern, religious/secular, liberal/conservative, and so on. Notice, for instance, that despite all his

---

[48] I am grateful to Prof. Vincent Cornell for alerting me to this insight.

[49] In any case, Ahmad Raza Khan did not even consider the Ottomans legitimate occupants of the caliphate because they did not trace their lineage back to the Quraysh.

anxiety over the preservation of an authentic Indian Muslim identity, it was the traditionalist Khan who adopted the more pragmatic position of engaging the British in a relationship of 'apparent' friendship and of avoiding war against them. By contrast, it was the modernist Azad who called for jihad against the British as well as the preservation and restoration of the caliphate, a desire often imputed exclusively to conservative/fundamentalist Muslims. On the other hand, while enraged at the public exaltation of Gandhi in Muslim sacred spaces and at the cultivation of Hindu–Muslim intimacy, Khan did not seem much perturbed by the absence of a Muslim caliphate. All this is not to endorse or undermine any of these positions, but just to highlight the conceptual fragility of categories like traditional, modern, liberal and conservative. While these categories might be useful for heuristic purposes, their limitations become all too obvious when set against the complicated discursive manoeuvres and strategies through which the boundaries of a discursive tradition are authoritatively contested. For instance, in the context of this essay, both Azad and Khan presented what they saw as normatively coherent understandings of tradition as they strived to articulate and defend their specific ideological and political projects. Rather than rushing to categorise their hermeneutical attitudes into readily-available binaries, it would be more productive to approach such moments of intra-Muslim contestation as what I would call 'competing rationalities of tradition', each with its own logic of how the memory of the prophetic past should inform the fashioning of a moral public in the present.

Second, even as Khan and Azad mobilised competing interpretations of the Qur'an and Muslim tradition, their polemic was made possible in the first place by the secularising conditions of colonial modernity. To begin with, the very public nature of their debate was largely a result of the modern technologies of print, the railways and the postal system. More importantly, Azad's and Khan's polemical encounter was informed and generated by a secular politico-conceptual terrain marked by the emergence of modern citizenship as a political imperative, the epistemic valorisation of secularism as a legitimate ideal and desire (as seen in Azad's reminder to the British of their secular responsibility), and the preponderance of what Sudipta Kaviraj has called an enumerated logic of identity, whereby identity can only be counted as such if it can distinguish itself from its competing 'others'. Even before they had entered the arena of this polemic, the conditions and rules that governed that arena had been put in place by the colonial state. Notice, for instance, that even while chastising the colonial state, Azad had fully internalised the modern secular premise that the state by its nature acts on 'behalf' of society and its citizens so that it should be boycotted when it fails to do so.[50] Similarly, Ahmad Raza Khan's anxiety over maintaining the purity of religious identity in the public sphere assumed the existence of a distinct, enumerated 'Indian Muslim public' that cried out to be reformed, warned and pastorally protected—a public that was not only countable, but also accountable to its identity in relation to its competing 'others'. Such an accountable notion of identity was in complete harmony with the promise of securing and maintaining the authenticity of a fully-defined religion that corresponded with an equally-defined public that 'belonged' to, and acted on 'behalf' of, that religion. Indeed, the reification of modern citizenship and that of religion went hand in hand.

While Azad and Khan were products of different lineages of Muslim thought in South Asia, their programmes were, albeit in different ways, haunted by the spectre of the modern

---

[50] Sudipta Kaviraj, *The Imaginary Institution of India: Politics and Ideas* (New York: Columbia University Press, 2010), p. 13.

secular. There was nothing new about the idea of two authoritative Muslim scholars contesting the import of Qur'anic verses or the limits of Muslim identity in relation to non-Muslims. What was decisively new, however, was the normative logic of what counted as authoritative as such, animated and inspired by the desires, aspirations and anxieties brought to life by the enveloping shadow of the modern colonial moment.

Booklets and *Sants*: Religious Publics and Literary History

FRANCESCA ORSINI, *School of Oriental and African Studies, University of London, UK*

The story of print and religious publics in colonial India has largely been told as one of reformist groups and religious polemics. But this covers only a small part of the story of religious print, which extends well beyond reformist groups. This essay focuses on the most systematic and long-lived project of publishing sant *orature (*bani*), the* Santbānī Pustakmālā *of the Belvedere Press, Allahabad. It examines its scope, aims and methods as well as its religious orientation and conceptualisation of a religious-devotional public in early-twentieth-century North India. Halfway between oral* bhajan *groups and the scholarly publications of the collected works (*granthavali*) of* sant *poets, throughout the twentieth century the Belvedere Press booklets have commanded tremendous currency as religious print-objects in the Hindi devotional public sphere. The results of one publisher's effort and investment, and of significant reorganisation of material from manuscript sources, these booklets have been extremely popular and lasting products in the extensive market for religious material, clearly a crucial technology for individual and group religious practice (*bhajan*), before which the lineages' own publishing efforts pale into quasi-insignificance.*

The story of print and religious publics in colonial India has largely been told in connection with reformist groups and religious polemics, yet anyone who has spent any time in the British Library calling up Vernacular Tracts (VT) cannot have failed to notice the large amount of religious publications of all hues that came out in the late nineteenth and early twentieth centuries.[1] Persian Sufi *risalas*, Urdu *munajat*, Hindi *bhajans* and *pothis*, Sanskrit texts, religious books were published both by specific *khanqahs* and *maths* (monasteries) and by generic publishers.[2] Studies in the 1990s focused on religious reform and polemics[3] and on the use of print for competitive and apologetic purposes, initially in connection with Christian missionaries and Hindu and Muslim reformers (who were also viewed as the first to draw up

---

[1] As I have suggested elsewhere, 'Strictly speaking, commercial publishing in North India includes the production and marketing of textbooks, religious books, and books for entertainment, since the same commercial publishers printed them all. Religious publishing spanned a wide range, from canonical texts, booklets of prayers and religious songs, polemical tracts, religious periodicals, and the texts of local or sectarian traditions. *It forms at least another history of print in North India, just as substantial in terms of bulk and variety of output, and as crucial in creating a reading public.* But it raises issues of content, audience, and religious transformation that the present book could not begin to address': Francesca Orsini, *Print and Pleasure: Popular Literature and Entertaining Fictions in Colonial North India* (Ranikhet: Permanent Black, 2010), pp. 3–4; emphasis added.

[2] For example, Gayaprasad booksellers of Chowk, Gorakhpur, sold *bhajans* and Krishna *pads* at four and a half annas; songbooks like *Chautāl Basant Bahār* and *Holī Bahār* and *Anūṭhī Kajlī* ranged between one and a half and three and a quarter annas; a collection of *barahmasas* at two annas; an Urdu-English primer at two and a quarter annas; and syllabaries in Devanagari and Urdu for half an anna or even less. Customers or hawkers who bought four books received a fifth one free. See *Chautāl Saṅgrah*, held in Bharati Bhavan Library, Allahabad.

[3] Kenneth Jones (ed.), *Religious Controversy in British India: Dialogues in South Asian Languages* (Albany: State University of New York Press, 1992).

expansive visions of *national* religious publics), though it became increasingly evident that, in fact, both 'traditionalists' and 'reformists' shared discourses, strategies and technologies, including print.[4] More recently, Nile Green's *Bombay Islam* (2011) has shown that in colonial Bombay, the world of Islamic print and publishing was constituted by both pan-Indian and transnational reformers and by small 'franchises' of local and regional saints and shrines. The result was an array of *old* and *new* texts and forms of address, which, he showed, combined to produce hybrid forms for the faithful in the colonial metropolis, forms that repay close individual study.[5]

This essay tells a similar story. Against the backdrop of early efforts at publishing *sant* orature (*bani*),[6] it focuses on the most systematic and long-lived project, the *Santbānī Pustakmālā* of the Belvedere Press. I examine its scope, aims and methods as well as its religious orientation and conceptualisation of a religious-devotional public in early-twentieth-century North India. Halfway between oral *satsang* groups and the scholarly collected works (*granthavali*) of the *sant* poets, the Belvedere Press booklets commanded tremendous currency as religious print-objects in the Hindi devotional public sphere throughout the twentieth century. The results of one publisher's effort and investment, and of his significant reorganisation of material from manuscript sources, these booklets have been extremely popular and lasting products in the extensive market for religious material, clearly a crucial technology for individual and group religious practice (*bhajan*), before which the lineages' own publishing efforts pale into quasi-insignificance.

Sants into Print

We know that the words of the North Indian *sants*—charismatic persons of spiritual accomplishments who delivered their message and teachings through songs and religious discourse ('do not consider this my song, consider it my thinking on Brahma', Kabir famously said)—circulated for centuries both orally and in manuscript form in very different formats as singers' notebooks and lineage books (*pothi* or *granth*).[7] And while lineages and the monasteries (*maths*) and seats (*gaddis*) they established were the chief agents in the systematic collation of *sant* aphorisms, song-poems and biographies—a crucial element in the constitution of the archive—their songs circulated orally beyond the *panths* (communities) through the agency of singers and in informal *bhajan* circles, where people got together, generally in the evenings, and sang devotional songs together with the accompaniment of cymbals and a drum, still a widespread practice and the main medium of circulation for devotional words. The Hindi poet Nirala's 'discovery' that, in the 1920s, illiterate Dalits in his own village had a deep and sophisticated embodied knowledge and aesthetic appreciation for

---

[4] Vasudha Dalmia, *The Nationalization of Hindu Traditions:Bhāratendu Hariśchandra and Nineteenth-Century Banaras* (Delhi: Oxford University Press, 1997).

[5] Nile Green, *Bombay Islam: The Religious Economy of the West Indian Ocean, 1840–1915* (Cambridge: Cambridge University Press, 2011).

[6] The term orature reverses the tendency to consider oral literature and traditions as inferior or marginal to literature and underscores the oral and aural qualities of much literary production and experience; written literature, from this perspective, is but a part of orature. See Ngugi Wa Thiong'o, 'Notes Towards a Performance Theory of Orature', in *Performance Research*, Vol. 12, no. 3 (2007), pp. 4–7.

[7] See W.M. Callewaert and Mukund Lath, 'Musicians and Scribes', in *The Hindi Songs of Namdev* (Leuven: Departement Oriëntalistiek, 1989), pp. 55–117; Christian L. Novetzke, *Religion and Public Memory: A Cultural History of Saint Namdev in India* (New York: Columbia University Press, 2008); and Tyler W. Williams, 'Sacred Sounds and Sacred Books: A History of Writing in Hindi', unpublished PhD thesis, Columbia University, 2014.

sant orature—indeed, deeper and more sophisticated than the high-caste 'Chaturvedi intellectuals' in the cities—finds powerful expression in his sketch, 'Chaturi the Cobbler'.[8]

The transfer of the *bani* of Awadh *sants* from the oral and manuscript traditions into print took place at the crossroads of quite different trajectories of multiple actors: European and Indian Christian missionaries, British Orientalists at Fort William College and in provincial administration, Hindi scholars and literary institutions, commercial publishers like the Belvedere Press or the Venkateshwar Press in Bombay, lineage holders, and Bengali literary figures like Kshiti Mohan Sen and Rabindranath Tagore. Unsurprisingly, the material product of these interventions also differed, though we see similarities in format and agenda emerge, partly because these actors were responding and reacting to one other.

For missionaries and colonial scholar-administrators, it was the *religious position* and message of the *sants*, and of Kabir in particular, that drew their attention, as well their popularity with the North Indian masses.[9] Already the Italian Capuchin friar Marco della Tomba, who was active in north Bihar in the late eighteenth century, had undertaken two (unpublished) translations of 'Cabirist' texts and had sought to understand their religious philosophy.[10] But the first time Kabir's poems appeared in print was in a lithographed anthology published in Calcutta aimed at providing teaching material for East India Company recruits, William Price's *Hindee and Hindostanee Selections* (1827). The nineteenth-century bazaar editions that followed consisted of compilations of the works of multiple saint-poets for devotional purposes, with little editorial intervention.[11] Other early publications were missionaries' translations and editions: E. Trumpp's 1877 translation of the *Guru Granth*; the 1890 edition of the Kabir *panth*'s *Bījak* by Rev. Prem Chand, a convert and Baptist missionary in Munger (Bihar); and its 1917 English translation by Rev. Ahmed Shah.[12]

The main Hindi literary institution, the Nagari Pracharini Sabha of Banaras (est. 1893), was another major force: its *Search for Hindi Manuscripts* reports alerted Hindi scholars and the Hindi public to the existence of texts and traditions and provided the building blocks for Hindi literary histories,[13] while its scholarly editions of Hindi 'classics' like

---

[8] S. Tripathi Nirala (N. Naval, ed.), 'Chaturī Chamār', in *Nirālā Rachnāvalī, Vol. IV* (New Delhi: Rajkamal Prakashan, 1983), pp. 74–83.

[9] As Purushottam Agrawal has recently argued, this shows that it is wrong to consider (and champion) Kabir as a marginal and subaltern voice, a brave but failed religious reformer. Kabir was not a marginal voice, but *the* most popular poet of the trading and artisanal classes, both in his time and in the following centuries. See P. Agrawal, *Akath Kahānī Prem kī: Kabīr kī Kavitā aur Unkā Samay* (New Delhi: Rajkamal Prakashan, 2009).

[10] Charlotte Vaudeville, *Kabir* (Oxford: Clarendon Press, 1974); and David Lorenzen, 'Marco della Tomba and the Brahmin from Banaras: Missionaries, Orientalists, and Indian Scholars', in *Journal of Asian Studies*, Vol. LXV, no. 1 (Feb. 2006), pp. 115–43.

[11] For these and other details about Kabir's printing and critical history, I draw upon Vaudeville, *Kabir*, p. 6 ff. She notes that the oldest of the popular editions of Kabir was in a collection with other devotional poems edited by Shankar Haribhai in Gujarati script in 1888, and four editions in Bengali translation with commentary appeared between 1890 and 1910 (p. 23fn). The Benares Light Press in Banaras had already brought out accessible lithographed editions of Kabir, Tulsidas and Surdas in the 1860s. See Francesca Orsini, 'Pandits, Printers and Others. Publishing in Nineteenth-Century Benares', in Abhijit Gupta and Swapan Chakravarty (eds), *Print Areas: Book History in India* (New Delhi: Permanent Black, 2004), pp. 103–38.

[12] Vaudeville, *Kabir*, pp. 11–2.

[13] The Nagari Pracharini Sabha's reports on its search for Hindi manuscripts mention not only Kabir and Raidas, but also Jagjivan Das and Malukdas, thus placing them within the purview of 'Hindi literature'. See, for example, Shyam Behari Mishra, *The Second Triennial Report on the Search for Hindi Manuscripts for the Year 1909, 1910, 1911* (Allahabad: Indian Press, 1914), pp. 182, 270. Mishra was one of the authors of *Hindī Navaratna* (*Nine Gems of Hindī*) (1910–11), which included Kabir, and of *Miśra–Bandhu Vinod* (Lucknow: Ganga Pustak Mala, 1928), a comprehensive survey of the Hindi literary tradition that drew extensively on the Sabha's search reports.

Shyamsundar Das's *Kabīr Granthāvalī*, based on two manuscripts preserved in the Sabha, provided new standards of publication.[14] At the same time, Ram Chandra Shukla's famously disparaging comments on Kabir and the *sants* in his *Hindī Sāhitya kā Itihās* (1929), which started life as an introduction to the Sabha's Hindi dictionary, provided the impetus for several more positive re-evaluations. This included the foundational monograph, *Traditions of Hindi Mysticism* (1936), by S. Das's student, Pitambar Datt Barthwal, the first scholarly treatment of *sant* philosophy and poetry, written in English and quickly translated into Hindi, on which more below. Outside the Hindi-speaking world, the Bengali scholar Kshiti Mohan Sen collected sayings and poems of Kabir from contemporary oral sources and published them in Bengali (*Kabir*, 1910), and it was from this volume that Tagore selected the poems for his influential translation, *100 Poems of Kabir* (1914).[15]

The result of this publishing activity was an overwhelming focus on Kabir, with an array of printed books at the top and bottom of the price range—English translations, scholarly editions and cheap bazaar anthologies. It is against this publishing landscape that Baleshwar Prasad's commercial-devotional printing effort at his Belvedere Printing Press in Allahabad from 1903 onward (he died in 1920, but his sons took over the concern) appears remarkably wide-ranging and systematic. His *Santbani Series* or *Santbānī Pustakmālā*, which remains in print to this day, included almost fifty titles. In the case of the 'lesser Sants' of the Eastern United Provinces (in boldface in Table 1), in most cases, it was until recently the *only* printed edition of their works.[16]

The *Santbani* Booklets

Compared to the miscellaneous collections of *sant* songs and verses that had been in the market since the 1860s, the scholarly editions brought out by the Nagari Pracharini Sabha, or the lineage *pothis*, the *Santbānī Pustakmālā* occupies a distinctive middle ground. These were booklets with a *modern look*, printed with movable type in codex format (unlike some ritual books like *vrat kathas*, which still imitate the horizontal manuscript format even today), with margins and indents and first-line indexes for easy retrieval of individual items (Figure 1).

We do not know much about the founder-manager of the Belvedere Press, Baleshwar Prasad, who belonged to an Agrawal service and business family that had moved from Punjab to Farrukhabad and then to Banaras in the nineteenth century. After serving as deputy collector, divan to the Raja of Banaras, and junior secretary to the Board of Revenue, in 1902 he retired and moved to Allahabad, where he set up a steam press in Belvedere House, next to the university in the Civil Lines area.[17] Baleshwar Prasad belonged to the Radhasoami community, and while his publishing efforts clearly reflect the catholic and inclusive approach of the movement, their diffusion went much beyond.[18] (The business is still in the family.)

Prasad's introduction to the series, which appeared behind the cover of every volume, sheds light on his motives, aim and methods. Regarding motivation, he speaks of retrieval and service to a generic community of readers (*sarvasādhāraṇ*)—a term I shall return to in the next section. Prasad then stresses the effort and investment put into finding, copying and collating

---

[14] These were based on the Dadu-*panthi* tradition, rather than the Kabir-*panthi Bījak*.

[15] For details, see Vaudeville, *Kabir*; and A.K. Mehrotra, *Songs of Kabir* (New York: New York Review of Books, 2011).

[16] The *Malūkdās Granthāvalī* only came out in 2006; see below for details.

[17] Details in the family history are taken from the book, *Agravāl Jāti kā Itihās*, Pt. 2 (Bhanpura, Indore State: Agrawal History Office, 1939), as reproduced on the Belvedere Printing Works website [http://www.belvedereprintingworks.com/family-history.html, accessed 15 April 2014]; all translations in this essay are mine.

[18] Mark Juergensmeyer, 'The Radhasoami Revival of the Sant Tradition', in Karine Schomer (ed.), *The Sants: Studies in a Devotional Tradition of India* (Delhi: Motilal Banarsidass, 1987), pp. 329–55.

TABLE 1. *Santbānī Pustakmālā.*

Kabīr Sāhib kā sākhī-saṅgrah
Kabīr Sāhib kī śabdāvalī aur jīvancharitr (4 pts)
Kabīr Sāhib kī jñān-gudṛī, rekhte aur jhūlne
Kabīr Sāhib kī akharāvatī
Dhanī Dharmadās jī kī śabdāvalī aur jīvan-charitr
Tulsī Sāhib (Hathras vāle) kī śabdāvalī may jīvan-charitr (2 pts)
Tulsī Sāhib (Hathras vāle) kā Ratna Sāgar may jīvan charitr
Tulsī Sāhib (Hathras vāle) kā Ghaṭ Rāmāyaṇ do bhāgõ mẽ, may jīvan charitr (2 pts)
Guru Nānak Sāhib kī Prāṇ-Saṅgalī saṭippaṇ, jīvan-charitr sahit (2 pts)
Dādū Dayāl kī Bānī, bhāg 1 [sākhī], jīvan-charitr sahit
Dādū Dayāl kī Bānī, bhāg 2 [śabd], jīvan-charitr sahit
Sundar-Bilās aur Sundardās jī kā jīvan-charitr
Palṭū Sāhib bhāg 1–kuṇḍaliyā aur jīvan-charitr
Palṭū Sāhib bhāg 2–rekhte, jhūlne, aril, kabitt aur savaiyā
Palṭū Sāhib bhāg 3–rāgõ ke śabd yā bhajan aur sākhiyāṃ
Jagjīvan Sāhib kī Śabdāvalī aur jīvan-charitr (2 pts)
Dūlan Dās jī kī Bānī aur jīvan-charitr
Carandāsjī kī Bānī aur jīvan-charitr (2 pts)
Gharībdās jī kī Bānī aur jīvan-charitr
Raidāsjī kī Bānī aur jīvan-charitr
Dariyā Sāhib (Bihār vāle) kā Dariyāsāgar aur jīvan-charitr
Dariyā Sāhib (Bihār vāle) ke chune hue Pad aur sākhī
Dariyā Sāhib (Mārvāṛ vāle) kī Bānī aur jīvan-charitr
Bhīkhā Sāhib kī Bānī aur jīvan-charitr
Gulāl Sāhib (Bhīkhā Sāhib ke guru) kī Bānī aur jīvan-charitr
Bābā Malūkdās jī kī Bānī aur jīvan-charitr
Gusāiṃ Tulsīdās kī Bārahmāsī
Yārī Sāhib kī Ratnāvalī aur jīvan-charitr
Bullā Sāhib kā Śabdasār aur jīvan-charitr
Keśavdās jī kī Amīghūṃṭ aur jīvan-charitr
Dharnīdās jī kī Bānī aur jīvan-charitr
Mīrā Bāī kī Śabdāvalī aur jīvan-charitr
Sahjo Bāī kā Sahaj-Prakāś jīvan-charitr sahit (3rd edn.)
Dayā Bāī kī Bānī aur jīvan-charitr
Santbānī Saṅgrah (2 pts)
Santbānī Saṅgrah charitr sahit

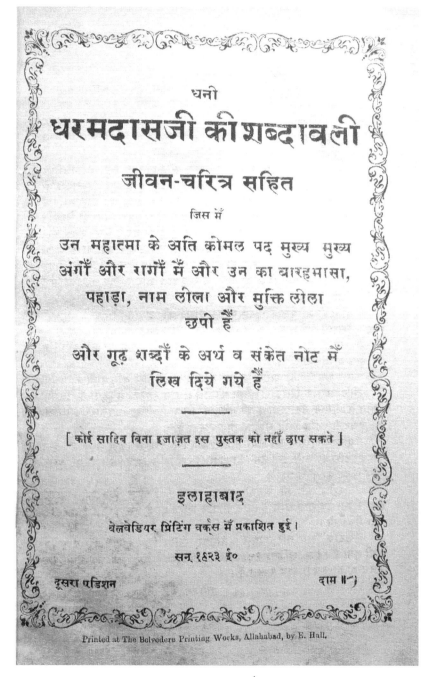

Figure 1. Second edition of *Dhanī Dharmadāsjī kī Śabdāvalī* (Allahabad: Belvedere Press, 1923).
Source: Author's own photograph.

the manuscripts in proper editorial fashion. The term he favours for the *sants* is a generic one, *mahatma*, and while his statement and the short biographies within each booklet talk at length of the *sants*' different communities (*sampraday, panth*) and provide lineage tables, the statement also reveals a strong standardising and generalising impulse, so that any theological difference or specificity of focus, or competition among *sants* and communities, is erased:

> The motivation for publishing the *Santbani* Book Series is to save the *bānī* and preaching/message (*upadeś*) of the world-famous *mahatmas* from disappearing. Among the *bānīs* that we have printed so far, several had never been printed before and some had been printed in such fragmented (*chhinn-bhinn*) and unorganised way that prevented one from drawing full benefit.
>
> In the last five years we have, with great effort and at great expense, asked for rare manuscript books and scattered verses from near and far away (*deś-deśāntar*); we either collect the originals or have copies made, and this activity is still going on. If possible we collect and print the whole texts (*granth*) and choose from their miscellaneous verses those *pad*/songs that will be beneficial to the general public (*sarvasādhāraṇ ke upkārak*). No book is published without comparing several scripts and without proper emendation, unlike the books others publish without any understanding and any checking (*besamajhe aur be jāṃche*). In correcting the spellings we ask knowledgeable followers of the *panth* of the *mahatmas* who authored the texts for help, and in choosing the words we are mindful that they should be in accordance with the taste of the general public (*sarvasādhāraṇ kī ruchi*) and should be attractive and heart-piercing, so that the heart may be pure and there be no need to avert one's eye.
>
> This book series has been published for several years and any shortcomings are gradually being remedied. We are providing glosses for difficult and rare terms, and printing a biography of the *mahātmā* in question alongside the text, as well as short accounts and wonderful occurrences (*kautuk*) in footnotes for the devotees and great men whose names occur in the *bānīs*.[19]

While Baleshwar Prasad shares a widespread perception of the fragility and perishability of oral traditions and appears keen to echo the Sabha's search efforts and scholarly standard of publication, his intended audience was not the Hindi literary public, but the devotional general public, who would benefit from reading and singing any of these works as part of either individual or collective *sadhna*.

It is instructive to compare these booklets to *Mahātmāõ kī Bānī* (1933), the printed edition of a manuscript that must have been a major source for Baleshwar Prasad.[20] The editor of the

---

[19] 'Manager, Belvedere Press' (presumably Baleshwar Prasad), 'Nivedan', *Gulāl Sāhib kī Bānī, Jīvan–Charitra Sahit* (Allahabad: Belvedere Press, 1910), pp. ii–iii. The sentiments were expressed in the book's subtitle as well: '*jismē un mahatmaō ke ati manohar aur bhakti baṛhāne vale pad aur sākhiyāṃ śodh kar mukhya mukhya aṅgō mē rakkhī gaī haĩ, aur gūṛh śabdō ke arth va saṅket bhī noṭ mē likh diye gaye haĩ*' (tr.: 'in which the extremely attractive and devotion-increasing songs and couplets are given after correction and arranged according to main categories, with the obscure words explained in footnotes').

[20] Ram Lagan Lal (ed.), *Mahātmāõ kī Bānī* (Bhurkura, Ghazipur: Ram Baran Das, 1933). The book was printed in Banaras by Baijnath Das; I have a facsimile version. The recent volume, *Rām Jahāj* (New Delhi: Naman Prakashan, 2005), published by Dr. Indradev, 'former Principal of Shri Mahant Ramashray Das Graduate College, Bhurkura, Ghazipur', appears to be a reprint of this book, though newly typeset and with extensive introductions by the editor and a subtitle that calls the community Satnami, rather than Bavri ('*Nirgun Satnāmī siddhapīṭh, Bhurkurā se sambaddh gyārah santõ kī bāniyõ kā saṅkalan*'), perhaps the result of a realignment of the *panth*?

volume praised Mahant Ram Baran Das of the Banvari Sahiba lineage in Bhurkura (Ghazipur)—who had just established a Sanskrit *pathshala* in Bhurkura—for his generosity in sponsoring the printing of the book, which was sure to 'benefit all good people'.[21] The thick, 483-page book was, therefore, a publication sponsored by the Mahant that reproduced in its entirety the 'old' and authoritative manuscript (*pothi*) preserved at the monastery. In the Bhurkura volume, all the poems are numbered sequentially, starting chronologically with the earlier gurus who had slim *oeuvre* such as Bavari Sahiba (one poem), Biru Saheb (two poems), Yari Saheb (twenty), Shah Faqir (seven) and Keshodas (ten). The longer *oeuvre* of Biru, Bula, Jagjivan, Dulan, Gulal and Bhikha is, instead, grouped by *raga* and by genre (e.g. *jhulna*, *arill*), often with similar compositions by different authors next to each other, an arrangement that may have corresponded to the rhythms of communal ritual and singing. Although the editor accompanied the text with a set of illustrations, individual biographies, a first-line index and occasional glosses *in the style of* the Belvedere Press (while the spellings tend to be more Sanskritised), the result was a very different, bulkier and less agile book, and one that does not seem to have been reprinted or circulated widely.

Whether the Bhurkura *math* brought out the volume in (silent) competition with the Belvedere Press booklets or not, it seems clear that the Belvedere Press rearrangement of the *Mahātmāõ kī Bānī* into individual portable booklets along a standard thematic pattern and with a handy apparatus was much better suited to, and successful in, reaching out to modern devotees far beyond those who belonged to each specific community. Indeed, arguably, the very doctrinal blandness of the enterprise facilitated diffuse and border-crossing readership. You did not need affiliation, initiation or commitment to a *sant* lineage to use and enjoy the poetry. Similarly, despite the fact that we can see some *sants* inclining towards certain oral forms, language registers and poetic strategies rather than others—Gulal towards Hori and spring songs, Bhikha and Bula towards Bhojpuri, Malukdas towards single-metaphor poems—the *Santbani* booklets de-emphasise any such specificity. All the *sants* fit the same pattern, all the volumes follow the same arrangement (thematically by *aṅga* and then by genre), and all their verses are 'attractive, devotion-arousing, and beneficial to the general public' in a similar way.[22] These very portable booklets could circulate singly and inexpensively—they still do—or be bound by readers into more durable volumes (Figure 2).

Even now, the family speaks of individual *sadhus* and devotees from distant regions who drop in to buy individual booklets, of bulk orders from bookstores and monasteries, and of the brisk commerce that takes place at religious fairs and railway stalls. This is a varied and diffuse distribution circle that extends all over North India, far beyond the domain of Hindi literary books and the collected works of *sants*.[23] If one of the great puzzles of the Hindi–Urdu publishing boom of the second half of the nineteenth century is its mismatch with the extremely sluggish growth in literacy and formal education statistics, I have argued elsewhere that the great expansion in cheap publications requiring only minimal literacy suggests that many people acquired literacy not at school, but 'on the side'.[24] That many religious publications, *Santbani* booklets included, belong to this category suggests that many

---

[21] Ram Lagan Lal (ed.), *Mahātmāõ kī Bānī*, n.p.g.

[22] The reference to the editorial purging of inappropriate words must remain obscure in the absence of manuscripts or oral tellings that reveal alternative readings, though, intriguingly, Gulal's caste-specific song-poems (on the four *varnas* and then on *kayath*, *ahir*, *baniya*, *khatri*, *sonar*, *lohar*, *bhat*, *pandit*, *molana*, *sanyasi*, *bairagi*, several kinds of *yogis*—*yogi*, *jangam*, *dandi*, *nirbani*—*darvesh*, *teli* and *kalvar*) are not included in the *Santbani* booklet of his works, *Gulāl Sāhab kī Bānī* (Allahabad: Belvedere Press, 1932). See *Mahātmāõ kī Bānī*, pp. 346–72.

[23] Interview with Anupam Agrawal, present owner of Belvedere Printing Works, Allahabad, April 2013.

[24] Orsini, 'Introduction', *Print and Pleasure*.

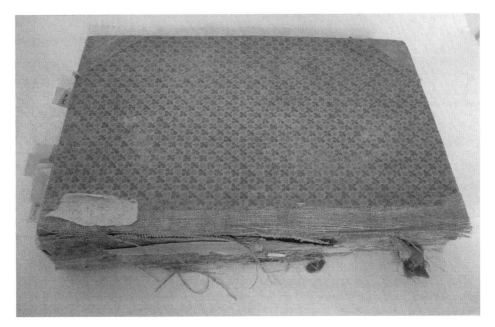

FIGURE 2. Collected and bound Belvedere *Santbani* booklets belonging to Saraswati Dalmia.
Source: Courtesy of Vasudha Dalmia. Author's own photograph.

religious/devotional readers were neo-literates. And if Chaturi the cobbler's descendants are literate today and still sing *sant* songs, these are the booklets they will purchase.

'Beneficial to the General Public': *Santbani* Booklets and Religious Publics

There are many *līlās* and miracles (*chamatkār*, elsewhere *karāmat*) regarding Bhikha Sahab and it is unnecessary to reproduce them all here because people invent so many stories after the *Mahatmas* disappear which in the eyes of reasonable people (*samajhdār*) do not increase one jot the *Mahatma* or devotees' glory despite the fact that ordinary people are enthusiastic about them (*vāh vāh karte haĩ*). Even so, here are two or three such stories.[25]

Let us return for a moment to Prasad's statements—his claim in the introduction to the *Santbani* booklets that he had selected songs that would be 'beneficial to the general public' (*sarvasādhāraṇ ke upkārak*) and, in the quote above, his contrast between 'reasonable people' and 'ordinary people'. Did Prasad see himself as part of a modernising elite and wish through his booklets to reform and improve a credulous public—an example of a 'split public', extending Rajagopal's useful concept?[26] Or does the last sentence—'Even so, here are two or three such stories'—suggest that this was just a gesture, and that the modern devotional public easily brushed aside scepticism and social divisions between educated and 'ordinary' people?

Let us start with *sarvasādhāraṇ*, a term generally used at the time to stress the openness and inclusivity of the 'public' (rather than the more cultural and community-loaded term *jāti*, which instead emphasised internal unity). *Sarvasādhāraṇ* could be used in a reformist

---

[25] *Bhīkhā Sāhib kī Bānī* (Allahabad: Belvedere Press, 1919), p. 2.
[26] Arvind Rajagopal, 'A "Split Public" in the Making and Unmaking of the Ram Janmabhumi Campaign', in *Politics after Television* (Cambridge: Cambridge University Press, 2001), pp. 151–71.

sense—the one seemingly implied here—or in a radical sense, to oppose restricted or hierarchical understandings of public.[27] But what does *sarvasādhāraṇ* mean in this particular context? Three aspects appear significant: first, publishing as publicity, making available in reliable editions valuable words that would otherwise disappear with frayed manuscripts in individual *maths*.[28] Booklets made verses and songs, so far only available either orally, in manuscripts or in expensive and unwieldy scholarly editions, accessible in agile and portable format for personal or group devotion. But, rather than viewing the printing of these booklets as a transition from orature to print and (silent) reading, we need to bear in mind that the booklets were and are meant to serve individuals or groups who recite or sing these verses. In this respect, the booklet should be rather understood as a technology of orature and an extension of it.[29] Second, *Santbani* booklets did make the words of the *sants* available *beyond* the purview of individual *sampradays*. While the *Santbani* project reflects Radhasoami attitudes (and, today, song-poems by *sants* like Malukdas are most likely to be quoted and commented upon by Radhasoami preachers), the booklets themselves did not carry or propound any obvious Radhasoami affiliation. They addressed and served a general public of devotees. Of course, the fact that the *sants* largely shared critiques of caste hierarchy and of other forms of organised religiosity made such general address easier (see also footnote 22 above). Third, the material form in which we find the booklets and the fact that wealthier readers bound these inexpensive booklets into handsome volumes underscore the fact that the audience the booklets reached was a wide one that encompassed *both* educated and ordinary readers. Finally, Prasad's disavowal of hagiography and belief in miraculous stories should arguably be read as only a gesture—a gesture repeated, but never completed ('Even so, here are two or three such stories'). This remains true to this day: whether it is scholarly treatments, critical editions like Baldev Vanshi's recent *Malūkdās Granthāvali* (2006), the *Santbani* booklets, the *Mahātmāõ kī Bāni* or a contemporary *pravachan* on a Malukdas poem, there is always an initial gesture towards historicity: 'We don't have the full history…sources were written quite a bit later….' But after this initial gesture, hagiographies are retold with full fervour.[30] So, while arguably by disaggregating *pothis* into individual authors the *Santbani* booklets encouraged a sense of individual authorship and historical personhood, it was and still remains a historical personhood invested with charisma. And despite the editor's mention of separate 'educated' and 'ordinary' readers, the booklet as a technology and an object did not produce a split public. Rather, by making inoffensive claims about the beneficial words of generic 'great souls', the *Santbani* booklets likely penetrated existing circles of devotional activity, extending their repertoires.

Not Poetic Enough? Orature, Religion and Literary History

There is another aspect of this story that intrigues me. While *sants* like Malukdas definitely fell within the purview of Hindi literary historians, aided by the Belvedere Press enterprise (it

---

[27] See Francesca Orsini, 'What Did They Mean by "Public"? Language, Literature and the Politics of Nationalism', in *Economic & Political Weekly*, Vol. 34, no. 7 (13–19 Feb. 1999), pp. 409–16.

[28] This emphasis is visible in the edition of the collected works of Malukdas recently sponsored by the successor to the *gaddi*, Yogiraj Nanakchand: 'As the Mahant of the holy *gaddi*…I consider it my duty to publish a reliable (*prāmāṇik*) collection of Malukdas's unavailable literature so that it can reach the general public (*jan sādhāraṇ*)'. See 'Do Śabd', in Baldev Vanshi (ed.), *Sant Malūkdās Granthāvalī* (New Delhi: Parmeshwari Prakashan, 2006), p. 5.

[29] For a similar argument about books as aids to orature and performance, see Novetzke, *Religion and Public Memory*, Chap. 3.

[30] '*Satsang Dada Mangharam Jeeti Baji Guru Pratapse Baba Malukdas*' [https://www.youtube.com/watch?v=wukY_6H0SBo, accessed 4 Sept. 2014].

seems hardly believable, but the most comprehensive scholarly study of North Indian *sants*, Parashuram Chaturvedi's *Uttar Bhārat kī Sant Paramparā* of 1950, drew upon the *Santbani* booklets instead of manuscripts for the Awadh *sants*), their literary status has remained much shakier. If Awadh *sants* have been discussed and valued, it has been as religious reformers and teachers, not as poets. Why so?

Colonial interest in bhakti, Vijay Pinch has argued, stemmed from a number of motivations. It paralleled the devotionalist ethic of late Victorian Britain and reflected a shift among Orientalists in India to a 'more comparative posture' in the 1860s and 1870s after the 'confident evangelism of the first half of the century'.[31] Moreover, if Orientalists believed that religion was crucial to any understanding of India, in polemic with Sanskrit Orientalists, scholar-administrators like George A. Grierson believed that studying bhakti yielded a better understanding of modern India—and earned the subjects' trust:

> Believe one who has tried it, that the quotation of a single verse of Tulasī Dāsa or of a single pithy saying of the wise old Kabīr will do more to unlock the hearts and gain the trust of our eastern fellow-subjects than the most intimate familiarity with the dialectics of Śaṅkara or with the daintiest verse of Kālidāsa. A knowledge of the old dead language will, it is true, often win respect and admiration, but a very modest acquaintance with the treasures—and they are treasures—of Hindī literature endows its possessor with the priceless gift of sympathy, and gains for him, from those whose watchword is *bhakti*, their confidence and their love.[32]

Bhakti presented British missionaries and scholars with a particularly congenial form of Indian religion. Grierson shared with Bishop Westcott and other missionaries the belief that bhakti—Kabir included—had derived from the spread of early Christianity.[33] And even when that particular theory was disproved, Christian vocabulary permeated Grierson's (and others') descriptions of bhakti, its saints, and poems (which he called hymns). Thus, for Grierson, bhakti taught 'the fatherhood of God and His infinite love and compassion';[34] Krishna worship taught 'the first, and great, commandment of the law; the second—though shalt love thy neighbour as thyself—it hardly touches';[35] Tulsidas' devotion 'is directed to a loving, all-powerful God, who offers Himself to His worshippers as the Great Example'.[36] Following Westcott, who had described Kabir as 'the Indian Luther of the 15th century',[37] Grierson spoke about Kabir in the idiom of reformation: '[t]hat some of [Kabir's] ideas, nay, many of

---

[31] Vijay Pinch, '*Bhakti* and the British Empire', in *Past & Present*, Vol. 179, no. 1 (May 2003), p. 175.

[32] G.A. Grierson, 'Modern Hinduism and Its Debt to the Nestorians', in *Journal of the Royal Asiatic Society of Great Britain and Ireland* (April 1907), pp. 327–8; quoted in Pinch, '*Bhakti* and the British Empire', p. 181.

[33] *Ibid.*; see also Vaudeville, *Kabir*, pp. 11–3.

[34] George A. Grierson, 'The Popular Literature of Northern India', in *Bulletin of the School of Oriental Studies, University of London*, Vol. 1, no. 3 (1920), p. 101.

[35] *Ibid.*, p. 102

[36] *Ibid.*, p. 112.

[37] G.H. Westcott, *Kabīr and the Kabīrpanthīs* (1908), quoted in Vaudeville, *Kabir*, p. 22. Grierson, who had already compared Bhakti to the reformation (with a small 'r'), wrote of Kabir that 'He was Musalmān who, attracted by the reformed Hinduism, founded a sect in which Islām and it were combined'. See Grierson's 1918 lecture to the School of Oriental and African Studies, 'Popular Literature of Northern India', p. 118.

his actual phrases, were borrowed either directly or at second hand from the Gospels cannot be doubted', he argued.[38]

Even Hindi scholars who did not share these Christian views shared some of the same epistemological premises. A 'new' religion like bhakti could only be described as a derivation, and combination, of elements from earlier philosophies and religions—indeed, it had to be so in order to prove that it was a 'real religion'. Similarities called for filiation, whether from Christianity or Vedanta or Sufism.[39] Particularly in the case of Kabir, 'birth determinism' meant that his birth and upbringing and his thought had to match—how could he know Hinduism and Vedanta so well if he was born a Muslim?[40] British and Indian modern scholars of Kabir shared this belief, Purushottam Agrawal has recently argued, because colonial modern epistemology viewed early modern Indian subjects as mere cyphers of their birth, caste and religion—so Kabir must have said what he said because of his background, not out of choice. Why, Agrawal asks, is it so difficult to imagine that the religious ideas of an early modern individual were the result of individual choice? 'It was not necessary to be born or converted into a religion to be familiar with the Nathpanth—people searched through study and *satsang*, they used their discrimination, they weighed and accepted or rejected it'.[41] So 'Kabir's discourse and ideas (*vaicāriki*) is not bound by genealogy', Agrawal argues, 'it is the outcome of the bold quest of a restless individual, it was an individual, rational choice'. Kabir was familiar with current religious idioms (*bahuśrut*, 'well-listened', if not *bahu-paṭhit*, 'well-read'),[42] but used them creatively to give expression to his own spiritual journey. It is in this spirit of creativity that we shall explore their poetic religious language below.

The historical view of bhakti as a direct product or consequence of Islamic 'invasion' was another premise that British and Indian scholars shared, and their words almost exactly mirror each other's. Thus, according to Grierson, bhakti came from the South 'in the same century as the battle of Thānēsar' and 'rapidly spread into Northern India, then gasping in its death-throes amid the horrors of alien invasion'; it 'came at this time as balm and healing to a suffering people, and we see this reflected in…lyric poetry'.[43] Ramchandra Shukla famously opened his chapter on the age of bhakti with an equally bleak picture of Muslim destruction

---

[38] Grierson, 'Popular Literature of Northern India', p. 119. Pinch argues that Grierson abandoned his view of the Nestorian Christian origins of bhakti after James Kennedy and J.B. Keith expressed scepticism and R.G. Bhandarkar showed evidence of the pre-Christian origin of bhakti theology in *Vaisnavism, Saivism and Minor Religious Systems* (1913), but we see in the 1918 speech that Christian vocabulary still governed Grierson's description of bhakti. See Pinch, '*Bhakti* and the British Empire', pp. 176–7.

[39] P.D. Barthwal, *Traditions of Indian Mysticism, Based upon the Nirguna School of Hindi Poetry* (New Delhi: Heritage Publishers, [1936] 1978), p. 15; see esp. Chap. 2, 'The Nirguṇi's Philosophy', pp. 18–89.

[40] 'Though brought up in a Muslim household', Shyamsundar Das stated, 'the fact that he is steeped in Hindu ideas gestures towards the fact that Brahmin, or at least Hindu, blood flowed in his veins'. See introduction to *Kabīr Granthāvalī*, quoted in P. Agrawal, *Akath Kahānī Prem kī*, p. 158. For Chandrabali Pandey, Kabir was instead a Muslim by birth and a radical Sufi by practice. Hazari Prasad Dvivedi set up an elaborate scheme that accounted for the varied strands of his religious idiom; according to Dvivedi, there had been a caste of Nathpanthi householders in northern and eastern India at the time who were either weavers or beggars, most of whom did not observe caste rules and worshipped a formless god; with the coming of Islam, they had gradually converted, and it was in such a family of neo-converted householder *jogis* that Kabir was brought up. The only problem, Agrawal notes, is that Kabir never called himself a *jogi*, but only a *julaha*, a *kori*, or 'neither Hindu nor Muslim': *ibid.*, p. 163.

[41] *Ibid.*, p. 174.

[42] *Ibid.*, p. 312.

[43] Grierson, 'Popular Literature', p. 101.

and Hindu despair.[44] In his monograph on the Nirguna School of Hindi poetry, Pitambar Datt Barthwal also began with this gloomy picture of 'Mohammadan conquest' and a stark polarity between the polytheist, idol-worshipping Hindus and the monotheist, idol-breaking Muslims ('There was thus a vast gulf of hatred separating the two races, that still needed being bridged'). In Barthwal's case, though, Hindu–Muslim hostility emphasised the contrast with the *sants* (and the Sufis, among Muslims) as men 'above all race-prejudices' who 'viewed this state of things with grave concern....'[45] The Nirguna School, therefore, answered the need of the hour; it was the reform movement that Medieval India 'urgently needed'. It 'would aim at sweeping away all ignorance and superstition, that gave rise to Mohammadan superstition and fanaticism on the one hand and iniquitous social fetters on the other and that stood in the way of communal rapprochement and social equities'.[46] Contemporary echoes would not have been lost on readers in 1930s North India who had witnessed the violent communal riots of the 1920s.

Religious and political questions therefore dominated discussions of Bhakti and the *sants*, and even for literary scholars they tended to overshadow serious engagement with *sant* poetry. Yet, even when they did discuss the poetry, they found it not to their liking. 'How earnestly one wishes that these Nirguṇīs knew and cared for the ordinary rules of grammar and prosody if not of rhetorics. Even a little bit of polish would have immeasurably enhanced the charm of their utterances', lamented Barthwal, and singled out the Dadu-*panthi* Sundardas as 'the only educated person among them perhaps'.[47] 'After acknowledging the greatness of [Kabir's] personality, when it comes to his poetic art the pen hesitates a little', wrote the Mishra brothers, who had placed Kabir among their 'nine jewels' of Hindi literature, but who, in literary terms, positioned him after Tulsidas and Surdas, 'between Matiram and Chandbardai'. They admitted that about 'a hundred pages' of Kabir's poems were of high quality, while the rest was repetitive and dull (*fikā*).[48] Echoing Barthwal, they conceded that '[h]ad Kabir Sahab composed books (*granth*) from a literary perspective, there is no doubt that given the level of his composition he could have written excellent ones. He had all the qualities of a good poet (*satkavi*), he only lacked the will. He did not even want to be a good poet, he was a sermon-giver and a religious preacher'.[49] Thus, Hindi scholars chose to think that Kabir and the other *sants could have been poets if they had wanted*, but that poetry was not their aim.

Intriguingly, both Barthwal and the Mishra brothers acknowledged that Tagore's translation had bestowed recognition as well as literariness on Kabir's verses. According to Barthwal, '[t]hough naturally enough poetic ideas cannot be faithfully translated into a foreign

---

[44] 'With the establishment of Muslim rule in the country there was no place left in the hearts of the Hindu people for pride, self-respect, and enthusiasm. Right before them their temples were destroyed, the statues of gods were demolished, and their venerable persons were humiliated, and there was nothing they could do'. See R. Shukla, *Hindī Sāhitya kā Itihās* (Kashi: Nagari Pracharini Sabha, [1929] 1988), p. 15, quoted and translated in Navina Gupta, 'The Politics of Exclusion? The Place of Muslims, Urdu and its Literature in Rāmcandra Śukla's *Hindī Sāhitya kā Itihās*', in H. Harder (ed.), *Literature and Nationalist Ideology: Writing Histories of Modern Indian Language* (New Delhi: Social Science Press, 2010), p. 268; translation slightly changed.

[45] Barthwal, *Traditions of Indian Mysticism*, p. 8.

[46] 'Thus did the needs of the times find their realisation in the Nirguṇa movement initiated by Kabīr. Nānak, Dādū, Prāṇanāth, Malūkdās, Palaṭū, Jagjīvan dās, Śibdayāl, Tulasī Sāhib and a host of other Sants took up his mission from time to time and worked for the propagation of this movement for unity and equity'. *Ibid.*, p. 17. As is well known, Ramchandra Shukla did not share this opinion of the *sants*, whom he considered—in line with Tulsidas—as spreading radical centrifugal ideas that went against the need of the hour, which was for unity among Hindus.

[47] *Ibid.*, p. 222.

[48] G.B., S.B. and S.D.B. Mishra, *Hindī Navaratna* (Hyderabad: Ganga Granthaghar, [1955], new ed. 1975), p. 421.

[49] *Ibid.*, p. 491.

tongue, yet in fact most of the poems of the Nirguṇī poets appear grander in translations than in the original, for it is not only poetic "aroma" but also crudeness of expression that evaporates in the process'.[50] 'Didactic religious treatises' was Grierson's verdict on Kabir's poems, whereas he had warmer words for Surdas, Tulsidas, Vidyapati and even Bihari.[51] 'Crudeness of expression', 'ruggedness', 'didacticism', lack of knowledge of poetic rules—or, in positive terms, 'well-arranged and beautiful language', 'here and there you can find [in Maluk Das] poetic construction (*pad vinyās*) and *kavitt* like in good poets':[52] even when Hindi critics meant to praise the artistry of the *sant* poets, they damned them with faint praise. Why was it so difficult—even for those who were critical of old poetic tastes and were looking for models to establish new ones, and who appreciated the content and popularity of the *sant* poets—to find the vocabulary to appreciate the *sant* poetic aesthetic?

For the Mishra brothers, with their keen taste in courtly poetry (*riti*), the answer is simple: the *sant* poets did not follow the established formal rules of poetry and did not know, or care, to play that particular poetic game. In the case of Barthwal and the Romantic ideals that underwrote his views of poetry, he could praise *sant* poetry as 'natural poetry' for its 'artlessness' and the direct and unsuppressable 'experience of inner life'.[53] He approved of their 'observation of nature', some 'delightfully melancholy images', and the symbolic love songs, but this ideal not only pushed the *sants*' poems towards Tennysonian maudlinism, but also made him distinguish between 'true poetry' and 'mere didacticism'.[54] As a result, he conducted surgical operations in an attempt to divide good verses from bad ones.[55] The combination of deep philosophical-religious meanings and aesthetic appreciation that Nirala recognised in Chaturi's illiterate but perceptive understanding of *sant* poetry was not to be found among modern Hindi literary critics who held definite ideas about poetry.

Yet, while early modern *and* modern canonical lists of Hindi poets snubbed the Awadh *sant* poets[56]—with the exception of Kabir in modern times—the *sant* poets of Awadh certainly viewed themselves as poets, and what they did as poetry, *kabitāī*.[57] As Bhikha wrote in this autobiographical poem, it was through 'writing, learning, and reading' and singing many *rekhta, kabitta, sakhi, sabda* and *dhrupad* that he had found his guru:

bahu rekhta aru kabitta sākhī sabda sõ mana māna
soi likhata sīkhata paṛhata nisu dina karata Hari guna gāna. (8)
ika dhrupada bahuta bicitra sonata bhoga pucheu hai kahāṃ
niyare Bhuṛkuṛā gram jāke sabda āpe hai tahāṃ. (9)[58]

---

[50] Barthwal, *Traditions of Indian Mysticism*, p. 223. 'There is no doubt that Kabir Sahab was a poet of high quality. The jewel poet of contemporary India himself, Rabindranath Tagore, has recognized him as a good poet and translated his verses (*pad*) in English. Even from reading that book of translations Kabir's literary height (*gaurav*) transpires': G.B., S.B. and S.D.B. Mishra, *Hindī Navaratna*, p. 491.

[51] Grierson, 'Popular Literature', p. 119.

[52] Shukla, *Hindī Sāhitya kā Itihās*, p. 63.

[53] Barthwal, *Traditions of Hindi Mysticism*, p. 225.

[54] *Ibid.*, p. 227

[55] *Ibid.*, p. 228. But, as A.K. Ramanujan cautions, '"spontaneity" has its own rhetorical structure'. See A.K. Ramanujan, *Speaking of Śiva* (London: Penguin Books, 1973), p. 38.

[56] *Sant* poets were beyond the pale of literariness for early modern Hindi treatises: both Lal Kavi's *Avadha Bilāsa* (*Delights of Ayodhya*) (1675), a Ram-*rasik* text composed in Ayodhya, and Bhikharidas' *Kāvya-Nirṇaya* (*Discrimen of Poetry*) (1746) mention Tulsidas and Surdas as poets, but not Kabir. The first 'Hindi *tazkira*', Shiv Singh Sengar's *Śiv Siṃh Saroj* (1878), does include Malukdas, however briefly, but quotes a courtly verse that seems at odds with his poetic voice.

[57] *Malūkdās kī Bānī* (Allahabad: Belvedere Press, 1920), p. 31.

[58] *Bhīkā Sāhib kī Bānī*, p. 12.

So many *rekhta*, *kabitta*, *sakhi* and *sabda* I wrote, learnt and read
in my mind, night and day I praised Hari/the Lord.
I heard a strange *dhrupada* song and asked—where is it from?
The *sabda* is by some who lives near Bhurkura village.

Yet, partly for reasons of caste and class, modern Hindi literary scholars preferred the old courtly aesthetic to the 'rough' aesthetic of *sant* orature. And appreciation for the humanist values of the *sants* thus took the place of literary evaluation.

Conclusions

Awadh *sant* orature, which was such an important and vibrant part of local religious and poetic life well into the twentieth century, did make it into the world of print. This essay has explored the material form the *sant* poets' *oeuvre* took in print, the agents involved in this transfer, and the religious public the printed booklets envisaged and reached out to. Apart from the material changes involved in the process, we also saw the larger religious and literary-historical discourses the Awadh *sants* were fitted into. So, while the most significant agent was a commercial publisher of devotional disposition, his enterprise needs to be read at the intersection of a number of initiatives and discourses around Bhakti and the *sants* at the time—by missionaries, Orientalists, Hindi literati, and literary institutions.

The Belvedere Press *Santbani* series has been extraordinarily successful and long-lived and much more successful than the lineages' own publications in reaching out to a broader religious public. The booklets have continued to spread the *sants*' words independently of the varying fortunes of their *panth* communities for over a hundred years, and have allowed the Belvedere Press to survive. Yet, while the *Santbani* series has ensured *some* visibility and long-term life in print for these poet-saints and their words, and I have argued that the cheap booklet format should be viewed as a technology aiding orature rather than superseding it, in terms of general visibility it has had a kind of penumbral existence. In Hindi literary histories and in religious compendia, the limited and generic coverage of the Awadh *sants* means that they are more often known as names than as authors—what Genette calls 'paratext without a text'.[59] In fact, I call Malukdas, Dharnidas, Gulal Saheb, Bhikha Saheb, Paltudas, Jagjivandas, and so on 'three-line poets' because literary histories usually contain little beyond a short biography with hagiographical tales and a list of their works. Further, by packaging the *sants* as generic *mahatmas*, retrospectively the *Santbani* series has diluted and generalised the *bani* of the *sants*. From a literary perspective, although the Belvedere Press booklets have remained the only source for the *sants*' *oeuvre*, on the whole they have failed to alert readers and students of Hindi literature to the poetic value and historical significance of this poetry. The original *Santbani* project aimed at suturing differences between literary and devotional poetics, between oral and manuscript traditions and print, and between *panth*-centred and 'generic' devotional publics. But whereas older bound collections indicate that the Belvedere Press booklets reached both 'educated' and 'ordinary' readers, at present their low-quality paper and smudged printing suggests that the booklets now cater primarily to 'ordinary' devotees. Whether an influential and modernising organisation like the Radhasoami *panth* has repackaged them for their middle-class followers remains to be seen.

---

[59] Gerard Genette, *Paratexts* (Cambridge: Cambridge University Press, 1997).

Ambedkar, Marx and the Buddhist Question

AJAY SKARIA, *University of Minnesota, Minneapolis, USA*

This essay tries to frame one question, which at its most abbreviated can be posed thus: why does Ambedkar convert to Buddhism? Given Ambedkar's militant secularism, to ask this question is also to ask: what assumption of responsibility does that conversion enable which exceeds secular responsibility? This essay tracks how Ambedkar's religion questions both the liberal concept of minority, and the dissolution of the minor that is staged in Marx's critique simultaneously of religion and secularism. Buddhism becomes in the process a religion of the minor.

Around March 1956, Dr. Babasaheb Ambedkar completes the manuscript, published posthumously, of *The Buddha and His Dhamma*.[1] On 14 October, he converts to Buddhism. And on 2 December, just four days before he dies, he completes the manuscript of the famous short piece, 'Buddha or Marx', and gives it for typing up.

In this essay, I shall try to frame one question, which at its most abbreviated can perhaps be posed thus: why does Ambedkar convert to Navayana Buddhism? I say 'frame' because I will not be able to answer the question. But perhaps framing, reframing and even unframing the question is itself a most necessary task.

We could start by reminding ourselves how and why this question becomes a question. As Talal Asad has suggested, 'religious conversion needs explaining in a way that secular conversion to modern ways of being does not'.[2] That need and even demand for explanation becomes all the more powerful in the case of Ambedkar, whose radical secularism is exemplified both in his efforts in earlier years to institutionalise a liberal civil society and public sphere through the Indian Constitution, and in the fact that he converts without disavowing his secularism.

Moreover the demand (and here I might find myself in disagreement with Asad) is not an ethnocentrism or Eurocentrism; it is not the privileging of some exclusively European considerations of secularity. As a young Marx says right at the beginning of the 'Contribution to the Critique of Hegel's Philosophy of Right', 'the critique of religion is the prerequisite of all critique'.[3] And such criticism of religion has often been especially empowering for marginalised groups. For example, it is precisely by drawing on secular categories that the

---

I thank Laura Brueck, Aishwary Kumar, Udaya Kumar, Gyanendra Pandey and Simona Sawhney for discussions and comments that have helped frame this essay. I also thank Anupama Rao and an anonymous reviewer for the detailed and thoughtful comments they provided as reviewers for *South Asia*.

[1] The full text of B.R. Ambedkar, *The Buddha and His Dhamma*, is available online at http://www.columbia.edu/itc/mealac/pritchett/00ambedkar/ambedkar_buddha/, accessed 6 Feb. 2015.

[2] Talal Asad, 'Comments on Conversion', in Peter van der Veer (ed.), *Conversion to Modernities: The Globalization of Christianity* (New York: Routledge, 1996), p. 263.

[3] Karl Marx, *Critique of Hegel's 'Philosophy of Right'* (Joseph O'Malley and Annette Jolin, trans. and ed.) (Cambridge: Cambridge University Press, 1977), p. 131.

very category Dalit has been constituted; that upper castes have been held responsible for their violence against Dalits; and that Dalits have simultaneously assumed *and* universalised the responsibility of struggling against that violence. So when somebody—especially an already secular being—converts to a public religion, this can seem an abdication of the responsibility to question injustice.

And yet, that demand for explanation is turned upon itself here, for Ambedkar converts to Navayana Buddhism precisely as an act of the greatest responsibility. Here, there is not only a criticism of religion (most of all, Hinduism, but also prior traditions of Buddhism), but also of secularism, and that criticism is articulated moreover as a religion.

I

So, a first framing: when we ask 'why does Ambedkar convert to Navayana Buddhism', we are asking how does his conversion involve a responsibility greater than that which he already exercises as a secular being? As that reframing suggests, I ask the question 'why' only on a very limited register. I am not for example concerned here with Ambedkar's conscious or unconscious intentions, with the social context of the conversion, or with the Dalit and lower-caste religions and conversions that precede his conversion and provide its genealogy. While attention to all these matters is absolutely essential, here I limit myself to the re-figuring of secularism involved in his conversion. This re-figuring, I would suggest, is at least as crucial to Ambedkar's Buddhism as the critique of Hinduism that precedes and suffuses this Buddhism.

It is symptomatic of this greater responsibility that Ambedkar converts not only as an abstract individual, nor even as an individual Dalit, but also as a Dalit leader (or, in his early formulations, a Mahar leader), as one whose actions form a collective Dalit or Mahar identity. Thus in his May 1936 speech to the Bombay Presidency Mahar Conference, he says: '[J]ust as the boatman does not collect luggage unless he gets an idea of the number of passengers boarding the boat, so also is the case with me. Unless I get an idea as to how many persons are willing to leave the Hindu fold, I cannot start preparation for conversion'.[4] He also insists there: 'If at all you decide in favour of conversion, then you will have to promise me organized and en-masse conversion. If the decision is taken in favour of conversion, and the people start embracing any religion they like individually, I will not dabble in your conversion'.[5]

Ambedkar's religion itself is social—this is why dhamma is both a religion and not quite a religion. *The Buddha and His Dhamma* notes that while dhamma is 'analogous' to 'what European theologians call religion', the latter is personal and 'one must keep it to oneself. One must not let it play its part in public life'. In contrast to religion, he goes on, 'Dhamma is social. It is fundamentally and essentially so.... [O]ne man, if he is alone, does not need Dhamma. But when there are two men living in relation to each other, they must find a place for Dhamma whether they like it or not. Neither can escape it'.[6]

And if I began by noting a distinctive concatenation of events in 1956, this was in order to indicate the two co-ordinates that frame the question here. First, *The Buddha and His Dhamma*, published posthumously in 1957. As we know, Ambedkar worked feverishly and obsessively to complete the book. This intense textual engagement suggests, as Simona Sawhney has recently

---

[4] B.R. Ambedkar, 'What Path to Salvation', speech delivered to the Bombay Presidency Mahar Conference, Bombay, 31 May 1936 [http://www.columbia.edu/itc/mealac/pritchett/00ambedkar/txt_ambedkar_salvation.html, accessed 7 Sept. 2014]. I thank Laura Brueck for comments that stressed the importance of this social dimension of Ambedkar's conversion.

[5] *Ibid.*

[6] Ambedkar, *The Buddha and His Dhamma*, Book IV, Part I, Section 2.

pointed out, that while Ambedkar's conversion is nothing if not deeply political, politicalness cannot here consist of the 'rational decision to achieve an external or prior end'.[7]

Ambedkar is of course aware of the 'material aspect' and even instrumental dimension of conversion. His May 1936 speech to the Bombay Presidency Mahar Conference describes this aspect as 'class struggle' and suggests that those who ignore it are 'stupid'; conversion will make Mahars part of the larger community and provide them with outside strength in case of a struggle. But this material or calculable aspect is for him itself framed by an incalculable aspect (and the incalculable cannot strictly speaking be an aspect)—the compulsion to respond in a consistent way (which is also to say rationally) to the challenges he faces as he questions the disempowerment and marginality of Dalits. This compulsion forces him to convert to Buddhism. Moreover, he does not convert to a pre-existing Buddhism, but to a Buddhism that he receives in the process of writing *The Buddha and His Dhamma*. If we are to get a sense of the late Ambedkar's politics, we must get a sense of his religion, this Buddhism that seizes him.

Second, to get a sense of this religion, we must attend to his engagement with Marx and Marxism. Ambedkar's most extended formulations on Marx occur in one very brief essay, 'Buddha or Karl Marx', which discerns a 'residue of fire' in Marx, and suggests that Buddha and Marx share a great deal. The essay reveals the stakes of this engagement for Ambedkar:

> Society has been aiming to lay a new foundation [which] was summarised by the French Revolution in three words, Fraternity, Liberty and Equality. The French Revolution was welcomed because of this slogan. It failed to produce equality. We welcome the Russian Revolution because it aims to produce equality. But it cannot be too much emphasized that in producing equality society cannot afford to sacrifice fraternity or liberty. Equality will be of no value without fraternity or liberty. It seems that the three can coexist only if one follows the way of the Buddha. Communism can give one but not all.[8]

Both Marxism and his Buddhism work, in other words, towards the promise of a world organised by equality, liberty, and fraternity, with equality as the key term. And Marxism is a particularly intense moment of the striving to keep that promise, even the most intense moment he is familiar with.[9]

But Ambedkar's most sustained engagements with Marx do not occur when he explicitly reads the latter. They occur rather where Marx's and his responsibilities traverse the same terrain. Such a traversal marks especially Ambedkar's thinking of the minor—the figure who is less than equal, but claims equality. Ambedkar's thinking of the minor re-orients Marx's simultaneous critique, articulated most forcefully in 'On the Jewish Question', of religion and secularism.[10] That re-orientation occurs in two ways, which are not so much different paths as the flip side of each other.

---

[7] Simona Sawhney, 'Ambedkar: The Inheritance of the Buddha', paper presented at the Annual South Asia Conference, Madison, 13 Oct. 2012. For an incisive interrogation of the scholarship that has read Ambedkar's conversion instrumentally, see Gauri Viswanathan, 'Religious Conversion and the Politics of Dissent', in Peter van der Veer (ed.), *Conversion to Modernities: The Globalization of Christianity* (New York: Routledge, 1996), pp. 89–114.

[8] B.R. Ambedkar, 'Buddha or Karl Marx', in *Dr. Babasaheb Ambedkar, Writings and Speeches, Vol. 3* (Bombay: Government of Maharashtra, 1987), p. 462, also available online [http://www.ambedkar.org/ambcd/20.Buddha%20or%20Karl%20Marx.htm, accessed 7 Sept. 2014].

[9] As Gail Omvedt notes, 'in seeing the Dhamma as a solution to exploitation, he was asking Marxist questions' and providing 'Buddhist answers'. See Gail Omvedt, *Buddhism in India: Challenging Brahmanism and Caste* (New Delhi: Sage, 2003), pp. 1, 3.

[10] 'On the Jewish Question', in *Karl Marx, Selected Writings*, David McLellan (ed.) (Oxford: Oxford University Press, 2nd ed., 2000), pp. 46–70.

Gyanendra Pandey and Anupama Rao amongst others have eloquently explored one of these ways. Rao writes how 'a new political collectivity was constituted by resignifying the Dalit's negative identity within the caste structure into positive political value'.[11] As her writing suggests, the concept of minority that organises the figure of the Dalit is quite different from that which Marx develops, since for the Dalit 'individual freedom was contingent on the emancipation of the community, rather than separation from it', or the dissolution of the minor that Marx envisioned.[12] Here, the Dalit as minority is constituted by a claim to equality that proceeds by secularising religion, or more precisely, by secularising and exploding caste. Both through the Constitution and through political struggles to demand that the state enforce Dalit rights, Ambedkar seeks to shore up the rights of this Dalit minority.

My concern in this essay is with the closely-related concept that Ambedkar intensifies by converting to Navayana Buddhism—that of the minor. If the minority is conceived in terms of measure, then the minor is conceived in terms of immeasure. The relationship between these two concepts—minority and minor—is excessive, rather than oppositional. To put it in Udaya Kumar's terms, even as the vocabulary of minority invokes measure and quantity, it 'exceeds them and turns them into signs of an intensive relationship. At the same time, the vocabulary of intensities has a relationship to what it rubs against, the world of measures and units'. Not only is 'the language of measure…challenged and affected by that of immeasure, but… immeasure nurses in its core a deep relationship to the impulse to measure'.[13]

One might add that what makes the pair 'minority-minor' so charged and destabilising, so unlike the pair 'majority-major' to which it could be opposed, is that the former is concerned constitutively with claiming equality as a minor. And since equality is not a transparent term, this claim involves not only thinking about what equality 'is', but also nurturing the life of both self and 'other' (whereas the pair 'majority-major' seeks to extinguish or subordinate the life of the other).

II

One way then of reframing the question could be: why in Ambedkar's writing must the minority of that radically secular figure, the Dalit, be supplemented by this radical religion of the minor, Navayana Buddhism?[14] What is the universal equality that this religion offers, which the French and Russian revolutions have failed to offer?[15]

---

[11] Anupama Rao, *The Caste Question: Dalits and the Politics of Modern India* (Berkeley: University of California Press, 2009), p. 2. Gyanendra Pandey points out succinctly the sense in which the term Dalit signifies a negative identity: unlike Muslims, Sikhs or Christians, he notes, Dalits 'gained their distinctiveness—at least until they were constituted into a legally recognised minority—precisely from the fact of their untouchability, that is, the discrimination they suffered at the hands of Hindu society'. See Gyanendra Pandey, 'The Time of the Dalit Conversion', in *Economic & Political Weekly*, Vol. 41, no. 18 (6 May 2006), p. 1781.
[12] Rao, *The Caste Question*, p. 23.
[13] Personal communication from Udaya Kumar, 10 Jan. 2015.
[14] My concern here is thus not so much the 'phenomenology of faith' involved in Navayana Buddhism, as the related question of the work this faith does in excess of conventional secularism. For a fascinating, if all-too-brief reading of this 'phenomenology', see Debjani Ganguly, 'Buddha, Bhakti and Superstition: A Post-Secular Reading of Dalit Conversion', in *Postcolonial Studies*, Vol. 7, no. 1 (2004), pp. 49–62.
[15] That Ambedkar's conversion is centrally about equality is forcefully recognised by Gauri Viswanathan, whose title for her chapter on Ambedkar is 'Conversion to Equality'. See Gauri Viswanathan, *Outside the Fold: Conversion, Modernity, Belief* (Princeton, NJ: Princeton University Press, 1998). Viswanathan suggests that Ambedkar's conversion 'produced a critique of secular differentiation as an ideology consistent with, rather than an alternative to, a social philosophy based on hierarchy' (p. 215). My essay elaborates on this theme of equality that Viswanathan's essay broaches.

Ambedkar's famous, never-delivered 1936 speech to the Jat Pat Todak Mandal, where he announces his desire to abandon Hinduism, already intimates what he sees as crucial to religion. There, condemning Hinduism as a 'religion of rules', he distinguishes between principles and rules:

> Rules are practical; they are habitual ways of doing things according to prescription. But principles are intellectual; they are useful methods of judging things. Rules seek to tell an agent just what course of action to pursue. Principles do not prescribe a specific course of action. Rules, like cooking recipes, do tell just what to do and how to do it. A principle, such as that of justice, supplies a main head[ing] by reference to which he is to consider the bearings of his desires and purposes, it guides him in his thinking by suggesting to him the important consideration which he should bear in mind. This difference between rules and principles makes the acts done in pursuit of them different in quality and in content. Doing what is said to be good by virtue of a rule and doing good in the light of a principle are two different things. The principle may be wrong but the act is conscious and responsible. The rule may be right but the act is mechanical. A religious act may not be a correct act but must at least be a responsible act. To permit of this responsibility, Religion must mainly *be* a matter of principles only. It cannot be a matter of rules. The moment it degenerates into rules it ceases to be Religion, as it kills responsibility which is the essence of a truly religious act.[16]

By insisting on responsibility as 'the essence of a truly religious act', this passage politicises religion in a very distinctive way. As the greatest responsibility, religion must now attend to questions of justice—of how best to accomplish 'liberty, equality, and fraternity'. Now religion becomes a profoundly public matter, rather than something limited to the private sphere.

Such responsibility requires moreover that religion be organised around the principle. Ambedkar's Buddha tells his followers that they 'were free to modify or even to abandon any of his teachings if it was found that at a given time and in given circumstances they do not apply. He wished His religion not to be encumbered with the dead wood of the past. He wanted that it should remain evergreen and serviceable at all times'.[17] Even *ahimsa* is a matter of principle: the Buddha 'did not make Ahimsa a matter of Rule. He enunciated it as a matter of Principle or way of life'. 'A principle leaves you freedom to act. A rule does not. Rule either breaks you, or you break the rule'.[18]

In insisting on a religion of the principle, Ambedkar makes a distinctive departure from modern conceptions of religion, and indeed of the principle. At least since Kant's insistence on autonomy, the principle has been a cardinal mark of the Enlightenment: to be principled is to retain the sovereign power of reason, and therefore to be able to modify one's convictions, and act in keeping with new circumstances. As such, the principle both institutes a distinction between the secular and the religious, and works primarily within the realm of the secular—religion, it is presumed, cannot be principled or a matter of public reason; it must be private.

---

[16] B.R. Ambedkar, 'Annihilation of Caste: With a Reply to Mahatma Gandhi', in *Dr. Babasaheb Ambedkar, Writings and Speeches, Vol. 1* (Bombay: Government of Maharashtra, 1979), p. 75, also available online [http://ccnmtl.columbia.edu/projects/mmt/ambedkar/, accessed 14 April 2015].

[17] B.R. Ambedkar, 'Buddha and the Future of His Religion', in *Dr. Babasaheb Ambedkar, Writings and Speeches, Vol. 17, Part 2* (Bombay: Government of Maharashtra, 2003), p. 98, also available online [http://www.clearviewproject.org/engagedbuddhistwriting/buddhaandthefutureof.html, accessed 7 Sept. 2014].

[18] Ambedkar, *The Buddha and His Dhamma*, Book IV, Part II, Section 3.

And in the relationship between the secular and the religious, we could say at the risk of some simplification, the principle has worked in one of two ways. First, in its most institutionally influential form, often at work in liberal or republican democracies, the distinction and relationship between the secular and the religious has been organised as one between the immanent and the transcendent.[19] Here, the implicit criterion is the degree to which religion can support the principle. For example, in *Religion Within the Limits of Reason Alone*, Kant, after insisting that 'for its own sake, morality does not need religion at all' and can be based on 'pure practical reason', goes on to suggest that the ends of religion 'cannot possibly be matters of indifference for reason'. And so, 'morality leads ineluctably to religion'. This moral religion moreover has a proper name: '[O]f all the public religions which have ever existed, the Christian alone is moral'.[20] Indeed, at this long inaugural moment of the modern concept of religion, as of secularism, for both Kant and Hegel in different ways, Christianity is the highest and most universal religion both because it gives birth to and institutes secularism and the principle in the public sphere, and because it recognises its own realm as that of the transcendent and therefore relegates itself to the private sphere. Here, religion is not opposed to the principle; each operates in its own realm and is complementary to the other.

Second, the more radical secularisms—such as those associated with Rousseau, Feuerbach and Marx—question the distinction between the immanent and the transcendent. They treat religion as always immanent, and consequently regard the immanent–transcendent distinction as itself an ideological mystification. Ambedkar makes this spirit his inheritance. Thus he insists in the late 1930s: 'In life and preservation of life therefore consists the religion of the savage. What is true of the religion of the savage is true of all religions wherever they are found for the simple reason that…life and the preservation of life constitute the essence of religion'.[21] Religion is now the realm of 'rules'. Relatedly, not all religions are equal—they are rather evaluated by the degree of divergence between these rules and those principles that autonomous beings might give themselves.

(In this spirit, Ambedkar also attacks the 'science of comparative religion': 'The science of comparative religion has broken down the arrogant claims of all revealed religions that they alone are true and all others which are not the results of revelation are false…. But it must be said to the discredit of that science that it has created the general impression that all religions are good and there is no use and purpose in discriminating [between] them'.[22] Comparative religion is here anti-colonial in that it refuses the claims of every revealed religion. And yet, anti-colonial relativism is not adequate for Ambedkar; his search for another universalism requires him to abandon not only Eurocentrism but also relativism.)

But as he makes radical secularism his inheritance, he also infuses it with a distinctive religion—a religion of the principle, or in other words a secular and immanent religion. This religion is difficult to think. It strives after all for the impossible: on the one hand to secure autonomy and sovereignty; and on the other hand to surrender precisely autonomy and sovereignty.

---

[19] The distinction between the immanent and the transcendent has been systematically explored (and even, one might say, affirmed) most recently in Charles Taylor, *A Secular Age* (Cambridge, MA: Harvard University Press, 2007).
[20] Immanuel Kant, *Religion Within the Limits of Reason Alone* (Theodore M. Greene and Hoyt H. Hudson, trans.) (New York: Harper Torchbook, 1960), pp. 5, 47.
[21] B.R. Ambedkar, *Essays on Untouchables and Untouchability: Religious* [http://www.ambedkar.org/ambcd/25.%20Essay%20on%20Untouchables%20and%20Untouchability_Religious.htm, accessed 7 Sept. 2014].
[22] *Ibid.*

So perhaps our question could also be framed this way: what is the religion of the principle that Ambedkar converts to?

What such a religion of the principle involves at its most elemental is indicated in Ambedkar's 1950 essay, 'Buddha and the Future of His Religion'. The new world needs a religion because '[i]n all societies, law plays a very small part. It is intended to keep the minority within the range of social discipline. The majority is left and has to be left to sustain its social life by the postulates and sanction of morality. Religion in the sense of morality, must therefore, remain the governing principle in every society'. Such a religion, he suggests, must be 'in accord with science'; 'its moral code must recognize the fundamental tenets of liberty, equality and fraternity'; and finally, it 'must not sanctify or ennoble poverty'.[23]

This religion of the principle, moreover, has a proper name: 'If the new world—which be it realized is very different from the old—must have a religion—and the new world needs religion far more than the old world did—then it can only be religion of the Buddha'.[24]

The impossible bringing together of the principle and religion is signalled again in the closing sentences of the speech that Ambedkar gives in May 1936 to the Bombay Presidency Mahar Conference. Trying to convince them 'to leave the Hindu religion', and yet not wanting them to do so 'only because I say so', wanting them to consent 'only if it appeals to your reason', Ambedkar wonders: 'What message should I give you on this occasion?' And then he recounts the message given by the Buddha to the Bhikku Sangha:

'What does the Sangh expect from me? Ananda, I have preached the Dhamma with an open heart, without concealing anything. The Tathagata has not kept anything concealed, as some other teachers do. So Ananda, what more can I tell to the Bhikkhu Sangh? So Ananda, be self-illuminating like the lamp. Don't be dependent for light, like the Earth. Don't be a satellite. Be a light unto thyself....'

I also take your leave in the words of the Buddha. 'Be your own guide. Take refuge in reason'.[25]

But of course, this begs the question: if one is a light to oneself, then what need does the principle have for religion? Why does the principle take *refuge* in reason? What is involved in making reason into a religion? In that transaction, what happens to reason's autonomy and to religion's surrender?

III

Ambedkar is scarcely the first to strive for a religion of the principle—secular traditions have long fantasised about such a religion. Kant, for example, after insisting that morality does not need religion, also adds: '[M]orality finds in the holiness of its laws an object of the greatest respect'.[26] And in the traditions of radical secularism, the famous penultimate chapter of Rousseau's *Social Contract* describes a 'civil religion'.

---

[23] Ambedkar, 'Buddha and the Future of His Religion'.
[24] *Ibid.*
[25] For a discussion of Ambedkar's invocation of this passage, see Christopher Queen's superbly meticulous reading of *The Buddha and His Dhamma* in his 'Ambedkar's Dhamma: Source and Method in the Construction of Engaged Buddhism', in Surendra Jondhale and Johannes Beltz (eds), *Reconstructing the World: B.R. Ambedkar and Buddhism in India* (New Delhi: Oxford University Press, 2004), pp. 132–50.
[26] Kant, *Religion Within the Limits of Reason Alone*, p. 7.

Our question then could also be framed thus: is Ambedkar's religion of the principle a civil or civic religion?[27]

The compulsions that produce the conceptual space for civil religion are indicated by the paradoxical relationship between the rights of man and the rights of the citizen. Hannah Arendt suggests in *The Origins of Totalitarianism* that the Declaration of the Rights of Man 'meant nothing more nor less than that from then on Man, and not God's command or the customs of history, should be the source of Law'.[28] But even though the rights of the citizen might seem derived from those of man, Arendt notes that the '"inalienable rights of man" must nevertheless find their guarantee and become an inalienable part of the right of the people to sovereign self-government':

> In other words, man had hardly appeared as a completely emancipated, completely isolated being who carried his dignity within himself without reference to some larger encompassing order, when he disappeared again into a member of a people. From the beginning the paradox involved in the declaration of inalienable human rights was that it reckoned with an 'abstract' human being who seemed to exist nowhere, for even savages lived in some kind of a social order.[29]

Because of this paradox, the 'Rights of Man, supposedly inalienable, proved to be unenforceable even in countries whose constitutions were based upon them whenever people appeared who were no longer citizens of any sovereign state'.[30] Indeed, 'we become aware of the existence of a right to have rights'—what she describes as 'the right of every individual to belong to humanity, [which] should be guaranteed by humanity itself'—'only when millions of people emerged who had lost and could not regain these rights because of the new global political situation'.[31] All of this is 'an ironical, bitter and belated confirmation' of Burke's assertion that 'human rights were an "abstraction", that it was much wiser to rely on an "entailed inheritance" of rights which one transmits to one's children like life itself, and to claim one's rights to be the "rights of an Englishman" rather than the inalienable rights of man'. 'The pragmatic soundness of Burke's concept seems to be beyond doubt in the light of our manifold experiences'.[32]

Responding to the force of that Burkean critique, Arendt in her later work—especially in *On Revolution* in 1963—emphasises a certain constitutionalism. Here, like Burke, Arendt is more sympathetic to the American Revolution than the French Revolution. But unlike Burke, she recognises that both revolutions are organised around the rights of man, that their divergence lies more in their constitutional histories, and the way these modulate the rights of man. Arendt, it might be said, seeks to conserve the abstract rights of man by making the

---

[27] The argument that it is such a religion has been made most systematically by Martin Fuchs: see especially his 'A Religion for Civil Society? Ambedkar's Buddhism, the Dalit Issue and the Imagination of Emergent Possibilities', in Vasudha Dalmia, Angelika Malinar and Martin Christof (eds), *Charisma and Canon. Essays on the Religious History of the Indian Subcontinent* (New Delhi: Oxford University Press, 2001), pp. 250–73.

[28] Hannah Arendt, *The Origins of Totalitarianism* (New York: Meridian Books, 1958), p. 290.

[29] *Ibid.*, p. 291.

[30] *Ibid.*, p. 293.

[31] *Ibid.*, pp. 297, 298. It would take us too far afield to take issue with Jacques Rancière's simplifications of Arendt's arguments. Suffice it here to note that Rancière's description of the rights of man (that 'the Rights of Man are the rights of those who have not the rights that they have and have the rights that they have not') and Arendt's description of the right to have rights are both very far and very close to each other: they could even be said to be respectively the an-archic and archic description of the same right. See Jacques Rancière, 'Who is the Subject of the Rights of Man?', in *South Atlantic Quarterly*, Vol. 103, nos. 2–3 (2004), pp. 297–310.

[32] *Ibid.*, p. 299.

constitution into an entailed inheritance, which through its publicness and gradualism, will clothe the nakedness of natural man. (As this distinction suggests, Arendt's public sphere, even if transparent, is anything but naked.)

This anxiety over the fragility of the rights of man (which leads to Arendt's emphasis first on the right to have rights, and later on constitutions)—is it not the same anxiety at work in the late nineteenth and early twentieth centuries, striving to institutionalise civil religions? Is not the striving for a civil religion an anxious recognition—analogous to the right to have rights—of the inadequacy by themselves of constitutional rights (those rights that are simultaneously human rights and political rights, but that depend on the political to defend the human)? Civil religion does for its exponents the work of concretising the abstractness of rights of man in a way that still avoids the descent into the particularity of nationalism, that still retains the universality of man. Very briefly, consider John Dewey, one of the two proponents of civil religion who have had considerable influence in twentieth-century India.[33] Dewey (who in Ambedkar's words 'was my teacher and to whom I owe so much'[34]) writes *A Common Faith* in the 1930s in his effort to articulate a democratic faith.[35] As Robert Westbrook notes, Dewey, unlike his associate William James, is not satisfied with a 'neutral public sphere, naked of all faith'. Dewey was 'a democrat and religiously so. And because Dewey believed that supernatural overbeliefs often threaten the democratic beliefs in which he vested his own faith, he tied the fate of democracy to the defeat of supernaturalism, and the growth of a catholic natural piety. His was a fighting faith'.[36]

Through civil religion, Dewey seeks to rescue the rights of man from fragility and abstract nakedness, to enshrine these rights themselves as religious. He works with a distinctive understanding of religion: 'Faith in the continued disclosing of truth through directed cooperative human endeavor is more religious in quality than is any faith in a completed revelation with democracy'.[37] He also says of his later writings that they 'are devoted to making explicit the religious values implicit in the spirit of science as undogmatic reverence for truth in whatever form it present[s] itself, and the religious values implicit in our common life, especially in the moral significance of democracy as a way of living together'.[38] By these criteria, the Universal Declaration of Human Rights is the 'religion of religions', as one admirer of Dewey enthusiastically declares in 1950.[39]

There is certainly enough textual warrant to treat Navayana Buddhism as one more moment in this tradition of civil religion. Like Dewey and Arendt, Ambedkar is acutely aware of the potentiality of the rights of man—the Indian Constitution is an extended testament to this. But perhaps even more than them, he emphasises the challenges of working it. Thus, in his Constituent Assembly speech on 25 November 1949, he stresses that 'however good a Constitution may be, it is sure to turn out bad because those who are called to work it, happen to be a bad lot. However bad a Constitution may be, it may turn out to be good if those who are called to work it happen to be a good lot. The working of a Constitution does not depend

---

[33] The other influential figure is William Salter, whose relationship with Gandhi is discussed in my *Unconditional Equality: Gandhi's Religion of Resistance* (Minneapolis: University of Minnesota Press, 2016.)
[34] Ambedkar, 'Annihilation of Caste', p. 79.
[35] John Dewey, *A Common Faith* (New Haven, CT: Yale University Press, [1934], 2nd ed., 2013).
[36] Robert Westbrook, 'An Uncommon Faith: Pragmatism and Religious Experience', in Stuart Rosenbaum (ed.), *Pragmatism and Religion: Classical Sources and Modern Essays* (Urbana: University of Illinois Press, 2003), p. 199.
[37] Dewey, *A Common Faith*, p. 24.
[38] Cited in H.M. Kallen, 'Human Rights and the Religion of John Dewey', in *Ethics*, Vol. 60, no. 3 (April 1950), p. 176.
[39] *Ibid*.

wholly upon the nature of the Constitution'.[40] Given this emphasis on the need to bring into being a society that can give force to the Constitution, one cannot rule out the possibility that Navayana Buddhism strives to create, in a spirit similar to and influenced by Dewey's, a civil religion that is also a 'fighting faith'.

IV

But even if Ambedkar were to explicitly set out to conceptualise a civil religion, his religion of the principle can never be only that, for the very presumptions he begins with exceed 'civil religion'. Most of all, Ambedkar questions the assumption—shared in different ways by Arendt and Dewey—that the rights of man are centred around natural man in his abstract nakedness, that it is these rights which need to be clothed. In order to elicit the distinctiveness of his questioning, perhaps we can take some cues from the young Marx. In 'On the Jewish Question', Marx conceives the relationship between the rights of man and the rights of the citizen in terms very different from those articulated by Burke. His implicit counterpoint is Hegel's *Philosophy of Right*, which suggests secularism can emerge only out of a specific Christian past, and is indeed the highest form of Christianity.[41]

Drawing on and radicalising Feuerbach's materialist inversion of Hegel (though Marx is yet to write 'Theses on Feuerbach'), Marx quite comprehensively reworks this Hegelian problematic and narrative. 'On The Jewish Question' begins with the argument that Jews already achieve 'political emancipation' where a secular state—as distinct from a Christian state—is established. Such emancipation occurs because the state emancipates 'itself from the state religion, i.e. by not recognizing, as a state, any religion, by affirming itself simply as a state'.[42] This political emancipation Marx describes as 'a great progress', as even 'the final form of human emancipation inside the present world order'.

But 'On The Jewish Question' goes on to point out that with 'political emancipation' or the establishment of secular states, religion not only proliferates, but is transformed by its repositioning. Thus, 'North America is the land of religiosity *par excellence*'; and 'the fact that even in the land of completed political emancipation we find not only the existence of religion but a living existence full of freshness and strength furnishes us with the proof that the existence of religion does not contradict or impede the perfection of the [secular] state. But since the existence of religion is the existence of a defect, the source of this defect can only be sought in the nature of the state itself'. The defect shows that 'the state can be a free state without man himself being a free man'. With this observation, 'On the Jewish Question' embarks on its famous reworking of the Hegelian distinction between civil society and state:

> The perfected political state is by its nature the species-life of man in opposition to his material life. All the presuppositions of this egoistic life continue to exist in civil society outside the sphere of the state, but as proper to civil society. When the political state has achieved its true completion, man leads a double life, a heavenly one and an earthly one, not only in thought and consciousness but in reality, in life. He has a life both in the political community, where he is valued as a communal being, and in civil society, where he is active as a private individual, treats other men as means, degrades

---

[40] Speech by Dr. B.R. Ambedkar in the Constituent Assembly, 25 Nov. 1949, *Constituent Assembly Debates: Official Report*, Vol. XI (New Delhi: Government of India, 1949), p. 975.

[41] G.W.F. Hegel, *Elements of the Philosophy of Right* (H.B. Nisbet, trans; Allen Wood, ed.) (Cambridge: Cambridge University Press, 1991), § 270, pp. 291–303.

[42] Marx, 'On the Jewish Question', p. 51.

himself to a means, and becomes the plaything of alien powers. The political state has just as spiritual an attitude to civil society as heaven has to earth. It stands in the same opposition to civil society and overcomes it in the same manner as religion overcomes the limitations of the profane world, that is, it must likewise recognize it, reinstate it, and let itself once more be dominated by it. Man in the reality that is nearest to him, civil society, is a profane being. Here where he counts for himself and others as a real individual, he is an illusory phenomenon. In the state, on the other hand, where man counts as a species-being, he is an imaginary participant in an imaginary sovereignty, he is robbed of his real life and filled with an unreal universality.[43]

Here, I wish to draw attention to only three points about the unruly spectrality that rustles through this and related passages. First, the spectrality undoes Hegel's categories of civil society, where the bourgeois individual exercises his rights of man, and political society, where the rights of the citizen are exercised. In Marx's reading, by contrast, civil society is marked by an illusoriness—though here man counts for himself and others as a real individual, though here he is 'free for himself', civil society is concerned with 'egoistic life'. Religion itself is in the process transformed: it 'is no longer the spirit of the state where man behaves, as a species-being in community with other men albeit in a limited manner and in a particular form and a particular sphere: religion has become the spirit of civil society, the sphere of egoism, the *bellum omnium contra omnes* (war of all against all). Its essence is no longer in community but in difference'.[44] And this spectrality suffuses the political community too—only the state is free, not man. 'The state is the intermediary between man and his freedom. As Christ is the intermediary onto whom man unburdens all his divinity, all his religious bonds, so the state is the mediator onto which he transfers all his Godlessness and all his human liberty'.[45]

Second, and relatedly, the spectrality also undoes Hegel's presumption of a complementary relationship between civil society and the rights of man on the one hand, and the higher universality of the state and the rights of the citizen on the other. In Marx's reading, political society must let itself once more be dominated by civil society—the very civil society that Hegel describes as concerned with ends that 'are in the first instance purely private, particular and contingent'. In other words, the secular state is not dominant where the modern complex of state and civil society establishes itself. Rather, civil society, organised around the pursuit of private freedoms (whether those involved in capital or in religion), dominates: the secular state must 'recognize it, reinstate it, and let itself once more be dominated by it'.

Third, in 'On the Jewish Question', the state is Christian again because of a distinctive spectrality (rather than because, as in Hegel's account, the concept of religion is the absolute truth of freedom and reason). Thus Marx argues: 'In the so-called Christian state it is alienation (*Entfremdung*) that is important, not man himself'. This is so because the most important man, the king, remains apart from other men and in direct contact with the divine. Nevertheless, 'it is not the so-called Christian state, that one that recognizes Christianity as its basis, as the state religion, and thus adopts an exclusive attitude to other religions, that is the perfected Christian state, but rather the atheist state, the democratic state, the state that downgrades religion to the other elements of civil society'.[46] And secular democracy is 'the perfected Christian state' because it spectralises this spirit of Christianity:

---

[43] *Ibid.*, p. 53.
[44] *Ibid.*, p. 54.
[45] *Ibid.*, p. 52.
[46] *Ibid.*, p. 55.

What makes a political democracy Christian is the fact that in it man, not only a single man but every man, counts as a sovereign being; but it is man as he appears uncultivated and unsocial, man in his accidental existence, man as he comes and goes, man as he is corrupted by the whole organization of our society, lost to himself, sold, given over to the domination of inhuman conditions and elements—in a word, man who is no longer a real species-being. The fantasy, dream, and postulate of Christianity, the sovereignty of man, but of man as an alien being separate from actual man, is present in democracy as a tangible reality and is its secular motto.[47]

The implications of this spectral relationship between state, civil society and religion have often remained unexplored in the way we have thought these categories. Marx himself, as we shall see, turns away from it already in 'On the Jewish Question'. And liberal traditions around the term civil society, of course, continue to remain within the tradition that Hegel elaborates with such precision. The spectrality identified in 'On the Jewish Question' remains largely unexplored also in current re-figurings of the Hegelian understanding of secularism as a sublation of Christianity (which term itself functions as shorthand for Western Christian traditions). Most of these re-figurings only invert the Hegelian sublation rather than spectralise it, as Marx does. When Carl Schmitt, for instance, argues that '[a]ll significant concepts of the modern theory of state are secularized theological concepts' not only because of their historical origin, but also because 'their systemic structure', the sociology he uses to make this argument, is organised by the terms that were set out by Hegel.[48]

There is however a curious affinity between Marx's spectral reading and the arguments offered in Partha Chatterjee's *Lineages of Political Society*. The book suggests that while 'the new republic was founded on a liberal democratic constitution, universal suffrage, and competitive electoral representation', 'the space of politics became effectively split between a narrow domain of civil society where citizens related to the state through the mutual recognition of legally enforceable rights and a wider domain of political society where governmental agencies dealt not with citizens but with populations to deliver specific benefits or services through negotiation'. Indeed, 'the domain of civil social institutions and modern representative politics was, in most parts of the colonial world, restricted to only a small section of the colonized population'.[49]

Here, Hegel's categories of state and civil society are fused into 'civil society', which is conceived in terms akin to Hegel's state, and a new category, 'political society', is posited as outside civil society. Thus, 'civil society' itself continues to be understood in broadly Hegelian terms, or in terms of 'normative political theory', as distinct from the spectrality that comes to mark civil society in 'On the Jewish Question'. Indeed, I would suggest that what Chatterjee describes as 'political society' is precisely the spectral logic that the young Marx sees as constituting 'civil society', where man is 'active as a private individual, treats other

---

[47] *Ibid.*, p. 57.
[48] Carl Schmitt, *Political Theology* (Chicago, IL: University of Chicago Press, 2010), p. 50f. Elsewhere, Schmitt's concept of the enemy is explicitly derived from Hegel. Cf. Carl Schmitt, *The Concept of the Political* (George Schwab, trans.) (Chicago, IL: University of Chicago Press, 2007), p. 63. Even in contemporary scholarship, this Hegelian reading continues to be influential. Taylor's *A Secular Age* is not isolated in remaining deeply Hegelian, unmarked by Marx, or even Feuerbach. Much recent 'post-secular' scholarship, when it has criticised secularism for its Christianity, has done so by only inverting Hegel; it would not be unfair to say that this scholarship remains within the Hegelian problematic, practising what in Marx's terms would be 'critical criticism', rather than critique.
[49] Partha Chatterjee, *Lineages of Political Society* (New York: Columbia University Press, 2011), pp. 13–4.

men as means, degrades himself to a means, and becomes the plaything of alien powers'. Perhaps then a careful reading of 'On the Jewish Question' might suggest a new set of questions: is it necessary today to revisit Marx's insistence that there is only a spectral civil society? If yes, why—and where—must this spectral civil society exist along with a more conventionally Hegelian civil society?

V

I have not yet been able to ascertain whether Ambedkar ever read 'On the Jewish Question'. But whether he did or not, the questions that Marx encounters would have been his too, at the very least analogously. Like Marx's Jew, the Dalit too is amongst those outside the political community. But Ambedkar cannot respond the way Marx does in his explicit formulations; Ambedkar cannot dismiss the rights of man as only abstract or formal. If indeed Ambedkar ever read 'On the Jewish Question', at least two things would have occasioned the most profound disquiet in him. First, there is the curious disappearance in the essay of the Jew. 'It is in the North American states—or at least a part of them—that the Jewish question loses its theological importance for the first time and becomes a really *secular* question. It is only where the political state exists in its complete perfection that the relationship of the Jew and of the religious man in general to the political state, and thus the relationship of religion to the state, can stand out in all its peculiarities and purity'.[50] With political emancipation, the only space left for the Jew is in civil society, as 'religious man in general'. 'Religious man in general', egoistic man, civil society—this is what becomes dominant with political emancipation. Unlike in a Christian state, the Jew now becomes indistinguishable from the Christian; he is resolved into 'religious man in general'; he is no longer a minor as a Jew.

We know our Indian history, or for that matter our European history, well enough to know that this resolution of the minor never occurs in the way that Marx's explicit formulations posit. Indeed, it is precisely because that resolution never occurs, because civil society is spectral, that liberalism must create its concept of the minority—the marked figure who has to constantly prove his or her citizenship, who requires always 'tolerance…as a supplement to equality rather than a mere extension of it'.[51] And it is precisely because that tolerance is unstable that Arendt must return to the question of the rights of man and the rights of the citizen. (Aamir Mufti notes Arendt's response in her Lessing Prize Lecture: 'I cannot gloss over the fact that for many years I considered the only adequate reply to the question, Who are you? to be: A Jew. That answer alone took into account the reality of persecution. As for the statement with which Nathan the Wise (in effect, though not in actual wording), countered the command: "Step closer, Jew"—the statement: I am a man—I would have considered as nothing but a grotesque and dangerous evasion of reality'.[52])

Like Arendt, Ambedkar could never have accepted this resolution of the minor. Indeed, what is most thought provoking for Ambedkar as well as in Ambedkar, what may perhaps be described as the provocation that leads to Ambedkar's massive originality, is precisely his struggle with the question of the minor who remains after political emancipation.

---

[50] Marx, 'On the Jewish Question', p. 50.
[51] Wendy Brown, 'Tolerance and/or Equality: The "Jewish Question" and the "Woman Question"', in *Differences: A Journal of Feminist Cultural Studies*, Vol. 15, no. 2 (2004), p. 21. See also Gyanendra Pandey, 'Marked and Unmarked Citizens', in Gyanendra Pandey, *Routine Violence: Nations, Fragments, Histories* (Stanford, CA: Stanford University Press, 2006), pp. 129–53.
[52] Aamir Mufti, *Enlightenment in the Colony: The Jewish Question and the Question of Postcolonial Culture* (Princeton, NJ: Princeton University Press, 2007), p. 54.

The second thing that will have occasioned disquiet: even though Marx has not yet arrived at his thinking of the proletarian revolution, or of class, he already affirms instead 'human emancipation'. 'It is only the critique of political emancipation itself that would be the final critique of the Jewish question and its true resolution into "the general problems of the age"'.[53] Ambedkar's relationship with political emancipation is more tortured: he is only too acutely aware of the empowerment it also offers.

Perhaps because of these two divergences, Ambedkar is more faithful to the spectrality of 'On the Jewish Question' than Marx. For one could well ask: if political emancipation is spectral in the sense that 'On the Jewish Question' identifies, then does not political emancipation itself constantly produce, along with 'religious man in general', the figure of the minor—the Jew, the Muslim, or the 'other' who cannot be subsumed within the category 'religious man in general'?

Conversely, in order to question the ascription of minority, is not a certain political emancipation always to come? And if political emancipation can in this sense never be completed (and this is not a horizontal incompletion—the bad infinity of there always being more to accomplish, of pursuing a constantly receding goal), and must constantly be re-visited and re-formulated, then must not human emancipation itself be re-thought? Human emancipation can no longer overcome or sublate within it the moment of political emancipation—political emancipation is too spectral for sublation. Perhaps human emancipation must now be conceived rather as the challenge of constantly questioning and supplementing political emancipation.

An acute sensitivity to these questions ripples through that posthumously-published essay, 'Buddha or Karl Marx'. There, Ambedkar articulates what makes him uncomfortable about the violent 'means' involved in communism. He is willing to accept revolutionary or law-making violence: 'Dictatorship for a short period may be good and a welcome thing even for making Democracy safe'. But he is made hesitant by the apprehension (which he shares with Arendt) that revolutionary violence may continue without end—that unlike the project of political emancipation, which, after the revolutionary moment, requires law-preserving violence, the project of human emancipation envisioned by Marx(ism) requires a permanent regime of revolutionary violence: 'a Russian Dictatorship would be good for all backward countries. But this is no argument for permanent Dictatorship'.[54]

The essay contemplates quite another relationship with the founding moment of revolutionary violence: 'Why should not Dictatorship liquidate itself after it has done its work, after it has removed all the obstacles and boulders in the way of democracy and has made the path of Democracy safe? Did not Asoka set an example? He practised violence against the Kalingas. But thereafter he renounced violence completely. If our victors today not only disarm their victims but also disarm themselves there would be peace all over the world'.[55] To that renunciation of violence, to that other universality, Ambedkar gives in the essay the names 'religion' and Buddhism.

What is involved in religion here is indicated by his remark in 'Philosophy of Hinduism', the typescript of which was found amongst Ambedkar's papers after his death: 'Philosophy is static because it is concerned only with knowing truth. Religion is dynamic because it is concerned with love of truth'.[56] Here, as Udaya Kumar suggests, love 'may need to be

---

[53] Marx, 'On the Jewish Question', p. 49.
[54] Ambedkar, 'Buddha or Karl Marx', p. 461.
[55] Ibid., p. 459.
[56] B.R. Ambedkar, 'Philosophy of Hinduism', in *Dr. Babasaheb Ambedkar, Writings and Speeches, Vol. 3* (Bombay: Government of Maharashtra, 1987), pp. 86–7, also available online [http://www.ambedkar.org/ambcd/17.Philosophy%20of%20Hinduism.htm, accessed 16 April 2015]. I thank Sanil V. for drawing my attention to and discussing this passage; my reading in what follows has also been shaped by a personal communication, cited earlier, from Udaya Kumar on 10 Jan. 2015.

understood in terms of a mode of subjectivation akin to that of passion, and "dynamic" in terms of "being affected by" as much as "acting on"'. Involved here, as in the call earlier to take refuge in reason, is the acknowledgment that a certain surrender of autonomy may itself be most proper to autonomy. And Ambedkar comes to Navayana Buddhism as the articulation of how this surrender should proceed. (Thus, in the unpublished preface to *The Buddha and His Dhamma*, he says: '[I]f a modern man who knows science must have a religion, the only religion he can have is the religion of the Buddha'.)

If we are to briefly indicate how Navayana Buddhism is such a religion of reason, or how reason works when it is not a civil religion but a refuge, perhaps we should attend to Ambedkar's rendering in *The Buddha and His Dhamma* of the moment when Siddhartha Gautama takes the oath of *parivraja* or wandering mendicancy and starts on the path that makes him the Buddha. Siddhartha is a member of the Sakya kingdom, which seems marked by at least some of the traits of political emancipation: '[T]he Sakyas had their Sangh (association). Every Sakya youth above twenty had to be initiated into the Sangh and be a member of the Sangh'.[57] The *sangh* moreover privileges fearless speech and truth-telling.

The *senapati* or warrior head of the Sakyas, the kingdom to which Siddhartha Gautama belongs, calls a meeting of the Sakya *sangh* to 'consider the question of declaring war on the Koliyas', a neighbouring kingdom whose inhabitants had been involved in clashes with the Sakyas over the waters of the river Rohini. Siddhartha opposes this, suggesting that both are at fault, and that the dispute should be settled. The *senapati* responds (and the spectre of Krishna is evident here) that 'the Kshatriyas cannot make a distinction between warriors and strangers. They must fight even against brothers for the sake of their kingdom'. Siddhartha replies: 'Dharma, as I understand it, consists in recognizing that enmity does not disappear by enmity. It can be conquered by love only'. The *senapati*'s resolution carries the day. At the next day's meeting, the *senapati* proposes that 'he be permitted to proclaim calling to arms' every Sakya between the ages of twenty and fifty. Now 'the minority who had voted against it had a problem to face. Their problem was—to submit or not to the decision of the majority. The minority was determined not to submit to the majority'.[58]

In this moment, *The Buddha and His Dhamma* shears away dizzyingly from the problematic of political emancipation. By not submitting to the majority, the minority abandons the protocols of political society and civil society, for these require that the minority must—even if it protests against or criticises the law—also do what the law or political society enjoins.[59] By not submitting, the minority refuses its part in political society, becomes no longer a minority.

But this refusal to submit to the majority carries its own entailments. The *sangh* can impose a social boycott on Siddhartha's family and confiscate his family lands. Wishing to avoid this, Siddhartha speaks to the *sangh*: 'Please do not punish my family…. They are innocent. I am the guilty person. Let me alone suffer for my wrong. Sentence me to death or exile, whichever you like. I will willingly accept it, and I promise I shall not appeal to the king of the Kosalas'. The *senapati* says that the *sangh* may face reprisals from the king even if Siddhartha voluntarily undergoes the sentence of death or exile. Siddhartha then suggests: 'I can become a Parivrajaka and leave this country. It is a kind of exile'.[60]

---

[57] Ambedkar, *The Buddha and His Dhamma*, Book 1, Section 13.
[58] *Ibid.*, Book 1, Section 15.
[59] These protocols are already implicit in Kant's injunction, 'Argue as much as you want and about what you want, but obey!'. See Immanuel Kant, 'An Answer to the Question: What is Enlightenment?', in Ted Humphrey (trans.), *Perpetual Peace and Other Essays* (Indianapolis, IN: Hackett, 1983), p. 42.
[60] Ambedkar, *The Buddha and His Dhamma*, Book 1, Section 15.

One must add: but only a kind of exile. Voluntary acceptance of death or exile: this would be to submit to the political community. Because that submission is not possible, Siddhartha becomes instead a *parivrajaka*, leaves the country. But as a *parivrajaka*, he submits not to the political community, but to the call to *parivraja*. If this is an exile, it is so only in the sense that it converges with the exile the *sangh* as a political community wants. Later in the narrative, moreover, his exile becomes only *parivraja*—the dispute is resolved, many in the Sakyan kingdom would like to have him come back, but now *parivraja* has seized him.

One must also add: Siddhartha can choose to appeal to the king of Kosala. If he successfully did so, he would re-make the political community, and become the majority. This option becomes even more forcefully available later in the narrative, when the king, Bimbisara, offers Siddhartha his army if necessary to fight foes. But Siddhartha again refuses. His defiance of the majority is in other words accompanied by a refusal to become the majority, or to overcome the existing majority.

In both these senses, Siddhartha Gautama seeks a curious role with the political society he questions. He does not destroy it; he does not have or want a part in it; he participates without a part. This participation without a part, without sovereignty—this is the first statement of the Buddha's religion.

That first statement must encounter and re-work itself through several questions. For now, in lieu of a conclusion, I wish only to note two. First, Ambedkar is acutely aware of his homelessness, his exile from India. The book is written after all by the man who famously tells Gandhi, 'Mahatmaji, I have no country'.[61] What is the relationship between this exile and the Buddha's *parivraja*? Second, as one of the authors of the Indian Constitution, Ambedkar writes the protocols of what Marx would call political society, and makes sure the minority has a part in it. What is the relationship between the part which the minority has, and its being minor, or its partless participation in *parivraja*?

---

[61] Cited in Viswanathan, *Outside the Fold*, p. 219.

Jurisprudence of Emergence: Neo-Liberalism and the Public as Market in India

RITU BIRLA, *University of Toronto, Ontario, Canada*

Highlighting legal–governmental techniques by which the public is conceptualised as the market and market activity as public agency, this article poses India as a key site for a globalised analysis of neo-liberal governance. It opens a genealogy for India's 'emerging market' governance that extends back to colonial modernisation, highlighting ties between a coercive state, its benevolent performance and the making of a market society. Such a long view challenges the free market vs. strong state opposition so central to contemporary neo-liberal thought. It also calls attention to the nexus between powers of emergency and emerging markets. Elaborating, the essay engages Foucault's analysis of neo-liberal political economy to read recent Indian jurisprudence on financial markets, the rule of law, and public interest.

In October 2013, six months before his ascent to India's prime ministership, Narendra Modi spoke via videoconferencing to the Global Meeting of Emerging Markets Forum in Washington, DC. As might be expected, his speech presented India as a global centre for democratic values. To further these, he conveyed an agenda for 'system-based and policy-driven' governance, explaining that people would be ready 'to accept tough decisions by governments once they are convinced [these] are for the greater good'. He emphasised that '[i]n a democracy, listening to people is a must' and that the real challenge for good governance 'is that we take government to be a *provider* and people as beneficiaries [and this]…is preventing people from being active partners in development'. Therefore, if 'today we talk about representative democracy', now 'we have to…move towards participatory democracy and increase the level of participation of people'.[1] Shifting the emphasis from democracy as a system of political representation to democracy as participatory economic development, Modi also referenced the colonial political economy and the construction of India as a market for British goods. He asserted that 'emerging markets' may not be an accurate reflection or productive title for the countries to which it refers, for it would be wrong to treat countries just as markets: 'Instead of calling these countries

---

I delivered a very early version of this article for the Carol Breckenridge Memorial Lecture at the New School University, New York, on 15 Sept. 2014. My thanks are due to the Department of History at the New School for Social Research and Eugene Lang College of the New School for Liberal Studies for this invitation and opportunity, and also to Arjun Appadurai, Cathy Davidson, Ritty Lukose, Oz Frankel and Jake Short for post-lecture inputs. The title is a play on an important study in Indian legal history that examines the state, but not markets: Nasser Hussain's *Jurisprudence of Emergency: Colonialism and the Rule of Law* (Ann Arbor: University of Michigan Press, 2003).

[1] Gyan Varma, 'Narendra Modi Stresses on Democracy at US Forum', livemint.com (14 Oct. 2013) [http://www.livemint.com/Politics/5ZjKXr0pgoH6yGZbtva2XI/Narendra-Modi-stresses-on-democracy-at-US-forum.html?utm_source=ref_article, accessed 26 July 2014].

markets, they can be called emerging growth centres'.[2] In other words, India should not be seen as *just* a market to be exploited and, therefore, as a global periphery as in colonial times; rather, it should be recognised as a centre in an emergent global market order, one that provides an exceptionally hospitable home for transnational capital.

Modi's vision of democracy evokes a foundational opposition in contemporary neo-liberal thought: the state and its coddling of the public on the one hand, and citizenship as market participation on the other. At same time, his fine-tuning of the concept of the 'emerging market' relies on an active interpretation of India's colonial history that at once performs an anti-colonial script in service of nativist pride (that is, India should not be perceived as just an exploitable consumer market) *and* a hyper-marketised world-view. Modi's reproduction, as well as fine-tuning, of neo-liberal ideas evinces the continued relevance of India's colonial history in contemporary political and economic imaginaries, global as well as local.

Attentive to this relevance, this essay emphasises that histories of colonial liberalism inform global genealogies of neo-liberal governing and contemporary globality itself. Informed by the Indian colonial legal institutionalisation of the market as the name for the public, a project undertaken as a benevolent implementation of the rule of law, I open a colonial genealogy of the neo-liberal public, understood as constituted by competitive market actors and entrepreneurs. In shifting from 'representative' democracy to 'participatory' democracy-cum-economic development, Modi's agenda can be located within India's long history of political economy as a master discourse of governing, one that dates to the origins of the British political economy and its prolific governmental laboratory, the English East India Company, and continues through its colonial liberal and then national developmentalist regimes. De-emphasising languages of popular sovereignty, representation and political rights, Modi foregrounds the people's economic agency as market actors—and, indeed, seeks to define the very concept of 'the people' through the agency of the market; political democracy here gives way to languages of economic freedom. To paraphrase Foucault, civil society becomes an arrangement of economic men.[3]

Foucault's potent formulation is to be found in his Collège de France lectures on 'The Birth of Biopolitics', which address political economy as the ground for liberal governmentality as well as for the emergence of neo-liberal thought and its political rationality.[4] Significantly, he emphasises that the discourse of governing that is political economy emerges just as late eighteenth-century languages of juridical sovereignty transform concepts of absolute sovereign right into the modern social contract. That is, just as the sovereignty of 'the people' and citizenship rights emerge to oust the coercive authority of absolute sovereignty, political economy's biopolitical techniques take centre-stage. I have argued that law is a key site for pursuing this play of juridical sovereignty and technologies of government and administration, most especially in the colonial contexts that Foucault leaves unaddressed. Elaborating, this essay considers first how the colonial legal coding of the public as market resonates with classical neo-liberal thought and, then, how it is incarnated in contemporary Indian jurisprudence, most especially in key questions that grapple with the

---

[2] *Ibid*.
[3] Michel Foucault, *The Birth of Biopolitics: Lectures at the Collège de France 1978–79* (New York: Palgrave Macmillan, 2008), Chap. 12. See also Colin Gordon, 'Governmental Rationality', in G. Burchell, C. Gordon and P. Miller (eds), *The Foucault Effect* (Chicago, IL: University of Chicago Press, 1991), pp. 1–52.
[4] Attentive to political economy's wide range of schools from the late eighteenth century, these lectures map it as a potent modern arrangement of power directed at managing political subjects as bodies and populations, ultimately through the production of an isolated sector of reality, that is, 'the economy'. Michel Foucault, 'Governmentality', in G. Burchell, C. Gordon and P. Miller (eds), *The Foucault Effect* (Chicago, IL: University of Chicago Press, 1991), pp. 87–104.

sovereign representation of public interest and the exercise of public agency—by the state *and* by market institutions.

More specifically, this investigation considers how a genealogy of the idea of public that is attentive to colonial market governance configures and challenges a foundational distinction articulated by neo-liberal thought: the distinction between an oppressive and/or interventionist state (socialist, communist, or liberal nanny-state) and the freedom of the market. When seen in a broad historical frame, the legal–political imaginaries emerging in India's economic liberalisation direct us to the intimacies between a strong, even authoritarian, state and the production of free market agency, as subjectivised in the name of 'the public' and mediated through the rule of law. I thus build on Foucault and important recent studies of the history of neo-liberal thought and policy, as well as the established study of liberalism and empire, to launch an examination of *neo-liberalism and empire*.

After a framing discussion in this vein, I delve into jurisprudence, highlighting an iconic case in the recent history of Indian public interest litigation that foregrounds globally-relevant moves in contemporary neo-liberal governing: moves that weave the state's responsibilities for representation and provision into those of market-based association. Launched in 1995 by the State of West Bengal on behalf of its poor citizens against fraudulent small savings and investment companies, this case exposes, counter-intuitively, a coding of citizens as market actors first and foremost. This relationship between a strong post-colonial state that at once performs benevolence and at the same time buttresses market society is echoed in a concomitant flurry of judgements concerning stock markets that I will also review. As such, I foreground the emergence of India's brand of neo-liberalism, one that both echoes and challenges neo-liberal orthodoxy by fuelling a liberalised marketplace through an assertive state, and by deploying the rule of law not as a limit to coercive authority, but as a medium for its force through the powers of administration.

Neo-Liberalism, Empire and the Rule of Law

Neo-liberal governmentality has been associated with the commercialisation and financialisation of public space, agencies and agency, and the erosion of political democracy.[5] As important recent work elaborating Foucault's approach emphasises, 'far from being an ideology or economic policy', neo-liberalism has emerged as a governmental rationality characterised by 'the generalisation of competition as a behavioral norm and of enterprise as a model of subjectivation', one that challenges and reconfigures the very notion of citizenship.[6] The neo-liberal turn marks a shift from a language of political to economic freedom: thus, as Keith Tribe has argued, for a foundational neo-liberal thinker like Friedrich Hayek, 'the "market" is an abstract, not a substantive, entity; the "perfect market" is the counterpart of the liberal state'. Thus, Hayek's 'road to freedom' runs 'through the [free] market to political liberty, and not the other way around'.[7] India is a significant site for examining such a shift and placing it in a global historical frame, not least because its colonial history demands close attention to the

---

[5] For a detailed theoretical elaboration of this argument, see Wendy Brown, 'Neoliberalism and the End of Liberal Democracy', in *Theory and Event*, Vol. 7, no. 1 (Nov. 2003), pp. 1–25. See also 'American Nightmare: Neoliberalism, Neoconservatism, and De-Democratization', in *Political Theory*, Vol. 34, no. 6 (Dec. 2006), pp. 690–714.

[6] Pierre Dardot and Christian Laval, *The New Way of the World: On Neoliberal Society* (New York: Verso Books, 2014), p. 4.

[7] Keith Tribe, 'Liberalism and Neoliberalism in Britain, 1930–1980', in P. Mirowski and D. Plehwe (eds), *The Road from Mont Pèlerin: The Making of the Neoliberal Thought Collective* (Cambridge, MA: Harvard University Press, 2009), pp. 68–97, quotation at pp. 76–7.

intimate workings of political and economic liberalism—and, indeed, the emergence of languages of political liberty *after* the implementation of the abstract market. Colonial authority institutionalised the public as a new, abstract site of governance: an all-India arena for the free circulation of capital, the economy.[8] After 1947, India moved from imperial subjecthood to a developmentalist bureaucratic–administrative nation-state marked by its authoritarian colonial ancestry, as condensed in the emergency powers written into its Constitution.[9]

In contrast, articulating a rupture from the colonial–national, policies of economic liberalisation, which officially launched India's emerging market brand in 1991, have expressed a heavy state versus market freedom distinction. Indeed, liberalisation's master script spoke of the dismantling of 'licence Raj', or the tangled web of bureaucratic rules regulating business in India. The language of economic liberalisation has thus celebrated a radical discontinuity from earlier periods of state interventionism. However, the long colonial view draws attention to the continuities between a strong state and the making of a market society.

The Indian story has much to offer the important new burst of research on the history of neo-liberal thought and practice. Recent studies focusing on the emergence of neo-liberal thought back to the 1920s have significantly elaborated on Foucault's mapping. They have supplemented his primary attention to the economic liberalism of the Chicago School and German Ordo-Liberalism by investigating differences in regional and national trajectories of the neo-liberal political economy; the work of key thinkers only touched upon by Foucault such as Ludwig von Mises and Friedrich Hayek; the role of think-tanks, institution-building and intellectual entrepreneurship; and by more extensively detailing the neo-liberal revision of classical liberalism.[10] Nevertheless, this new work attests to Foucault's prophetic instincts in investigating the shift from liberal to neo-liberal governmentality, and its long history, which is not to be seen as just a late twentieth-century phenomenon. Indeed, recent research has sought to further extend the genealogy of neo-liberalism from the 1920s back to the late nineteenth century.[11] This important gesture demands multi-sited, grounded attention to the defining global formation of this era, one that remains largely absent from current studies—

---

[8] Ritu Birla, *Stages of Capital: Law, Culture and Market Governance in Late Colonial India* (Durham, NC: Duke University Press, 2009).

[9] Important discussions of the shift and continuities from developmentalist to neo-liberal state can be found in Niraja Gopal Jayal, *Citizenship and Its Discontents: An Indian History* (Cambridge, MA: Harvard University Press, 2013); Atul Kohli, *Democracy and Development in India: From Socialism to Pro-Business* (New Delhi: Oxford University Press, 2010); and Subir Sinha, 'Lineages of the Developmentalist State: Transnationality and Village India, 1900–1965', in *Comparative Studies in Society and History*, Vol. 50, no. 1 (Jan. 2008), pp. 57–90. On developmentalist to neo-liberal political economy, see Francine R. Frankel, *India's Political Economy, 1974–2004: The Gradual Revolution* (Oxford: Oxford University Press, 2005); on the post-Independence national economy, see Manu Goswami, *Producing India: From Colonial Economy to National Space* (Chicago, IL: University of Chicago Press, 2004). For an excellent comparative reading of the emergence of the neo-liberal political economy in Chile, Mexico, Britain and France, see Marion Fourcade-Gournichas and Sarah L. Babb, 'The Rebirth of the Liberal Creed: Paths to Neoliberalism in Four Countries', in *American Journal of Sociology*, Vol. 8, no. 2 (Nov. 2002), pp. 533–79.

[10] See P. Mirowski and D. Plehwe (eds), *The Road from Mont Pèlerin: The Making of the Neoliberal Thought Collective* (Cambridge, MA: Harvard University Press, 2009); Angus Burgin, *The Great Persuasion: Reinventing Free Markets since the Depression* (Cambridge, MA: Harvard University Press, 2012); Daniel Stedman Jones, *Masters of the Universe: Hayek, Friedman, and the Birth of Neoliberal Politics* (Princeton, NJ: Princeton University Press, 2012); and Nicholas Gane, 'The Emergence of Neoliberalism: Thinking Through and Beyond Michel Foucault's Lecture on Biopolitics', in *Theory, Culture and Society*, Vol. 31, no. 4 (July 2014), pp. 3–27. Gane has emphasised that Foucault's reading of liberalism remains narrow, with a focus on Smith and Bentham and no attention to thinkers such as J.S. Mill.

[11] Gane, 'The Emergence of Neoliberalism', pp. 3–27.

that is, empire.[12] Working from colonial and post-colonial sites illuminates not only new trajectories of neo-liberal governmental rationality, it also highlights aspects of it that may go less noticed in the context of Europe and the United States. Thus, by addressing the relationship of liberalism and neo-liberalism via India and its history of colonial market governance, I foreground here the operation of a key feature of classical neo-liberal thought that remains unelaborated in recent studies, though it is very robustly engaged by Foucault himself: the operation of the rule of law and its relationship with administration. I will now briefly highlight this significant thread in his analysis as an outline for the reading of the Indian case law to follow.

A Juridico-Economic Order: Resonances of Colonial Liberalism

Foucault's attention to the rule of law emerges in his explication of the role of juridical sovereignty in neo-liberal governmental rationality, which poses itself against authoritarian fascist and communist states as well as interventionist liberal ones. Did neo-liberals, therefore, call for weak states, as contemporary iterations seem to demand? In fact, as Foucault and recent research has emphasised, classical neo-liberals did not abandon the idea of a strong state, but conceptualised one that would perform itself as a backdrop to the market order, a non-interventionist framework enabling the re-casting of the social as the theatre of market competition, constituted by entrepreneurs. As such, the draft of the Statement of Aims presented by the first meeting of the Mont Pèlerin Society in 1947 asserted that 'the preservation of an effective competitive order depends upon a proper legal and institutional framework'. Its final version called for 'the redefinition of the functions of the state so as to distinguish more clearly between the totalitarian and the liberal order', demanding 'methods of reestablishing the rule of law' for this purpose.[13]

The rule of law thus becomes a powerful medium for the inscription of the public as market. Indeed, Foucault emphasises that neo-liberalism is at its heart a *juridico-economic order* built on a tight bond between law and economy apparent even in its ancestors, founders of utilitarianism such as Jeremy Bentham. Discussing a key moment in the birth of neo-liberal thought, the Walter Lippman Colloquium of 1939, he finds that 'the juridical gives form to the economic, and the economic would not be what it is without the juridical.... [I]nstead of distinguishing between an economic belonging to the infrastructure and a juridical-political belonging to the superstructure, we should in reality speak of an economic-juridical order'.[14] Significantly, and outside Foucault's purview, the institutionalisation of the economy as the primary object of governance in British India also evinced a powerful juridico-economic order. This was manifest in an intense flurry of law and jurisprudence directed at enforcing the free circulation of capital that standardised procedures for companies, trusts, negotiable instruments, finance and speculation, all the while delegitimising the embedded networks of the bazaar as anachronistic

---

[12] One exception is Dieter Plehwe, 'The Origins of Neoliberal Development Discourse', in P. Mirowski and D. Plehwe (eds), *The Road from Mont Pèlerin: The Making of the Neoliberal Thought Collective* (Cambridge, MA: Harvard University Press, 2009), pp. 238–79. Plehwe addresses post-colonial developmentalism, which is a key channel for post-war liberal imperialism in projects such as the US Marshall Plan. Tribe, 'Liberalism and Neoliberalism in Britain', pp. 68–97, also takes account of the pressures of empire in the inter-war period.

[13] 'Draft of the Statement of Aims of the Mont Pèlerin Society, 7 April 1947, and final Statement of Aims, 8 April 1947', cited in P. Mirowski and D. Plehwe, *The Road from Mont Pèlerin: The Making of the Neoliberal Thought Collective* (Cambridge, MA: Harvard University Press, 2009), pp. 23–5.

[14] Foucault, *Birth of Biopolitics*, p. 163. Foucault's embrace of Weber to finesse historically determinist Marxism is clear here. The Walter Lippman Colloquium was organised by French philosopher Louis Rougier. Its prominent attendees included the American journalist after whom it was named, Ludwig von Mises, Friedrich Hayek and Alexander Rüstow. For more on this history, see Burgin, *The Great Persuasion*, pp. 55–78.

cultural practices to be governed by personal law. Legitimised as a benevolent civilising mission, colonial market governance in the period from about 1870 to 1930 installed the rule of law in the name of 'general public utility', and so installed the market as the site for an all-India public.[15] Colonial market governance thus offers a genealogical link across classical economic liberalism/*laissez-faire*, utilitarian government, and the neo-liberal.

The relationship between law and economy provides a sharp historical as well as analytical lens for investigating neo-liberal conceptualisations of governing, which forged ties between ideas of market freedom, competition and vigilance. As Foucault illuminates, neo-liberals were less interested in *laissez-faire* than they were in a panoptical vigilance, which was tied closely to their fortified concept of social competition. Competition was not to be seen as an anti-social force; instead, it marked the very ground for social vitality and progress. For this reason, neo-liberals confronted monopoly, which they understood as a coercive arm of the state (like the East India Company and other early joint stock monopolies), rather than as part of the very economic and historical logic of capitalist markets.[16] Monopoly was to be combatted by ensuring the ongoing play of competition, which would be accomplished by producing a *legal framework* to buttress and motivate it. Through a special emphasis on the rule of law as framing the market, these classical neo-liberal thinkers *promoted vigilance even as they staged the freedom of the market as radically distinct from state coercion*.[17] And this was their innovation: overarching vigilance, they asserted, was not the same thing as authoritarian state control. Vigilance belonged to the realm of law, which they distinguished from the coercive exercise of direct sovereignty that is police power.[18]

To position market society as the result of a *legal order*, neo-liberals emphasised 'a difference of kind, effect, and origin between on the one hand, laws, which are universally valid general measures and in themselves acts of sovereignty, and on the other hand, the particular decisions of public authorities'.[19] Here, the rule of law operates as a prophylactic against a coercive, interventionist and/or authoritarian state because it articulates sovereignty and renders it necessarily distinct from the powers of administration and policing (that is, the 'particular decisions of public authorities'). Neo-liberals thus distinguished between the rule of law and the practices of administration, which, if merged, would produce an arbitrary police state.[20] Indeed, this distinction is a key contribution of British liberalism (and empire) to the neo-liberal fold: Foucault emphasises that in the United Kingdom (unlike in Germany and France), there is no system of administrative courts because public appeals against the state cannot be arbitrated by the state itself; instead, 'the Rule of Law is a state in which citizens can appeal to ordinary justice against the public authorities'.[21] This legal history lives robustly, as we shall see, in recent Indian jurisprudence on the public interest.

The inauguration of neo-liberal thought was thus characterised by fortification of the rule of law as *a limit* to state-based public authority. With its focus on the rule of law, the early neo-liberal world-view speaks directly to colonial market governance. In mid twentieth-century United States, Britain and Europe, the rule of law was posited as the antithesis of the coercive

---

[15] On the installation of the public and the modern public/private distinction as an economy/culture distinction, see Birla, *Stages of Capital*.

[16] Foucault, *Birth of Biopolitics*, pp. 133–4.

[17] *Ibid.*, pp. 136–7. The question of a juridico-legal framework, which depoliticises as it structures and conveys power, evokes the process of what Timothy Mitchell has called 'enframing'. See Timothy Mitchell, *Rule of Experts: Egypt, Techno-Politics, Modernity* (Berkeley: University of California Press, 2002).

[18] Foucault, *Birth of Biopolitics*, pp. 133–4.

[19] *Ibid.*, p. 169.

[20] *Ibid.*, pp. 169–70.

[21] *Ibid.*, p. 170.

state. However, in colonial India, the seat of liberalism and empire, the rule of law had been the very manifestation of an authoritarian state, while the juridico-economic order it instituted—the public as market—emerged in consonance with a regime of policing and coercive, if not obviously despotic, authority. Colonial market governance sheds light on the ways in which the rule of law, articulated as a civilising mission, may operate as a technology of governing that fortifies absolute sovereignty through powers of administration, rather than democratic representation, thus coding the public *as subjects of a benevolent authority and, at the same time, as instruments of market policy*. We must remember that colonialism's utilitarian investment in the rule of law, a major story in the globalisation of contract law, sought to install modern forms of social association grounded in the contractual relations of individual subjects, who were coded first and foremost as economic actors.[22] The very inscription of the market coincided with the production of an abstract, all-India public, not a citizenry, but the object of the paternal civilising project of colonial policy. Moreover, as the colonial state gave way to the developmentalist nation-state, it may be argued that the rule of law fortified, rather than limited, bureaucratic–administrative authority, again in the name of public agency.

A product of this history, India's brand of neo-liberalism challenges the logic of classical neo-liberal orthodoxy *and* exposes its workings by deploying the rule of law, not as a limit to sovereignty, but *as a medium for its force through the powers of administration*. Moreover, this fortification of administrative power, which is enabled by judicial activism and operates in a language of liberal benevolence, introduces and buttresses the neo-liberal coding of society as a free market. These processes are starkly illustrated in a dense and significant moment in the consolidation of India's public interest law, a 1995 Calcutta High Court judgement on a petition launched by the Government of West Bengal in the name of the public interest to protect countless poor, extremely small depositors against a class of fraudulent institutions in the early years of economic liberalisation. Delving first into this case, I then briefly review recent cases on stock markets and their public duties to elaborate on the relationship between public interest and market agency being forged in India's emerging market jurisprudence.

Liberalising Markets/Publics: *The State of West Bengal vs. Union of India and Others, 1995*

Distinguished by its adjudicating bench as a rare and potent case in the unique history of public interest litigation in India, *The State of West Bengal vs. Union of India and Others, 1995*, saw the West Bengal government petition the Government of India *on behalf of* depositors for relief against 'mushrooming' Residuary Non-Banking Companies (RNBCs).[23] These were

---

[22] Birla, *Stages of Capital*.

[23] *State of West Bengal vs. Union of India and Others, 1995*, AIR 1996 Cal 181. For a critical mapping of the emergence of public interest litigation in India as a mechanism of judicial activism, dissimulation of populist ideals, and sovereign exceptions after the Emergency, see Anuj Bhuwania, 'Courting the People: The Rise of Public Interest Litigation in Post-Emergency India', in *Comparative Studies of South Asia, Africa, and the Middle East*, Vol. 34, no. 2 (Nov. 2014), pp. 314–5. Bhuwania reads public interest litigation, or PIL, through tensions found in the Indian Constitution between the Directive Principles and the Fundamental Rights, via Uday Mehta's analysis. Mehta poses the Directive Principles as motivated by the project of social revolution, legitimising the powers of sovereignty (as in the French Revolution), while the Fundamental Rights articulate limits to sovereign power. See Uday Singh Mehta, 'Constitutionalism', in Niraja Gopal Jayal and Pratap Bhanu Mehta (eds), *The Oxford Companion to Politics in India* (Oxford: Oxford University Press, 2010), pp. 15–27. Attending to the genealogy of the public as market elaborates the legal–constitutional analysis of the authoritarian incarnations of state, for, as I argue here, it is neo-liberal governmentality, grounded in market sovereignty, that stages both these constitutional projects concomitantly, *through* the language of the rule of law. For a review of PIL from a predominant liberal social-welfare narrative, see Surya Deva, 'Public Interest Litigation in India', in *Civil Justice Quarterly*, Vol. 28, no. 1 (June 2009), pp. 19–40.

small deposit/investment companies that received 'large deposits from the members of the public and specially from ignorant small depositors having little capital of their own' and then siphoned off funds, 'rendering the small depositors penniless and deprived of their life savings'.[24] West Bengal petitioned the Government of India to apply the 1987 Reserve Bank of India Directions for RNBCs. These were federal directives promulgated in service of the public interest, to safeguard small depositors. Furthering and citing a wave of judicial activism beginning in the early 1980s that had initiated the very concept of public interest litigation in India, the Calcutta High Court ultimately supported the State of West Bengal in its request, resulting in what seemed to be the state's triumphant protection of its citizens.

At first glance then, here, the public appears first and foremost as citizens represented actively by a strong and benevolent state enacting the responsibilities of a liberal social-welfare regime. Members of the public are not conceived as market actors subject to the contingencies of market fluctuations in the name of limited liability, which protects companies under company law. But in its long deliberation of the case, the Calcutta High Court's careful review of the RNBCs' points of opposition to the petition reveals a more complex picture. Here, in an extensive elaboration of precedents on public interest, the Court's logic and deployment of precedent evinces an intimate relationship between the state and the liberalising market, marking the inheritance of a strong colonial–national state at the official launch of India's liberalisation and neo-liberal market society.

The RNBCs' two main oppositions concerned, first, the authority of the West Bengal state to even institute the petition to the Government of India; and, second, the appropriateness of public interest litigation in the first place because, the RNBCs claimed, *they were not public institutions*. The first claim argued that the State of West Bengal had absolutely no cause for action (*locus standi*) because the very subject matter of the litigation could not be pursued by the state—only citizens (as enabled by the Constitution) could initiate writ petitions to demand such remedies.[25] Citing an earlier precedent, the respondents emphasised that public interest litigation is 'about the content and conduct of governmental action in relation to the Constitutional or Statutory rights of segments of Society'.[26] The RNBCs argued that the state, therefore, could not initiate public interest litigation, for this legal process is meant specifically as a check on 'governmental action' and state power. Thus, they asserted that in this case, *the state had illegitimately tried to launch public interest litigation against itself* because West Bengal had called upon the Government of India to exercise federal directives against the RNBCs. Concomitantly, they also argued that public interest litigation, which is a process of public law, has no bearing on non-governmental institutions like RNBCs.

---

[24] *State of West Bengal vs. Union of India and Others, 1995*.
[25] Articles 32, 139 and 226 of the Indian Constitution govern writ petitions. Article 32, part of the Constitution's Fundamental Rights section, is itself a fundamental right that empowers citizens to petition the Indian Supreme Court to issue writs to remedy the breach of any fundamental right. Article 139 allows the Supreme Court to enforce rights other than fundamental rights. Article 226 outlines the power of the High Courts to issue writs in the case of the state's breach of fundamental rights and 'for any other purpose'. The petition in the case being discussed here calls for the Supreme Court to issue the writ of mandamus (Latin: 'we command'), which gives the right to secure the performance of a public duty. The question here, then, is whether the RNBCs are considered to have a public duty. The very language of the writ—of authority and command—sits comfortably here with the project of public duty.
[26] The respondents here cited Justice J. Venkatachaliah's statement in *Sheela Barse vs. Union of India and Ors on 29 August, 1988*, JT 1988 (3) 15, which confronted the Supreme Court's procedures and claims to administer the public interest. This 1988 case was a follow-up to a precedent-setting 1986 public interest case, *Sheela Barse and Another vs. Union of India, 1986*, AIR 1773, on the detention of minors.

Building a rigorous state versus market distinction, the RNBCs also asserted that the Reserve Bank of India Directions that the state wished to activate could not be implemented through the public interest mechanism, for these directive principles could only be 'applicable in making laws' and not for instituting litigation and/or securing the relief of depositors. Put differently, the arguments of the RNBCs here echoed the classic neo-liberal call to the rule of law as the *limit to* sovereignty, thus distinguishing between the correct use of the Reserve Bank of India Directions—the right to make laws—and their incorrect deployment as instruments of government administration. However, at the same time, the representatives of the RNBCs also reinforced the authority of the state, arguing that institutions of state, and not market, are the media for public agency. Here, in their second major claim, they asserted that public interest litigation could not apply against RNBCs because these financial institutions *are not public institutions*. Because RNBCs had been incorporated under the Companies Act, they should be addressed under this statute, which governs limited liability companies. With this response, the RBNCs asserted that the state's petition actually sought to extend the instruments of state by defining RNBCs as public institutions with public responsibilities, which they are not.[27]

The Court addressed these claims first by asking whether 'a public interest litigation can be initiated by the State when normally…it is initiated by a public spirited person or association'.[28] The judgement proceeded by systematically mapping key precedents in the history of public interest litigation that had defined the concept of public interest very broadly in order to render the concept applicable to a wide range of institutions that could include the state itself. To buttress the state's claim to the public interest cause, the bench argued for a robust application of the rule of law: 'the rule of law must win the aggrieved person for the law Court and wean him from the law-less street. In simple terms, *locus standi* (or the cause for action in the public interest) *must be liberalised* to meet the challenges of the times'.[29]

The Court's logic belies a new version of the public to suit 'the challenges of the times': *economic liberalisation required a liberalisation of the idea of the public*, one that at once strengthened the powers of state *and* coded market institutions as having public duties. In this vein, citing an Indian Supreme Court case from 1981, where the terminology of public interest had been deployed for the first time, the Calcutta High Court employed an established principle of equity law and a governmental–legal tool for the fortification of administrative (as opposed to representative) powers. This was the principle of *ubi jus ibi remedium*—'where there is a right there is a remedy': an injury to a right produces a reciprocal requirement, the application of a remedy.[30] Referring to an earlier Supreme Court judgement, the Calcutta decision here argued that *ubi jus ibi remedium* 'must be enlarged to embrace all interests of public-minded citizens or organizations with serious concern for conservation of public resources and the direction and correction of public power'.[31] The interests of 'all public-minded citizens' are here economised as an interest in the management of resources, and the 'direction and correction of public power' presents a potent promotion of the judiciary's

---

[27] Respondents' argument, *State of West Bengal vs. Union of India and Others, 1995*.

[28] *State of West Bengal vs. Union of India and Others, 1995*.

[29] *Fertilizer Corporation Kamgar Union vs. Union of India, 1980*, 1981 AIR 344, cited in *State of West Bengal vs. Union of India*; emphasis added.

[30] The etymology of the word 'administration' includes in its earliest usages the idea of the application of a remedy, medicine, and treatment. See 'Administration', *Oxford English Dictionary Online*.

[31] *Fertilizer Corporation Kamgar Union vs. Union of India*, cited in *State of West Bengal vs. Union of India and Others, 1995*.

primary role in the conduct or direction of conduct.[32] The protection of fundamental economic rights in this case operated in two ways: first, to activate the historically established developmentalist state directed at poverty alleviation; and, second, at the same time, to pose market institutions as responsible to a public coded economically, and so, as representative of public interest. A neo-liberal coding of the public as market, that is, not just as the ground for political citizenship, is here initiated by an arm of the state itself, one particularly keen on fortifying administrative powers as a medium for the application of the rule of law. [33]

Pursuing this line, the judgement also cited a foundational post-Emergency Supreme Court decision establishing the independence of the judiciary, in which the concept of public interest was 'crystallize[d]'. In *S.P. Gupta vs. President of India, 1981*, the Supreme Court had asserted that 'a vast revolution is taking place in the judicial process...and the problems of the poor are coming to the forefront. The Court has to innovate new methods and devise new strategies for the purpose of providing access to justice to large masses of people who are denied their basic human rights and to whom freedom and liberty have no meaning'.[34] This judgement had occurred shortly after the re-election of Indira Gandhi in 1980, after her suspension of political rights during the Emergency in the name of poverty control, and upon the return of her Congress. This case reflects the translation of the politics of Emergency into a biopolitics of poverty reduction, articulated benevolently through the ventriloquising of the subaltern.[35] It is telling that in 1995, at the moment of the emergence of 'the emerging market', the Calcutta High Court found precedents in this jurisprudence influenced by the politics of Emergency.

From Emergency to emergence: this is how we might begin to characterise the Indian take on the genealogy of neo-liberalism, a key contemporary global characteristic of which is the strengthening of the judiciary, over and above mechanisms of political representation.[36] Concluding the judgement by further exercising judicial activism, the Calcutta High Court then addressed the second set of responses from the RNBCs, that they were not public institutions, and cited a range of precedents that allowed for the expansion of the definition of public interest itself. Turning to the 1987 Directions of the Reserve Bank of India, the Court

---

[32] I am drawing from Foucault's elaboration of 'the conduct of conduct' in liberal and neo-liberal governmentality. For an elaboration of '*conduite*' or direction and the conduct of conduct, see Michel Foucault, *Security, Territory, Population: Lectures at the Collège de France* (New York: Palgrave Macmillan, 2007), pp 190–5.

[33] In a rich reading of neo-liberalism and citizenship, Niraja Gopal Jayal pursues a related question through an examination of social and economic rights as distinct from political and civil rights in India, asking: 'does the use of the language of rights imply a substantive rather than rhetorical advance over the older language of state paternalism and official largesse?' Here, I place the language of state paternalism in a genealogy from colonial liberalism to neo-liberalism. The judicial fortification of powers of administration in the service of economic remedy and in the name of the rule of law, which poses a porous boundary between state paternalism and market citizenship, supplements Jayal's important critical reading of the operation of social and economic rights in neo-liberalism. See Jayal, *Citizenship and Its Discontents*, p. 167 and Chap. 6 generally.

[34] *S.P. Gupta vs. President of India and Others, 1981*, also cited as *P. Gupta vs. Union of India*, AIR 1982 SC 149, cited in *State of West Bengal vs. Union of India*.

[35] This benevolent ventriloquising, in which the Supreme Court speaks for victims deploying discourses of suffering to fortify its own agency, is mapped by Veena Das in an article that was published in the very same year as the *State of West Bengal vs. Union of India* judgement, on the legal dimensions of the 1984 Union Carbide gas leak disaster in Bhopal. Veena Das, 'Suffering, Legitimacy, and Healing: The Bhopal Case', in Veena Das, *Critical Events: An Anthropological Perspective on Contemporary India* (New Delhi: Oxford University Press, 1995), pp. 137–74. For a close reading of the intertwined history of the Emergency and the launch of public interest litigation, see Bhuwania, 'Courting the People'.

[36] For an elaboration, see Boaventura de Sousa Santos, 'The Gatt of Law and Democracy: (Mis)Trusting the Global Reform of Courts', *Oñati Papers*, Vol. 7 (1999), pp. 49–86.

asserted that these Directions conferred upon these financial institutions a 'public duty to depositors'. In short, by liberalising the channels for the expression of public interest, the Court expanded the domain of *public duty* that had been previously monopolised by the state and its languages of citizenship. Public duty was mapped onto non-governmental institutions, including market institutions.[37] The next section considers the ramifications of this move through a brief review of related cases that deliberate on whether stock exchanges— historically constituted as associations of private interests—can be construed as imbued with public duties.

The Stock Exchange: Market Exchange as Public Agency?

To buttress its decision in *West Bengal vs. Union of India and Others*, the Calcutta High Court had revitalised a foundational 1990 Bombay High Court Case, *Mrs. Sejal Rikeen Dalal and Others vs. The Stock Exchange Bombay*. This case, decided just as economic liberalisation was emerging as official policy, held that a writ of mandamus—the kind of writ at play in the *West Bengal vs. Union of India and Others* case, in which the court can demand the performance of certain public duties—was applicable to the Bombay Stock Exchange. At its heart, this case grappled with the question of whether the stock exchange could be conceived like the state itself, as imbued with the public duty and the responsibility of public welfare, that is, not just as an association regulating private interests. On the one hand, the question seems to be motivated by the protectionist aims of a strong welfare state, on the other, its logic seems to pose market exchange as the very ground for public agency.

The case had been launched by a joint family firm seeking to deploy constitutional protection against the stock exchange, which had rejected the firm's request to replace a deceased stock exchange member with another member of that firm. The firm, Harishondas Dalai, was 'of long standing' and had been in existence since before Indian Independence. One of its members, Mr. Pradip Harishondas Dalai, had died in a plane crash; he was a member of the Bombay Stock Exchange. The firm had been engaged extensively in speculative activities since 1970, and it was in debt (to a total of just over Rs32 lakhs, or Rs3.2 million) to 90 fellow stock exchange members. The members of this firm, which included Pradip's son and daughter-in-law, Mrs. Sejal Rikeen Dalai, asked that she take the firm's seat as member of the Bombay Stock Exchange. In addition, the firm also had a subsidiary in which Pradip had been a senior partner, Messrs. Harishah & Co. The governors of the Bombay Stock Exchange argued that this subsidiary firm had also long been a front for dangerous speculative business. Citing concerns about speculative-cum-gambling activity in both firms, the governing board of the Bombay Stock Exchange had voted by a 15–2 majority to prevent the admission of Mrs. Sejal Rikeen Dalai as a member. She then became the first petitioner in this petition to the Bombay High Court, which also included a second, third and fourth: in order, Pradip's son, his widow, and his granddaughter.[38]

The petitioners called upon the fundamental rights enshrined in the Indian Constitution, specifically Article 19, which outlines freedoms and guarantees the economic right to carry on trade and occupation. Claiming the exchange had prevented them in these endeavours, the petitioners sought to deploy Article 226 to force the exchange to offer Mrs. Sejal Dalai

---

[37] *State of West Bengal vs. Union of India and Others, 1995*. For an argument on the language of duty operating through a language of rights in India from the post-independence developmentalist period, see Jayal, *Citizenship and Its Discontents*.

[38] *Mrs. Sejal Rikeen Dalal and Others vs. The Stock Exchange Bombay, 1990*, AIR 1991 Bom 30. The case is named Dalal, although the family's name is Dalai.

membership. Article 226 allows for the High Courts to issue writs *to any institutions of state or those with public responsibilities* to enforce the fundamental rights of any citizen. The petition thus argued that the stock exchange, as an institution with such public duty, could be subject to Article 226, and the Indian Constitution could thus be used to override the stock exchange's formal rules of procedure. In response to the petition, the Bombay Stock Exchange asserted that it was not a public 'authority' within the meaning of Article 226 and, therefore, the petition would have to be dismissed. As might be expected, the Bombay Stock Exchange affirmed its status as a market association under the private law governing companies and societies, thus insisting on a classical state versus market distinction.[39] But the Bombay High Court did not deploy this straightforward line of argument, even though, in the end, it dismissed the petition. Instead, it delved into the operations of the Bombay Stock Exchange, turning the case into investigative grounds for the assessment of the role of stock exchanges in society. To begin, the Court refused to engage the petitioner's claim, for its claim to access fundamental rights was at its inception 'bad in law'—that is, overreaching and not legally logical. Even still, it sought to assess the application and meaning of the stock exchange rules, to investigate whether the stock exchange's rejection of the petitioner's request had been bona fide. With this aim, the bench cited a 1989 Indian Supreme Court decision that had affirmed that 'the term "authority" used in Article 226...*must receive a liberal meaning*...and not be confined only to statutory authorities and instrumentalities of State. They may cover any other person or body performing public duties'.[40] Deploying this precedent masterfully, the bench, Justice M.S. Manohar, transformed this case into a project of judicial activism posing the stock exchange as obligated to the public, here conceptualised as a domain of market exchange and profit. The Court instituted a liberalisation of the responsibility of state—a familiar neo-liberal move—while through its judicial activism also fortifying the administrative authority of the state. This occurred at a time of accelerated global financialisation, at the moment of the computerisation of the stock markets, of which, in India, the Bombay Stock Exchange was the most significant and globally influential.

The Court thus contended that the stock exchange's decision to reject Mrs. Dalai could be affirmed if it had been made on the grounds of public duty. This called for a review of exchange rules, bye-laws and procedures. The judgement thus highlighted that the stock exchange bye-laws were statutory bye-laws approved by the Government of India under the Securities Contracts (Regulation) Act, 1956, a key statute of post-Independence administrative law. Among the main objects of the Bombay Stock Exchange's governing rules were: 'To support and protect in the public interest the character and status of brokers and dealers and to further the interests both of brokers and dealers and of the public interested in securities; [and] to assist, regulate and control in the public interest dealings in securities'.[41]

The Bombay High Court interpreted the objects of the Bombay Stock Exchange very liberally, arguing that the exchange had a responsibility to protect the public from rapacious and immoral commercial activities. As such, even though this was not a case of public interest litigation, the Court proactively strengthened the powers of the judiciary to oversee market transactions in the name of the public: it affirmed the stock exchange's decision primarily on the grounds that this organisation had a duty to protect the public from potentially devastating

---

[39] *Ibid*.
[40] The Bombay High Court here summarises *Shri Anadi Mukta Sadguru Shree Muktajee Vandas Swami Suvarna Jayanti Mahotsav Smarak Trust & Ors. vs. V.R. Rudani & Others, 1989*, 1989 (2) SCC 691; emphasis added.
[41] Governing rules of the Bombay Stock Exchange, as cited in *Mrs. Sejal Rikeen Dalal and Others vs. The Stock Exchange Bombay, 1990*.

speculative activity.[42] In this way, a case that was judged at the outset as an illegitimate constitutional claim became a much-cited precedent on market exchange as an expression of public interest and agency. This public interest was identified by administrative procedure—through the judicial review of administrative action—rather than by constitutional right or electoral representation. The rule of law, incarnate in an active judiciary, operates here as the medium for a strong state, rather than as its limit: again, the neo-liberal turn institutes an extension of governmental authority via an identification of the public interest with market interest. The economic 'subject of interest' here enables the expansion of sovereign right, writing over the political subject of democratic rights.[43]

Mrs. Sejal Rikeen Dalal and Others vs. The Stock Exchange Bombay came to be robustly appropriated and rejected in a range of succeeding cases all after 1995, the year of the *West Bengal vs. Union of India and Others* public interest litigation. All these contemplate the public duties of stock exchanges. A potent case that summarises these trends is *Rajendra Rathore and Another vs. Madhya Pradesh Stock Exchange*, a 1999 judgement in which the Madhya Pradesh Stock Exchange is affirmed as a 'public authority' and even *as an arm of the state itself*.[44] In this case, a variety of petitioners claimed different reliefs against this exchange; the key feature of the case was that these petitioners 'contended that the stock exchange had all the trappings of "State" and was an "authority" of the State…inasmuch as its entire functioning was governed and regulated by the Securities Contracts (Regulation) Act, 1956…[which] confer[red] power on the Central Government to direct and regulate its functioning every inch'.[45] The representatives of the exchange responded that it was 'only an association of brokers engaged in buying and selling of securities and was not performing any public duty as such'.[46] Contesting this modest self-characterisation, the Court asserted that 'a superficial understanding of the nature of the stock exchange operations would suggest that it is not engaged in discharge of any public duty as such, so long as it deals with dealing and buying and selling of company shares. But there is more to it than meets the eye'.[47] It first reviewed precedents from the two decades before that mapped the birth and growth of public interest litigation in India, and so the increasing power of the courts to determine public duty and responsibility. Then it emphasised that stock exchanges do indeed offer a public good—the free circulation of capital: they provide 'facilities to liquefy capital to enable a person to

---

[42] It is important to note here that the moralising stance of the Indian government relies on a distinction between the 'legitimate' speculation that occurs under the formal rules of the exchange and 'illegitimate', high-risk speculation associated since the 1870s with informal, customary markets run by joint family firms. Formal speculative market practices can be just as, if not more, risky than informal ones. The Court's moralising articulates the benevolent performance of a strong state, one that produces the administrative architecture of speculative markets. See Ritu Birla, 'Speculation Illicit and Complicit: Law and Market Governance from the Colonial to the Emergent Neoliberal', in Laura Bear, Ritu Birla and Stine Simonsen Puri (eds), 'Speculation: Futures and Capitalism in India', special section of *Comparative Studies of South Asia, Africa and the Middle East*, Vol. 35, no. 3 (Dec. 2015), forthcoming.

[43] For a discussion of the distinction between the subject of interest and rights, see Foucault, *Birth of Biopolitics*, esp. Chap. 11.

[44] *Rajendra Rathore and Another vs. Madhya Pradesh Stock Exchange, 1999*, 2000 102 CompCas 300 MP. Another 1995 decision, the same year as *West Bengal vs. Union of India and Others*, in the Andhra Pradesh High Court had also used writ jurisdiction to regulate the Hyderabad Stock Exchange, which had moderated the grading of its entry tests after they had been completed, under the newly-established (1992) Securities and Exchange Board of India. It established the right to do so on the stock exchange's public duty and as an instrument of state. See *Rakesh Gupta and Others, Etc. vs. Hyderabad Stock Exchange Ltd., 1996*, AIR 1996 AP 413.

[45] *Rajendra Rathore and Another vs. Madhya Pradesh Stock Exchange, 1999*.

[46] *Ibid.*

[47] *Ibid.*

convert his/her investment made in a company into cash by disposing of the shares held to some one else, [thus giving] mobility to the capital in the absence of which the capital invested in the form of shares would be locked up'.[48]

Moreover, because securities contracts 'sometimes also carry the risk of degenerating into speculative transactions amounting to pure gambling which could subvert the main object of the stock exchange', the Government of India had established the Securities Contracts Regulation Act, 1956, which regulates the procedures of exchanges.[49] This statute was followed by the establishment of the Securities and Exchange Board of India in 1992, which approves the addition of new bye-laws within the exchanges. In addition, the 1956 Act also empowers the central government to 'supersede the governing body of a recognized stock exchange and *even to suspend its business in case of emergency and it could also prohibit contracts in certain areas to prevent undesirable speculation*'.[50] Here, the governmental investment in speculative transactions—affirmed in its proliferating infrastructure of administrative law for securities—reinforced anxiety about the possibly unsavoury effects of speculation. This in turn legitimised the state's right to claim and define an emergency in order to suspend the business of an exchange, as articulated in the Securities Contracts Regulation Act.[51] These 'emergency powers' are then deployed to affirm that the stock exchange is tied intimately to the mechanisms of state and is a 'public authority': 'It goes undisputed that the existence and functioning of the stock exchange is provided for and regulated by the Act and the rules made thereunder…have the consequence of making it a public authority if not statutory body in the strict sense of that term'.[52] Understood as not exactly the state itself, but very close, here the stock exchange was thus made partly amenable to writ jurisdiction. The case highlights an intimate relationship between neo-liberal governmentality, processes of financialisation and the fortification of authoritarian power, one also evocative of a long colonial history.

This jurisprudential trend of tying the public duty of stock exchanges with market protection and emergency powers was not without its detractors. In 1995, the Kerala High Court, and then in 1998, the Madras High Court stated clearly that writ jurisdiction does not apply to stock exchanges. In the Kerala case, *Satish Nayak vs. Cochin Stock Exchange Ltd.*, a terminated general manager of the exchange's Administrative Department sought to deploy Article 226 to contest his dismissal. The Kerala High Court, significantly, assessed whether the exchange counted as 'the State' under Article 12 of the Constitution of India, which defines the meaning of 'the State'. Unlike the Madhya Pradesh High Court, the bench did not take a liberal interpretation of public responsibility, and outwardly rejected the decision in *Mrs. Sejal Rikeen Dalal and Others vs. The Stock Exchange Bombay* as 'not correct' in 'our view'.[53] Here, the Court understood the subject matter of the case to be 'purely contractual in character': 'the issue relating to the termination of services of an employee are purely in the realm of contract' and, therefore, only subject to the principles of the civil law governing relations between individuals, as governed by companies law and its related domains. As such, the 'extraordinary jurisdiction under Article 226 is not the proper forum for the reliefs prayed for'.[54]

Interestingly enough, it was the High Court of a long-time communist-dominated state that was arguing for the interpretation of the stock exchange as a purely market mechanism and so

---

[48] *Ibid.*
[49] *Ibid.*
[50] *Ibid.*; emphasis added.
[51] Government of India, Securities Contracts Regulation Act, 1956, Article 12.
[52] *Ibid.*
[53] *Satish Nayak vs. Cochin Stock Exchange Ltd., 1995*, AIR 1995 Ker 373.
[54] *Ibid.*

articulating what might sound like a classically neo-liberal resistance to state involvement in market relations. The Madras High Court concurred, citing this logic and arguing similarly in a case of a man seeking entry into the Madras Stock Exchange, who claimed he held all the necessary qualifications, but was prevented membership due to established and vested interests in the exchange.[55] And, fascinatingly, in a judgement written by Justice S. Rajendra Babu, the Karnataka High Court in 1995 once again rehearsed all the arguments for the reason for a stock exchange, the various kinds of speculative contracts it is allowed to enter into, its regulation by central government statute and the Securities and Exchange Board of India, but came to a wholly different conclusion than the Bombay and Madhya Pradesh cases. The Karnataka case also concerned an alleged fraudulent transaction involving various members of the exchange. Here, the judgement clearly states that in order for the Court to interfere, a public duty must be at stake, and in this case, the writ of mandamus cannot be deployed 'to order admission or restoration to an office that is essentially of a private character, as in the present case, [or to order the] restoration of membership of a stock exchange that is essentially of a private character, nor, in general, will it lie to secure the due performance of the obligations owed by a company towards its members, unless it be that it is a case to secure performance of statutory duty, which is not the position in the present case'.[56] Again, in this case, even if the law could concede that market activities may have public import, they were here understood as the decisions of private individuals.

A Jurisprudence of Emergence/Emergency

The jurisprudence of India's emerging market tells a story about the techniques through which democratic languages of citizenship rights and public good, especially social and economic rights, are translated into the emergent juridico-economic order of neo-liberal governing. In the name of market-publics, the rights and powers of citizenship metamorphise into the potentially coercive authority of sovereign right. The *State of West Bengal vs. Union of India and Others, 1995*, and the debates about the status of stock exchanges throughout India in the 1990s are evocative starting points for the detailed study of such processes. In these cases, an expanded concept of the public as an economic formation sees a key instrument of neo-liberal thought, the rule of law, deployed to strengthen rather than circumscribe the administrative powers of the state, especially the authority of the judiciary. Classical neo-liberal thought operates on a distinction between the coercive state and the free market and finds in the rule of law a limit to the forceful potential of sovereignty: a prophylactic against the police state, the rule of law separates formal sovereignty from its powers of administration. In contrast, the Indian genealogy of liberalism and empire, and its characteristically strong state—colonial and national—legitimised by the application of the rule of law, exposes how neo-liberal governing may be understood to fuel the unmediated expression of sovereign authority *via the powers of administration*. Significantly, in India, this neo-liberal assertion and consolidation of a strong state via the re-coding of the public as market is reflected in the state's claims to represent and protect the masses: the paternal benevolence of colonial political liberalism and nationalist developmentalism reincarnates in neo-liberal governmental rationality through its call to 'good governance' and, as Modi's 'Emerging Markets' speech demonstrates, languages of participatory economic democracy.

---

[55] *A. Vaidyanathan vs. Union of India (Uoi) and Anr., 1998*, 2000 101 CompCas 224 Mad.
[56] *R. Jagadeesh Kumar vs. P. Srinivasan and Others, 1995*, ILR 1995 KAR 954.

A Different Kind of Flesh: Public Obscenity, Globalisation and the Mumbai Dance Bar Ban

WILLIAM MAZZARELLA, *University of Chicago, Chicago, USA*

Why did Mumbai's famous dance bars have to close in 2005? This paper analyses the ban and its aftermath in terms of (1) a colonial and post-colonial genealogy of the regulation of allegedly obscene public performances in India and (2) the provocative location of the dance bars vis-à-vis the cultural politics of consumerist globalisation. Combining a reading of arguments around the ban with first-hand ethnographic vignettes, the paper is a contribution to a critical analysis of the politics of publicity in India.

The famous dance bars of Mumbai were, aptly enough, closed down on Indian Independence Day: 15 August 2005.[1] In these establishments, also sometimes called beer bars, young women, many of them from the poorer hinterlands of the state of Maharashtra and beyond, danced with varying degrees of animation to the hit Hindi film song of the day.[2] An almost exclusively male clientele sat drinking, sometimes gazing raptly at a favourite dancer, occasionally summoning one over to exchange some currency notes for a few minutes of more exclusively directed attention. Every now and then, a male bar employee or a customer would step out in front of the stage and perform the 'money shower', a sudden and spectacular burst of small-denomination bills, either in the general direction of the dancers or directly over the head of a chosen muse.

By the time they were banned, the dance bars had become iconic of Mumbai nightlife, featured in Hindi movies like *Chandni Bar*[3] and given transnational literary circulation by Suketu Mehta's hypnotised description in *Maximum City*.[4] Formally, bar dancing referenced

---

The field research on which this essay builds was made possible by funding from the Social Science Research Council. For invaluable critical commentary, I would like to thank Shannon Dawdy, William Elison, Dianna Frid, Thomas Blom Hansen, Rama Mantena, Christian Novetzke, Francesca Orsini, Rupa Viswanath and Karin Zitzewitz. An earlier version of this article will appear in Brinda Bose and Shilpa Phadke (eds), *Explode Softly: Sexualities in Contemporary Indian Visual Cultures* (Kolkata: Seagull Books, forthcoming).

[1] The law that closed the dance bars, the Bombay Police (Amendment) Act of 2005, was passed by the state legislature of Maharashtra on 21 July 2005.

[2] Research conducted around the time of the ban by teams from SNDT Women's University and other institutions concluded that the bar dancers' origins were mixed: some of them came from traditional performing communities, some of them were the daughters of industrial workers who had been laid off during the Mumbai textile mill closings of the 1980s and 1990s, and some of them were domestic and piece workers looking to improve their meagre incomes.

[3] *Chandni Bar*, dir. Madhur Bhandarkar, 2001.

[4] Suketu Mehta, *Maximum City: Bombay Lost and Found* (New York: Vintage, 2004).

mujra,[5] popular Maharashtrian performance idioms like *tamasha* and *lavani*,[6] and Bollywood bump and grind. The dance bars were certainly not strip joints, although, accurately or not, the suggestion of sex work clung to the dancers. Clothes stayed on and most of the dancing was relatively demure. Facts and figures are contested. Some claimed that as many as 2,500 dance bars were operating in Maharashtra, collectively employing 72,000 women.[7] Having evolved out of the 'permit rooms'[8] and hotel bar cabarets of the 1960s and 1970s, the dance bar phenomenon started to take off in the 1980s, catering, at a wide variety of price points, to a socio-economically mixed clientele.

Why did the dance bars have to die? The preamble to the law that closed them, the Bombay Police (Amendment) Act of 2005, claimed that dance bars contravened the licensing terms for places of public amusement by 'permitting performance of dances in an indecent, obscene or vulgar manner', that this was 'giving rise to the exploitation of women', and that the dancing was both 'derogatory to the dignity of women' and 'likely to deprave, corrupt or injure the public morality or morals'.[9] When the Act was challenged in the Mumbai High Court in 2006, the state government further sweepingly submitted that bar dancing was 'having ill effects on society and in particular on safety, public health, crimes traceable to material welfare, disruption of cultural pattern, fostering of prostitution, infiltration of crime, problems of daily life of customers and their dependents and self-abasement apart from the degradation of the women themselves'.[10]

There are good reasons to be sceptical of these moralising justifications. Empirical research subsequently cited in court showed, for example, that the links between bar dancing and sex work were occasional, rather than characteristic.[11] Very few of the bar dancers were under 18 years of age. And if the issue really was indecency and obscenity, then why was provocative dancing in other venues—from popular *lavani* or *tamasha* shows to nightclubs in fancy hotels—not being outlawed?[12] Certainly, the dance bar ban was not in any simple sense

---

[5] A form of North Indian light classical dance developed and typically practised by courtesans during the Mughal period.

[6] Sharmila Rege, 'The Hegemonic Appropriation of Sexuality: The Case of the Lavani Performers of Maharashtra', in *Contributions to Indian Sociology*, Vol. 29, nos. 1–2 (Jan. 1995), pp. 23–38; and Sharmila Rege, 'Conceptualising Popular Culture: "Lavani" and "Powada" in Maharashtra', in *Economic & Political Weekly*, Vol. 37, no. 11 (16 Mar. 2002), pp. 1038–47.

[7] These were figures cited by the Bharatiya Bar Girls' Union in their challenge to the ban, *Indian Hotel and Restaurants Association and Others vs. State of Maharashtra on 12 April 2006* (henceforth *AHAR 2006*), Para 3. In the same case, the state government claimed that there were only 345 licensed dance bars in the state (Para 46) [http://indiankanoon.org/doc/1434517/, accessed 18 Aug. 2014].

[8] A 'permit room' is a space, usually within an establishment serving food, which is licensed to serve alcohol under the Bombay Prohibition Act of 1949.

[9] *AHAR 2006*, Para 14.

[10] *AHAR 2006*, Para 11.

[11] The desire to discover whether bar dancers were 'really' prostitutes was itself problematic. As Svati Shah points out, the moralism of reformist and abolitionist discourses on prostitution in India (as elsewhere) obscures the recognition of sex work as one among a range of strategies that poor migrants to a city like Mumbai might undertake at various points in their lives and in various combinations with other kinds of labour. See Svati Shah, *Street Corner Secrets: Sex, Work, and Migration in the City of Mumbai* (Durham, NC: Duke University Press, 2014). Sonia Faleiro, in her journalistic portrait of 'Leela', a Mumbai bar dancer, writes: 'Although they all did it, no bar dancer ever admitted to galat kaam [bad/wrong work, i.e. sex work]'. See Sonia Faleiro, *Beautiful Thing: Inside the Secret World of Bombay's Dance Bars* (New York: Black Cat, 2011), p. 12.

[12] Mumbai-based activist lawyer Flavia Agnes, who was closely involved with the legal defence of the bar dancers, gives a vivid impression of the puerile misogyny that characterised the debate on the bill in the State Assembly in July 2005. She also notes that at least one participant in the debate wanted to seize the occasion to close down not just the dance bars, but also 'hotels with three stars…five stars, disco dancing…belly dancing…all that is vulgar… every thing should be banned, except ['classical' Indian dance forms] Bharatnatyam and Kathak'. See Flavia Agnes, 'Hypocritical Morality: Mumbai's Ban on Dancers', in *Manushi*, No. 149 (2005), pp. 10–9.

only a symptom of the kind of Right-wing cultural policing that Mumbai's Shiv Sena party had made a central plank of its public profile in the mid 1990s; if anything, the dance bars flourished during the high-water mark of the Shiv Sena's decency crusades against films, television shows, magazine articles and art exhibitions.[13] Since the late 1990s, the increasingly extortionate regime of bribes, licences and taxes that state governments and the city police force had imposed on the dance bars had prompted dancers and bar owners to organise and seek legal protection against the authorities' predations. Some, therefore, interpreted the ban as a kind of tantrum thrown by the Maharashtra state government as its ability to profit from the dance bars came under increasing public pressure.

No doubt attending to this kind of *realpolitik* helps us to understand the exact timing of the ban. Indeed, it seems that the scales may have been tipped in the spring of 2005 because of the embarrassing public disclosure by the president of the Indian Hotel and Restaurants Association (AHAR) of a Rs120 million (then about $2.7 million) bribe demand from the Home Ministry to extend dance bar opening hours—a bribe that the AHAR president had apparently, at least initially, been willing to pay. But what I have in mind for this essay is a rather different register of inquiry; perhaps, one might call it a genealogy of the dance bar ban. By situating the dance bar ban vis-à-vis a series of precedents reaching back into colonial times, we will get a more expansive view of both the compellingly uncomfortable singularity of the dance bars in an age of globalisation and a longer history of the categories through which they were apprehended and shut down.

In the late nineteenth and early twentieth centuries, British colonial authorities insisted on a legal distinction between public places and places of Indian tradition. By contrast, a basic normative presumption of Indian nationalism was that the Indian and the public should coincide. In practice, however, post-Independence cultural politics have involved constant struggles over what kinds of practices, identities and performances may legitimately claim a public place. Judging an object or a practice as 'obscene' means, among other things, marking it as unfit for public visibility. Such a judgement involves not only a question regarding the cultural location of the object or practice in question—Is it art? Is it craft? Is it traditional? Is it Indian?—but also a problem regarding the relationship between any empirically existing audience—these particular people in this particular place—and the virtual projection that we call a 'general public'. As we shall see, bar dancing troubled these boundaries in particularly acute ways. At the same time, the dance bars were very much iconic of the uneasily democratised consumer erotics of the 1990s and 2000s. Especially insofar as they threatened to become objects of transnational touristic fascination, they interrupted the smooth semiosis of 'Incredible !ndia', the globally-branded destination in which the placeless global imaginary of immaculate office towers, freeways and shopping malls somehow also nourished a picture-postcard village India, populated by wizened, but smiling peasants in colourful turbans.[14]

I should also offer a word or two about the textual strategy that I have chosen for this essay: a formal separation between passages of legal and political analysis and segments of first-person ethnographic narrative. Although my ethnographic passages are certainly not

---

[13] As self-styled custodians of Maratha regional pride, the Shiv Sena's relationship to the dance bars was deeply ambivalent. On the one hand, Maratha masculinity was, according to Sainik ideology, predicated on non-indulgence in the kind of 'decadent' courtly entertainments from which bar dancing was clearly descended and which had, so the story went, contributed to the effeminacy which had caused the Peshwas to cede control of Maratha territories to the British in 1818. On the other hand, the Shiv Sena-led state government of the late 1990s certainly profited handsomely from the dance bars, even as it promoted a 'respectable' revival of *lavani*- and *tamasha*-based performances in upscale Maharashtrian concert halls.

[14] See Ravinder Kaur, 'Post-Exotic India: On Remixed Histories and Smart Images in the Contemporary Global', in *Identities: Global Studies in Culture and Power*, forthcoming.

'raw' field notes, I have decided to juxtapose them (rather than integrate them) with the analytic parts of the essay so as to preserve something of the disorientation and confusion that I experienced as someone who encountered Mumbai's dance bars at a time when I had no way to explain them. My hope is that the analytic parts of the essay will provide a retrospective reflexive framework for what, in the narrative sections, I did not yet understand I was experiencing. If the result at times might seem to lack the empathetic resonance that is supposed to be the watchword of the ethnographic method, then I can only plead a spontaneous failure of sensuous absorption—a failure that I would not invoke were it not, I want to suggest, indicative of the peculiarity of the dance bar as, to borrow a phrase, a 'discomfited emblem of modernity'.[15]

***

As a rank anthropological novice in Mumbai, I visited the dance bars several times in the autumn of 1997. A good friend and informant of mine was temporarily addicted to their charms and felt that it behoved him to introduce me, a foreigner in his city, to one of its more distinctive features. On my first visit, we arrived after official closing time, at around 1am. The shopfronts were shuttered and the main road was largely deserted. Pulling up in a taxi, my friend and I were immediately approached by a tout cajoling us to enter. But just as we were beginning to cross the road, the tout stopped us short with an urgent whisper: 'Wait a minute, wait a minute!' A police jeep had pulled up outside the entrance and now sat idling, apparently keeping watch. My friend suggested to the scout that the policeman might be offered a suitable consideration. The scout frowned, motioning us to be patient, and, eventually, the jeep moved away. The two of us were ushered down a pitch-black narrow lane between buildings that eventually brought us to a small side door. As we stepped inside, blinking in the sudden brightness, a glittering line of heavily made-up, giggling young women swept past us and on into a room emanating Hindi film music, cigarette smoke and coloured light. I was trailing my friend up a flight of stairs when a young man with longish curly hair and a white shirt stuck his considerable arm across my chest and barked: 'You're not Indian, are you? Not allowed in here!' Bewildered as I was by the whole scene, for a few moments, I took him at his word and earnestly began calling up the stairs for my friend to come down and extricate me. Later, the same young man approached me in the dance bar, slapped me on the back with some violence, and grinned: 'No hard feelings, eh?'

***

In April 2006, the Bombay High Court overturned the dance bar ban. The challenge to the ban was led by AHAR, but also pulled in petitions from a panoply of social justice-oriented non-governmental organisations (NGOs), including the Bharatiya Bar Girls' Union (representing the dancers), Aawaaz-e-Niswan (representing the interests of Muslim women), Akshara and the Women's Research and Action Group (women's rights groups), the India Centre for Human Rights and Law and HIV/AIDS-STD activists.

This is not the place to explore each legal dimension of the case; suffice it to say that Justices Rebello and Dalvi found that the ban amounted to an arbitrary restriction on the bar dancers' constitutionally guaranteed freedom to practise their profession. The ban had baldly stated that the 'holding of a performance of dance, of any kind of type, in any eating house, permit room or beer bar is prohibited'. By this logic, then, any kind of dancing that took place in a dance bar was inherently offensive simply because it took place in a dance bar. To

---

[15] Davesh Soneji, *Unfinished Gestures: Devadasis, Memory, and Modernity in South India* (Chicago, IL: University of Chicago Press, 2012), p. 11.

underline the point, the ban went on explicitly to exempt other kinds of venues, specifying that the restriction would not apply to:

> The holding of a dance performance in a drama theatre, cinema theatre [or] auditorium; or sports club or gymkhana, where entry is restricted to members only, or a three starred or above hotel or in any other establishment or class of establishments which, having regard to (a) the tourism policy of the Central or State Government for promoting the tourism activities in the State; or (b) cultural activities, the State Government may, by special or general order, specify in this behalf.[16]

These exemptions constitute a useful inventory of the performative spaces that the state government, for one reason or another, considered legitimate: spaces that were either 'private' (members' clubs) or spaces in which the sensuous provocation of dance could be sublimated by referring it to the interests of art or culture, whether the intended audience was imagined as culturally local or foreign/touristic. It would seem, then, that the obscenity of bar dancing—which clearly did not consist of anything particularly explicit—had to do with its singular failure to conform to these officially authorised performative dispensations.[17] In overturning the ban, Justices Rebello and Dalvi further asked why, if the Mumbai city police and magistrates were satisfied with their existing ability to regulate auditoria, fancy nightclubs and *tamasha* theatres, they needed extra legislation to cope with dance bars?[18] And if dance bars were inherently corrupting places for the women who danced there, then what about other female employees such as waitresses? How could the state government claim, as it did, that '[t]here is no arousing of lust when women serve the customers in the eating house…that happens only when the women start dancing'?[19]

On the face of it, the dance bar ban smacked of plain old class discrimination. Why should bar dancers be prosecuted, many critics asked, when more provocative dancing was allowed in fancy hotels, clubs and expensive restaurants? Was this not simply yet another example of the kind of hypocritical moralism that targeted popular pleasures while permitting high-end obscenity? The problem with this argument was that the ban did not in fact discriminate in only this way. To be sure, it exempted up-market venues, so as not to disturb the playgrounds of the rich and the flow of foreign currency at authorised tourist traps. But it also left down-market venues alone, as long as what took place there could be justified as 'traditional'. The problem with bar dancing, it would seem, was that it fitted neither the high cultural requirements of 'classical' dance, nor the definitively global profile of cabaret or 'modern' dance, nor yet state-sponsored popular idioms.

The need to locate bar dancing within some plausible narrative of Indian cultural tradition dominated its defence—even as these invocations of tradition invariably had to rehearse the cultural laundering that, in the first half of the twentieth century, had rendered Indian dance and music idioms long associated with courtesan performance 'respectable' in such a way as

---

[16] Cited in *AHAR 2006*, Para 1.

[17] For a more comprehensive development of the concept of 'performative dispensations', see William Mazzarella, *Censorium: Cinema and the Open Edge of Mass Publicity* (Durham, NC: Duke University Press, 2013).

[18] For example, the Bombay Police (Amendment) Act of 2005 modified Section 33 of the Bombay Police Act (1951), which already gave the city police the right to license and regulate places of public amusement other than cinemas (which are covered by the Cinematograph Act) 'in the interest of public order, decency or morality or in the interest of the general public, the employment of artists and the conduct of the artists and the audience at such performances' [http://www.pdfqueen.com/pdf/po/police-act/6/, accessed 7 April 2010].

[19] *AHAR 2006*, Para 68.

to conform to the public cultural requirements of a reformist bourgeois nationalism.[20] Justices Rebello and Dalvi noted, in general terms, that dancing, even erotic dancing, was at least potentially eligible for constitutional protection as a form of expression and as an occupation. Perhaps even more fundamentally, they also deemed dance central to Indian cultural traditions, both ancient and modern. Several of the groups attacking the ban tried to extend this cultural justification by likening bar dancing to modern popular entertainments: 'ladies undertaking dance performances for the entertainment of men is part of the cultural tradition of Maharashtra, e.g. *Lavanis*, *Tamashas* etc.'.[21] Even the Hindi cinema, since it was such a palpable source of inspiration for bar dancing moves, was mobilised in challenges to the ban as both a cultural reference point and a yardstick for obscenity.[22]

Perhaps the most explicit attempt to locate bar dancing in a 'deep' Indian cultural context was that of Varsha Kale, who represented the bar dancers' union in their challenge to the ban. Speaking to a journalist at the time of the ban, she argued that many of the dancers 'have been taught *mujra* from their childhood and have a professional approach to their work in the bars. They touch the floor in a *namaskar* before they begin. Many have demonstrated the *chumkar* or whirling step to me and asked "*Aap isko kala bolenge ki nahin?*" ("Wouldn't you call this folk art?")'.[23] At the same time, other petitioners on behalf of the dancers stressed precisely their limited skills in order to show that the ban was an unreasonable restriction on the work of women who would not be able to find work elsewhere: '[B]ar dancers are capable of dancing to existing Hindi film tunes. This is the only skill most of them possess, and at the highest is a profession and/or vocation or occupation' (and thus rising neither to the status of art nor of any other kind of constitutionally-protected 'expression').[24]

The Mumbai police commissioner's argument against the dancers was, conversely, that their activity was not sophisticated enough to count as a 'skill', but that this meant that, as unskilled labourers, the dancers should be able to find other kinds of work.[25] The state government asserted that bar dancing was 'neither entertainment nor art' and that the attempts to dignify it by giving it any kind of Indian cultural pedigree was spurious: 'The dancing girls invariably used to be clad in dresses, apparently for name's sake traditional, but truly revealing female anatomy'.[26] Unredeemable as culture, entertainment or art, bar dancing was, in the state's discourse, reducible to a kind of null category of bare smut whose purpose could only be crudely instrumental.

By way of comparison, the cabaret dancer prosecutions that started gathering steam in the early 1970s involved acts that were far more explicit than what later transpired in the dance bars. In the oft-cited case of a dancer who performed at the Blue Nile club in Colaba, Bombay, in 1970 under the names of Joyce Zee and Temiko, the evidence records that, wearing only panties, she and her co-dancers 'swished their backs and breasts against the customers, pushed

---

[20] Soneji, *Unfinished Gestures*; and Amanda Weidman, *Singing the Classical, Voicing the Modern: The Postcolonial Politics of Music in South India* (Durham, NC: Duke University Press, 2006).

[21] *AHAR 2006*, Para 54. Such proto-dance bar scenes appear in several classic Marathi films that feature *lavani*, for example *Lok Shahir Ram Joshi*, dir. Baburao Painter, 1947; *Amar Bhoopali*, dir. V. Shantaram, 1951; and *Sangte Aika*, dir. Anand Mane, 1959. Thanks to Christian Novetzke for these references.

[22] Flavia Agnes records a public protest by the bar dancers in which they demanded to know why they were being harassed for performing the same dances as mainstream Hindi film heroines. Agnes, 'Hypocritical Morality', pp. 10–9. Of course, during the 1990s in particular, these actresses and their directors were by no means themselves immune to prosecution for obscenity. See Raminder Kaur and William Mazzarella (eds), *Censorship in South Asia: Cultural Regulation from Sedition to Seduction* (Bloomington: Indiana University Press, 2009).

[23] Freny Manecksha, 'Dancers in the Dark', *Infochange India* (Sept. 2005) [http://infochangeindia.org/women/features/dancers-in-the-dark.html, accessed 1 Mar. 2015].

[24] *AHAR 2006*, Para 30.

[25] *Ibid.*, Para 55.

[26] *Ibid.*, Para 37.

their nipples in the mouths of some and imitated sexual acts'.[27] Or consider Sadhna and her colleagues, Delhi cabaret dancers, who, during a 1979 performance, 'were wearing nothing except under wears (*sic*) and brassieres and were vibrating the various parts of their bodies'.[28] These were, in short, actions that by Indian standards would certainly be deemed explicit. But the dance bars were different. As Suketu Mehta puts it in *Maximum City*:

> I started going to the beer bars because I was puzzled. I couldn't figure out why men would want to spend colossal amounts of money there. On a good night a dancer in a Bombay bar can make twice as much as a high-class stripper in a New York bar. The difference is that the dancer in Bombay doesn't have to sleep with the customers, is forbidden to touch them in the bar, and wears more clothes on her body than the average Bombay secretary does on the broad public street.[29]

Where was the obscenity in this?

***

Having ascended the stairs to the second floor, my friend and I entered a small room with tables arranged in two rows down the middle and around the edges. On two sides were low stages, upon which groups of women—the same sparkly women, it turned out, who had swept past us in the entryway—danced to blaring Hindi film music cassettes. Some of the women evinced a certain verve in their imitation of film song dance moves, but most of them shuffled around on the spot in a desultory holding pattern, casting searching glances out into the room. Seated at the tables was an assortment of Indian men, one of whom would later beamingly greet me in the toilet: 'Welcome to our country!' Most of the patrons were middle-aged and pot-bellied; a few of them looked like college kids. The room was small enough that the dancers were no more than a few feet away from any table. At this point, I had no idea what was going to happen or what the implications of looking might be, so I tried to balance due ethnographic diligence with keeping my eyes to myself.

My friend ordered us drinks and gave the waiter an extra Rs100 bill. The waiter returned promptly, having converted the bill into a small stack of tens, one of which he immediately received back for his trouble. Waving a couple of tens at several of the women in turn, my friend succeeded in bringing them over to the table, where they would take the money and then return to the stage without any (to me) apparent effect on their demeanour. 'So what happens?' I asked. 'That's it', my friend replied. 'They kind of dance for you'. As they danced, the women clutched substantial bundles of bills in their fists—money to attract money. I wondered whether I was missing something. Next to the stage to our right was a small booth, where a DJ selected cassette tapes from an enormous series of stacks behind him. At the end of each song there was an awkward silence and some clicking noises from the PA system before the next selection lurched into gear.

Most of the time, the dancers seemed to respond to donations in the manner of slot machines: a few bills would add some energy to their moves for a minute or two and then it was back to the bored shuffling. My friend must have sensed my bewilderment because the next time a dancer came over to grab his proffered bills, he whispered something in her ear, whereupon she bent over the table and caressed my cheek with the edge of the money he had given her before wandering back to the stage. Only big spenders seemed to elicit anything more energetic. One man in a corner of the room was whooping it up, throwing heaps of

---

[27] Cited in *Sadhna vs. State 1981*, Para 2 [http://indiankanoon.org/doc/661129/; accessed 18 Aug. 2014].
[28] *Ibid.*, Para 1.
[29] Mehta, *Maximum City*, p. 269.

money at a particularly comely dancer, who was giving him the full belly-dancing treatment, smiling, extending sinuously longing arms in his direction, lip-syncing sentimentally romantic words, as her sponsor sat slapping his thighs and laughing uproariously.

At one point, a short uniformed employee walked right up to the edge of the dance floor. Pulling a big pile of bills out of his pocket, he proceeded to send them, in an artful simulation of slow motion, flying out at the dancers in a profuse cascade. This evoked no discernible response from the dancers, but a few customers soon proceeded to enact their own, generally more modest versions of the money shower. Some would ejaculate bills quickly and frontally, in a burst of compressed energy. Others would stand next to a particular dancer, smilingly gyrating their hips and nodding in the rhythmic manner of Hindi film choreography, while slowly letting individual banknotes billow over the head of their chosen woman. Thus selected, the dancer would preen as if in response to the most flattering admiration. Once the stack was exhausted, with the music still blaring, another uniformed employee scurried around the floor, hastily shoving bills onto a large silver tray.

My friend remarked that the roles enacted by the dancers strongly referenced the stock courtesan character in Hindi films: the refined prostitute with a heart of gold and a soft spot for the respectable but reckless hero who, in the dance bar, was represented by the customer. Emotionally intimate but socially distant, the courtesan and the hero can of course never make a life together; nor can the courtesan, qua fallen woman, ultimately be allowed to survive. Often, she finds a way to pay tribute to her lover in the very act of sacrificing her own life. The hero mourns her for a while, before wandering off into the sunset with his virginal bride. The social order is restored, with a twist of melancholy.[30]

Next to the DJ booth were two vertical rows of numbered pigeon-holes. Each number corresponded to one of the women; occasionally, one of them would wander over from the stage and deposit a fistful of money into her designated slot.

***

Regulating public performance means imagining, invoking and attempting to impose a moralised relationship between public space and cultural value. Any such moralised relationship has its histories; the dance bar ban was, as we shall shortly see, unintelligible without reference to the colonial and post-colonial precedents by which the dance bars could be recognised as public spaces of performance and by which bar dancing could be marked as obscene. Spatially, the dance bar ban invoked several different scales simultaneously: a Maharashtrian politics of cultural patronage; a national register of 'decent' publicness; and a global field of consumerist aspiration and touristic recognition. And as an attempt to regulate public *performance* (as opposed to defining and managing public space as such), the dance bar ban confronted the full ambiguity of locating obscenity: was it in the dance qua object, was it in the dance bar qua context, or was it in the audience qua subject?

As the appeal against the High Court decision moved up to the Supreme Court in May 2006, the state government knew that its gambit had failed. Prosecuting obscenity under Sections 292 and 294 of the Indian Penal Code is a notoriously slippery business—and by seeking to criminalise dance bars as dance venues, rather than having to prove the obscenity of the dancing itself, the ban was quite deliberately an attempt to get around the problem. Satisfying the legal definition of obscenity is tricky enough because it requires proving that a given image, text or object has a 'tendency' to corrupt those who may come into contact

---

[30] Faleiro notes the iconic status, for many of Mumbai's bar dancers, of the titular performance of the legendary Hindi film actress, Rekha, in the courtesan drama, *Umrao Jaan*, dir. Muzaffar Ali, 1981. See Faleiro, *Beautiful Thing*, p. 107.

with it.[31] But when it comes to obscene *acts*, as covered by Section 294, matters get still more complicated.[32]

Section 294, which covers 'obscene acts and songs', specifies: 'Whoever, to the annoyance of others, (a) does any obscene act in any public place, or (b) sings, recites or utters any obscene song, ballad or words, in or near any public place, shall be punished with imprisonment of either description for a term which may extend to three months, or with fine, or with both'.[33] In addition to the problem of establishing the obscenity of the act, then, Section 294 requires the prosecution to show that the venue in which the act took place was a 'public place' and that the act in question took place 'to the annoyance of others'.[34]

Between the 1870s and the 1970s, a radical reversal appears at first sight to have taken place in the Indian legal understanding of what constitutes a 'public place' vis-à-vis potentially provocative performances. The Dramatic Performances Act of 1876, oriented as it was toward the regulation of modern proscenium theatre, defined a public place as 'any building or enclosure to which the public are admitted to witness a performance on payment of money'.[35] Conversely, by the time of the Joyce Zee cabaret judgement in the early 1970s, the Blue Nile nightclub was found *not* to be a public place precisely because patrons paid— and paid dearly—to enter. As a high-end nightspot, catering primarily to elites, the Blue Nile was in this instance assumed to operate outside of a post-colonial public sphere in which no one should be expected to pay for access.

Colonial legislation tended to invoke a split between the kind of in-principle universal access offered by an 'open' or general market for tickets to the 'closed' or particular performative publics of Indian custom, to which one might be admitted by virtue of one's membership in a socio-cultural community or one's relationship to a patron. Anti-colonial nationalist cultural activism was premised on the abolition of this split; only by reconciling 'Indian' and 'general' publics could, it was presumed, a genuinely national public culture be forged. But in practice, around the turn of the twentieth century, a new kind of division began to appear within this nationalist project. On the one hand, cultural activists politicised what the British had designated as Indian 'custom' by taking it to the streets and thus laying a direct, and directly 'Indian', claim on public space.[36] On the other hand, reformers were busy

---

[31] Brinda Bose (ed.), *Gender & Censorship* (New Delhi: Women Unlimited, 2006); and Mazzarella, *Censorium*.
[32] The dance bar ban did not in fact draw on Section 294, so why am I invoking it here? First, as I have noted, the case against the dance bars was quite consciously constructed as a way of getting around the onerous evidentiary requirements of Section 294 and was as such in a strong sense defined by its terms. The ban was proximately preceded by an April 2005 case before the Nagpur Bench of the Bombay High Court in which the judges found, against the Nagpur police, that bar dancing did not satisfy the requirements of Section 294. Second, although Section 294 was not directly at issue in the 2005–06 dance bar struggle, the longer history of cases prosecuted under Section 294 had fundamentally conditioned and inflected the ways in which key terms like obscenity, indecency, publicness and audience could be mobilised. Section 294 operated, one might say, as a spectral constituent of the dance bar ban.
[33] *Indian Penal Code, 1860* (Allahabad: Law Publishers [India] Pvt. Ltd, 2003), p. 146.
[34] *Ibid.*
[35] The Dramatic Performances Act, 1876, 3(c) [http://indiankanoon.org/doc/1511172/, accessed 18 Aug. 2014].
[36] Sandria Freitag, *Collective Action and Community: Public Arenas and the Emergence of Communalism in North India* (Berkeley: University of California Press, 1989); Raminder Kaur, *Performative Politics and the Cultures of Hinduism: Public Uses of Religion in Western India* (New Delhi: Permanent Black, 2003); William Mazzarella, 'A Torn Performative Dispensation: The Affective Politics of British World War II Propaganda in India and the Problem of Legitimation in an Age of Mass Publics', in *South Asian History and Culture*, Vol. 1, no. 1 (2010), pp. 1–24; Christopher Pinney, *'Photos of the Gods': The Printed Image and Political Struggle in India* (London: Reaktion, 2004); and Christopher Pinney, 'Iatrogenic Religion and Politics', in Raminder Kaur and William Mazzarella (eds), *Censorship in South Asia: Cultural Regulation from Sedition to Seduction* (Bloomington: Indiana University Press, 2009), pp. 29–62.

producing the kind of sanitised performance traditions that would, after Independence, readily be recognised and patronised by the new nation-state as its ostensibly 'classical' cultural heritage.

From a regulatory standpoint, the British colonial authorities had—whatever the predations of their actual practices—generally upheld a principle of non-interference in what they understood as the life-worlds of Indian custom. By contrast, the post-colonial state, since it was ideologically premised on full overlap between Indian custom and Indian public culture, did not have to concern itself with any such scruples. One might say that the British colonial authorities sequestered the very cultural category of 'Indian custom' from which political challenges immediately began to issue. But by the same token, the post-Independence Indian state staked its legitimacy on the prospect of a unified national public culture whose standards of propriety necessarily produced a popular remainder that was perpetually under suspicion for obscenity and indecency.

Today, the law of the land, when it comes to obscenity, is a historical palimpsest of colonial and post-colonial concerns. On the one hand—in line with the colonial principle of non-interference—Section 292 of the Indian Penal Code exempts objects from the charge of obscenity if they can plausibly be redeemed according to religious–traditional values ('bona fide...religious purposes'). On the other hand—in line with the modernising mission of the post-colonial project—the imputation of obscenity may also be obviated according to secular–cosmopolitan standards ('science, literature, art or learning or other objects of general concern').[37] These are not just discursive formations, they are also ways of imagining two types of citizens who, respectively, are supposed to enjoy two kinds of moral prophylaxis against the menace of obscenity and indecency: on one side, the 'naive' integrity that comes from immersion in purportedly traditional life-worlds and, on the other side, the reflexive judgement promised by education and worldly experience.

Obscenity law, then, imagines ideal-typical subjects who are, as it were, anchored in either a 'traditional' or a 'modern' way, and thus protected from potential corruption. At the same time, the general public is implicitly imagined as perpetually at risk, precisely because there is no guaranteed overlap between publicness, *in its generality*, and the particular insulations that either 'bona fide...religious purposes' or 'science, literature, art', etc., might confer. This is where the weight placed on ticketing, as a marker of the publicness or otherwise of a performance, becomes indicative of the ambiguous relationship of culture and citizenship in a post-colonial democracy: is the substantial price of a ticket to a provocative entertainment a reassuring index of aesthetic cultivation, or does it simply buy immunity from the law? The state government of Maharashtra invoked the former argument to justify the exemption granted to fancier hotels in the dance bar ban: 'The persons visiting these hotels or establishments stand on a different footing and cannot be compared with people who attend the establishments which are popularly known as dance bars. They belong to different strata of society and are [a] class by themselves'.[38] But by this logic, as Justice Padmanabhan had already observed in the mid 1980s, any cinema hall or other performance venue could easily 'be converted into a private place by restricting entry to rich persons who alone could afford the luxury'.[39] Similarly, in a second Blue Nile judgement in 2003, Bombay High Court

---

[37] *Indian Penal Code*, p. 143; see also Mazzarella, *Censorium*.
[38] *AHAR 2006*, Para 37.
[39] *Deepa and Ors. vs. S I of Police and Anr. on 27 November 1985*, Paras 6, 8 [http://indiankanoon.org/doc/391886/, accessed 11 Mar. 2015].

Justices Desai and Kakade noted: 'The result will be that any obscenity which is prohibited to the poor will not be a prohibited obscenity for the rich. That will lead to a very unhappy situation'.[40] Justice Padmanabhan had ruled that a place was public as long as no category of person was a priori prohibited entry. But what might that mean in practice? Could exclusion on the basis of an (in)ability to spend, or on the basis of other classed or gendered markers of (non)belonging, amount to a priori prohibition of entry?[41]

Recall that Section 294 specifies not only that the obscene act must occur in a public place, but also that it must do so 'to the annoyance of others'. Built into this phrase is the implicit assumption that these 'others' are in fact representative of the general public and that because they are representative, their annoyance thus also becomes a representative reflex of generally held moral values. Now, of course, there is a kind of prima facie plausibility to the principle that the reactions of those actually present at an event should be given the greatest evidentiary weight. As Justice Jain put it in the case of *Sadhna vs. State, 1981*: '[I]t would not be possible to convict a cabaret dancer merely because a section of the people *not* attending such shows equate them, perhaps rightly, with pornography'.[42] But what was one to make of the apparent non-annoyance of actual customers at a provocative show?[43] Some were inclined to interpret it, as we have seen, as an index of the aesthetic maturity of those who were in a position to pay for such entertainments—evidence of their membership in a 'class by themselves'. Others argued that the act of buying a ticket, whether or not it defined the difference between a public and a non-public place, was a sovereign act of consumer-citizenship, a pre-emptive act of consent to whatever the entertainment might involve. But how, still others asked, could one reasonably consent to the unreasonable—i.e. to obscenity? Might not a willingness to spend money on such entertainments in fact confirm the moral eccentricity, even incompetence, of the patron? As Justice Padmanabhan further observed, if the patron's competent consent could be assumed from his purchase of a ticket, then 'an obscene performance could be had with impunity before an exclusively willing crowd even in a public place. That will not be conducive to public order, decency or morality'.[44]

***

The last time I went to a dance bar, I went in the company of a few friends from the advertising agency where I was doing fieldwork. Again, gaining entry involved negotiating what seemed like an uneasy truce between patrolling police cars and furtive doormen. Again, the outside doorway was small and dingy, but having passed through a series of two or three other doorways manned by burly bouncers, we found ourselves in the kind of palatial marbled hall, complete with sweeping staircase, that has long been a stock setting for the more opulent variants of Hindi film melodrama. The staircase led us up to a smaller set of air-conditioned rooms with mirrors on the walls and a bar at one end, the predominant textures marble and onyx. Extravagantly expensive drinks were served. We were shown to cushions arranged

---

[40] *Narendra Khurana and Ors. vs. Commissioner of Police and Anr. on 18 December 2003*, Para 12 [http://indiankanoon.org/doc/1945094/, accessed 18 Aug. 2014].

[41] This is pretty much the situation in India with exclusive gymkhanas and sports clubs which, by charging exorbitant annual fees, can control their customer profile and define themselves as private members-only establishments. Such clubs are, of course, places of amusement, but, legally, they are not places of *public* amusement. As such, they do not fall within the terms of Section 294 or of the city authorities' definition of places of public amusement. In policing practice, this distinction has not always been observed.

[42] *Sadhna vs. State, 1981*, Para 2, emphasis added.

[43] The judge in the Joyce Zee case, for example, held not only that the Blue Nile was not a public place, but also that there was no evidence that anyone in the audience had been annoyed when Joyce Zee and her colleagues performed (see reference in *Sadhna vs. State, 1981*).

[44] *Deepa and Ors. vs. S I of Police and Anr., 1985*, Para 13.

around the perimeter of the room, much as dignitaries might once have assembled in a wealthy merchant's home for a nautch. *In front of us stood low tables with glass tops supported by arch-backed miniature caryatids.*

After my first couple of visits to dance bars, Mumbai friends both male and female had been curious to hear what I had made of it all. I said, truthfully, that the dance bars made me uncomfortable. My friends typically assumed that my discomfort had to do with some kind of moral disapproval of the performance. But that was not really it. My reaction was in truth more one of alienation: seldom had I felt more foreign in India, seldom had I felt less successfully interpellated than I did at the dance bars. Their erotics were clearly not intended to be intelligible to me, or to hail me as a spontaneously assenting member of their public.

By playing the responsible ethnographer, I gradually became able, of course, to 'situate' their semiotics according to a set of cultural references, but for me, this work of interpretation remained largely devoid of sensuous resonance. At these points, I felt more distant than ever from my local friends: sipping my exorbitantly priced glass of Coke, I glanced at the person sitting next to me. Having secured the temporary attention of a favourite dancer, he sat leaning forward, eyes at once glazed over and locked onto the dancer, clutching a stack of bills, a small smile on his lips and a tiny waggle of the head registering quietly awed appreciation. As a senior executive put it to me later in the evening, leaning over to make himself heard through the filmi *din, 'It's a different kind of flesh'.*

Intensely conscious of my white face and my disorientation—'You're not Indian, are you? Not allowed in here'/'Welcome to our country!'—I only gradually came to appreciate how the dance bars were emerging as an obligatory site for the discriminating cultural tourist in Mumbai. The object of this touristic desire was not simply the mise en scène *of the dance bar itself, but also the regime of bribery and corrupt policing that surrounded it. One late night, I begged off going to a dance bar, but several of my friends and acquaintances—including an American expat—went ahead. Early the following morning, I received an excited call from my American friend who had just been released by the police after a raid. The police had swooped after he and the others had been at the dance bar for about twenty minutes. Employees had herded them, along with the other customers, into a small room where this motley assortment of executives, entrepreneurs, college students and the odd expat had enjoyed a largely jolly couple of hours as the management attempted to negotiate with the cops downstairs. The air of lifeboat conviviality suffered only a minor setback when a large Gujarati businessman, not bothering to disguise the Smith & Wesson pistol poking out of his pocket, tried to move in on my American friend's date. Despite the best efforts of the management, the police eventually insisted—quite politely, it seemed—that everyone come along to the station, where they all gave fake names and addresses.*[45] *By then, it was early in the morning, and the core party moved on to breakfast at the Hotel President at Cuffe Parade. My friend sounded quite charged up by his night: 'One of my top three experiences in India!'*

***

Perhaps, it was not surprising that the money shower should again and again have been singled out as an iconic précis of the obscenity of bar dancing: the spectacular equation of money and

---

[45] My friend had thus become part of the strategy used by the Mumbai police, whereby each separate arrest counted as a distinct offence. This is how the police were subsequently able to present impressive prosecution figures in court to support the ban.

lust was at once irredeemably instrumental and sinfully profligate.[46] The money shower performatively quoted an ostensibly archaic form of sovereignty and sponsorship: that of the feudal lord and patron. In mainstream Hindi cinema, such relations of patronage could be staged as a romantically nostalgic invocation of a courtly courtesan aesthetic displaced by the rise of the secular–democratic nation-state. But in the eminently contemporary spaces of the dance bars, the money shower literalised, in an uncomfortable way, the ambiguity of the consumer-citizen as patron: at once lofty lord of the dance and common customer, at once sovereign and spendthrift. This citational re-enactment of the forms of feudal patronage, then, became intolerable precisely as an expression of popular desire—something like a generally intelligible public culture.

I think it is important to distinguish the dance bar ban from the earlier cabaret cases, even as they belong to the same genealogy. Stripping could easily be marked as foreign or, failing that, a symptom of Mumbai urban excess. Just like the vamp in 1970s Hindi films, the cabaret dancer represented something essentially foreign.[47] As such, her provocation, while regularly prosecuted, could also more easily be excused. As a performative type, the cabaret artist, while decadent, did not fundamentally trouble the boundary separating the global from the authentically Indian.

Bar dancing did not fit into either of these categories. During my doctoral dissertation fieldwork in the late 1990s, I was regularly told that the mark of Indian globalisation was the new confidence with which Indian young people were now mixing and matching global and Indian products.[48] From *tandoori* pizza to 'Hinglish' advertising copy, the cultural ideology of globalisation gleefully combined the 'traditional' and the 'modern', but always in such a way as to reassert the reified integrity of the opposition: the office towers featured in the advertisements were always as shiny as the ones in Singapore and Dubai, the Indian villagers were never drab or listless.

The dance bars, by contrast, were scrappy and a little rough around the edges. Their emergence as transnationally-feted objects of touristic fascination, as noted in the 2006 challenge to the dance bar ban, was always going to irritate the sentinels of 'Brand India': 'The establishment[s] are frequented by tourists from all over the world who come to watch the dance. Impressed and inspired by the dance bars of Mumbai, restaurants and bars having music and dance have opened up in Dubai, Singapore, London, Malaysia, Muscat, Bahrain, Sri Lanka etc, where dancers are specially taken from India and other parts of the world to perform there'.[49]

---

[46] Responding to the congeries of interest groups that challenged the 2005 amendment to the Bombay Police Act, the state government focused on the money shower as a particularly insalubrious feature of the dance bar *habitus*. This complaint is recorded in the 2013 Supreme Court judgement as follows: 'With regard to the form of remuneration, learned senior counsel submitted that remuneration to dancers in banned establishments is generally made out of the money which is showered on them. This creates an unhealthy competition between the dancers to attract the attention of the customers. Therefore, each dancer tries to outdo her competitors in terms of sexual suggestion through dance': *State of Maharashtra & Anr. vs. Indian Hotel & Restaurants Assn. & Ors. on 16 July 2013*, Para 27 [http://indiankanoon.org/doc/38033723/, accessed 18 Aug. 2014]. Implausibly, Varsha Kale, representing the bar dancers' union, had tried to claim that 'a TV clip portraying a woman dancing as hundreds of currency notes are thrown her way has done immense damage: "It is a huge exaggeration, possibly one that took place in a South Mumbai [and thus more high-end] bar on a rare occasion"'. See Manecksha, 'Dancers in the Dark'.
[47] Ranjani Mazumdar, *Bombay Cinema: An Archive of the City* (Minneapolis: University of Minnesota Press, 2007); and Jerry Pinto, *Helen: The Life and Times of an H-Bomb* (New Delhi: Penguin, 2006).
[48] William Mazzarella, *Shoveling Smoke: Advertising and Globalization in Contemporary India* (Durham, NC: Duke University Press, 2003).
[49] *AHAR 2006*, Para 36.

This, perhaps, was the cardinal sin of the dance bars at the level of cultural location: they threatened to globalise that popular Indian language of public desire which, as Christopher Pinney observes, finds its objects in 'the melodies of Hindi film songs, the curves of Amitabh's or Madhuri's body, the vivid materiality of popular visual culture'.[50] For all the much-touted globalisation of Bollywood during those years, the films that have been aimed at diaspora markets determinedly fetishised either 'global' urban life-worlds (*Kal Ho Naa Ho*,[51] with its yuppie Manhattan *habitus*) or 'traditional' family values (the sentimental conservatism of a *Kabhi Khushi Kabhie Gham*[52]). Against such authorised export-quality alloys of the transnational and the Indian, the dance bars were disastrously 'off brand'.

***

The State Government of Maharashtra appealed against the overturning of the dance bar ban and the Supreme Court of India admitted the appeal in May 2006, ordering that the dance bars remain closed until it could render a decision. Not until July 2013 did the Supreme Court finally uphold the Bombay High Court's judgement that the ban was unconstitutional.[53] Bar dancers had been forced, during the intervening seven years, to find alternative sources of income. There were reports of suicides, of transitions into full-time sex work, but also of returns to the kinds of menial manual jobs that many of them pursued before they began dancing: construction, rolling *bidis*, domestic service, rag-picking. A few dance bars continued operating despite the ban, paying five times the usual bribe for the privilege.[54] At the time of this writing, the latest development is the June 2014 passage of a bill in the Maharashtra state legislature that comprehensively criminalises bar dancing in *all* venues, from roadside shacks to five-star hotels. Further legal challenges are no doubt on the horizon. In a minor key, then, the memory of the dance bars has become another epitaph for the troubled cosmopolitanism of a great city.

---

[50] The reference here is to Hindi film superstars Amitabh Bachchan and Madhuri Dixit. See Christopher Pinney, 'Introduction: Public, Popular, and Other Cultures', in Rachel Dwyer and Christopher Pinney (eds), *Pleasure and the Nation: The History, Politics, and Consumption of Public Culture in India* (New Delhi: Oxford University Press, 2001), p. 1.
[51] *Kal Ho Naa Ho*, dir. Nikhil Advani, 2003.
[52] *Kabhi Khushi Kabhie Gham*, dir. Karan Johar, 2001.
[53] William Mazzarella, 'Where Court Stops Short', *The Indian Express* (25 July 2013) [http://archive.indianexpress.com/news/where-court-stops-short/1146213/, accessed 18 Aug. 2014].
[54] Faleiro, *Beautiful Thing*, p. 159.

Commissioning Representation: The Misra Report, Deliberation and the Government of the People in Modern India

RUPA VISWANATH, *University of Göttingen, Göttingen, Germany*

Commissions of inquiry are unique tools of modern governance that represent 'the people', but in a manner quite unlike parliaments and other forms of elected political representation. Using as its example the 2007 Misra Report, this paper reveals how, in the production of a commission report, scores of non-state actors—'stakeholders' from a wide range of social strata—are enlisted to produce the policies that will then redound upon those very stakeholders. In thus consulting the people and eliciting their speech, commissions serve to publicly enact, in a controlled setting, the deliberative ideal of democracy that is otherwise absent in India. In this particular instance, the problematic status of Dalits is subsumed under the normative religious identity of the post-colonial Indian nation, a conclusion whose emergence through reasoned debate is publicly enacted in the form of the commission.

Introduction

In the present age of the nation-state, the legitimacy of rulers depends everywhere on the claim to govern in the name of the people. Whether liberal or authoritarian, capitalist or socialist, states today almost invariably characterise themselves as 'democratic'.[1] Such is the prestige of popular sovereignty that, as John Dunn has pointed out, even those few functioning monarchies that still exist 'strive to ingratiate themselves as best they may as the instruments of their people's purposes, [and as] tools of the Demos'.[2] In reality, of course, nowhere in the world do 'the people' actually rule. They are represented, both in the sense of having others decide authoritatively for them and in the sense of being portrayed and interpreted.[3]

Does the state truly represent the will of the people? This question is central to the legitimacy of modern states inasmuch as an affirmative answer must be continually demonstrated. The hegemonic institutional form through which it is demonstrated—through

---

This essay has benefitted from the astute comments of participants at the Rethinking Publics conference held at Northwestern University in 2014, and I would especially like to thank its organisers, Bart Scott, SherAli Tareen and Brannon Ingram. Peter van der Veer offered valuable criticism on an early version, and Srirupa Roy asked searching questions of a late draft. Extended conversations with Nate Roberts were essential both to the formulation of the introductory sections and to the overall thrust of the argument. Finally, I am grateful to the two anonymous reviewers for *South Asia*.

[1] John Dunn, *Western Political Theory in the Face of the Future* (Cambridge: Cambridge University Press, 1988).
[2] *Ibid.*, p. 1.
[3] Hanna F. Pitkin, *The Concept of Representation* (Berkeley: University of California Press, 1967); and David Runciman, 'The Paradox of Political Representation', in *Journal of Political Philosophy*, Vol. 15, no. 1 (2007), pp. 93–114.

which 'the people' are at once portrayed and invited to speak—is, today, the representative assembly (the parliament or other legislative body, such as the US Congress). Thus, a massive literature in philosophy, political theory and political science focuses on the representative function of elected bodies endowed with the task of creating law.

This paper, by contrast, offers a different perspective on the problem of representation by way of a comparatively marginal institution, the commission of enquiry. But as is often the case, by focusing on the marginal, we are able to perceive that which is central and hegemonic in a new light. Since at least the late Victorian era, when commissions became the primary means of addressing what were newly understood as 'social questions' in Britain—namely, poverty, labour, education, public health and other typical targets of state welfare—critics have alleged that commissions in Westminster-style parliamentary systems are sops that give the mere appearance of action in order to placate the public, and that membership of them is often politically-stacked.[4]

While there is no doubt a good bit of truth to such accusations, the purpose of this paper is not to debunk, but to understand; commissions do not always—indeed, very rarely—deliver on their promises, but they are nevertheless effective, as I will show. In this paper, I focus on one particular commission, the 2007 Misra Commission, and its report, which is also known as the *Report of the National Commission for Religious and Linguistic Minorities* (*NCRLM*). The report's most significant sections concern India's lowest castes, and the question that animates it—without ever being directly stated—is the problematic relationship of these outcaste groups to the national whole.[5] What is at stake is the very idea of 'the people' as such.

The fact that any national population will comprise multiple and competing interest groups is well known. The task of a parliament and other institutions of representative government is conventionally seen as being to discover, through the deliberation of representatives, the common national interest that is assumed to exist above and beyond the apparently conflicting interests of its members. The conceit that such a transcendental whole exists—and that irreducibly antagonistic divisions do not[6]—is the unthought of national ideology that the political practice of 'representing the people' seeks to affirm. Since at least the early twentieth century, however, it has been obvious that the ideal of open-ended deliberation that is the intellectual foundation of parliamentary democracy fails entirely to characterise the actual operation of existing bodies of elected representatives.[7] As Carl Schmitt has put this, deliberation

---

[4] Classics of this kind of analysis include F. Burton and P. Carlen, *Official Discourse: On Discourse Analysis, Government Publications, Ideology and the State* (London: Routledge & Kegan Paul, 1967); and A.P. Herbert, *Anything But Action? A Study of the Uses and Abuses of Committees of Inquiry* (London: Barrie & Rockliff, 1960).

[5] The Misra Commission Report displays highly generalisable features characteristic of the first of two broad sub-types of commission in post-colonial India, namely those that address social questions. The other type of commission, which does not necessarily display the features discussed here, investigates major allegations of criminal wrongdoing by state officials (see examples in fn. 12). The full text of the *Report of the National Commission for Religious and Linguistic Minorities (Ranganath Misra Commission Report) Vols. I & II* is available at http://www.minorityaffairs.gov.in/sites/upload_files/moma/files/pdfs/volume-1.pdf, and http://www.minorityaffairs.gov.in/sites/upload_files/moma/files/pdfs/volume-2.pdf, accessed 23 Feb. 2015.

[6] Nathaniel Roberts, 'Puzzles of Representation: Vote Buying and "Fraudulent" Conversion in a Chennai Slum', invited paper at Department of Anthropology, University of Pennsylvania, 2 Jan. 2009.

[7] Talal Asad, *Formations of the Secular: Christianity, Islam, Modernity* (Stanford, CA: Stanford University Press, 2003), pp. 4–6; Alasdair MacIntyre, 'Politics, Philosophy and the Common Good', in Kelvin Knight (ed.), *The MacIntyre Reader* (Notre Dame, IN: University of Notre Dame Press, 1998), pp. 235–52; and Carl Schmitt (Ellen Kennedy, trans.), *The Crisis of Parliamentary Democracy* (Cambridge, MA: MIT Press, 1988). Anglo-American political theorists have recently debated the relative merits of deliberation over other decision-making procedures and considered what makes some kinds of deliberation properly democratic. A good overview may be found in Amy Gutmann and Dennis Thompson, *Why Deliberative Democracy?* (Princeton, NJ: Princeton University Press, 2004), Chap. 1.

does not mean simply negotiation…[but] an exchange of opinion that is governed by the purpose of persuading one's opponent through argument of the truth or justice of something, or allowing oneself to be persuaded of something as true and just.[8]

In actually existing parliaments and comparable assemblies, by contrast:

parties…do not face each other today discussing opinions, but as social or economic power-groups calculating their mutual interests and opportunities for power, and they actually agree to compromises and coalitions on this basis. The masses are won over through a propaganda apparatus whose maximum effect relies on an appeal to immediate interests and passions. Argument in the real sense that is characteristic for genuine discussion ceases…. [I]t is no longer a question of persuading one's opponent of the truth or justice of an opinion but rather of winning a majority in order to govern with it.[9]

One need not accept Schmitt's alternative to recognise the plain truth in the gap he identifies between practice and precept. The fact that deliberation is absent from the globally hegemonic institutional form of representative government does not, however, mean that it has been banished entirely from modern statecraft. The argument of the present paper is that, having been marginalised in parliaments and comparable bodies, deliberation reappears in another—institutionally marginal, but politically critical—representative body, the commission. It is here, rather than in parliaments, that the symbolic labour of discursively conjuring up (or discovering) the people as a whole is performed. In a carefully circumscribed setting, the range of opinions on potentially antagonistic social divisions are publicly called forth and reconciled. The purpose of the present essay is to demonstrate in some detail how this effect is achieved. I underscore that my own aim is not normative: I do not consider commissions a solution to what some call 'deficits' of democracy in India.[10] I am interested in how the commission's representative function serves to highlight both the fissures in the national whole that a representative regime must resolve in order to maintain legitimacy, and also the deliberative consensus-making activity through which solutions to 'social questions' are authoritatively constructed.

The term 'commission' refers to both an institution and the document that the institution produces, also called the commission report. As documents, these are very deliberately crafted, unlike all other papers in the official archive, to serve a specifically *public* function.[11] Commissions are a particular form of public event and, indeed, from

---

[8] Schmitt, *Crisis of Parliamentary Democracy*, p. 5. Schmitt's favoured term for what others call deliberation is 'open discussion', and he sometimes uses 'deliberation' in a contrastive sense that is at odds with current usage in democratic theory. To avoid confusion, I use deliberation consistently throughout.
[9] *Ibid.*, pp. 6–7.
[10] As I note in this essay's conclusion, such a position would entail understanding deliberation as *essentially* democratic, a view I do not share.
[11] It is true that when their findings are too controversial or politically inconvenient for ruling parties and interests, the release of commission reports in India is delayed or suppressed. But this does not affect my overall argument about their form and function.

Shah to Mandal, Misra to Nanavati, and Sri Krishna to Sachar,[12] the political history of the post-colonial state could well be written as a history of commissions and the public talk they occasion.[13] Textually, as I will show, a commission enacts the representation of the people's collective deliberation, the making of reasoned consensus that is at the normative core of modern democracy.[14] In graphic form, it displays the amassing of a variety of opinions, including, importantly, those of representatives of the groups whose problems the commission might be addressing.[15] Commissions are never short documents, running into hundreds of pages of opinion, nor is the style of exposition concise. Because they record or report upon the views of many persons on the same topic, much of the substance is highly repetitive. Indeed, like much ethnographic writing, the accumulative repetitiveness and concern with minutiae play both a rhetorical and epistemological role. They embody what anthropologists call 'thick description',[16] in contrast to the discursively thin soup of national elections, the political equivalent of a multiple-choice survey. The result is a graphic clamour of voices in debate, all permitted to speak—indeed, made to speak. The commission then guides these voices to consensus, even when it strategically showcases, to great rhetorical effect, disagreement along the way, as I will soon show. The commission is not, however, just one instance of the state consulting the people to determine the nature of and solutions to their own problems—it publicly calls attention to the very processes of consultation and consensus in both

---

[12] The Shah Commission investigated the excesses of Indira Gandhi's regime during the Emergency of 1975–77 and was published in 1978; the Mandal Commission created a furore in 1987, when then Prime Minister V.P. Singh sought to implement its recommendations on reservations for Other Backward Classes (OBCs); the Nanavati Commission of 2000 inquired into the 1984 anti-Sikh riots in Delhi that followed Indira Gandhi's assassination and led to the resignation of a cabinet member; the Sri Krishna Commission studied the Hindu–Muslim riots in Mumbai in 1992–93, following the demolition of the Babri Masjid; and, finally, the Sachar Committee report was ordered by Prime Minister Manmohan Singh in 2005 to study the condition of Muslims in India. All of these commissions occasioned extensive and heated public debate.

[13] Yet, the form of the commission has received no scholarly attention from South Asianists, except for an article by Thomas Hansen, which discusses the Sri Krishna Report and its role in restoring faith in the idealised face of the state as the benevolent and neutral arbiter of social conflict. See T.B. Hansen, 'Governance and Myths of State in Mumbai', in C.J. Fuller and V. Bénéï (eds), *The Everyday State and Society in Modern India* (London: Hurst, 2001), pp. 31–67.

[14] My point here is only that deliberation which results in some form of rational compromise through persuasive argument is a widespread ideal, a theory of democracy best exemplified in works such as J. Habermas, *Between Facts and Norms: Contributions to a Discourse Theory of Law and Democracy* (Cambridge, MA: MIT Press, 1996), and it is this variety of deliberation that the post-colonial state enacts in commissions. But there is no agreement on either the necessity of deliberation for a just democracy, or on the idea that deliberation must ultimately result in consensus. Thus, Gutmann and Thompson argue that even when agreement cannot be reached, deliberation is superior to purely aggregative forms of decision-making (see Gutmann and Thompson, *Why Deliberative Democracy?*), while deliberation as an ideal is itself questioned in, for instance, Lynn Sanders, 'Against Deliberation', in *Political Theory*, Vol. 25, no. 3 (1996), pp. 347–76; and Iris Marion Young, 'Activist Challenges to Deliberative Democracy', in *Political Theory*, Vol. 29, no. 5 (2001), pp. 670–90.

[15] Commissions are thus also representative in the sense of being politically incorporative: the problems posed by some sub-populations to the unity of the people are represented as amenable to solution within the frame of the nation-state. The commission, therefore, acts as both instrument and index of political conciliation. See Adam Ashforth's examination of the use of official discourse (not only commissions) in the South African regime's attempts at subduing the 'natives' in his *The Politics of Official Discourse in Twentieth-Century South Africa* (Oxford: Oxford University Press, 1990). Similarly, Oz Frankel describes the incorporation of Native American tribes in the United States in the nineteenth century through print media in his *States of Inquiry: Social Investigations and Print Culture in Nineteenth Century Britain and the United States* (Baltimore, MD: Johns Hopkins University Press, 2006).

[16] Clifford Geertz, 'Thick Description: Toward an Interpretive Theory of Culture', in *The Interpretation of Cultures* (New York: Basic Books, 2000), pp. 3–30.

institutional and discursive respects. In this sense, it represents not just a range of actual opinions, but the idealised form of political representation itself. It represents the deliberative processes that are so conspicuously lacking in all modern parliaments and other bodies of elected representatives.

Determining the Religion of Caste

I myself in my own person claim *to represent* the vast mass of the Untouchables (Gandhi, 1931).[17]

The true significance of Gandhi's (in)famous claim resides not, as most commenters have tended to assume, in either its hubris or the obvious fact that he is not an untouchable. While likeness between representer and representative is certainly a worthy goal and has important political implications, representatives are in fact always different from those they stand for, and necessarily so.[18] What is significant stems rather from what Gandhi does not say, and which goes without saying: that he represents not only untouchables, but also caste Hindus. For in claiming to represent both untouchable and caste Hindu, Gandhi asserts the nationalist dogma that there is no fundamental antagonism between the two, that there is a 'whole' capable of being represented, and that this encompassing whole is in some fundamental but unspoken way a Hindu one.[19]

To grasp the significance of the Misra Report, we must situate it in terms of the historically shifting relationship between religion and caste, from which the new administrative category of Scheduled Caste emerged as a temporary and unstable solution to the problematic status of untouchables within the nation as a 'whole'. Caste and religion are most often described in academic accounts as two distinct *kinds* of social difference that cleave the populace in modern India. An enduring problem is the point at which this categorial logic meets its limit, and that is with respect to Dalits, who in fact are defined by both. In the administrative language of the state, most Dalits primarily appear under the rubric Scheduled Castes (SCs), so called because they are included on a schedule or list first prepared in 1935 for purposes of legal and administrative identification.[20] In legislation, Dalits are described in official terms as those who are victims of 'untouchability', by which is meant degrading treatment and social and physical exclusion that is supposed to derive its legitimacy from a Hindu biomoral conception of these groups as permanently 'polluted'. Yet, they are also almost to a number descendants of unfree agrestic servants, a fact that is historically central,[21] but which the official accounts of the post-colonial state never acknowledge. While religion and political

---

[17] Mahatma Gandhi at the Round Table Conference in 1931, quoted in Eleanor Zelliott, 'Gandhi and Ambedkar: A Study in Leadership', in *From Untouchable to Dalit: Essays on the Ambedkar Movement* (New Delhi: Manohar, 3rd ed., 2010), p. 166, emphasis added.

[18] As Bernard Manin has powerfully demonstrated, it is not only that representative governance is linked historically and conceptually to aristocratic rule. Rather, by their very nature (and not just empirically), elections entail the selection of elites who are at least in some respect different from those they represent. See Bernard Manin, *Principles of Representative Governance* (Cambridge: Cambridge University Press, 1997).

[19] Cf. Nathaniel Roberts, 'The Power of Conversion and the Foreignness of Belonging', unpublished book manuscript, Chap. 3.

[20] Though often used as a synonym for Dalit, the category Scheduled Castes does not include all Dalits; Christian and Muslim Dalits are specifically excluded. See Rupa Viswanath, 'A Textbook Case of Exclusion', *The Indian Express* (13 July 2012) [http://www.indianexpress.com/news/a-textbook-case-of-exclusion/973711/0, accessed 10 Jan. 2015]. We return to this point below.

[21] Rupa Viswanath, *The Pariah Problem: Caste, Religion and the Social in Modern India* (New York: Columbia University Press, 2014), Chap. 1.

economy might appear, then, to present contrasting ways of *accounting* for Dalits' subordination—and social scientists cite both in equal measure as 'factors'—scholars continue implicitly to *define* Dalitness specifically in terms of religious denigration, for instance by privileging their ritually untouchable status as the single unambiguous index of what it means to be Dalit and, relatedly, by linking caste ontologically to Hinduism.[22] This structuring assumption, shared by both academics and officials, is reflected in the very name 'untouchable', which foregrounds ritual prohibition at the expense of other aspects of their subordination.[23]

In the self-representation of political Dalits since at least the early twentieth century, they exist in an ongoing antagonistic relationship with the rest of Indian society and with Hindus. But because of their demographic importance in electoral politics, both the Congress Party and its primary rivals in the Hindu majoritarian camp have long insisted on definitionally incorporating them within the Hindu fold, which, I should note, plentiful evidence shows was not at all obvious prior to the early twentieth century.[24] While the conception of Dalits as a religiously-defined sub-population, and the political importance of their constituency, emerged in the colonial era, becoming fully hegemonic only after Gandhi adopted this view, what is not often publically acknowledged is that the post-colonial state has been instrumental as well in legally and administratively securing Dalits as an integral part of a specifically Hindu body politic.[25]

The most effective of these means is first, as Marc Galanter and Duncan Derrett have pointed out, that the legal definition of Hinduism is above all remarkably capacious.[26] In personal law, anyone practising or professing anything at all, even ardent atheism, is a Hindu—so long as she refrains from explicitly adhering to Christianity or Islam—and this applies as well to Dalits. In this way, the majority of Dalits were defined as Hindus as a matter of law. At a stroke, the law accomplishes what many tried to do at the turn of the century by political means, and what outfits like the RSS (Rashtriya Swayamsevak Sangh) continue to do today. In defining Hinduism in exactly the same way as it is defined by the Hindu majoritarian ideology known as 'Hindutva', India's otherwise liberal judiciary testifies to the pervasive agreement on the relationship of Dalits to Hinduism that exists across the political divisions that make up the post-colonial state.

The counterpart to these measures of administrative incorporation is a series of disincentives to out-conversion accomplished by the fact that 'Scheduled Castes' and,

---

[22] For documentation of the ubiquity of this trend in the South Asianist anthropology of caste, see Nathaniel Roberts, 'Caste, Anthropology Of', in William Darity (ed.), *International Encyclopedia of the Social Sciences, Vol. 1* (New York: Macmillan Reference USA, 2008), pp. 461–3. I have traced the emergence of this discourse to Protestant missionaries in nineteenth-century Madras. See Viswanath, *The Pariah Problem*, Chap. 2 and 5.

[23] The effect of this spiritualised view of Dalit subordination on state policies is detailed in *The Pariah Problem*. David Washbrook has suggested that post-colonial policy continues to favour symbolic, rather than structural measures to redress caste inequality. See his 'Caste, Class and Dominance in Modern Tamil Nadu: Non-Brahmanism, Dravidianism and Tamil Nationalism', in Francine Frankel and M.S.A. Rao (eds), *Dominance and State Power in Modern India, Vol. 1* (New Delhi: Oxford University Press, 1989), pp. 204–64.

[24] Cf. Rupa Viswanath, 'Dalit/ Ex-Untouchable', in Knut Jakobsen (ed.), *Brill's Encyclopedia of Hinduism, Vol. 4* (Leiden: Brill, 2012), pp. 779–87.

[25] See Rupa Viswanath, 'Silent Minority: Celebrated Difference, Caste Difference and the Hinduization of Independent India', in Steven Vertovec (ed.), *Routledge Handbook of Diversity* (London: Routledge, 2015). On Gandhi's role in popularising the now common-sense opinion that Dalits are Hindus, see Roberts, 'The Power of Conversion and the Foreignness of Belonging'.

[26] See Marc Galanter, 'Hinduism, Secularism and the Indian Judiciary', in *Philosophy East and West*, Vol. 21, no. 4 (Oct. 1971), pp. 467–87; and J. Duncan M. Derrett, *Religion, Law and the State in India* (London: Faber, 1968), p. 52.

therefore, the policies of reservation which apply to those, refer *only* to Hindu, Sikh and, as of 1990, Buddhist Dalits. To openly convert to Christianity or Islam is to exclude oneself from access to preferential treatment in education and government hiring and to lose eligibility to stand for office in a reserved electoral constituency. Moreover, Dalits stripped of SC (Scheduled Caste) status because they convert also lose protection under the Prevention of Atrocities Act, so depriving Dalit converts of any special protection from retribution at the hands of caste Hindus.[27] Both the post-colonial state's capacious definition of Hinduism, as well as the disincentives to out-conversion secured by reservation policy, thus serve to place, and then help retain, Dalits within the Hindu fold. In defining SC status by religion, the post-colonial state reinforces the consensus that Dalitness is a specifically Hindu phenomenon, and that the existence of discrimination against Dalits by non-Hindus is simply residual.

The denial of SC status to Dalit Christians and Muslims has angered civil rights and Dalit activists for decades. For one thing, the idea that Dalits no longer need protections upon conversion implies that Dalits cease to be Dalits, with all that entails, just because they are no longer officially Hindu. But there is no evidentiary basis for this presumptive logic. Indeed, there is evidence aplenty of just the reverse, namely that Dalits are often targeted for additional abuse just for converting. Yet, the opposition to Muslims and Christians benefitting from state aid is so deeply entrenched among one section of India's political class, and passively accepted by the other, that most Muslim and Christian Dalits had come to regard their cause as hopeless.

Then, in 2007, something quite unexpected happened. The Misra Commission Report made for the first time an official statement that the category Scheduled Caste should be amended to include Christians and Muslims. At the end of a lengthy inquiry, and on the basis of evidence presented by academics, community leaders and human rights activists, as well as discussions of constitutional validity, the Commission concluded that there was no justification for the exclusion of Christian and Muslim Dalits from the SC category, not least in a state committed to equal treatment of religions. The initial impression of observers was that, although implementing this recommendation might be opposed, and even possibly delayed, given the political strength of Hindu majoritarian parties in India, the problem itself had been definitively resolved and a longstanding injustice rectified. The expected fruits of the Commission's findings, however, have still to be tasted—the Misra Report appeared in 2007, and the legal definition of SC has yet to be amended—lending credibility to the frequent charge that commissions are a specific mode of state inaction.

But a commission is not, thereby, simply a dead letter. The Misra Commission accomplishes something quite other than that which it officially claims for itself due to the discursive *form* and *manner of production* of the commission. What does it mean that it is specifically a commission that has produced this new truth about Dalit subordination? I will focus on four aspects of the Misra Report to elucidate.

Self-Narration

The first is historical self-narration. Common to colonial-era commissions and to those of the post-colonial state is the prominent place assigned within the body of the commission to a history of the commission's own emergence, which takes the form of a history of state

---

[27] It should be noted, however, that lack of enforcement and the exceedingly high rate of acquittal mean these legal protections exist mainly at a theoretical level and not in fact. See Smita Narula (ed.), *Human Rights Watch, Broken People: Caste Violence against India's "Untouchables"* (New York: Human Rights Watch, 1999) [http://www.hrw.org/reports/1999/india/, accessed 21 Dec. 2014].

solutions to the particular problem in question. The state is invariably represented as having long recognised the problem. An exhaustive accounting is then taken of prior state efforts to resolve it, which are said to have been, however valiant, inadequate. The problem, we are told, must therefore be posed anew, and this time to a wide battery of those known in modern developmental statist parlance as 'stakeholders'.

In the case of our example, the Misra Report must explain to its readers how and why Scheduled Castes have been categorised according to religion. The Misra Report, and not only that Report, but a wide range of other official and semi-official post-colonial documents, assert that the term Scheduled Caste was linked to religion from *the very first time* it appeared, namely in the 1935 Government of India Act. As the Report asserts, 'the test applied [for inclusion in the schedule] was the social, educational and economic backwardness *arising out of the historical custom of untouchability*'.[28] Untouchability, the religiously-defined prejudice against Dalits perpetrated by caste Hindus, is identified as the source of the 'backwardness' to which the state should attend: religion is the generative source of social ills, and this is presumed in the making of the administrative term Scheduled Caste, according to the Misra Report. But no particular part of the 1935 Act, or any other document, is ever cited as the specific source of the claim.

The Government of India Act of 1935 does indeed contain the first official attestation of the term Scheduled Caste, and it does include a schedule, or list, of castes to whom this designation should apply. And, by default, the only persons included in the category are Hindus, but that was because Christians and Muslims already had their own reserved seats in colonial legislatures. This is quite distinct from ontologically linking SC status with Hinduism. Contrary to what all post-colonial commentators have claimed, the Government of India Act, then, does not link SC status to a religious point of origin, saying only that '"the scheduled castes" means such castes, races or tribes or parts of or groups within castes, races or tribes…which appear to His Majesty in Council to correspond to the classes of persons formerly known as "the depressed classes"'.[29] What the Government of India Act does is simply to refer us back to an earlier administrative category—which was itself never linked to religion and routinely included Christians in the distribution of welfare.[30] There is no mention of the ritual logic of untouchability *per se* in the 1935 Act. Yet, this is what the Misra Commission states, and earlier post-colonial commissions on the Scheduled Castes have done the same. What this false identification does, since this way of thinking about Dalit subordination has been identified in Misra as an error, is to firmly locate the source of the error in an administrative logic framed prior to the post-colonial regime's foundation.

The historical narratives that introduce Misra and other Indian commissions are best understood as specifically moral statements, a feature of narrative often linked to its teleological structure.[31] The moral dimension is evident in how commissions provide justification for state intervention as well as a rationale for the particular kind of intervention proposed. In the Misra Commission Report, the state is rhetorically construed as *separate from*

---

[28] *Report of the National Commission for Religious and Linguistic Minorities* (henceforth *NCRLM*), *Vol. I*, p. 39, emphasis added [http://www.minorityaffairs.gov.in/sites/upload_files/moma/files/pdfs/volume-1.pdf, accessed 23 Feb. 2015].

[29] Government of India Act of 1935, Chap. 2, First Schedule, Para 26 [http://www.legislation.gov.uk/ukpga/1935/2/pdfs/ukpga_19350002_en.pdf, accessed 12 Dec. 2014].

[30] See Rupa Viswanath, 'Rethinking Caste and Class: "Labour", the "Depressed Classes", and the Politics of Distinctions, Madras 1918–1924', in *International Review of Social History*, Vol. 59, no. 1 (2014), pp. 1–37.

[31] Cf. Alasdair MacIntyre, *After Virtue: A Study in Moral Theory* (Notre Dame, IN: University of Notre Dame Press, 1981); and Hayden White, 'The Value of Narrativity in the Representation of Reality', in *Critical Inquiry*, Vol. 7, no. 1 (1980), pp. 5–27.

the problem it addresses. Yet, it is in fact its constitutive source. For the problem is, after all, entirely a matter of how the state has categorised and differentially tended to national sub-populations on the basis of religion—namely, in a manner that reveals its own investment in promoting one category of persons (Hindus) against others (Dalits and non-Hindus). While a false start is assigned to the colonial regime, the Misra narrative stresses that the post-colonial Constitution is the right instrument to fix the social problem. The chapter in Misra which describes the state policy of providing benefits to Scheduled Castes begins:

> The spirit of equality pervades the provisions of the Constitution of India as the main aim of the founders of the Constitution was to create an egalitarian society wherein social, economic and political justice prevailed and equality of status and opportunity are made available to all. However, owing to historical and traditional reasons certain classes of Indian citizens are under severe social and economic disabilities that they cannot effectively enjoy either equality of status or of opportunity. Therefore, the Constitution accords to these weaker sections of society protective discrimination in various Articles....[32]

'Tradition' is credited with producing untouchability and the latter is thereby placed beyond the blame of the post-colonial nation-state. By positioning itself as the solution to a problem whose source lies elsewhere, underscoring the autonomy of the state from the society in whose name it governs, the Report displaces culpability.

It is striking too that the first and only Dalit activist to be mentioned as a significant player in the history of solving this social problem in the Misra Report's introduction is B.R. Ambedkar—after all difficult to ignore since he was a principal author of the Constitution. Dalits' own political and social interventions and forms of mobilisation in different regions of India since at least the end of the nineteenth century are entirely omitted. In this way, the Misra Commission constructs a historical narrative of social intervention conducted under the auspices of the people, but decidedly and solely by the agency of the state. The Report's argument for intervention is based on the (moral) claim that the founding of the nation-state came with a promise of equality and that it is the citizen's duty to evince loyalty to that promise just as it is the state's to fulfill it. In Misra's narrative, moreover, while the members of the Commission are not all state actors, they were called to action by the post-colonial state. The narrative that frames every commission fixes the legitimate provider of solutions to crises as the state, which acts, by means of the commission's collection of opinion, on the will of the people.

Social Science, Relays and Representation through the Achievement of Consensus

The second feature of commissions I want to examine is the connections made, by means of the commission's procedures, among ordinary persons, forms of activism, and professional social science. These concrete mechanisms that produce the commission as a replica of consensus-making are by no means a secret, but they are conspicuously missing from the sections of commissions that narrate their own emergence. How did the question that most interests me among those the Misra Commission was charged to answer—namely, the issue of whether Dalit Christians and Muslims should be awarded Scheduled Caste status, thereby becoming eligible for state protections and benefits—come to be included in the

---

[32] *NCRLM, Vol. I*, p. 114.

Commission's mandate? The answer shows the operation of a complex relay between the state, democratic politics, formal institutions of higher education, and practices of representation.

The issue of according SC status to Christians and Muslims was not, in fact, even one of the original aims of the Commission, but was added to its tasks at a later stage; the Commission was originally conceived only as a general inquiry into the conditions of religious and linguistic minorities. This additional task was assigned to the Commission not because a past error had now come to be recognised, but as the result of a series of writ petitions made to the government. A writ petition is a document written by or on behalf of a citizen and ratified by a judge in the Supreme Court, and in post-colonial India, these have increasingly been used to uphold citizens' rights, enlisted by activists as a way of calling the state to account. In this case, the writ petition was filed by a particular Dalit Christian activist, to whom we will return shortly, and concerned the findings of the Supreme Court in a landmark judgement made in response to an earlier writ petition that would appear to have settled the question regarding the SC status of Dalit Christians. That earlier petition concerned a Dalit Christian cobbler in Madras (now Chennai) named Soosai (a common Tamil Catholic name), who was to be awarded a free lean-to as part of the state's SC welfare measures. Soosai was first promised this service and then denied it because he was a Christian, and his own case became the subject of the earlier writ petition filed in 1985.

That petition went up to the Supreme Court, but was ultimately denied, the reason being the lack of reliable social scientific evidence. Here is what the justice said:

> To establish that…the…(Scheduled Castes) Order [of] 1950 discriminates against Christian members of the enumerated castes it must be shown that they suffer from a comparable depth of social and economic disabilities and cultural and educational backwardness and similar levels of degradation within the Christian community necessitating intervention by the State under provisions of the Constitution. It is not sufficient to show that the same caste continues after conversion. It is necessary to establish further that the disabilities and handicaps suffered from such caste membership in the social order of its origin—Hinduism—continue in their oppressive severity in the new environment of a different religious community. No authoritative or detailed study dealing with the present conditions of Christian society have been placed on the record in this case.[33]

In fact, there was never any lack of social scientific evidence of the kind the judge alleged. But the authority of the judge is an instance of sovereign and not democratic power in modern polities. The judge had no training in social science, but his claim that the 'social science is lacking' was not up for debate. In the normal course of things, the issue might have disappeared, as it did in fact for almost the next twenty years. Yet, in pinning his decision to social scientific knowledge, the judge unwittingly provided an opportunity for activists. In denying the adequacy of existing social science (however falsely), the court was simultaneously calling for more—for ever more authoritative and detailed studies that would tell it what the condition of society was.

And this, not coincidentally, is precisely what a state-sponsored commission sets out to do. In a very critical respect, therefore, Soosai the cobbler and the activists and politicians and non-governmental organisations (NGOs) that rallied around him produced the Misra Report: a complex relay of events and agents links activists, state agents, the courts, politicians and

---

[33] *Soosai Etc vs. Union Of India And Others, 30 Sept. 1985*, AIR 1986 733, 1985 SCR Supl. (3) 242 [http://indiankanoon.org/doc/1724190/, accessed 20 Feb. 2015].

social science, culminating in the Commission's performance of democratic deliberation. What began in colonial India with the recognition of Dalits as a sub-population requiring intervention was deemed inadequate by citizens—first Soosai himself and then Dalit activists and civil rights organisations. This, in turn, provoked a judgement pointing to a dearth of social scientific verifiability. Complaints about that judgement were elicited and formally filed on behalf of the citizenry as a writ petition in the early 2000s, which was itself the result of the dogged efforts of a single man: a Tamil Dalit activist by the name of Franklin Caesar, a Catholic, who painstakingly sought and won the endorsement of various state- and national-level politicians. Caesar's action redounded upon the state, which commissioned social scientific inquiry in the form of the Misra Commission Report. The Commission's members then turned to consult 'the people', calling forth the astonishing series of conferences, workshops, discussion groups and reams of reports that were subsequently produced at the most prestigious institutions of higher learning in India, including Jawarharlal Nehru University (JNU), Delhi University and the Tata Institute of Social Sciences (TISS) in Mumbai.[34]

The vast volume of data thus accumulated means that the Commission Report is nothing if not prolix. In both rhetorical form and in authorship, then, it may be contrasted to the other far more ubiquitous type of modern government document, namely, what we may call, following Max Weber, the 'file'.[35] Where the file is terse and exclusionary, the commission operates according to an incorporative principle by opening itself—rhetorically, if not in fact—to all relevant voices and opinions. In contrast to the file, the Misra Commission required two volumes and over four hundred dense pages to reach its conclusions—which is one reason such documents are so popular among historians. According to the Commission's own self-representation, formal recommendations are reached only after all parties have been made to speak.[36]

In the first volume, the chapters describe the history of the Commission's own emergence, the condition of different minorities, the history of reservation (the affirmative action policies that target SCs), and provide statistics, tables and charts drawn from data produced by social scientists and administrators, on behalf of the Commission, hailing from all of India's states and union territories. The second volume provides corroboration for all these results, including copies of the questionnaires sent out to the states, and a list of community and religious leaders with whom discussions were held—these were representatives of about

---

[34] The importance of social science to modern commissions specifically has rarely provoked comment, despite the well-known importance of social science to both colonial and post-colonial statecraft more generally. A few have simply evaluated how well social science serves the commission's ends from the perspective of studies of public policy. See Martin Bulmer (ed.), *Social Research and Royal Commissions* (London: George Allen & Unwin, 1980), a collection which mostly contains the reflections of commission directors and members; and more recently, K.S. Louis and R.J. Perlman, 'Commissions and the Use of Social Science Research: The Case of Safe Schools', in *Science Communication*, Vol. 7, no. 1 (1985), pp. 33–62.

[35] Max Weber (Guenther Roth and Claus Wittich, eds), *Economy and Society: An Outline of Interpretive Sociology* (Berkeley: University of California Press, 1978), pp. 956–8. Patrick Joyce discerns the very core of the nineteenth-century British imperial state's functioning in the file, and historians of former colonies largely agree. See Patrick Joyce, *The State of Freedom: A Social History of the British State Since 1800* (Cambridge: Cambridge University Press, 2013), esp. Chap. 4; Ilana Feldman, *Governing Gaza: Bureaucracy, Authority and the Work of Rule (1917–67)* (Durham, NC: Duke University Press, 2008); and Matthew Hull, *Government of Paper: The Materiality of Bureaucracy in Urban Pakistan* (Berkeley: University of California Press, 2012).

[36] The potential exploitation by interested state officials of the ambiguity between an official recommendation for legal action and actual legal indictment led to severe denunciations of commissions as early as the infamous 1849 London pamphlet by the city lawyer, J. Toulmin, entitled 'Government By Commission Illegal and Pernicious'.

twenty of the most important national religious organisations of minorities, including Christians, Muslims, Buddhists and Jains. Also included are summaries of the reports of visits to each of India's states and union territories conducted by employees of the Commission, which would have involved the co-operation of a large number of state-level employees. And, lastly, there are summary reports on the findings of studies sponsored by the Commission, which, as I have said, came from a range of academic institutions, think-tanks and NGOs, in order to accumulate detail on a vast array of sub-topics: thus, Jamia Millia Islamia University reported on the effects of madrasas in 'mainstreaming' Muslims into secular education; the Centre for Research, Planning and Action in New Delhi carried out a study in 151 cities to assess the socio-economic conditions of minorities; the Agricultural Finance Corporation performed a 'Rapid Assessment of the Role of Financial Institutions in the Upliftment of Minorities in the Country'; the Baba Saheb Ambedkar National Institute of Social Sciences in Mhow considered the 'Selection of Criteria and Identification of Social and Economic Backwardness among Religious Minorities'; the Tata Institute of Social Sciences inquired into the educational status of minorities; and the International Population Sciences Institute in Mumbai performed a 'situational analysis' on the condition of religious minorities. Numerous workshops were held: for instance, at the Delhi School of Economics, to consider 'alternatives to depoliticising backwardness'; at JNU, to assess the impact thus far of reservations policies; while the Tata Institute of Social Sciences organised an 'open-ended discussion' on the conferment of Scheduled Caste status to Dalit Christians and Muslims. Typically at such events, each attendee is invited to express an opinion until every single voice has been heard and duly recorded.

The profusion of social science that commissions elicit can even culminate in an entirely new political constituency: with the redefinition of SC will come a new sub-population to be represented, another voice to add to those that will make up the next commission. Historians have focused much critical attention on the relationship between administration and information gathering in the colonial period, when ethnographers and administrators were of course often the very same persons. But in post-colonial India, where professionalised social science has proliferated, the specifically *representational* logic by which it operates in a formal democracy, through the mechanism of the commission, has escaped notice. The often overlooked, but nevertheless intimate, relationships among politicised demands for state accountability, the incorporation of difference through a representation function, and the production of social science in the form of the commission have followed similar circuits now for well over a century and a half in India. Their links to the representative function of government have only been ramified in post-colonial India.

Recursivity

Consider, thirdly, the strange power according to which commissions reproduce themselves. We know that for the kinds of state intervention which concern problems of social difference, the consent of politically influential persons is necessary, and commissions have been a means to acquire this successfully since the colonial period. But why the sheer regularity with which they are instituted?

At least part of the answer is that commissions demand the repetition of their own form: commissions inevitably spawn commissions. Thus, we have a report like that of the Misra Commission, which investigates and discovers solutions to a social problem. To keep matters straight, let us call this an investigatory commission. But a 'commission' can also refer to a government body intended to oversee and ensure that the recommendations of an investigatory commission are implemented: this type I will call an oversight commission. In this case, the oversight commission is the National Commission for Minorities (also known as the Minority Commission). Oversight commissions also produce voluminous reports, this time on the extent to which the findings of investigatory commissions have been properly executed. While the main task of oversight commissions is to track implementation, the instrument for fulfilling this role is producing reports rather like those of investigatory commissions; the oversight commission, therefore, *also* produces reports on the basis of research conducted through sustained interaction with citizens, non-state experts and social scientists. And, of course, the reports of an oversight commission will become the evidentiary basis of a future investigatory commission. The Minority Commission has since, incidentally, produced an excellent report on the conditions of Dalit Christians and Muslims, which draws both upon primary research as well as the wealth of ethnographic sources that already exist, and was run by one of India's most eminent sociologists, definitively putting paid to the claim of lack of evidence in the judgement of the Soosai case.[37] Through a relay of state and non-state agents, the social science demanded by a judge in 1985 has now been produced and incorporated into the annals of the state, with the capacity to recursively produce more commissions.

Deliberation, Consensus and the Recalcitrance of Religion

I want to ask a final question of the Misra Commission Report. How is disagreement and consensus achieved within it, and what can this illuminate about democratic deliberation in modern states? The Commission was instructed to discover whether in fact Christian and Muslim Dalits face discrimination of an order comparable to their unconverted caste fellows. It did not take much for Misra's inquirers—the many agencies I referred to above—to conclusively demonstrate, first, that Dalit Muslims and Dalit Christians face the same discrimination after converting as before, and that by all possible measures—education, literacy, poverty, employment, and so on—they are in a comparable situation to their caste fellows of whatever religion. Contrary to the judge in the Soosai case, there always had been plenty of social science to support this view. What is interesting, then, is how this persistence of discrimination following conversion was explained. The Report concludes:

> On a careful examination of [the] prevalence of the caste system among various sections of the Indian citizenry we have concluded that caste is in fact a social phenomenon shared by almost all Indian communities irrespective of their religious persuasions.[38]

A little later, it reiterates:

> We recommend that the caste system should be recognized as a general social characteristic of the Indian society as a whole, without questioning whether the philosophy and teachings of any particular religion recognize it or not…. [T]he Indian brands of certain faith traditions like Christianity and Islam have never assimilated many puritan principles of those religions…[so] singling [them] out for a differential treatment is unreasonable and unrealistic.[39]

---

[37] Satish Deshpande, with the assistance of Geetika Bapna, 'Dalits in the Muslim and Christian Communities' [http://ncm.nic.in/pdf/report%20dalit%20%20reservation.pdf, accessed 5 Oct. 2014].
[38] *NCRLM, Vol. I*, p. 153.
[39] *Ibid.*, pp. 153–4.

Recall that the Report refers to the duty of the post-colonial nation-state to uphold the promise of equality enshrined in the Constitution and the fact that the colonial state is held responsible for wrongly assuming untouchables must be Hindu to face discrimination. The Commission provides what at first sight might appear to be a quite different etiology of this social problem. Caste, it asserts, has been incorrectly construed as a purely religious matter, when it inheres in fact in *society*.[40] Yet, even here, where it might appear that caste is being distinguished from religion, the Commission subtly reaffirms the Hinduness of Dalits, irrespective of what religion they profess. For we are told that in the face of Hindu society, imbued with its principles of caste, other religions like Christianity and Islam cannot exhibit themselves in their pure form, but are reduced to the status of 'Indian brands'—in comparison, we must suppose, to their original expressions found elsewhere. Islam and Christianity, in effect, have been nationalised by the very fact of their being Hinduised, which (in a subtly circular logic) is proven by their recognition of caste.

The Commission goes on to recommend that the Constitution be amended to grant reservations to Dalit Christians and Muslims, and this recommendation, as the Report repeatedly both shows and states, is arrived at via the consensus of the members of the Commission, and as a result of their discussion with and readings of the reports of the many official and non-official interlocutors whose opinions were solicited. So it is highly unusual, as the official members themselves remark, that the secretary of the Commission, one Asha Das, a woman whose post is explicitly defined as administrative as opposed to advisory, decided to write a 'Note of Dissent', which is included in the Report. Das' sole contention in a Report on a wide array of issues amounting to over four hundred pages of summary is the recommendation to amend the Scheduled Castes Article. This attests to the deep-rooted anxiety regarding the place of Dalits in national society, but what I want to focus on is the effect of Das' 'Note of Dissent' as an addition to the Commission Report as a whole. In it, the most obvious counter-arguments to the Commission's recommendations, common-sense assumptions on which ideas about SC status have long relied, are displayed and then contained. The inclusion of the 'Note' thus illustrates the representative logic of the Commission. The Commission members' counter-note, which follows Das', remarks: 'We are not sure of the propriety of this Dissent Note against the unanimous recommendations of the rest of the Commission (as member secretaries of Commissions are generally not members in their own independent capacity but ex officio members by virtue of their administrative position), but yet we have not raised any objection to it'.[41] It may not be proper, but it is a dissenting voice, and it is not silenced, graphically demonstrating the Commission's impartiality. What are the counter-arguments the 'Note of Dissent' illustrates and, most importantly, what assumptions does Das share with those from whom she is dissenting?

First, Das too asserts, like the judge in the Soosai case, that sociological data on Christian Dalits are lacking, this despite the four-hundred-odd pages in which her 'Note of Dissent' is contained. In this, therefore, she flatly denies the adequacy and impartiality of the Commission's collection of data—favouring a single nineteenth-century missionary report over the Commission's. But, importantly, she concurs with the dominant view on *the nature of evidence* that should be adduced and in *the kind of expertise* that is required. The 'Note of Dissent' confirms the legitimate form in which the people can participate in the solution of social problems.

---

[40] This is not the first time such an analysis has been made in an official document: the first time caste was ascribed to the realm of the social was in the late 1910s, at the very time when, as I have argued, social questions became a mark of good governance. See Viswanath, *The Pariah Problem*, Chap. 9. But regardless of its originality, it would seem to be one of the most significant findings of the Commission.

[41] *NCRLM, Vol. I*, p. 169.

Das' objection also rhetorically delimits the arena of acceptable debate. Since the Scheduled Castes order excludes Christianity and Islam from a list that includes Hinduism, Buddhism, Jainism and Sikhism, what is at issue is the national origin of religions. Religions originating in India are assumed to be less likely to produce forms of life that will quarantine adherents from Indian social conditions than are religions understood as foreign in India, namely Christianity and Islam. If Das unproblematically underscores the alleged foreignness of Indian Christians and Muslims, she also accords dubious internal—that is, *de facto* Hindu—status to Sikhism and Buddhism, explaining that these 'were primarily home-grown sects within Hindu religion rather than being independent religions in the nature of Christianity or Islam'.[42] The counter-note from the members of the Commission is quick to denounce this denial of the autonomy of Sikhism and Buddhism, as well as the treatment of Islam and Christianity as foreign:

> The statement made in the Dissent Note that 'Sikh and Buddhist religions were primarily home-grown sects within Hindu religion rather than being independent religions' is deplorable as it offends the religious sensitivities of the Sikh and Buddhist citizens of India who have always regarded their faiths as 'independent religions'.... Equally deplorable is the volatile attempt made in the Dissent Note to place 'religions which originated outside India' on a footing different from those born in India. As it introduces an absolutely un-Constitutional distinction between the two self-created categories of religions prevailing in India, we denounce it in the strongest possible terms.[43]

While I am in agreement with the conclusions and recommendations of the Commission, it is nevertheless important to point out that it is not only Das who makes a point of distinguishing, with direct political and policy-making consequence, Christianity and Islam from home-grown varieties of religion. If, for Das, they represent a foreign body in the body politic, and therefore are imagined negatively, for the Commission writers, they are Indian brands of foreign faiths, not *really* foreign, having never risen to the levels of purity attained in their sites of origin. One view is exclusionary, the other assimilationist, and both in different ways serve to reaffirm India's quintessentially Hindu national character. Disagreements within commissions, however indignantly expressed, in fact define a shared evidentiary and normative basis for the nation as a whole.

In the Misra Commission, then, what are represented as the farthest poles of opinion held by the influential political classes on the relationship of Dalits and religion are given voice. Insofar as commissions showcase democratic deliberation and serve to produce the people, Misra and other commissions tell us that the people can surmount internal disagreement. The compatibility of the people among themselves never entirely founders; there is no *total* dissensus, as the inevitable arrival of every commission at its final recommendations makes clear. In this case, the inherent Indianness of all the members of the population, including Christians and Muslims, who, we are assured, bear the traces of their Hindu pasts, is definitively preserved.

Conclusion

The commission as a genre of official writing is an institutional and textual form that is essential to the practice of modern statecraft, especially in relation to the state's function as an apparently neutral body serving to mediate and transcend the social divisions that cleave the

---

[42] *Ibid.*, p. 164.
[43] *Ibid.*, p. 169.

body politic.[44] This peculiar form long predates the modern state, rising to prominence in the Tudor period, where it played a critical role in the longstanding political contest between parliament and monarch.[45] In Tudor England, parliaments were called to secure fealty from powerful elites whose support for the royal regime was crucial to its fiscal and especially military success.[46] Commissions were an occasion when parliamentary debate was called forth and recorded, and while it had no legislative power, it was assumed these debates would shape the decisions of the monarch; parliamentary papers are therefore a form of commission.[47] Intervention in society—what the commission recommends—appears as a collective mandate that has been arrived at through deliberation, and in the post-colonial democratic state, this is the people's mandate. This aspect of the commission's operation shows one critical strand of continuity between post-colonial regimes and those that preceded them, since representation is a critical element of governance not only in democratic regimes, but in monarchies as well.[48]

Commissions also widely publicise a conception of the social problem in the form that will then likely govern administration and, very often, public talk. Commissions, after all, are designed to cast their net over scores of state and non-state agents, who, as we have seen, will disseminate its forms of talk in the courts, universities, boardrooms, NGOs and newsdesks over which they preside. What is not widely known is that in contemporary India, as elsewhere, it is a bailable offence to defame commissioners or the workings of a commission: 'If any person, by words either spoken or intended to be read, makes or publishes any statement or does any other act, which is calculated to bring the Commission or any member thereof into disrepute, he shall be punishable'.[49] The commission, an officially-sanctioned, but nevertheless independently-produced—and, therefore, putatively more credible—account of a social phenomenon, allows the official form of the social problem to become pervasive on pain of punishment.

The state's immense powers to define the sub-categories of the national population have long been sorely lamented by scholars. But it is crucial that these powers do not present themselves as the arbitrary exercise of administrative or judicial fiat because, in modern India, the state's decisions are ultimately justified on the basis of social scientific truth, and the public display of consensus and deliberation, especially when the subject of official concern is populations whose existence has been a matter of national anxiety since the foundation of the

---

[44] Cf. Frankel, *States of Inquiry*. This view is also compatible with Thomas Hansen's account of the work of the Sri Krishna Commission in post-riot Mumbai. See Hansen, 'Governance and Myths of State in Mumbai', pp. 31–67.

[45] Historians of policy will frequently refer to the Domesday book of 1086 as the first commission, but the form fulfilled a new function, similar to its modern role, only in the Tudor period. The earliest commissions, like the Domesday Book, were primarily intended to collect information to assist in taxation. See Thomas J. Lockwood, 'A History of Royal Commissions', in *Osgoode Hall Law Journal*, Vol. 5, no. 2 (Oct. 1967), pp. 172–209; and Harold F. Gosnell, 'British Royal Commissions of Inquiry', in *Political Science Quarterly*, Vol. 49, no. 1 (1934), pp. 84–118.

[46] Parliament at that time was of course the arena in which popular support was garnered, but this must be distinguished from the popular *sovereignty* with which parliaments are associated today, since popular sovereignty was not the source of political legitimacy.

[47] H.M. Clokie and J.W. Robinson, *Royal Commissions of Inquiry; The Significance of Investigations in British Politics* (New York: Octagon, [1937] 1964), esp. pp. 24–41.

[48] Manin, *Principles of Representative Governance*.

[49] Commissions of Inquiry Act, 1952, Section 10(2). It was a report on the workings of the Act published ten years after the Act's publication—a commission on commissions, as it were—that successfully urged the inclusion of these penalties for defamation. See Ministry of Law, Government of India, *Law Commission of India: Twenty-Fourth Report (Commissions of Inquiry Act, 1952)* (Dec. 1962) [http://lawCommissionofindia.nic.in/1-50/Report24.pdf, accessed 20 Feb. 2015], p. 10.

polity. The commission's importance in India has only grown with the passage of time. More significant in the late colonial period than the earlier, with the transition to formally democratic rule that came with Indian Independence, commissions have proliferated and taken on unprecedented scope.

Insofar as commissions embody what Timothy Mitchell has called 'the rule of experts', a technocratic form of governance that bases itself ultimately on the state's competence to efficiently and fairly administer to the needs (moral as well as material) of the population, they would seem to fit with a mode of statecraft political theorists and historians of India have typically seen as standing in contrast to that apparently more democratic institution of representative government, parliament. Throughout this paper, I have pursued a different line of thought, insofar as I have identified commissions as fulfilling a specifically representative function. By attending to the representational logic at work in both the commission and representative assemblies, it becomes evident that the 'relays' (as I have called them) between the people and state authority are more complex than is realised in theories that contrast the 'democratic' realm of electoral politics to a realm of technocratic 'rule by experts'. In analysing commissions in terms of the logic of representation—that is, as an institutional form in which a mute society is made to speak through purposeful deliberation—I do not intend to claim, however, that commissions are in any obvious sense democratic.[50] After all, the primary actors in commissions very much remain 'The Great and The Good', as indeed the list of men eligible to serve on commissions was explicitly labeled in nineteenth-century Britain.[51] But this is hardly different from parliaments.

---

[50] It is significant that like representation, the origins of deliberation are also aristocratic. See the discussion of Edmund Burke in Gutmann and Thompson, *Why Deliberative Democracy?*, pp. 8–9.

[51] P. Hennessy, *The Great and the Good: An Inquiry into the British Establishment* (London: Policy Studies Institute, 1986), discussed in George Gilligan, 'Royal Commissions of Inquiry', in *Australian & New Zealand Journal of Criminology*, Vol. 35, no. 3 (Dec. 2002), pp. 294–6.

Postscript: Exploring Aspects of 'the Public' from 1991 to 2014

SANDRIA B. FREITAG, *North Carolina State University, Raleigh, USA*

This essay suggests the expanded scholarly terrain created to analyse 'the public' that has been mapped between an initial special issue of the journal South Asia: Journal of South Asian Studies *(published in 1991) and this current essay collection (of 2015). In the process, it suggests not only what new scholarly interests and skills, as well as new sites for analysis, have opened up, but also points to issues yet unaddressed, along with elements of visual culture that scholars interested in 'the public' could consider. For the realm of the visual remains, even after 25 years, largely unconnected to analyses of 'the public', despite its centrality to the ways in which public issues, enactments and interests are expressed and debated. To provide overarching ways to think about how the essays presented here treat 'the public', as well as to draw attention to issues still not addressed that offer future challenges, this essay suggests conceptualising the subject around four aspects that emerged when the authors met together: the public as enacted; the public as envisioned; public space, both rhetorical and actual; and concepts of the public expressed as belief, interpretation, understandings, values and 'public opinion'—that is, as concepts understood to motivate and influence their audiences.*

Introduction

The journal *South Asia*, in a special issue published in 1991, brought together six articles approaching the concept of 'the public' in different ways.[1] This essay collection emerged when we had only an article by Jürgen Habermas to prompt us to think in new ways about the public sphere.[2] As my 'Introduction' suggested in 1991,[3] the goal in juxtaposing these articles was to investigate alternative locales (to those suggested by Habermas) for seeking 'the

---

[1] This issue included Dipesh Chakrabarty, 'Open Space/Public Place: Garbage, Modernity and India'; Faisal Devji, 'Gender and the Politics of Space: The Movement for Women's Reform in Muslim India, 1857–1900'; Sandria B. Freitag, 'Enactments of Ram's Story and the Changing Nature of "The Public" in British India'; David Gilmartin, 'Democracy, Nationalism and the Public: A Speculation on Colonial Muslim Politics'; Jim Masselos, 'Appropriating Urban Space: Social Constructs of Bombay in the Time of the Raj'; and Pamela Price, 'Acting in Public versus Forming a Public: Conflict Processing and Political Mobilization in Nineteenth Century South India'. See special issue of *South Asia: Journal of South Asian Studies*, 'Aspects of "the Public" in Colonial South Asia', Vol. 14, no. 1 (1991).
[2] Jürgen Habermas, 'The Public Sphere: An Encyclopedia Article (1964)', in *New German Critique*, Vol. 3 (Autumn 1974), pp. 49–55. Habermas' book, *The Structural Transformation of the Public Sphere: An Inquiry into a Category of Bourgeois Society*, was not published in English until after the essays in the 1991 special issue of *South Asia* had been written.
[3] Sandria B. Freitag, 'Introduction: "The Public" and its Meanings in Colonial South Asia', in *South Asia: Journal of South Asian Studies*, Vol. 14, no. 1 (1991), pp. 1–13.

public', not least because we feared that the shaping of the Western-oriented analytical category of 'public sphere' would point scholars only in certain directions, simultaneously implying that other parts of the world were somehow deficient if they did not fit this normative characterisation.[4] In complementary ways, the articles on context-specific understandings of urban public space (Masselos and Chakrabarty), on enactments connected to 'public interests' and 'public opinion' played out in those spaces (Freitag and Price), and on ideological and social constructions of the 'public good' (Gilmartin and Devji) broadened significantly the ways in which analysts might reconstruct understandings related to 'the public' from India's colonial past. Perhaps most striking about this collection were the sites under study and, by extension, the kinds of primary source materials examined.

Over the last 25 years, much has been published on elements of India's public sphere, yet this current special issue of *South Asia* is perhaps the first systematic reconsideration of 'the public' in South Asia. A comparison of the two issues of the journal is thus illuminating in several ways, helping to track changes in the field over the quarter century. First, the increased capacity of scholars to move among numerous South Asian languages and texts has enabled scrutiny of many more sources and perspectives on efforts to influence and express 'public opinion', capturing especially debates about the concepts and processes involved as participants worked to construct what they regarded as 'modern' issues and values. This has facilitated more sophisticated understandings about the roles, insights and place of 'text' in a way not possible in the early 1990s—and leading to a delineation of what we might call a range of varying 'public(s)'. In turn, this poses a new challenge for tracing the interrelationships of such 'publics' that we have not yet addressed.

Second—perhaps as a reflection of changes in the larger world over the last 25 years—we have excavated much more deeply the connections between a range of practices and understandings labelled 'religion' and how these have affected participation in 'the public'. While these connections, too, have yet to be systematically analysed, the range of case studies in this new essay collection points us in some promising directions, to which we will return below. Third and finally, we have now a fascinating depth of explorations regarding the relationship between the law, the state, and others who make claims in the name of 'the public'. While recognition of the importance of law and legal institutions was provided in 1991, especially by Pamela Price's essay, the articles included here uncover a much broader array of ways in which public morality, public interests, the state's assertion of its role on behalf of the public, and related issues are pursued through the courts and other state institutions, such as the formally-constituted commissions. Indeed, the implicit connection between the detached individual able to judge impartially among public-interest issues, and the claim by the state to act impartially on behalf of the public, is something that ought to be examined quite explicitly. As we conduct future such scholarly examinations, we also need to keep in mind that notions of 'the public' are constituted in adversarial as well as official ways that then enter as naturalised and, often, internalised understandings to inform the various perspectives we study.

Shared Understandings of 'the Public': As Conceptual/Imagined Entity and as Enactment

Despite the many changes in the field between these two journal issues, however, there also have been shared understandings. Key among these understandings are two complementary,

---

[4] In time, critiques of Habermas by Europeanists suggested that the categories were, in fact, too abstracted and normative to fit even the characteristics of British or German society, to which they were first directed.

but distinct ways in which 'the public' is expressed: as conceptual/imagined entity and as enactment. Both connect, in differing ways, to processes of identity formation and the resulting identity narratives that are created, expressed and revised to fit changing circumstances, for both individuals and collectivities. The two special issues of *South Asia* have addressed this package of associations connected to understandings of 'the public'; in certain respects, then, we benefit from bringing together all these essays to see the underlying analyses as parts of a single, coherent whole. This would help suggest the new directions still needed, both in deepening the trajectories proposed in the research already undertaken and in clarifying the different ways in which conceptualisations and actions contribute to understandings over time.

Perhaps, most immediately obvious is the recognition of how affect and emotive appeals studied in the current collection have added to the earlier collection's discussion of space; we now have references to friendship as well as the impact of visual evidence to recognise and incorporate into our emerging analytical framework. The more we can track these kinds of appeals, the more recognition we can accord to the underlying *tension* between that emotive side and the exercise of reason (more often invoked in textual references) that Gilmartin calls to our attention in his discussion of the sovereign and 'enchanted' individual. Similarly, the different viewpoints on the contestatory assertions and referents to authority and legitimacy, especially in relation to behaviours exhorted for audiences being addressed, help us to incorporate the depth of research already accomplished on 'custom' and 'reform' as those play out in new texts, sermons and other efforts to motivate action and to alter behaviour. Indeed, the awareness and expansion of *audience itself* is a key element to incorporate into our understandings of the multiple meanings of 'the public', a subject which is addressed below.

As suggested, the deeper examination of 'the public' is facilitated by the ways in which particular sites (such as dance bars in this collection) as well as spaces through which participants move (such as different neighbourhoods and central-city districts, examined in the earlier collection), to use two examples from Mumbai (formerly Bombay), clarify for us the constructed meanings of 'public spaces' being evoked. We are, now, in a position to approach in a more systematic way the constructed meanings and their contexts that such sites engender, and how they point to changes over time: how do these relate to each other? When and what changes can we identify as crucial to alterations in these meanings? How might we 'map' such changes over time for these meanings as well as their contexts? If, in the process of addressing these issues, we also bring together into a single field both print debate and visual expressions, the juxtapositions also enable us to understand continuities, as well as disjunctures, before and after Partition/Independence in 1947.

By including case studies on both sides of 1947, we get a glimpse at these continuities and disjunctures. Given the long reach of colonial precedents, as well as the tendency of studies of contemporary India to see 'the modern' as distinctly post-colonial, this collection is an especially valuable contribution to building a more comprehensive overview and a systematic, ultimately comparative, treatment of the larger patterns at work.

Where We Are Now: Aspects of 'the Public'

Both the shared understandings, and the expanded approaches charting progress made between 1991 and 2014, have mapped out promising research agendas for the future. My own hope is that we might collectively do that in a way that not only makes clear the characteristics of South Asian understandings of 'the public,' but that creates an analytical vocabulary (as well as systematic methodologies and range of evidence) serviceable for comparative purposes as well. Unquestionably, it is important to first have a critical mass of studies on South Asia from which

FIGURE 1. The Public as Conceptual Entity. 'Goddess Battles the [British] Demons', newspaper insert, 1870s, presents a frame composed of photographic busts of the first generation of nationalists with a traditional story of a goddess trampling demons, with a gloss (through labels) that identifies the demons as the British.
Source: Reproduced with kind permission of the British Library, OIOC.

FIGURE 2. Public as Enacted. Procession in Jaipur, probably related to a cow festival. Photograph included in Presentation Album given to the viceroy, Lord Curzon (ca. 1905), by the Maharaja of Jaipur; photographs by Rajputana Studio.
Source: Reproduced with kind permission of the British Library. Photo 430/36 (19) & (20).

to work, but part of our goal should be the ability to move beyond such regional foci so that the 'public sphere' is not identified solely with the patterns that have characterised the West.

Towards those ends, I suggested after our discussions of the papers at the conference[5] that we had (at least implicitly) delineated at least four different pathways or routes into understandings of 'the public' that I would like to explore here. At the same time, I called attention to an area that has continued to be neglected over the last 25 years: the contribution made to all of these pathways by visual culture. That is, it is not that no one has worked on elements of popular visual culture (especially posters),[6] but those who have worked on other elements, especially ones that fell within print capitalism as new modalities for suasion and contestation, have neglected to recognise the connections between, for instance, the texts they

---

[5] The conference, 'Imagining the Public in Colonial India: Print, Polemics and the People', took place at Northwestern University, Illinois, in May 2014.

[6] Among the number of essay collections on poster and calendar art are Richard Davis (ed.), *Picturing the Nation: Iconographies of Modern India* (New Delhi: Orient Longman, 2007); and Sumathi Ramaswamy (ed.), *Beyond Appearances? Visual Practices and Ideologies in Modern India* (New Delhi: Sage India, 2003); monographs include Patricia Uberoi, *Freedom and Destiny: Gender, Family, and Popular Culture in India* (New Delhi: Oxford University Press, 2006); and Christopher Pinney, *'Photos of the Gods': The Printed Image and Political Struggle in India* (London: Reaktion, 2004).

studied and the visual-culture contributions made, often in conjunction with those texts.[7] This section, therefore, treats both texts and visual culture together in four ways:

- As *enacted* (by which we may understand not only 'performance', but also 'participation', even behaviour and clothing as statements);
- As *envisioned* (or what has been called here 'the imaginaire');
- As *space, both rhetorical and actual* (that is, built environments, pictured and real, which operate 'in public' and/or with public access, serving as stages for performing the polity, as well as statements on what constitutes 'the public' and who falls within it);
- As *belief, interpretation, understandings, values, 'public opinion'* (that is, as concepts understood as motivations for actions, as forms to influence popular conceptualisations, and as expressions of shared views).

This list provides us not only with promising pathways to understanding 'the public', but also to some key meeting grounds or intersections for visual culture and popular participation in shaping the polity as a way of calling out the broader and more inclusive array of South Asian 'public(s)'.[8] In the course of our considerations of these pathways, I hope it also will become obvious that the focus on the visual, communicating as it does across literacy and language divides, reveals how much more inclusive this realm is—this is not just a bourgeois public sphere, as Habermas and others have seen it; it is tied intimately to the reach and nature of print capitalism as this developed in British India and elsewhere. That inclusiveness is demonstrated especially when one sees together evidence drawn from images (posters, calendar art, photographic landscapes and portraits), along with evidence from performances and other observances that contribute to narrative constructions, as those come to express both individual and collectivities' meaning-making. We should add to these the various built environments, and their interactions with bodies and urbanscapes, that convey a sense of place as well as anchors for meaning-making and related narratives. Taken all together, these elements of visual culture not only open up concepts of 'the public' to many different kinds of contributions, but also alert us to other sites of action/participation. Let us explore the list given above:

Public(s) as Enacted: Enacted publics range from *bhajans* (as in the collective and embodied use of *bhajan* texts analysed here by Orsini), to processions (such as that pictured in Figure 2, where the situating of an individual and/or a group in local society and amidst power structures may be performed, or refuted, by presenting alternatives),[9] to the women voters in Old Delhi (such as a wonderful photograph of Muslim women in white burqas, standing in line during India's first elections).[10] Crucial for our analysis is a focus on the meeting ground of larger, ideological meanings attributed to actions in the aggregate, and the individual actions connected to (the 'enchanted') individual's meaning-making. Also related to the

---

[7] Fascinating exceptions to this are two essays in another *South Asia* special section, 'The Visual Turn in South Asian Studies', published in Sept. 2014. See Sujata Mody, 'Visual Strategies for Literary Authority in Modern Hindi', in *South Asia: Journal of South Asian Studies*, Vol. 37, no. 3 (Sept. 2014), pp. 474–90; and Robert Phillips, 'The Urdu-Language *Kushtar Ramayan*: Verbal- and Visual-Narrative Repertoires and "Sense of Place"', in *ibid.*, pp. 454–73.

[8] I have used this formulation of 'public(s)' because scholars have also not come to grips with the problem of whether we should refer analytically to a single 'public' or a public world constituted of multiple 'publics'.

[9] That is, even ostensibly passive observers, by their contributions to the density of the crowd, the level of noise (cheering, musical accompaniment, etc.) and the exercise of their gaze still contribute actively to the making of meaning(s) created by such enactments.

[10] Space constraints prevent reproduction of this image, to be found in Sabeena Gadihoke (ed.), *India in Focus: Camera Chronicles of Homai Vyarawalla* (Delhi: Alkazi Foundation for the Arts *et al.*, 2014), p. 181.

FIGURE 3. Public as Space. Sufi saints and their shrines. Represented here, from bottom left, are Baba Farid (Pakpattan in Pakistan); Khwaja Qutbuddin Bakhtiyar Kaki (Mehrauli, outside Delhi); Khwaja Moinuddin Chishti (Ajmer Sharif); Hazrat Chaus-e Azam (Baghdad); Hazrat Bu Ali Sharaf (Panipat in Haryana, India); and Hazrat Nizamuddin Aulia (Nizamuddin Sharif, in Delhi).
Source: Reproduced with kind permission of Brijbasi.

staging of various enactments, of course, are the underlying issues regarding who can control these exercises; with whom they are associated; and who can demonstrate influence by shaping such demonstrations (including the refusal to hold an observance). Perhaps, most significantly, including a focus on visual-culture elements allows analysts to move beyond a single moment of production to cyclical and repetitive observances over time. What matters for us is not just production of an image, but the interactions between viewer and image; not just a single performance, but repeated observances on the same occasions over time. In this way, we not only may apply the same questions and measures to different moments in time to see what has changed, but we can contextualise each of these occasions to reconstruct made-meanings as they adapt to new circumstances.

Public(s) as Envisioned: Identifying the implicit connections between the two processes of interaction and contestation may be among the most important contributions that can be made when including visual-culture evidence within any particular case study. Regretfully, space constraints prevent the inclusion here of what may be the most provocative example of this interaction: Homai Vyarawalla photographed both the debate and voting by Congress representatives on the momentous decision to support the 'two nations' and resulting partition approach, *and* the general public massed on Delhi's *maidan*, awaiting the vote's outcome.[11]

---

[11] While, in retrospect, we may see as the obvious narrative presented here the two perspectives (that of politicians and that of the general public) on the challenge of making such a decisive move regarding the 'two nations', yet Vyarawalla's observations tell a very different story: she noted that very few people were actually at the meeting (only those in Delhi, while 'India is so big: they should have taken the consensus of people…that they didn't do'). She also felt that Gandhi should have opposed Partition; he was, instead, 'notably absent' in the words of her biographer. See Sabeena Gadihoke, *India in Focus: Camera Chronicles of Homai Vyarawalla* (Ahmedabad: Mapin Publishing, 2010), p. 78.

IMAGINING THE PUBLIC IN MODERN SOUTH ASIA

FIGURE 4. Public as Space. 'The Equality of Religions', Belgium Glass House, Ludhiana, 1974. This is one of a pair of images that gloss India's self-designated theme in the Nehruvian period of 'unity in diversity'. This image—with a light at the top and women in clothing and buildings behind them that give each a religious identity—shows all religious beliefs in India connecting to the same 'light' that we might take to be Indian democracy. The second print in this series depicts male figures tied to a cow (described below in the 'Public(s) as Envisioned' section).
Source: Reproduced with kind permission of Patricia Uberoi, Uberoi Collection.

Many posters also posit—and debate—the nature of the polity, such as various 'unity in diversity' themed posters, including school charts of boys in various regional and religiously-coded dress (calling to our attention the reliance on visual stereotypes for these forms of identity). Figure 4 has been paired with a contesting image (not included here) that substitutes the cow for the shining light to which the human figures are tied; in that case, the male figures also have coded dress (especially in terms of headwear) and are pictured with their buildings of worship behind them. Taken together, this pair of images clearly debates the relevance of

Indian 'secularism' to the values of the polity and thus implies the place of non-Hindus in that polity.[12]

Implicit in *envisioning* the public are the acts of 'seeing' and rendering 'visible'. Especially with protests, resistance and the pursuit of alternative visions, being 'seen' is to gain recognition that a group and its causes have significance for the government and/or for local society; that such groups have the authority to 'speak' on 'public' issues.[13] This exercise of the gaze is, of course, two-way in its efficacy and its analytical importance. The gaze plays a key role in sovereignty, as discussed by Gilmartin; it is worth observing here that, indeed, surveillance over the state is an important form of 'seeing' and of the public *as envisioned*.

Public as Space, Both Rhetorical and Actual: Built environments, and especially cityscapes, are spaces that function as both contexts and stages. Urban spaces and landscapes are important for enacting a polity, in the process expressing ideologies and values in order to motivate actions. The fact that a polity is envisioned and unfolds, in part, because it occurs 'in public' or in places with public access (access to which may, in fact, become part of what is being contested) is suggested by the conflict that continues to arise over statues of B.R. Ambedkar, both official and folk. (One set of images shows a folk statue being first installed in a village space and then broken; the story accompanying those pictures describes broken Dalit bodies as well.[14]) Moreover, the interactions between bodies and buildings and/or landscapes show us how important it is to analyse these interactions as they change over time in response to the changing status, authority and legitimacy of those involved, and the changing ways in which the pasts of these locales are imagined. Even beyond interactions between bodies and buildings is the association of the two in various kinds of posters. Most often, this association emerges with shrines and similar sacred spaces, underlining for us the role of these built environments as spaces of authority—encompassing shrines, temples, palaces, courts, etc.

The convention in poster/calendar art of including together in the same poster both pictures of a saint and the building that often stands in for him (Figure 3) is but the most obvious example of this body-and-building interaction. A similar practice of association, but using ordinary people, can be seen in Figure 4 (and the other half of the pair, debating what should be pictured at the top, as described above). In these posters, the inclusiveness of the claimed focal point is demonstrated by including religious buildings pictured behind each of the 'representative' figures.

As with many images, pictures of a built environment provide mental prompts for a particular story, but do so with enough ambiguity that the meanings involved are open to viewers' (re)interpretations to fit individual needs as well as (changing) local and current contexts. In so doing, the pictures possess the potential to craft a sense of place that makes room for both shared and individualised understandings of that place.

Public(s) as Belief, Interpretation, Understandings, Values, 'Public Opinion': that is, as concepts understood and available as motivations for actions and as expressions of shared views. When calling attention to how visual culture treats larger concepts, in my presentation

---

[12] See both images (Figures 5 and 7) in Patricia Uberoi, '"Unity in Diversity?": Dilemmas of Nationhood in Indian Calendar Art', in *Contributions to Indian Sociology*, Vol. 36, nos. 1–2 (2002), pp. 191–232.

[13] Lisa Mitchell's work makes this point very convincingly. See, for instance, Lisa Mitchell, 'The Visual Turn in Political Anthropology and the Mediation of Political Practice in Contemporary India', in the special section of *South Asia: Journal of South Asian Studies*, 'The Visual Turn in South Asian Studies', Vol. 37, no. 3 (Sept. 2014), pp. 515–40. This collection has also been published as an edited volume, *The Visual Turn: South Asia Across the Disciplines* (Abingdon: Routledge, 2015).

[14] See, for instance, the statues, both folk and official, included in Nicolas Jaoul, 'Les statues d'Ambedkar en Inde', in *Gradhiva*, Vol. 11 (2010), pp. 30–5.

FIGURE 5. Canvas 'studios' of itinerant photographers outside Jaipur's Albert Hall Museum, ca. 2003.
Source: Photograph by Sandria B. Freitag.

to our conference, I juxtaposed three photographs: (1) a picture of the artist Husain (known for his stylistic representations of horses, both in gallery logos he designed and in his oil paintings), literally painting a live horse. The horse would then perform his role as Duldul in the observances of Muharram; (2) Ram Rahman's art photo of huge Ram Navami figures during the enactment of Ram's story in Delhi; and (3) a close-up of a garlanded, enlarged bust poster-portrait of Ambedkar and a figure of a man with the garlands sitting next to the poster-portrait at a Dalit rally in Delhi (also by Ram Rahman). The juxtaposition was intended to underscore how beliefs, as well as efforts to shape and express public opinion, are expressed through visual culture. Perhaps equally revealing is the importance of these 'religious' enactments taking place *in public*—that is, in public spaces and through public interactions with the figures at the centre (horse, effigy, hoarding). At the same time, the juxtaposition demonstrates the seamless connections between narrative construction and cosmologies. Too often, such 'cosmologies' are most often understood in visual culture as representing *specific* religions;[15] the juxtaposition suggests how much more revealing it would be to employ a larger and more encompassing structure of meanings. In other words, visual-culture evidence helps us see how 'religion' operates in public arenas, not just as systems of belief, but also as the larger context within which various belief systems operate simultaneously—as the broader world in which many belief systems become expressed. Indeed, it is by virtue of a shared cosmological frame that debates about values and behaviours can be expressed. Such a larger

---

[15] Virtually all of the scholarship tries to 'explain' posters by relating them to Hindu beliefs and gods/goddesses. Yet, very similar interactions with posters by those with different religions suggest the inadequacy of these explanations.

FIGURE 6. Sample of a 1942 calendar by Oriental Calendar Mfg. Co., prepared for marketing to shopkeepers. The text around the picture of Krishna and Radha exhorts shopkeepers to 'promote Indian art' and 'encourage Indian artists', and gives the cost for printing an advertisement (for a shop) in more than one colour.
Source: Author's collection.

understanding of 'cosmology' also enables us to compare across civilisational systems the working of many visual cultures and, especially, to place within this frame the various cultural expressions of 'the public', where meaning-making and identity narratives can be seen to prompt emotive responses leading to action in their own right.

Conclusion

Both the underlying connections of visual evidence to textual and other formats as well as the interocularity of visual-culture media themselves (nicely illustrated by Figure 1, combining as it does photographs bordering drawn images) make the case that neglecting the visual leaves us much impoverished in understanding, especially, the emotive appeals to understandings about various aspects of 'the public' and the intersection of individual and collective participation in a polity.

Not least of the revelations made possible by the many forms and inclusiveness of visual culture—ranging as it does from itinerant photographers' accessibility for lower-class and -caste consumers (Figure 5), through free calendar-art posters given away by shopkeepers to many different levels of shoppers (Figure 6), to participation as audiences or marchers in processions (Figure 2)—is the need to analytically recognise that the shaping of aspects of 'the public' is not limited to the bourgeois inhabitants of a Western-style public sphere. Even the textual case studies included in this collection suggest many ways in which members of 'the public' interact, shape and otherwise affect the understandings that emerge from these texts, whether by hearing them read aloud, singing their words, or being exhorted about them in sermons and other forms of debate, let alone by bringing collective pressure to bear or by alternative glosses on the understandings derived. Indeed, the tensions that animate such understandings reflect the intimate connections among these many forms of 'public' participation, whether participants join in the form through critique or validation.

Our case studies help us see processes by which 'public opinion' can be persuaded as well as expressed and debated. They suggest the varied contexts in which 'a public' may be delineated and represented, or constructed from more or less inclusive definitions of a polity. And they suggest the very broad range of those who would speak on behalf of such 'public interests'. The array of contexts and types of 'language' in which such public expressions may be expressed still challenge us to construct a larger frame for understanding how these aspects of modern, democratic India fit within a comparative framework of public life and values, as well as participation and polity.

Index

Adcock, C.S. 4, 11, 24
Addison, C.G. 40
al-Afghani, Jamal al-Din 49
Aga Khan case (1866) 22
Agamben, G. 12
Agnes, F. 126, 130
Agrawal, A. 86
Agrawal, P. 81, 90
Ahmadiyya sect 49
Ahmed, S. 67
Ahmed, S.K. 60
Akbar's parliaments of religion 8
'Ali, Khurram 50
'Ali, Maulvi Hakim 63, 70
Ali, Meer Hassan 51
Ali, Sayyid Imdad 52
Aligarh *see* custom, critique of
All India Muslim League 57
Ambedkar, B.R. 10, 12, 94–109, 147, 164, 165
Ambedkar, Marx and Buddhist question 10, 12, 94–109; civil or civic religion 100–3; civil society 94, 103–6, 108; comparative religion 99; equality, fraternity and liberty 96, 98, 100; immanent and transcendent 99; minority and minor 96–7, 106–9; political society 104, 105–6, 108–9; poverty 100; principles and rules 98, 99
Anstey, Thomas 37, 40–1, 42
Appadurai, A. 2, 15
Arendt, H. 101–2, 103, 106, 107
Arya Samaj 4, 11, 24, 57
Asad, T. 94, 140
Australia 39
Azad, Abul Karim 63–73, 75–8
Al-Azmeh, A. 66

Babb, S.L. 113
Bacon, F. 46
Bader, V. 54
Bagehot, W. 8
Baljon, J.M.S. 55
Banerjee, S. 10
Bapna, G. 151
Barthwal, P.D. 82, 90, 91–2
Barz, R. 43, 44
Bayley, Lyttelton 42, 43
Bayly, C.A. 5–6, 8, 19
Bear, L. 122
Beltz, J. 100
Belvedere Press – booklets and *sants*: religious publics and literary history 6, 14, 79–93
Bénéï, V. 142
Bennett, P. 43, 45
Bentham, J. 114
Benton, L. 21
bhakti/devotion 28, 41, 89–91, 93
Bhargava, R. 5, 7
Bhattacharya, N. 7, 51
Bhuwania, , A. 116, 119
Birla, R. 11, 35, 113, 115, 116, 122
Bohman, J. 16
Bombay Gazette 36, 37, 45
booklets and *sants*: religious publics and literary history 6, 14, 79–93
Bose, B. 133
Breckenridge, C. 2, 15
bribes 127, 136, 138
Brizratanji, Jadunathji: Maharaj Libel case 13–14, 22, 31–46
Brown, W. 106
Brueck, L.R. 7
Buddhism 153; Ambedkar, Marx and Buddhist question 10, 12, 94–109

169

INDEX

built environments 161, 164
Bulmer, M. 149
Burchell, G. 111
Burgin, A. 113, 114
Burke, E. 18, 101, 155
Burton, F. 140

calendar art 160, 161, 164, 166, 167
Calhoun, C. 7, 8, 24, 53
caliphate 67, 76, 77; Ottoman 64, 65–7, 68, 69
Callewaert, W.M. 80
Carlen, P. 140
Carter-Ruck, P.F. 39
caste 6–7, 10, 19, 24, 43, 46; Bombay 35–6; Dalits 7, 10, 80–1, 95, 96–7, 106, 143–53, 165; Misra Commission and Report *see* commissioning representation; *sant* orature 80–1, 88, 90, 93; visual culture 165, 167
Chakrabarty, D. 2, 5, 156, 157
Chakravarty, S. 81
Champakalakshmi, R. 51
Chand, Prem 81
Chatterjee, P. 2, 105
Chaturvedi, P. 89
Christianity 89–90, 99, 103, 104–5, 144, 145, 147–53
Christof, M. 101
cinema 10, 35, 127; dance bars 125, 130, 132, 135, 137, 138
citizenship 111, 112, 134; consumer- 135, 137; religious identity and secular (Abdul Kalam Azad) 64, 65–7, 68, 69, 77
civil religion *see* Ambedkar, Marx and Buddhist question
class 6, 16, 20, 24, 93, 96, 135; consumerism 28; critique of custom 48, 52–3, 54, 58; dance bar ban 129; visual culture 167
Clokie, H.M. 154
Cohn, B.S. 18, 57
colonial authorities: non-interference principle 11, 51, 134
colonial and pre-colonial 'publics' 5–6
colonialism and neo-liberalism *see* jurisprudence of emergence: neo-liberalism and the public as market
commissioning representation 9, 13, 139–55; deliberation, consensus and recalcitrance of religion 151–3; determining the religion of caste 143–5; recursivity 150–1;

self-narration 145–7; social science, relays and representation through achievement of consensus 147–50
competition 115
conceptual/imagined entity: 'the public' 157–8
Congress Party 144
constitution(s) 102; Indian 94, 97, 102–3, 109, 120–1, 130, 138, 145, 147, 152
consumer-citizen 135, 137
consumerism 28
contract law 116
conversion 145, 151; Ambedkar, Marx and Buddhist question *see separate entry*
Cooke, G. 40
Cornell, V. 68, 76
courts and law 157; as central to emerging public in India 19–25; dance bar ban 126–7, 128–31, 132–5, 138; imperial and colonial sovereignty 18; Maharaj Libel case 13–14, 22, 31–46; *State of West Bengal vs. Union of India and Others* (1995) 116–20, 124; stock exchanges and public duties 120–4; writ petitions 148, 149
Cow Protection Movement (1893) 57
Crone, P. 67
cultural regulation 11
custom, critique of 13, 47–62; clothing 60–1; comparing Aligarh and Deoband 48–50; 'custom' in late colonial India: three overlapping frames 50–1; Islamic legal critique of custom: normativity, rationality and public 'signs' of Islam 48, 56–61; liberal critique of custom: rationality, civility and power of print 48, 52–6; rationality/reasoning 48, 50, 53–4, 59
customary law 51

Daechsel, M. 28
Dalal and Others vs. The Stock Exchange Bombay 120–2, 123
Dalits 10, 80–1, 95, 96–7, 106, 143–53, 165; literary group 7
Dalmia, V. 6, 32, 80, 101
dance bars: public obscenity, globalisation and Mumbai dance bar ban 4, 13, 125–38, 158
Dardot, P. 112
Darity, W. 144
Das, Asha 152–3
Das, Shyamsundar 82

170

INDEX

Das, V. 119
Datla, K. 25
Davis, R. 160
defamation *see* Maharaj Libel case
Defoe, D. 33
deliberation 10, 140–1, 142–3, 149, 155; consensus, recalcitrance of religion and 151–3
democracy 8, 10, 102, 104–5, 107, 110–11, 112, 124, 134, 139; deliberation 10, 140–1, 142–3, 149, 153, 155; and mobocracy 27
Deoband *see* custom, critique of
Derrett, J.D.M. 144
Deshpande, S. 151
Deva, S. 116
Devji, F. 10, 49, 53, 54, 61, 62, 156, 157
Dewey, J. 10, 102, 103
Dihlavi, Sayyid Ahmad 50–1
Dirks, N. 8, 51
Dodson, M. 2
Donagh, W. 40
Doniger, W. 2
Douglas, I. 65
Dunn, J. 139
Dwyer, R. 23, 138

East India Company 81, 111, 115
economic-juridical order *see* jurisprudence of emergence: neo-liberalism and the public as market
elections 11–12, 25, 27, 142, 155, 161
emerging markets 110–11
empire, neo-liberalism and rule of law 112–14
enactment, 'the public' as 157–8, 161–2
etymology of 'the public' 5

Faleiro, S. 126, 132, 138
Faruqi, Ziya ul-Hasan 50
fascism 28
Feldman, I. 149
feminism 8, 32
Feuerbach, L. 99, 103
films 10, 35, 127; dance bars 125, 130, 132, 135, 137, 138
Foucault, M. 111, 112, 113, 114, 115, 119, 122
Fourcade-Gournichas, M. 113
France 8
Frank, J. 12
Frankel, F.R. 113, 144
Frankel, O. 142, 154

Fraser, N. 7, 24
Freitag, S.B. 2, 3, 7, 10, 14, 19, 22–3, 24, 45, 57, 133, 156, 157
Frere, B. 9
friendship in colonial Muslim India, contesting 13, 63–78; duplicitous stratagems 72–3; friendship and its perils 70–1; good non-Muslim, bad non-Muslim 68; imperial hermeneutics 73–5; negotiating religious identity and secular citizenship 65–7; preserving a moral public 75–6; promise and responsibility of secularism 69–70; tampering with Shari'a 71–2
Fuchs, M. 101
Fuller, C.J. 142

Gadihoke, S. 161, 162
Galanter, M. 144
Ganachari, A. 40
Gandhi, Indira 119, 142
Gandhi, M.K. 26–7, 32, 63–4, 66, 69, 71, 72, 73, 75, 109, 143, 144, 162
Gane, N. 113
Ganguly, D. 97
Garcin de Tassy, J. 51
Geertz, C. 142
gender 6, 10, 21, 24, 32, 48, 135
genealogical method 3–7
Genette, G. 93
al-Ghazali, Abu Hamid 67
Ghosh, A. 6
Gilligan, G. 155
Gilmartin, D. 11, 17, 25, 51, 61, 156, 157
globalisation, public obscenity and Mumbai dance bar ban 4, 13, 125–38, 158
Gopal, S. 51
Gordon, C. 111
Gosnell, H.F. 154
Goswami, M. 113
Green, N. 35, 51, 80
Grierson, G.A. 89–90, 92
Gupta, A. 81
Gupta, C. 10
Gupta, N. 91
Gutmann, A. 140, 142, 155

Haberman, D.L. 32
Habermas, J. 5, 7–8, 12, 16–17, 19, 22, 23, 24, 28, 33, 52, 53, 142, 156, 161

INDEX

Hadley, E. 12
Hali, Khvajah Altaf Husain 52, 58
Hamilton, W.R. 40
Hansen, K. 6
Hansen, T.B. 142, 154
Harder, H. 91
Hasan, F. 5
Hassan, M. 67
Hastings trial, Warren 8, 18
Hatcher, B. 2
Hayek, F. 112, 113, 114
Haynes, D. 9, 41
Heesterman, J.C. 17
Hegel, G.W.F. 99, 103, 104, 105
Heimsath, C. 32
Herbert, A.P. 140
Hinds, M. 67
Hinduism 5, 21, 59–60, 144–5, 146, 152, 153; Ambedkar 95, 98; Ganesh festival 10, 35; Maharaj Libel case 13–14, 22, 31–46; public arenas, law and oversight of religion 22–4
Holt, F.L. 39
Hull, M. 149
human rights 101–2, 103, 119
Husain 165

Ibn 'Abidin 74
Ikram, S.M. 49
imaginaire 161, 162–4
imagined/conceptual entity: 'the public' 157–8
Indian National Congress 18–19, 57, 63–4, 66
Ingram, B.D. 6, 58
inheritance court cases 20–1
Iqbal, M. 29–30
Iqtidar, H. 22
Islam/Muslims 5, 21, 79–80, 90–1, 144, 145, 147–53; Aga Khan case (1866) 22; clothing 60–1; custom, critique of see separate entry; friendship in colonial Muslim India, contesting 13, 63–78; Iqbal 29–30; public arenas, law and oversight of religion 22–5; Qur'an see separate entry; sovereignty 17; Sufism 5, 21, 28, 47, 61, 79, 90, 91
Isma'il, Muhammad 50

Jaffery, Y. 6
Jainism 153
James, W. 102

Jaoul, N. 164
Jayal, N.G. 113, 116, 120
Jondhale, S. 100
Jones, D.S. 113
Jones, J. 53
Jones, K.W. 6, 79
Joyce, P. 149
Juergensmeyer, M. 82
jurisprudence of emergence: neo-liberalism and the public as market 4, 8, 11, 110–24; judicial activism 116, 117, 119–20, 121–2; juridico-economic order: resonances of colonial liberalism 114–16; jurisprudence of emergence/emergency 124; liberalising markets/publics: *State of West Bengal vs. Union of India and Others* (1995) 116–20; neo-liberalism, empire and rule of law 112–14; public interest 112, 115, 116–22; Stock Exchange: market exchange as public agency? 120–4

Kabir 80, 81, 82, 89–90, 91–2
Kale, Varsha 130, 137
Kallen, H.M. 102
Kant, I. 98, 99, 100, 108
Kantorowicz, E.H. 12, 17
Kapila, S. 32
Kaur, R. 10, 11, 35, 127, 130, 133
Kaviraj, S. 59, 77
Keddie, N. 49
Khaksars 28
Khan, Ahmad Raza 63–5, 69–78
Khan, Ali Bakhsh 52
Khan, N. 29
Khan, Sayyid Ahmad 4, 47–56, 57–8, 59, 60–2
Khilafat movement 64, 65–6, 69, 70–3, 75
Kinra, R. 8
Kohli, A. 113
Kuczkiewicz-Fras, A. 52
Kumar, U. 97, 107–8

Lajpat Ray, L. 33
Lal, Ram Lagan 85, 86
Lath, M. 80
Laval, C. 112
Le Bon, G. 50
Lelyveld, D. 6, 52
Leonard, K. 51
libel: Maharaj case 13–14, 22, 31–46

INDEX

liberal critique of custom: rationality, civility and power of print 48, 52–6
liberalism 3, 7–10, 27, 33–4, 57, 106; neo-liberalism and *see* jurisprudence of emergence: neo-liberalism and the public as market
Lippmann, W. 10, 114
literacy 16, 86–7
Lockwood, T.J. 154
Lorenzen, D. 81
Louis, K.S. 149
Ludden, D.E. 57
Lütt, J. 32, 46

MacIntyre, A. 62, 140, 146
Maclean, D.N. 60
McLellan, D. 96
MacPherson, A.J. 39
Mah, H. 16, 24, 53
Mahadevdass, Gopalldas 44
Mahajan, G. 57
Maharaj Libel case 13–14, 22, 31–46; genealogies of libel law 38–40; making the Bombay public 34–8; manifestly divine 43–5; public spirit 33–4; reputation: property and honour 38–40, 41, 43; secularism 42; unbecoming Krishna 40–3
Majumdar, R. 2
Malabari, B.M. 46
Malik, H. 55
Malinar, A. 101
Manecksha, f. 130, 137
Manin, B. 143, 154
Mantena, K. 8, 9
Mantena, R.S. 6
Marfatia, M. 45
market, neo-liberalism and the public as 4, 8, 11, 110–24
Marx: Ambedkar, Marx and Buddhist question 10, 12, 94–109
Mashriqi, Allama 28
mass media 10
Masselos, J.C. 35, 156, 157
Masud, M.K. 60
Masuzawa, T. 21–2
Maussen, M. 54
Mazumdar, R. 137
Mazzarella, W. 10, 11, 129, 130, 133, 134, 137, 138

Mehrotra, A.K. 82
Mehta, M. 32
Mehta, P.B. 116
Mehta, S. 125, 131
Mehta, U.S. 8, 116
Mendieta, E. 53
Merwanjee, J. 40
Metcalf, B.D. 49, 59
Metcalf, T.R. 8
Mill, J.S. 55–6, 113
Miller, P. 111
Minault, G. 6, 48, 51, 53, 64, 66
minorities: National Commission for Religious and Linguistic Minorities (NCRLM) *see* Misra Report: commissioning representation
Minority Commission 151
Mir, M. 29
Mirowski, P. 112, 113, 114
Mises, Ludwig von 113, 114
Mishra, G.B. 91, 92
Mishra, S.B. 81, 91, 92
Mishra, S.D.B. 91, 92
Misra Report: commissioning representation 9, 13, 139–55; deliberation, consensus and recalcitrance of religion 151–3; determining the religion of caste 143–5; recursivity 150–1; self-narration 145–7; social science, relays and representation through achievement of consensus 147–50
missionaries 79, 81, 89, 93, 152
Mitchell, L. 164
Mitchell, P. 39
Mitchell, T. 115, 155
mobocracy and democracy 27
Modi, Narendra 110–11, 124
Mody, S. 161
Moin, A.A. 4, 12, 17
monopoly 115
Moors, A. 54
Morgan, W. 39
Motiwala, B.N. 31
movies 10, 35, 127; dance bars 125, 130, 132, 135, 137, 138
Mufti, A. 106
Muhammad, S. 55
Mukherjee, A.P. 10
Mukherjee, M. 12, 18, 26

173

INDEX

Mulji, Karsandas 4; Maharaj Libel case 13–14, 22, 31–46
Mumbai dance bars: public obscenity, globalisation and Mumbai dance bar ban 4, 13, 125–38, 158
Munshi Dayaram Sahib, S. 33
Muslims *see* Islam

Nagari Pracharini Sabha of Banaras (est. 1893) 81–2
Naim, C.M. 51
Nanakchand, Y. 88
Nanautvi, Muhammad Qasim 49, 50
Narula, S. 145
National Commission for Minorities 151
natural law 18
Navayana Buddhism: Ambedkar, Marx and Buddhist question 10, 12, 94–109
Nayak vs. Cochin Stock Exchange Ltd 123
neo-liberalism, public as market and 4, 8, 11, 110–24; judicial activism 116, 117, 119–20, 121–2; juridico-economic order: resonances of colonial liberalism 114–16; jurisprudence of emergence/emergency 124; liberalising markets/publics: *State of West Bengal vs. Union of India and Others* (1995) 116–20; neo-liberalism, empire and rule of law 112–14; public interest 112, 115, 116–22; Stock Exchange: market exchange as public agency? 120–4
newspapers 4, 6, 16, 58; inheritance court cases 20; *see also* Maharaj Libel case
Nirala, S.T. 80–1, 92
Non-Cooperation movement 63–4, 66, 69, 70–3
non-governmental organisations (NGOs) 128, 148, 150, 154
Novetzke, C. 5, 80, 88, 130

obscenity, globalisation and Mumbai dance bar ban 4, 13, 125–38, 158
Oddie, G. 40
O'Hanlon, R. 19
Omvedt, G. 96
Orsini, F. 4–5, 79, 81, 86, 88
Ottoman caliphate 64, 65–7, 68, 69
oversight commissions 150–1

Pakistan Movement 28, 29
Pandey, G. 97, 106

Panipati, M.I. 49, 50, 52, 53, 54, 55
Patel, Alka 51
performance: public arenas, law and oversight of religion 22–5; public obscenity, globalisation and Mumbai dance bar ban 4, 13, 125–38, 158; sovereignty and the 'people': public as 25–30
Perkins, C.R. 4
Perlman, R.J. 149
Pernau, M. 6, 48, 57
Perry, E. 36
Phillips, R. 161
photography 161, 162, 165, 167
Pinch, V. 89, 90
Pinney, C. 23, 44, 133, 138, 160
Pinto, J. 137
Pitkin, H.F. 139
Platts, J.T. 34
Plehwe, D. 112, 113, 114
poetry *see sant* poets
Post, R.C. 38, 39
posters 160, 161, 163–4, 165, 167
Powell, A. 6, 55, 56
Prakash, G. 35
Prasad, Baleshwar 82–5, 87–8
pre-colonial and colonial 'publics' 5–6
Price, P.G. 20, 21, 156, 157
Price, W. 81
print 23, 26, 57, 58, 77, 160–1; booklets and *sants*: religious publics and literary history 6, 14, 79–93; culture 6, 16; liberal critique of custom: rationality, civility and power of 48, 52–6; networks of 19; newspapers *see separate entry*
processions 23, 161, 167
property disputes: court cases 20–2
public interest 112, 115, 116–22
public obscenity, globalisation and Mumbai dance bar ban 4, 13, 125–38, 158; earlier cabaret dancer prosecutions 130–1, 137
public opinion 9, 15, 51, 53–4, 58, 157, 161, 164–7; caste 10
public space 161, 164
Purohit, T. 22, 35
Pushtimarg: Maharaj Libel case 13–14, 22, 31–46

Queen, C. 100
queer theory 8

INDEX

Qur'an 60, 61, 66, 70, 78; Surah Mumtahana (verses 8 and 9) 64–5, 68, 71, 75
Qureshi, N. 64

Rahman, F. 49
Rahman, M.R. 53
Rahman, Ram 165
Rajagopal, A. 6, 11, 87
Ramanujan, A.K. 92
Ramaswamy, S. 160
Ranchhoddas, R. 38
Rancière, J. 101
Rao, A. 97
Rao, M.S.A. 144
Rapoport, Y. 67
Rast Goftar and Satya Prakash 36, 37–8, 44
Rathore and Another vs. Madhya Pradesh Stock Exchange 122–3
reason 16, 17, 18–19, 20, 21–2, 25, 26, 27, 28, 30; Muslim India: critiquing 'custom' 48, 50, 53–4, 59; principles 98; religion 100, 108
Rege, S. 126
Reifeld, H. 5, 7
Relg, W. 16
religion 3, 4, 6, 10, 11, 157; Akbar's parliaments of 8; Ambedkar, Marx and Buddhist question 10, 12, 94–109; booklets and *sants*: religious publics and literary history 6, 14, 79–93; Christianity 89–90, 99, 103, 104–5, 144, 145, 147–53; court cases and reconstruction of 19, 21–2; Hinduism *see separate entry*; Islam *see separate entry*; Maharaj Libel case 13–14, 22, 31–46; National Commission for Religious and Linguistic Minorities (NCRLM) *see* Misra Report: commissioning representation; public arenas, law and oversight of 19, 22–5; visual culture 165–7
representation by commission of inquiry *see* commissioning representation
Roberts, N. 140, 143, 144
Robinson, F. 57
Robinson, J.W. 154
Roe, J. 8
Rosenbaum, S. 102
Rosenberg, N.L. 39
Roth, G. 149

Rougier, L. 114
Rousseau, J.-J. 99, 100
Roy, Ram Mohan 4
rule of law 26, 112–16, 118, 122, 124
Runciman, D. 139
Rüstow, A. 114

Saha, s. 43
Sanders, L. 142
sant poets 6, 14, 79–93; 'beneficial to the general public': *santbani* booklets and religious publics 87–8; not poetic enough? orature, religion and literary history 88–93; *santbani* booklets 82–7; *sants* into print 80–2
Santos, B. de S. 119
Sanyal, U. 70
Sarkar, T. 22
Sartori, A. 2, 8
Sawhney, S. 95–6
Schmitt, C. 10, 105, 140–1
Schomer, K. 82
Scott, J.B. 4, 9, 21, 32, 33, 36, 42
secularism 42, 69–70, 77–8, 164; Ambedkar 94–5, 96–7, 98–9, 103, 104, 105
self-rule (*swaraj*) 26–7, 30, 32
Sen, A. 8
Sen, Kshiti Mohan 81, 82
Sevea, I.S. 29
Shah, Ahmed 81
Shah, S. 126
Shahidganj Mosque 28
Sharafi, M. 40
Sharar, Abdul Halim 4, 51
Sharif, Ja'far 51
Shiv Sena party 127
Shodhan, A. 32, 35, 36
Shukla, R. 82, 90–1, 92
Sikhism 153
Simonsen, S. 122
Sinha, S. 113
Smith, W.C. 30
Soneji, D. 128, 130
sovereignty, caliphal 76
sovereignty, Muslim imperial 73–5
sovereignty and the public 12, 15–30, 111, 158, 164; court cases, 'private' realm and reconstruction of sovereignty 20–1; courts and law as central to emerging public in India 19–25; Habermas, sovereignty

175

INDEX

and public sphere 16–17; imperial and colonial sovereignty 18; legitimation and governance 16–17; reason 16, 17, 18–19, 20, 21–2, 25, 26, 27, 28, 30; sovereignty and the 'people': public as performance 25–30; sovereignty, society and state: public as discourse 18–19
The Spectator 52
Stark, U. 9
State of West Bengal vs. Union of India and Others (1995) 116–20, 124
Stietencron, H. von 32
Stock Exchange: market exchange as public agency 120–4
Stokes, E. 8
Sturman, R. 21
Subrahmanyam, S. 6
Sufism 5, 21, 28, 47, 61, 79, 90, 91
Sullivan, W.F. 11
swaraj (self-rule) 26–7, 30, 32

Tagore, Rabindranath 81, 82, 91–2
Tahzib al-Akhlaq (*The Refinement of Morals*) 52–6, 57
Tarakeswar murder case (1873) 22
Tatler 52
Taylor, C. 25, 36, 99, 105
Tayyib, Q.M. 60, 62
Thakkar, U. 32
Thakore, D.K. 38
Thanvi, Ashraf 'Ali 4, 47–9, 50, 51, 56–62
Thiong'o, Ngugi Wa 80
Thompson, D. 140, 142, 155
Thoothi, N.A. 36, 43
Tilak, B.G. 10
The Times of India 36, 37, 45
Tomba, Marco della 81
Toulmin, J. 149
translation of 'public' into South Asian languages 4–5, 33–4, 45
Tribe, K. 112
Troll, C. 49, 50
Trumpp, E. 81
Tupper, C.L. 51

Turner, V. 24
typological method 3–7

Uberoi, P. 160, 164
ubi jus ibi remedium 118
United Kingdom 8, 115–16, 140, 154, 155
United States 115–16
Universal Declaration of Human Rights 102
utilitarianism 114

Vallabhacharya, Shri 43–4, 45
Van der Veer, P. 8, 94, 96
VanAntwerpen, J. 53
Vandravandas, P.R. 45, 46
Vanshi, B. 88
Varma, G. 110
Vaudeville, C. 81, 82, 89
Venkateshwar Press 81
Vertovec, S. 144
visual culture 160–7
Viswanath, R. 143, 144, 146, 152
Viswanathan, G. 96, 97, 109
voluntary societies 9–10
voting 25, 27, 161; secret ballot 11–12
Vyarawalla, Homai 162

Warner, M. 5, 8, 33, 36, 48, 52
Washbrook, D. 144
Weber, M. 149
West Bengal vs. Union of India and Others (1995) 116–20, 124
Westbrook, R. 102
Westcott, G.H. 89
White, H. 146
Williams, T.W. 80
Wilson, John 31
Wittich, C. 149
writ petitions 148, 149

Yelle, R. 11
Young, I.M. 142

Zaman, M.Q. 59
Zelliott, E. 143